National Intelligencer and *Washington Advertiser* Newspaper Abstracts 1800-1805

Joan M. Dixon

HERITAGE BOOKS
2006

HERITAGE BOOKS
AN IMPRINT OF HERITAGE BOOKS, INC.

Books, CDs, and more   Worldwide

For our listing of thousands of titles see our website
at
www.HeritageBooks.com

Published 2006 by
HERITAGE BOOKS, INC.
Publishing Division
65 East Main Street
Westminster, Maryland 21157-5026

Copyright ' 1996 Joan M. Dixon

All rights reserved. No part of this book may be reproduced or transmitted in any form or by any means, electronic or mechanical, including photocopying, recording or by any information storage and retrieval system without written permission from the author, except for the inclusion of brief quotations in a review.

International Standard Book Number: 978-0-7884-0392-3

NATIONAL INTELLIGENCER NEWSPAPER
WASHINGTON, D C
1800-1805

TABLE OF CONTENTS

Daily National Intelligencer-1800--1
Daily National Intelligencer-1801--13
Daily National Intelligencer-1802--67
Daily National Intelligencer-1803--116
Daily National Intelligencer-1804--159
Daily National Intelligencer-1805--210

American Citizens of Md detained on British ships—3-4
American Seamen detained by the British—256-260

American Seamen in Kingston, Jamaica—42-44
American vessels at Cape Francois, Feb 12, 1802—73

American vessels captured by British cruizers—32
American vessels captured by the Spaniards—268

American vessels in the port of Spain—130

Appointments by the President—22; 28-29; 30-31; 35; 82-85; 124-125; 163-164; 169; 170; 195-196; 201; 246

Citizens of the U S at Cape Francois—45; 81
Claims under Louisiana Convention—249-250

Commencement at Dickinson College, Carlisle, Pa—260
Commencement at St John's College, Annapolis, Md—8

Commencement at Princeton College, New Jersey—105
Court Martial of Capt Geo Little—59

Deserters—34
Forces in the Mediterranean—245-246

Grand Jurors, Balt Co, Md—140
Impeachment trials—215-217

Impressed Seamen on American vessels—156-157
1st Leg of Militia-D C—90

Justices of the Peace for the Territory of Columbia—80

Ladies with letters in the Post Ofc—38; 55; 67; 76; 88; 106; 116; 136; 145; 161; 171; 181; 196; 224; 234; 253

Land Grants—25; 65-66; 67
Longevity in Virginia—229

Meeting at Rhodes Tavern, Wash City—213
Members of Congress—5

Members of 8th Congress—145-147
Members of Congress—266-267

Midshipmen—96
Militia under Gen Shee—137

Navy Officers—169
Nelson's Fleet—233

N Y fire sufferers—144
Nominations by the President—19; 20

Officers on the Phoenix-killed—261
Officers of the U S Gov't—46-50; 99-103

Officers on the ship President—249
Officers under Cmdor Ed Preble—219-220

Prince Georges Co, Md-tax list—238-239
Sale of Kentucky land for taxes—39

Scholars of Columbia Academy, Georgetown, D C-148-149
Ships under Sir Robt Calder—251

Trial of Edw Kearney for high treason, Dublin—149
U S expenditures—15

Washington City Council—86; 133
Washington City-tax list—187-189

Index--[1]

PREFACE
Daily National Intelligencer Newspaper Abstracts
1800-1805
Joan M Dixon

The National Intelligencer & Washington Advertiser is hereafter the Daily National Intelligencer. It was the first newspaper printed in Washington, D C; Samuel H Smith, the originator. The same was transferred to Jos Gales, jr on Aug 31, 1810; on Nov 1, 1812, the paper was under the firm of Jos Gales, sr, & Wm W Seaton. The Library of Congress has microfilm of the paper from the first issue of Oct 31, 1800 thru Jan 8, 1870, the final paper.

The Evening Star Newspaper of Jan 10, 1870 reports: The Intelligencer is discontinued: the proprietor, Mr Alex Delmar, says that having lost several thousand dollars, & being in poor health, he has resolved to discontinue its publication.

Included in the abstracts are advertisements; appointments by the President; Hse o/Rep petitions; passed Acts; legal notices; marriages; deaths; mscl notices; social events; tax lists; military promotions; court cases; deaths by accident; prisoners; & maritime information-crews. Items or events which might be a clue as to the location, age or relationship of an individual are copied.

No attempt has been made to correct the spelling. Due to the length of some articles, it was necessary to present only the highlights of same. Chancery and Equity records are copied as written.

All surnames and *land/tract names* are included in the index.

ABBREVIATIONS:
AA CO	ANNE ARUNDEL COUNTY
CO	COMPANY/COUNTY
CMDER	COMMANDER
CMDOR	COMMODOR
D C	DISTRICT OF COLUMBIA
ELIZ	ELIZABETH
ELIZA	ELIZA
MONTG CO	MONTGOMERY COUNTY
PG CO	PRINCE GEORGES CO
WASH	WASHINGTON

BOOKS IN THE NATIONAL INTELLIGENCER NEWSPAPER SERIES: 1800-1805/1806-1810/1811-1813/1814-1817/1818-1820/1821-1823/1824-1826/1827-1829/1830-1831/1832-1833/1834-1835/1836-1837/1838-1839/1840/1841/1842/1843/1844/1845/1846/
SPECIAL: CIVIL WAR 2 VOLS, 1861-1865

> *The National Intelligencer and Washington Advertiser*
> *Printed by Samuel Harrison Smith, NJ Av, nr the Capitol.*

Washington, DC 1800

FRI OCT 31, 1800   NO. 1
Copy of a ltr by John Adams to Tench Coxe, Quincey, Mass-May 1792. Last winter the Leg of Mass, upon the petition of North Parish in Braintree, separated it from the rest of the town, erected it into a new one & gave it the name of Quincey depriving me of my title of *"Duke of Braintree"*. My friends should write me in future as an inhabitant of Quincey. So much for the brimborion.

Mr Pinkney, Ambassador to England; his family has had their eyes fixed upon the Embassy to St James for many yrs.

Candidates chosen to represent the western dist of Vt in Cong: Gregg, Brown, Muhburg, Stewart, Hanna, Bard, Rpblcns; Hemphil & *Edie, Federalists. [*Corr of Nov 3-Mr Edie shd have been Mr Boude]

Gen C C Pinckney, chosen Senator in Leg of S C, Charleston Dist-632 votes.

3rd Middle Dist of Mass: Nathan Read to represent them in Congress, Mar next; a Fed candidate he had 1567 votes; Mr Crowinfield had 1364 votes.

Israel Smith, Rpblcn candidate; to rep the Western Dist of Vt in Cong of U S.

Isaac Tichenor is elected Governor & Paul Brigham Lt Gov, of Vt.

Forty Dollars reward for negro man, Nace, age 30 yrs. -Zachariah Sothoron Chas Co, Md, nr Benedict, Oct 31.

Boarding & Lodging-2 hses in sq 690, NJ Av opposite hse presently occupied by Thos Law, esq. -Robt W Peacock, Wash City.

MON NOV 3, 1800   NO. II
In Massachusetts a 2nd trial has been had in the dist formerly represented by Dwight Foster-the votes recd in Worcester on Oct 22 gave Mr Lincoln, Rpblcn candidate, 817 votes; Mr Upham, Federalist, 577 votes.

For the information of the ctzns of Wash, we publish the act of the President of the U S dated Jun 5, 1796, permitting the erection of frame bldgs until the 1st Mon in Dec next, after which day it will be illegal to erect any bldgs not of stone or brick, the walls shall not be higher than 40 ft to the roof, in any part of the city, or lower than 35 ft on any of the aves. -Jun 25, 1796 Geo. Washington.

Gentlemen to represent Connecticut
Roger Griswold	Samuel W Dana	Wm Edmond
John Davenport Jr	Elizur Goodrich	John C Smith

Elias Perkins
Unsuccessful gentlemen:
Wm Hart	Gideon Granger, Jr,	Sylvester Gilbert
Colvin Goddard	Benj Talmage	Simeon Baldwin
Timothy Pitkin, Jr	Wm Mosely	Epaphroditus Champion
Chaunchey Goodrich	Jonathan Brace	

WED NOV 5, 1800   NO. III

Richard Howel, re-elected Gov of NJ on the 30th, they procceded to the choice of electors of Pres & VP, when the votes stood: Isaac Smith, Hunterdon-38; Wm Griffith, Burlington-34; Richd Stockton, Somerset-36; Dr Sam Stanhope Smith, Middlesex-35; Joshua L Howell, Gloucester-35; Matthias Williamson Jr, Essex-35; Thos Sinnickson, Salem-36; Jas Mot, Monmouth-14; Moore Furman, Burlington-14; Wm Woodhull, Morris-10; Wm Helms, Sussex-14; Saml Hay, Essex-13; Henry Southard, Somerset-15; John Cobb, Morris-13. [The first 7 men formed the Federal tkt]

Thos Lowndes, esq, elected rep of Charleston, SC, Vice Maj Pinckney, who declined re-election. Gen C C Pinckney, elected to rep city of Charleston in the Senate of SC. John Dayton is Lt Gov of SC.

Died: Sarah Lea, age 102 yrs, Oct 21, N Wilmington, Del, at the poor hse. Her son was at Broddocks defeat-then age 21.

From Aug 21 to Oct 25:1800-1,197 people died at Balt. [978 adults]

FRI NOV 7, 1800   NO. IV

Life of Benjamin Franklin: son of a tallow-chandler who emigrated from Eng for his religious opinions & established himself in Boston, where Benj was born Jan 17, 1706; Benj at age 14 remvd to Phil about 1720 & was taught printing; went to Eng about 1724 & worked with the late Mr Watts; returned from Eng & mrd, had a son, Wm, & a dght-she mrd Richard Bache, mrchnt in Phil. He wrote a ltr to Miss Hubbard on loss of his bro, John of Boston, who was Miss Hubbard's fr-in-law. Mr F died Apr 17, 1790, age 85 yrs.; left his grandson, Wm Temple Franklin, a grant of land in Ga.

Boston Oct 29. *"Essex"*, Capt Jenkins, arvd at Newburyport.

The Brig, *"Union"* Capt Billington, arvd in NY, 39 days from Belfast.

New-Haven, Conn - Oct 31, 1800. Electors for Pres & VP have been chosen by our legislature: i.e, Gov Trumbull; Lt Gov Hon J Treadwell; Jesse Root, Jonathan Sturges, Steph. M Mitchell, Jonathan Ingersol, Tapping Reeve. Judges of Supreme Crt: Matthew Griswold, esq & Jonathan O. Mosely, esq.

Saml Duvall, Frederick-town, Oct 15, had his house wantonly assailed with stones, window broken. -Reward, $50.

Leg of Vt. re-elected Elijah Paine, Senator of the U S-97 votes; S R Bradley received 68 votes.

Mbrs of present Congress who have declined being considered as candidates :
John Lawrence	Theo Sedgwick	Saml Lyman
John Read	Harrison G Otis	Bailey Bartlett
Jas H Imlay	Robt Goodloe Harper	Thos Pinckney
Wm Gordon	John Wilkes Kittera	Jonathan Brace
Jonathan Freeman	Thos Hartley	Chauncy Goodrich
Christopher G Champlin		

Mbrs of Congress-Ga: Messrs Jones & Talliaferro.

Wash Artl Co, to meet at my hse. -John Kearney, 2d Lt.

Election of electors, for Wash City, to meet on Capitol Hill on Mon & thence to Bladensburg where the election will be held. -Federal Rpblcn Candidate
-Francis Deakins [Washington]

MON NOV 10, 1800 NO. V

Capt Jas Barron is apptd command of U S Ship, *Warren*.

Paris Oct 3, 1800: Convention of amity & commerce, bet the French Republic Claret, Fleurieu, & Riederer & the Americ commrs, Oliver Elsworth, W R Davey & W V Murray.

Strayed or stolen, a black mare, $4 reward -Jas Usher, Greenleaf's Point, Wash City, Nov 10, 1800.

WED NOV 12, 1800 NO. VI

Electors of Pres & VP were chosen in Md. Gtwn Dist, T Duckett, Rpblcn Cand-152 votes; J F Deakins, Fed Cand-138 votes. Montg Crt Hse-Mr Deakins had 3/4s of the votes; at Marlborough the votes were nrly equal; at Bladensburg, including Wash City, Mr Deakins had 201 votes & Mr Duckett 91 votes. No doubt of the elec of Federal candidate, Mr Deakins.

Dept of State. Wash, Oct 30, 1800. List of men, who alledge they are Americ ctzns born in Md & are detained on board British ships of war; for want of proof of their American ctznship; from Baltimore:
John Davist	Wm Floyd	Richd Walker
John Stafford	Henry Clay	Jas Cooper
Wm Hulson	Edw Carter	Thos Butters
Andrew Craig	Benj Harris	Barney Galdy
Henry Galdy	Henry Long	Jas Smith
All unknown:		
Wm Ford	John Simmonds	John Herner
Geo Ramsey	Jas McLinnan	Jas McLaring
Horatio Gates	John McDonald	

Wm Screvern	Queen Ann's Co	Henry Clay	Harford Co
Archibald Hunt	Cecil Co	John Shields	Sussex Co
Wm Moore	Eastern shore	John Somers	Dorset Co
Wm Stanford	Caroline Co		

Election for town of Balt: G Duvall, Rpblcn cand, over J T Chafe, Fed cand Balt co: N R Moore, Rpblcn cand, over T C Hunt, Fed cand. Electors of Pres & VP-N J: Kensey Johns, Chief Justice of Sup Crt for Newcastle co; Capt Saml White, Kent Co; Gen Nath'l Mitchell, Sussex Co-all good Fedrls.

Mr Wolcott, among the ctzns to first reach the fire in the War Office. -Wash City.

For sale: brick hse & lot nr Union Tavern-also a # of lots; one nr Mr Jos Peck's bldg; part of sq in Thos Beall's Addition to Gtwn; part of sq improved by Wm Smith; also a lot across from resid of Jos Nourse. -Jonathan Jackson

FRI NOV 14, 1800 NO. VII

Reps in Congress: counties of Jefferson, Montgomery, Wash., Hancock, Burke, Warren, Scriven & Wilkes: Jas Jones-4000; Benj Talliaferro-2500; Francis Willis-1000; all esqs.

John Barnes has for sale from Phil: teas, spices, liquors & coffee; store just opened opposite Mr Semmes's Tavern in Gtwn.

Frederick, Co, Md: Mr Murdock, Fed cand, 2,084 votes, Dr Dyler, Rpblcn cand, 1,724 votes.

NY candidates for the chair: Saml Osgood 62 votes & Mr Ten Broeck-31 votes. Gen John Armstrong, elected U S Senator, in the room of John Lawrence, esq, 99 votes and 2 for Peter Ganevoort, Jr. Nominated in Senate:

Rpblcns

Isaac Ledyard	Queen's Co	Anth'y Lipinard	NYC
P Van Cortlandt	W Chess. Co	Jas Burt	Orange Co
Gilb't Livingston	Dutchess Co	Peter Van Ness	Dutchess Co
Robt Ellis	Saratoga Co	John Woodworth	Renssalaer Co
J Van Renssalear	Albany Co	Jacob Eacker	Montg. Co
Wm Floyd	Suffolk Co		

Federal tkt.

John M Smith	John Outhour
Richd Morris	Jonathan Hasbrouck
Peter Sylvester	John DeWitt
Amos Hall	Jas Cocheran
Jos Kirkland	Abraham Ten Broeck
Aaron Lane	Cornelius Van Vechten

Mon Nov 17, 1800   No. VIII

Chosen Md electors: Gabrial Duval, J Gilpin, Mr Moore & P Spencer, all Rpblcns & Messrs Murdoch, Dickins, Plowden & J Doane, Feds. Benj Ogle unanimously re-elected Gov of Md.

Mr Ridout chosen mbr of council in room of Mr Wilmore, resigned.

N Carolina electors: Absalom Tatom, Gideon Allston, Jos Taylor, Judge McCoy; first three are Rpblcns & McCoy is a Federalist.

Raleigh, Nov 4. Electors: Col Taylor, anti-Fed-301 votes; Henderson, esq, Fed candidate-266 votes.

S Caroline: Mr Sumpter, Gen Butler & Mr Moore, all Rpblcns, elected to Hse of Reps for SC.

For sale: lot 9 sq 122, west of Pres. sq, indisputable title. -John Kearney. Also, lot 4 sq 491, on Pa Av -J K.

Forty-four mbrs of Congress assembled today-Nov 17: Messrs:

Foster	Shephard	Freeman
Sedgwick	Wadsworth	Varnum
Williams	Bishop	John C Smith
Davenport	John Smith	Cortland
Platt	Glen	Thompson
Baily	Lieb	Thomas
Heister	Brown	Muhlenberg
Woods	Smilie	Bear
Craik	Christie	Nicholson
John C Thomas	Powel	W C C Claiborne
Sumter	Page	Nicholas
Dawson	New	Jackson
Holmes	Reed	Silas Lee
Dent	Macon	Stanford
Allston	Huger	

Senate-13 mbrs appeared:

Anderson	Baldwin	Brown
Cocke	Chipman	Langdon
Livermore	Tracy	Wells
Howard	Foster	Hillhouse
Schureman		

R I: Fed tkt:-Gov Green, Geo Champlin, Edw Manton & Oliver Davis; Rpblcn tkt-Gov Fenner, Benj Johnson, Jas Helm & Constant Taber.

Washington book-store. Rapine, Conrad, & Co. corner of So B St & N J Ave, nr the Capitol.

Notice is hereby given that I have applied to the Genrl Assembly of Md for an act of insolvency. -Patrick Sim. Nov 7.

NC Electors: Alsalom Tatom, Gideon Allston, Jos Taylor & Judge McCoy.

WED NOV 19, 1800 NO. IX
Robt Liston, Minister of Gr Britain, arrv'd here on Mon last.

14th Regt of Militia of Md, requested at Mr Stille's Tavern in Wash City; Fri the 21st instant at 11 o'clock.

Mass. Elections for Hse of Rep: Dr Wm Eustis, Rpblcn; Nathan Read & Menassah Cutler, Federal. 1st Southern Dist: L Williams, 130 votes from 3 towns. Mr Bishop, Rpblcn-783 votes, Mr May-237 votes, Mr Bullock-148 votes from 8 towns. 2d Middle Dist: Mr Varnum, Rpblcn, 1007 votes against Mr Bigelow. 4th W Dist: Mr Upham, Fed, 836 votes, Mr Lincoln, Rpbl-825 votes.

Ltr from Bennington, Vt, to correspondent in Wash, Nov 3: Electors: Elijali Dewey, Jonathan Hunt, Genrl Chamberlain & Roswell Hopkins, all Federal.

Md has elected 4 Rpblcn & 4 Fed electors. Mr Kerschner, Rpblcn-19 votes; Mr Lynchecomb, also Rpblcn, is elected.

Jas Thompson Calender has applied to Genrl Crt of Va to be released from confinement under the sedition law by Habeas Corpus; answer made that it is improbable that any relief can be granted.

John Langdon, esq, Sen of NH, writes a ltr to Samuel Ringgold, esq, Hagerstown, Md-dated, Portsmonth, Oct 19, 1800. "I am now packing my bagage, shall set out in the stage tomorrow morning for the city of Washington, hope to be in Baltimore the beginning of next month-"

Congress-Hse of Reps, arrived in addition to those numerated yesterday, viz:

Wm Cooper	Lucas Elmendorg	Jas H Imlay	Robt Waln
Elijah Goodrich	Roger Griswold	Saml Smith	Henry Lee
Thos Evans	John Trigg	Franklin Davenport	Wm Edmond
R D Spaight	Jonathan Dickson	Benj Talliafaro	

Ltr to the late Dr Mather of Boston. Rev Sir-written by B Franklin, Passy, May 12, 1784, France. [Excerpts] You mention being in your 78th yr; it is now more than 60 yrs, I remember well both your fr & grfr, having heard them both from the pulpit; I visited your fr in Pa in 1724; I long much to see again my ntv place; I left in 1723, visited in 1733, 1743, 1753 & 1763; in 1773 I was in Eng. In 1775 I had a sight of it, but could not enter, it being in possesion of the enemy.
-B Franklin

Arrived in Wash: John C Smith, a new mbr from Conn, was sworn.

Messrs Mason & D Foster appeared.

FRI NOV 21, 1800 NO. X
Tho McKean is Govnr of the Commonwealth of Pa.

Rep in Congress for SC: counties of Georgetown & Cheraw Dist, Benjamin Huger-603 votes, Saml Benton-411 votes.

Terr nw of Ohio, Reps in Congress: Wm McMellon in the room of W H Harrison; & Paul Searin [Fearin].

Benj Goodhue has resigned his seat in the Senate.

NC electors: Gen Brown, Fed cand.-341 votes, Samuel Ashe, Rpblcn-6 votes. Newbern Dist: Wm Sheppard, Fed cand-70 votes.

Mr Robertson, Fed cand, chosen elector for Md & not Mr. Lynchcomb as stated in our last.

MON NOV 24, 1800 NO. XI
Middlebury, Vt. Legislature of Vt have passed an act incorporating a Univ at Middlebury, under the superintendency of Mr Jeremiah Atwater, who is appointed President.

John Bacon & Phanuel Bishop, Rpblcns, elected mbrs of Hse of Reps of U S for Mass.

Conrad & McMunn have opened hses of entertainment, 200 yds from the capitol in NJ Av -City of Wash-Nov 24, 1800.

For sale: ironmongery, cutlery, sadlery, brass wares & bldg materials, store on NJ Av, sq 600. -Henry Ingle

Meeting at Trenton, NJ; election for choosing 5 persons as Reps in 7th Cong of the U S to take place on Mar 4; Hon Isaac Smith-Chrmn & Gen John Beatty-Sec; to promote the election of Aaron Ogden, Wm Coxe Jr, Jas H Imlay, Franklin Davenport & Peter De Vroom, as Reps in the next Congress.
Committee to prepare an address to ctzns of NJ:

Mmbr	*County*	*Mmbr*	*County*
John Outwater	Bergen	Elisha Boudinot	Essex
John Neilson	Middlesex	John Lloyd	Monmouth
Frederick Frelinghuysen	Somerset	Geo Anderson	Burlington
Thos Heston	Gloucester	Wm Wallace	Salem
Saml Ogden	Cumberland	Parsons Leaming	Cape May
Isaac Smith	Hunterdon	Wm Campfield	Morris
Pete R Sharp	Suffex		

-Isaac Smith, Chrmn,   John Beatty, Sec.

WED NOV 26, 1800 NO. XII

J Rutledge, re-elected mbr of Hse of Reps-784 votes; C J Colcock-510 votes.

Electors of Va for Pres & VP:

Wm Newlum	Princess Anne	Edmund Pendelton, Sr	Caroline
Wm H Cabell	Amherst	Jas Madison, Jr,	Orange
John Page	Gloucester	Archib'd Stuart	Augusta
Thos Newton, Jr,	Norfolk Borough	Carter B Harrison	Pr Geo
Gen Jos Jones	Dinwiddie	Wm B Giles	Amelia
Greed Taylor	Cumberland	Thos Reed, Sr	Charlotte
Geo Penn	Patrick	Walter Jones	Northumberland
Richd Brent	Pr Wm	Wm Ellzey	Loudoun
Andrew Moore	Rockbridge	Gen John Brown	Hardy
Gen Jon Preston	Montg	Hugh Holmes	Frederick
Geo Wythe	Richmond City		

Electors of NC for Pres & VP:

Bryan Whitfield	Newbern Dist	Thos Wynns	Northampton
Gideon Alston	Halifax	Jos Taylor	Raleigh
Absalom Tatom	Hillsborough	Jos Winston	Rockingham
Wm Tate	Morgan	Nathan Mayo	Edgcombe
Thos Brown	Wilmington	Wm Martin	Fayetteville
Spruce Macay	Salisbury	John Hamilton	Edenton Dist

For sale: Dec 10 at Wm Tunnicliff's Hotel; 100 lots situated eastward of the Capitol.   -Geo Walker, Wash, Nov 26.

Commencement Nov 12th for conferring degrees in St John's College, Annapolis, Md:
1-Latin oration by Mr Richd Brown, of Va.
2-Oration on character by Mr C Stone, of Md.
3-Oration on modern philosophy by Mr Walter Fernandes, of Md.
4-Oration on study of history by Mr Jas Boyle, of Md.
5-Oration on ridicule, as test of truth, by John Sanders
6-Oration on party spirit, Mr Philip Thomas, of Md.

Degree of Bachelor of Arts:

Robt C Stone	Walter Fernandes	Jas Boyle
John Sanders	Philip Thomas	Thos Rogers
Richd Brown	Jas S Grant	Thos Dorsey

Master of Arts: [alumni of St John's]

Chas Alexander	Thos Chase	John B Ducket
John C Herbert	John H Tschudy	Richd Harwood
Wm Cooke	Robt H Goldsborough	Francis Key
Daniel Murray	John Shaw	C Whiling

Ltr from Col Wade Hampton, SC, to Col Holmesin, Va, Nov 11, "Mr Jefferson will have every vote here, but there is great danger that Gen Pinckney will also."

Boarding & Lodging; hse on NJ Ave, Mr Law's former residence. -Saml Bootes.
Meeting at Albany, Nov 8, 1800. Richd Hatfield, Chrmn; address to his Excellency John Jay who writes of his intentions for the past years to retire from the cares of public life.

Boston, Nov 13-Choice of electors:
Saml Phillips-166 votes
1st Western Dist-David Rosseter
3d Western-John Hooker
1st Southern-Walter Spooner
3d Southern-Wm Baylies
2d Middle-Francis Dana
4th Middle-Theophilus Bradbury
1st Eastern-Samuel Sumner Wilde

Edw H Robbins-210 votes
2d Western-Ebenezer Hunt
4th Western-Jos Allen
2d Southern-Wm Sever
1st Middle- Thos Dawes
3d Middle-Samuel Sewall
3d Eastern-Andrew P Fernald
2d Eastern-Lemuel Weeks

Gentleman with small family wishes lodgings in either Gtwn or Wash City. Apply to Mr Claxton, dr-kpr of Hse of Reps.

FRI NOV 28, 1800 NO. XII
Thos Jefferson, VP, arvd in Wash, Nov 27, & took up his lodgings in Messrs Conrad & McMunn's apartments.

Taneytown, Md-Nov 24, 1800. The factory for public arms belonging to Mr Mathias Shroyer, the contractor, burnt down.

Mass.-John Codman chosen Sen of U S in rm of Benj Goodhue resigned. Jonathan Mason, previously elected, declined. [Dec 1st - Corr: Jonathan Mason was chosen not John Codman]

Info wanted of Alexander Innes, hatter by trade, sometime ago was on the frig *Constellation* & in 1798 in Norfolk, Va. Not heard from since. -Robt Innes, Jr, merchant Easton, Pa.

Notice: 2 tracts of land in Pickering, Miss Terr, & adjoining the land of Adam Bingaman, are attached by a foreign attachment at the suit of Jos Calvet for $2,063.50. -Jos Calvet.

For sale: Brick hse & lot nr Union Tavern; also unimproved lots; 1 adjoining above, 1 nr Jos Peck's bldg; 1/4th of a sq in sq in Thos Beall's Addition to Gtwn, improved by Wm Smith; also lot at diagonal corner from resid of Jos Nourse sq in Wash. -Jonathan Jackson.

Hse of Reps: Elections committee reported: Nathan Read elected in place of Saml Sewall; John C Smith vice Jonathan Brace; Lyttleton W Tazewell vice John Marshall; Wm McMellon vice H W Harrison.

Boston, Nov 17. Sat, anchored in Nantasket Rds, U S frig, *Boston*, Geo Little, Cmder, with her prize, French Nat'l Corvette, *La Berceau*, commanded by Louis Andre Senes, captured Oct 12. Killed on the *Boston:* Wm Ford, John Higgins, Matthias Jafey & Wm McKee. Wounded: Saml Young, purser, Thos Hartley & Nath'l Dill, [since died]. Wounded & likely to recover: J M Haswell, Geo Groom, Gavin Wilkinshaw, Francis Rice, John Runlet, Francis Francis, John Alford & John Collins. French lost 35 & many wounded. The prize is now commanded by Lt Haswell, 1st Lt of the *Boston*. Saml Young had connections who reside in Bridge-Water.

Meeting of citizens of Phil City & County included: Capt Jas Gamble-chrmn; Wm Duane-sec; Hugh Ferguson, John Leib, Edw Pole, John Smith & John L. Irwin, committee; to consider conduct of the legislature.

MON DEC 1, 1800   NO. XIV
Jas Brindley, born at Tunsted, parish of Wormhill, Derbyshire, in England. Was the ingenious protector of the present system of canal Navigation.

WED DEC 3, 1800   NO. XV
John Michin, boot maker, from Phil, has rmv'd from nr Eastern Branch, to NJ Ave, on the hill. [Wash]

FRI DEC 5, 1800   NO. XVI
Benj Williams is re-elected gov of NC. 54 votes were given to Jos Taylor & John B Ashe. Electors of RI: Geo Chamblin, Edw Manton, Oliver David, & Wm Green.

Thomas Herty has opened an office nr the capitol, NJ Ave, -Legal Matters: Wills, Mortgages, Leases, Land Conveyances.

Geo Jackson is elected sen of U S for Ga.

MON DEC 8, 1800   NO. XVII
Electors of Ga: Gen John Morrison, Dr Dennis Smith, Henry Graybill, & John Lumpkin.

Richmond, Va-Richard Kennon chosen Spkr of Sen & Larkin Smith, Spkr of Hse of Reps.

Electors of Pa: Federal, nominated by the Senate-Frederick Kuhn, Jas Armstrong, Geo Ege, John Hubley, Wm Hall, Samuel W Fisher, Jas Crawford Sr. Rpblcns, nominated by Hse of Reps-Robt Whithill, Samuel Wetherill, John Kean, Jonas Hartzell, Gabriel Heister, Presly Carr Lane, Nathaniel B Boileau, Isaac Van Horne.

Died: Charles Adams, Dec 1, at NY, son of Pres of the U S.

Mbrs of Fed Lodge No. 15 to meet in dwelling hse of Mr Cunning Ham in NJ Av, from whence to Church of Rev'd Bro Andrew Thos Mc Cormick. Alex'r Cochran, Sec'ry, Wash City.

Boarding & Lodging: Wm O'Neal, apply to Mr Claxton, or at the Three Bldgs, 4 doors east of the Navy Ofc.

WED DEC 10, 1800   NO. XVIII
Jas Lloyd, Sen of U S for Md, rsgnd; [Dec 12] Wm Hindman, to fill the vacancy.

FRI DEC 12, 1800   NO. XIX
Lost-Red Morocco Pkt Bk, deliver to Mr Smith's Printing Ofc-NJ Av, receive a liberal reward.   -Thos Town.

Rpblcn Electors of S C: Robt Anderson, John Hunter, Arthur Simkins, Wade Hampton, Andrew Love, Theodore Gaillard, Paul Hamilton, Jos Blythe, Gen Washington, John Wood. Electors of Ky: Chas Scott, John Coburn, Isaac Shelby, & John Pope.

John Brackenridge, chosen Sen of U S for Ky, in the rm of H Marshall, whose time expires on Mar 3 next.

For sale: Lots in Wash City, also a few lots to be let on lease for 99 yrs nr the Navy Yd.   -Wm Prout.

Died: John Nicholson, at Phil.

MON DEC 15, 1800   NO. XX
Capt Richard Derby, apptd command of U S Ship of War *Connecticut;* vice Capt Moses Tryon, resigned.

Died: Henry Osborse, St Simon's, Ga, Nov 9.

WED DEC 17, 1800   NO. XXI
Kid, Eliot & Co. Rec'd an assortment of hard ware & iron mongery, for sale at their store opposite the Great Hotel. Wash city.

Philip N Nicholas, chosen Atty Gen of Va.

FRI DEC 19, 1800   NO. XXII
Thos Calvert, late Cmder of U S Frig *Norfolk*, is apptd Cmder of the frig *Eagle*.

Ran away, negro-Fidelio, could be lurking about Mrs Young's where he has a wife.   -Jas R Dermott

To rent: 2 story brick hse on sq 701.   -Benjamin More, Wash.

Mon Dec 22, 1800   No. XXIII
For rent: I shall attend at the Eastern Branch Ferry, Dec 29, for purpose of renting the *Fishing Landing*. -John Wallace, of Wm. Dec 22, 1800-Washington.

Thos Carpenter, taylor, in partnership with Chas Varden, like wise from Phil, on Capitol Hill, opposite Mr Carrol's bldgs, Pa Av Military, Naval & Fancy Dresses & Ladies Habits.

Ran away from A. Lindo, living in Frederic Co, Va, a mulatto boy, Tom, about 20 yrs of age; his mother is a black slave of Mr Frederick Conrad, living in the Federal City.

Wed Dec 24, 1800   No. XXIV
Salem, Dec 11-the ship *Brutus*, Wm Brown, Cmder, in 32 days from Gibraltar, & 40 from Algiers, informs that the U S Frig, *Geo Washington*, Capt Bainbridge, sailed for Constantinople on Oct 19.

Fri Dec 26, 1800   No. XXV
Oliver Ellsworth has resigned the Office of Chief Justice of U S & John Jay has been nominated by the Pres as his successor.

Died: Thos Hartley, Dec 21, at York-Town, Pa, mbr of Congress for Pa; age 52.

Died: Gustavus Scott, in Wash, one of the Commissioners.

Mon Dec 29, 1800   No. XXVI
Beef-Steak & Oyster Hse, on Capitol Hill, City of Wash, in hse lately occupied by Brown & Snowden as a printing office, nr the Capitol. -Wm Tonkin.

Boarding & Lodging, nr the end of the new gravel walk on NJ Av -Jas Vansandt.

Charleston, Dec 5. Yesterday was burnt pursuant to sentence, Ben, negro, belonging to Mr Creggmiles, for the murder of Mr Wm Maxwell, in a barbarous manner, nr 13-mile-hse.

Oliver Ellsworth, one of the American Envoys to France, arrived in London Oct 29.

Wed Dec 31, 1800   No. XXVII
Cabinet & Chair Manufactory. Wilson & Handy, have commenced their business at their shop on NJ Av between Episcopal Church & Sugar Hse.

President has nominated Samuel Dexter, Sec of Treas, vice, Oliver Wolcott resigned.

The National Intelligencer and Washington Advertiser
Washington, DC 1801

MON JAN 5, 1801
This day published: *Considerations on the Government of the Territory of Columbia* signed-Epaminondas. For sale at Michl Robert's Book-Store, Gtwn & at Rapine Conrad & Co.

Priv sale: 2-three story brick hses, adjoining ea other, lot 6 sq 586, in Wash. Apply: Danl Carrol or in Balt-Henry H Carrol.

Just arvd at Barneys Tavern, Gtwn, J B Dumoutet, from Phil, with an elegant assortment of jewelery.

Hse o/Reps: Crape is to be worn for the memory of Thos Hartley, a mbr.

Pres of the U S has recognised J H C Heineken as commercial agent to the Batavian Rpblc.

The Senate confirmed the nomination by the Pres of Saml Dexter, as Sec o/the Treas, vice Oliver Wolcott, rsgnd.

WED JAN 7, 1801
Notice: to creditors of John Dixon, meeting on Feb 17, at hse of Geo O'Hara, inn-kpr in Morris-Town, Morris Co, NJ, to ascertain debts due to each creditor; dividend of the said Dixon property will be made on Jul 9th next.
-Wm *Cramfield, assignee, Morris-Town, Dec 27, 1800. [*Canfield-Jan 16th newspaper]

Died: Peter J Van Berkel, late minister from United Netherlands, at Newark, NJ.

For sale-nr the county wharf, cologne mill stones. Jesse Hollingsworth-Balt, Md,

In chancery. Walter W Harwood, an insolvent of PG Co, application as a trader, praying the benefit of an *Act for the relief of sundry insolvent debtors.*
                        -Saml H Howard, Reg. CC.

Geo Dent, of Md, declines re-election as mbr of Hse o/Reps of U S.

In Chancery. John Hepburne, of Chas Co, Md, *Act for relief of sundry insolvent debtors.*   -Saml H Howard, Reg. CC.

Va: Hugh Jones is said to have been tried, condemned & executed by a foreign crt-martial; committee to investigate.

FRI JAN 9, 1801
Pres has nominated Wm Cranch a comr of Wash in room of G Scott, decd.

Ran away-apprentice girl, Rebecca Wood, age about 13 yrs, brown skin.
-Mary Hoffman, Bladensburg.

Northumberland, Pa. meeting regarding the leg system o/Pa, *Of What Use is the Senate?* Signed-

County			
Northumberland	John Bull	Danl Montgomery	Thos Cooper
	Wm Borham	Wm R Cozens	Robt Irwin
	John Mackey	Christopher Dering	Jos Priestley Jr
Sunbury	Saml Roberts	Jesse Moore	Jacob McKinney
	John Simpson	Henry Vanderslice	Jas Cummings
	Jacob Haller	Theodore Kiehl	Jos Alder
	Jacob Breyfogel	Jeremiah Simpson	Solomon Markley
	Andrew Grove		
Danville	Wm Montgomery	W. Montgomery Jr	D. Montgomery Jr
Chilisquaque	Thos Strawbridge	Saml Bond	
Selins Grove	Ch Drum	Geo Kremer	John Epler
Milton	Danl Vincent	Bethuel Vincent	Jas Dougal
	John Cohran	Jared Irwin	
Derrtown	Henry Spyker	John Metzgar	Lawrence Kemble
	Jas Webb	Jas Duncle	Andrew Albright
	John Webb		
Buffaloe & Whitedeer	Saml Dale	Wm Chamberlain	John Kelly

Americ Philosophical Soc, Phil, Jan 2, 1801:

Pres	Thos Jefferson		
VPs	Caspar Wistar	Robt Patterson	Andrew Ellicott
Secs	John Redman Coxe	Adam Seybert	Jos Clay
	Burgess Allison		
Cnslrs	Jonathan B Smith	Wm Gurrle	Saml Wheeler
	P S Duponceau		
Curators	C W Peale	J R Smith	Robt Leslie
Treas	John Vaughan		

WED JAN 14, 1801
Died: Jas Jones, age 32 yrs, Jan 12th in Wash City; mbr of Hse o/Reps of Ga.

Ltrs from N Hunter, an acredited agent of Cato West, Geo Brandon, Hugh Davis, Ebenezer Smith, Saml H Gibson, John Foster, Wm Erwing, Jos Calvit, John Bolls, Thos Calvit, Felix Hughs, Thos M Green, Ebenezer Gayton, Francis Smith & David Greenleaf-styling themselves a committee chosen by inhabitants of Mississippi Terr, for purpose of petitioning for a redress of grievances.

The Pres has nominated & the Senate confirmed Bartholomew Dandridge, Cnsl for the U S for the southern dist of St Domingo to include Aux-Cayes & Jeremie.

For sale: cheap lumber; lumber yards north end of Lamberton & at the Old Sturgeon Pond, above Richards Wharf. I intend establishing a lumber yd in Wash; apply to subscriber or with Wm & Anthony M Buckley, or Benj W Morris & Co, merchants, Phil.   -Nathan Combs.

Justices o/the Peace for Adams Co, Sep 15, 1800: Wm Dunbar, Thos Wilkins, Abraham Ellis, John Collins, Hugh Davis & Wm Kenner. Signed-Peter Walker, clk of the Crt of Gen Quar Sessions. [Miss Terr]

Miss Terr: Adam Co expenses for 1799 included: inquests held on the bodies of Ann Daugherty; & Duncan by L Evens, before the appointment of Melling Woolley as coroner.

FRI JAN 16, 1801
Expenditures of the U S included monies for: [Those with names only were extracted:]
Robt Purviance, coll at Balt,
Mr. David Caldwell, clk of the Dist Crt of Pa
Saml Meredith, receiver of monies from sale of public lands undercontract with John Cleves Symmes pursuant to Act of Mar 2, 1799.
Aquila Giles, marshal for the Dist of N Y.
Capt Thos Tingey, sales of sundry armed French vessels.
Wm Marshall, clk of the Dist Crt of Va, do.
Nath'l Goodale, clk of the Dist Crt of Mass, sales of the French armed vessels *L'active* & *L'mutine*.
Saml Bradford, marshal for the Dist of Mass.
Wm Peck, marshal for the Dist of R I, for sales of the schrs *Betsey* & *Flying-Fish*.
Isaac Parker, marshal for the Dist of Maine; sale of ship *Mac*.
John Hall, marshal for the Dist of Pa
Chas Wharton, late deputy commissary genr'l, for bal due by him.
Edw Carrington, late deputy Qrtr-mstr Genrl, for public prop sold.
Saml & Jos Sterett, late agents for erecting fortifications at Balt.
Jos Williams, late contractor at Chestertown, Md.
Jonathan Dayton, late Spkr of the Hse of Reps.
Scott & Ernest, late contractors for supplying the Army w. provisions.
Timothy Pickering, late Sec of State.
Theodore Sedgwick, spkr of the Hse of Reps.
                    -Jos Nourse, Reg Treas Dept, Dec 5

Meeting of the ctzns of Alexandria, Jan 13, 1801. Elisha C Dick, chrmn; Henry Moore, sec. Subject-genr'l regulations for Terr of Columbia.

Sarah McKaraher, mantua mkr & seamstress, has remv'd to the hse of Mr De France, one door of Mr Smith's printing ofc-Wash.

Rpblcn meeting at Phil City & Co. Col John Barker, chrmn, John Smith, sec.
Cmttee of Arrangement:

Hugh Ferguson	Danl Boehm	John Smith
Michl Bright	Thos Leiper	Andrew Kennedy
Peter S Duponceau	Jos Worrell	Jas Gamble
Jas Ker	Wm Rush	Robt Porter
Gen Jacob Morgan	Wm Coates	Dr John Porter
Frederick Wolbert	Casper Sneider	John Dover
Manuel Eyre, Jr	Ebenezer Ferguson	Isaac Hozey
Robt McMullen	Michl Freytag	Jas Ingle
Geo Goodwin	Philip Peltz	Heath Norbury
Nathan Jones.		

Mrs Dempsey, from NY, mantua-making, has commenced business in Wash, NJ Av, 5 doors from Mr Smith's printing ofc-Wash.

MON JAN 19, 1801
Lucius Horatius Stockton, nominated Sec of War, by Pres of U S.

WED JAN 21, 1801
John Marshall, nominated Chief Justice of U S, by Pres of U S.

Federalists of NY, have resolved to support Stephen Van Rensellear, present Lt-Gov, as Gov of the State.

FRI JAN 23, 1801
For sale or rent: 2 story brick hse nr the Little Hotel.-Jonathan Pancoast, Washington.

Levi Lincoln, elected Rep for 4th Western Dist of Mass. Mr Bacon is elected Rep for Mass in the next congress.

Jacob Carpenter, Rpblcn, elected treas of Pa, over Peter Baynton, Fed candidate.

Congress of U S-Hse of Reps: 1-Petition of H Pesinger, to be placed on the pension list was barred by statute of limitation. 2-Nathan'l Holmes, praying for expences in preparing & marching a detachment of militia to Trenton in 1794-referred. The following petitions were presented & referred: 3-Paul McDermot; 4-Shadrach Inman; 5-P C L'enfant, 6-John Pitchlynn; 7-Benj Law; 8-Chas Tonkins; 9-Wm Milton; 10-Pleasant Henderson; 11-Jas Coleman & others; 12-Solomon Boston. 13-Petition of N J Roosevelt was referred. 14-Leave given to Stephen Wock; 15-& to Eliz Jameson, to withdraw their petitions. Petitions rejected: 16-Thos Jenkins & sons; 17-Saml Trigg; 18-Nathan Sanborn; 19-Andrew Shepherd; 20-P C L'enfant; 21-Blagden; 22-Benj Law.

Partnership between Phelan & Noyes, is dissolved; business will be continued by Levi Noyes. [Washington]

Tutor wanted: to take charge of school abt 30 miles distant; apply at the bar of J H Barney in Gtwn.

MON JAN 26, 1801
Isaiah Wells, kpr of the prison of Montgomery Co: the prisoners commend Wells on their treatment and tell of brutality while in prison in Phil; They recd an executive pardon: Henry Jarrit, Conrad Mark, I. I. Eyermann, Valentine Kuder, Anthony Stahler, Henry Schmidt & Henry Shanwiler.

Notice: With astonishment, I read the dissolution of the partnership of the firm of Phelan & Noyes, without my consent-all persons are forbid trusting Levi Noyes.
-John Phelan.

Henry Latimer, sntr at Dela, will resign his seat in the senate, Mar 3d.

WED JAN 28, 1801
Will sell or exchange: land nr the Blue Ridge, Northumberland Co, Va, 1163 acs, divided into 2 plantations, brick dwelling hse 50 X 33, & 2 brick offices, 24 X 16. Framed hse 20 X 16 for an overseer. Mr Spencer Ball living thereon will show the whole & can make sale therof.   -Jas V Ball.

FRI JAN 30, 1801
High Crt of Chancery: to be sold at public auction, lot 1 sq in Wash, with the sugar hse & materials & other bldgs on said lot. Purchase money to pay & satisfy debt, int & costs due by mortgage from Jas Piercy to Thos Law.
-Jas D Barry, trustee.

Hse of Reps: Wm Smith Shaw, to be pd for his expences on a mission from Phil to Mt Vernon, on public business-$50.

The Pres has nominated Roger Griswold-Sec of War.

MON FEB 2, 1801
Providence, R I: Fire burnt the stores of: John Corlis, Saml Arnold, Thos L Halsey, John T Clark, Green & Barker, J Olney, & Jas Peck. Mr Peck lost his store & house. Loss is computed at $500,000.

Lt Gov Van Renselaer declines as candidate for Gov of NY. [Feb 9: Mr Van Rensselaer, agreed to stand as candidate]

In Chancery. Levi Butler, insolvent of Chas Co, trader, prays for "Act for the Relief of Sundry Insolvent Debtors". Resid of Md for 2 yrs; using the trade of merchandise.   -Saml H Howard, Reg. CC.

WED FEB 4, 1801
John Stewart elected to supply the vacancy in present congress occasioned by the death of Thos Hartley, Rep of Pa.

Hse of Reps: Petition of Lawrence Erb, late Col of Rev in Northhampton, praying to be released from confinement for having converted public monies to his own use. [Referred]

Christopher Hoxie, of Hudson, has invented a wheat machine, it will thresh & clean from 20 to 100 bushels in a day.

Fine Liverpool sale & pork-in barrels for sale at Barry's Wharf, by Redmond & G Barry, Washington.

Nail Manufactory: F St, Washington, John Jack

FRI FEB 6, 1801
Mr Pierpont Bacon, who lately died at Colchester, has left the whole of his prop- $30,000, to the 1st Society of that town, for the support of a school.

For sale: 30 barrels of shad & 115,000 bricks. -McCormick & Cochran. Wash.

Reward-$2 for Jack, 16 yrs of age, negro.   -Geo Andrews, Wash.

Vermont paper: Lewis R Morris is re-elected to rep the eastern dist of that state in congress.

MON FEB 9, 1801
Robt Greenhow, merchant in Williamsburg, Va. desirous to with draw from business, offers for sale the whole of his well know genr'l & valuable assortment of merchandise.

Committee of Fed Freeholders of NYC: Cornelius Ray; Robt Troup; Richd Harrison; Jas Watson; Archibald Gracie; Wm M Woolsey; Jas McHughes. [all esqs]

WED FEB 11, 1801
Died: Ann Hutchinson, age 101 yrs 9 mos 7 days, Jan 4, 1801, at hse of Robt Wilson, esq, in East-Windsor Township, Middlesex Co, w/o the late Wm Hutchinson; mthr of 13 chldrn, grmthr, ggrmthr, & gggrmthr, to the amt of as is known, of 375 Persons & a no. of them of the 5th generation.

For sale: hse & lot in Wash, cld *"The Cottage"*, on slope of the hill appropriated for the Nat'l Univ, nr Commissioners Wharf, at present occupied by Mr Knapp of the Auditor's Ofc. Terms, apply to Dr Wm Thornton, one of the comrs of Wash, to Mr Philip Fitzhugh, or Presly Thornton. Wash City.

FRI FEB 13, 1801
Return of votes for Pres & VP: Jefferson-73; Burr-73; Adams Pinckney-64; Jay-1. Reps of Hse, returned to chambers to chose one.   One ballot: Jefferson 55 votes & Burr 49 votes. 30th ballot was taken, next ballot tomorrow.

Addletong & Fome's, groc good store, NJ Av, nr the sugar hse, Wash.

Savannah, Jan 2-meeting of Rpblcn ctzns; Maj Wm Brown, chrmn; Col Tatnall, Maj Harden, W Bulloch, esq & Messrs Glass & Shaffer, committee. Regarding their high estimation of the administration of his Excellency Jas Jackson, Gov of the State of Ga.

MON FEB 16, 1801
John Harrison, boot & shoemaker, has remv'd from Alexandria, to Washington. Shop on Pa Av, nrly opposite bridge leading down to Greenleaf's Point. Washington.

John Chew Thomas, Rep in Congress for this dist, had a number of his constituents recommending him to vote for Thos Jefferson.

WED FEB 18, 1801
The 36th ballot was taken & Thos Jefferson was elected Pres. Jas A Bayard is nominated by the President Minister Plenipotentiary to the French Republic.

FRI FEB 20, 1801
Nominations of the Pres:
Judges of 1st Crct: John Lowell-Mass; Benj Bourne-R I; Jeremiah Smith-NH;
2d Crct: Egbert Benson-NY; Oliver Wolcot-Conn; Saml. Hitchcock-Vt.
3d Crct: Jared Ingersol-Pa; Richd Bassett-Dela; Wm Griffith-NJ.
4th Crct: Chas Lee, Atty-Genrl of U S Chief Judge; Philip B Key-Md; Geo Keith Taylor-Va. Theophilus Parsons, Mass, Atty Gen U S vice Chas Lee, nom. a Judge. John Davis, Dist Judge of Mass, vice John Lowell, nom. for promotion. Harrison G Otis, Atty for Dist of Mass, vice John Davis nom. a Judge. Ray Greene, Sen of R I, Judge of Dist of R I vice Benj Bourne, nom. for promotion. Edw St Loe Livermore, of NH, Atty of Dist of NH, vice Jeremiah Smith, nominated a Judge.
John W Kittera, of Pa, Atty of the Dist, vice Jared Ingersol, nom. a Judge.
New Consuls nominated: Henry Prebble, of Mass,-Cadiz.
John Jones Waldo, of Mass,-Nantes, France.
Isaac Coxe Barnet, of NJ,-Bourdeaux.
John M Forbes, of NY,-Havre-De-Grace.
Wm Lee, of Mass,-Marseilles.
Geo Rundle, of Pa,-Brest.
Thos Waters Griffith, of Md,-Rouen.
Wm Foster, Jr, of Mass,-Morlaix.
Geo Stacy, Acting Agent in Isle of France, to be consul at that place & Isle of Bourbon.
Jas H Hove, of Columbia,-Dunkirk.

Ranaway, Robert, negro, formerly prop of Parson Buckens of Stafford Co & by him sold to Mr Jas Patten of Alex; Patten sold him to Wm Broch, barkpr; age abt 23 yrs; was seen in employ of Jas R Dermot. -Richd Sandford, Orange Co, Va.

Wish of the bro of Richd Dempsey to know what has become of him & where he resides. Dempsey arrv'd in this country from Ire in County of Antrim, nr Barrymanock abt 9 yrs ago. He is supposed to be in West Pa. -John Dempsey, Wash.

Decision bet Pa & Conn, regarding boundary, was signed in Pa by: Wm Whipple, Wm C Houston, Eavid Brerely, Welcome Arnold & Cyrus Griffin.
-Trenton, Dec 20, 1782.

MON FEB 23, 1801
Elias Boudinot, esq, is director of the mint.

Hse of Reps: Petitions of Mathias Shroyer & Mgt Culbertson were presented & referred to committee of claims.

Hse of Reps: Spkr of the Hse does not have the authority to direct the Sgt at Arms to expel Saml Harrison Smith, ctzn of the U S, from the gallery; this right can only be forfeited by disorderly behaviour.

WED FEB 25, 1801
Chas Campbell, watch-maker, from Phil, intends remaining in Wash. a few days. May be spoken with at Tunnicliff's Hotel.

Nominations by the Pres:
Thos Bee, SC,-Chief Judge; John , NC, & Jos Clay, Ga,-Judges in 5th Crct of U S;
Wm McClung, Ky,-6th Crct of U S; Jacob Read, Sen at SC,-Judge in place of Judge Bee;
Wm H Hill, Mbr of Hse of Reps at NC,-Judge in place of Judge Sitgreaves;
Saml Blackbourn,-Atty for Western Dist of Va;
Robt Grattan, Staunton, Va,-marshal for Western Dist of Va;
Thos Gray, East Tenn,-marshal of said dist;
Chas J Porter, East Tenn,-marshal of said dist;
Wm Pitt Beers, Albany,-Atty of U S for Dist of Albany;
Jas Dole, Troy in Dist of Albany,-marshal of said dist;
Jas Clole Mountflorence,-Commercial Agent for U S at Paris.

Apptd by Gov St Clair. Indiana Terr: Wm Clark,-Chief Justice; Henry Vanderburgh,-2d Judge; John Griffin,-3d Judge.

For sale: 3000 weight of firkin butter.   -John Kearney, Wash.

New York-Jan 1, 1801. Report on prison expenditures; submitted by: Robt Bowne, Geo Warner, John Murray Jr, Jotham Post, Thos Eddy, Leonard Bleecker & Thos Franklin.

FRI FEB 27, 1801

Partnership of Wilson & Handy-cabinet & chair makers, is dissolved by mutual consent.   -Thos Wilson, Shop-NJ Av

Elias Boudinot is director of the mint of the U S; Jos Richardson is assayer to the mint of the U S.

MON MAR 2, 1801

Jonathan Booth, offers reward for his stolen great coat.

Died: Mrs Mgt Silvester, age 78, ntv of Boston, Mass, Feb 27.

Public sale of lots at Wm Tunnicliff's Hotel.-Geo Walker.

For sale: lots in Wash; or lease on ground rent.-John Stickney, from his bldg opposite Rhodes Tavern, Pres Sq.

Robert Ellis has wines, etc, for sale at the hse lately occupied as the Little Hotel.

Hse of Reps: Capt Philip Sloan, praying to be reimbursed money advanced for him by the Banking Hse of Bacris & Co of Algiers; to procure his ransom from captivity - Referred to Committee.

WED MAR 4, 1801

Wm Miller is comr of the revenue; Joshua Johnson is superintendent of stamps; Saml Dexter is sec of treas.

Proposals for disposing of an estate cld *"Blue Plains"*, on Md bank of Potomac, 500 acs, valued at $40,000. dwelling hse, 57 X 32. Wm Mackall, esq, gives a clear title.   -Wm Bayly.

This day at 12 o'clock, Thos Jefferson, took the oath of office as Pres of U S, in the Senate Chamber. Aaron Burr, VP of U S, took his seat in the Senate, as Pres of that body.

FRI MAR 6, 1801

Appointments: Jas Madison, Jr, esq, of Va, Sec of State; Henry Dearborn, esq, of Maine, Sec of War;
Levi Lincoln, esq, of Mass, Atty Genrl of U S; Robt R Livingston, esq, of NY, Minister Pleni. to French Republic.

John Chew Thomas informs his fellow-citizens of PG & AA Cos, & Annapolis, he will serve them if elected in cong of U S.

Lost: Black memorandum bk   -Mr John Barnes, of Gtwn.

In Chancery: Petition of John Conaway, of AA Co, Md-"Act for Relief of Sundry Insolvent Debtors".   -Saml H Howard, Reg CC.

MON MAR 9, 1801

Died: Jas Madison, father of Jas Madison, Sec of State.

Saml White-apptd Sen. in Cong. for Dela. vice, Henry Latimer, resigned.

Apptd by the late Pres of the U S: [John Adams]. Thos Johnson, esq, to be Chf Judge of the Dist of Col.. Wm Cranch & Jas Marshall, esqs, to Assist Judges. Jas M Lingan, esq, to be marshal.
Wm Hammond Dorsey, esq, to be Judge of the Orphans Crt in D C.
John Peters, to be Reg of Wills for D C.
John Herbert, esq, to be Judge of Orphans Crt for Alexandria Co.
Cleon Moore, esq, of Alexandria, to be Reg of Wills for same.

Justices o/the Peace for Wash Co, D C:

Abraham Boyd	Thos Sim Lee	Thos Peter
Tristram Dalton	Wm Marbury	Benj Stoddert
Thos Addison	Uriah Forrest	John Mason
John Laird	Danl Carrol	Richd Forrest
Jas Barry	Wm Thornton	Marsham Waring
Thos Beall	John Threlkald	Lewis Deblois
Danl Reintzel	Wm Hammond Dorsey	Robt Brent
Jos Sprig Belt	Cornelius Cunningham.	

Justices o/the Peace for Alexandria Co:

Wm Fitzhugh	John Potts	Robt Townsend Hooe
Jonah Thompson	Richd Conway	Wm Harper
Chas Alexander	Jonathan Swift	Geo Gilpin
Abraham Faw	Francis Peyton	Chas Alexander Jr
Geo Taylor	John Herbert	Dennis Ramsay
Cuthbert Powell	Simon Summers	Jacob Haughman
Cleon Moore		

Saml Hanson of Saml, to to be Notary Public for Wash. Henry Moore to be Notary Public for Alexandria. Cleon Moore to be Reg of Wills for Alex.

WED MAR 11, 1801

Acts Passed by Cong: 1-Relief of Solomon Beston; 2-the discharge of Saml Lewis, Sr from his imprisonment; 3-relief of Nathaniel Holmes; 4-relief of Arnold Henry Dorhman or his legal reps.

Littleton W Tazewell has declined being a candidate for Rep in next congress, Saml Tyler has offered his svcs.

For sale or rent: 2 brick hses on Pa Av   -Owen Roberts

In Chancery: Thos B Clements-insolvent of Chas Co, Md, applies as a trader, for benefit of "An act for relief of sundry insolvent debtors".
                                -Saml H Howard, Reg CC.

Lost or mislaid, cloth directed to Chas Varden, taylor, sent from Bryden's Stage Ofc, Balt, Md. Forward as directed, or to be left at McLaughlin's Stage Ofc-Gtwn, with line to Thos Carpenter, Wash City.

FRI MAR 13, 1801
In Chancery: Saml Boots, of PG Co, Md, trader, prays for benefit of an act of relief of sundry insolvent debtors.   -Saml H Howard, Reg CC.

Albany, NY-Appointments: Sheriffs:-Thos Stevens, for Essex; Guy Maxwell, for Tioga; Roger Sprague, for Ontario; [Blank] Greaves, for Clinton. Nominated but negatived for Orange Co: Benj Jackson & Col Wm Falconer; for Schoharie: Wardell Green, John Ingold & Benj Miles.

Candidates for Gov of NY: Geo Clinton & Stephen Van Rensselaer. Jeremiah Van Rensselaer has been agreed upon as a fit person for Lt Gov

To be rented: brick hse in sq 104, Wash City.   - Wm King.

MON MAR 16, 1801
Solomon Boston, confined in public jail of Kent Co, Delaware, to be released from all claim or demand o/the U S. Signed:-Theodore Sedgwick, Spkr-Hse of Reps. Thos Jefferson, VP of U S. John Adams, Pres of U S. Aprv'd Jan 30, 1801.

Married: Maj David Hopkins, marshal of Md, to Miss Isabella Ford, young lady lately from Jamaica, Mar 15, by Rev Mr McCormick.

Died: Mr Wm Milns, age 40 yrs, at Boston, formerly a school mstr in NYC.

Died: Rev Hugh Blair, at Edinburgh, Scot, Prof of Rhetoric & Belles lettres in Univ of Edinburgh.

Election of Gov in NH: Timothy Walker-447 votes, John T Gilman, 101 votes.

Firm of Andrew Rutherford & Co is dissolved. Jas Thompson & Andrew Rutherford. Washington.

Thos Johnson declines the ofc of Chief Justice of the Dist of Col.

Charlottesville, Va-Mar 4, 1801. Toasts were given at dinner in the Eagle Tavern by:

Col F Walker, Pres	Jas Barbour, VP	
Dr Ward Caw	H B Trist, late of Phil	P Carr
Col Lindray	D Yancy of Louisa	D Carr
M Dinsmore	Wm D Allen of Jas City	Chas Yancey
Capt B Harris	F Harris of Louisa	Wm D Meriwether
Wm Alcock	T W Lewis	I Carr
E Garrett	J Yancy	E Garland

Rev John Hargrove is the minister of the New Jerusalem Chr, Balt, Md.

WED MAR 18, 1801
For sale: *"Earnhill"*-20,574 acs & framed hse; *"Wickham Goodeville"*-2711 acs & framed hse; Montg. Crt-Hse, Md. -Honore Martin. Montg Co, Md.

Winchester, Va, paper-Feb 23. Act passed to incorporate a company for a turnpike rd from Savage Rvr to nrst western navigation. Subscriptions to be recd by: Chas Simms & Wm Hartshorn, Alexandria. Alexander White & Jas Stephenson, Berkley, Edw McCarty & Lewis Dunn, Hampshire. John Webster, John Prunty & Maxwell Armstrong, Harrison Co. John Steally, Henry Deering & Hugh McNeally, Monongahela. Archibald Magill, Adam Douglass & Robt Macky, Winchester.

Died: Jos Russell, Mar 9, age 70 yrs, merchant of Phil.

Revised list from Mar 9, 1801.
Appointments by the present Pres of U S: [Thos Jefferson]
John Shee, esq, marshal of Eastern Dist of Pa.
Alexr J Dallas, esq, atty for the same dist.
Presly Kerr Lane, esq, marshal of Western Dist of Pa
Jas Hamilton, esq, Atty for Western Dist of Pa
David Fay, esq, atty for Dist of Vt.
John Willard, esq, marshal for Dist of Vt.
Gen Wm Irwine, superintendant of military stores.

Justices o/the Peace for Wash Co: Danl Reintzell
Thos Corcoran   Danl Carol   Cornelius Cunningham
Thos Peter   Robt Brent   Thos Addison
Abraham Boyd   Benj More   John Mason
Wm Thornton   Benj Stoddert   Jos Sprigg Belt
Thos Sim Lee   Wm Hammond Dorsey [all esqs]

Justices o/the Peace for Alexandria Co:
Geo Gilpin   Wm Fitzhugh   Francis Peyton
Richd Conway   Elisha Cullen Dick
Chas Alexander   Geo Taylor   Jonah Thomson
Abraham Faw   John Herbert   Alex'r Smith
Cuthbert Powell   Peter Wise Jr   Jacob Houghinen,
Thos Darne, [all esqs]

Pres of U S has remitted the remainder of the sentence of Jas Thompson Calender, convicted last summer of libel, in Va; & also David Brown, convicted of similar offence: Crct Crt of Mass.

For sale: land lying below Fredericksburg, Va, 533 acs & hse; bounded by lands of Gen A Spotswood, Messrs Wm Herndon, Mann Page, Francis Taliaferro, & tract I live on.   -Laurence Brooke

FRI MAR 20, 1801
Ran away-my apprentice-boy, Walter Manly, abt 9 yrs of age; robbed me repeatedly. -John Minchin, NJ Av, Wash.

Hse hold furn for sale; to be sold-at hse of & by Saml Jackson.

Journeyman hair-dresser, Christopher Gird, Alexandria.

Phil, Mar 16, 1801 Supreme Crt-Timothy Pickering v Jas Reynolds, M.D. A civil action grounded on a paragraph in the Aurora charging Pickering with illegally receiving $5 for a passport delivered at his ofc.

MON MAR 23, 1801
For sale at public vendue for cash: sundry hsehold furn.-Jos Taylor, living in the Twenty Bldgs, Wash.

WED MAR 25, 1801
Grants of lands appropriated for the refugees from British Prov of Canada & Nova Scotia enacted by Sen & Hse of Reps of U S.
Following persons entitled to land:

2,240 Acs	Maria Walker wid of Thos Walker; John Edgar; P Francis Cazean; John Allan; Seth Harding.
1,280 Acs	Jonathan Eddy; Col Jas Livingston; Parker Clark; heirs of John Dodge
960 Acs	Thos Faulkner; Edw Faulkner; David Gay; Martin Brooks; Lt Col Bradford; Noah Miller; Joshua Lamb; Atwood Sales; John Starr; Wm How; Ebenezer Gardner; Lewis F Delesdernier; John McGown ; Jonas C Minot; heirs of Simon Chester
540 Acs	Jacob Vander Heyden; John Livingston; Jas Crawford; Isaac Danks; Maj B Von Heer; Benj Thompson; Jos Bindon; Jos Levitre; Lt Wm Maxwell; J D Mercier; Jas Price; Seth Novle; Martha Bogart; John Halstead; relict of Abraham Bogart, & formerly relict of Daniel Tocker.
320 Acs	David Jenks; Ambrose Cole; Jas Cole; Adam Johnston; wid of & heirs of Col Jeremiah Duggan; Daniel Earl Jr; John Paskell; Edw Chinn; Jos Cone; John Torreyre.
150 Acs	Saml Fales [Sales]

Official-Wm Kilty, Chief Judge of the Crct Crt of the Dist of Col.
Danl Carroll Brent, marshal of same. John Thomson Mason, atty of do.

Corrections-Mr Muhlenberg is not apptd coll of the port of Phil in room of Geo Latimer. Mr Dawson is not apptd Minister to Portugal in room of Mr Smith.

FRI MAR 27, 1801
Crct Crt of DC has appointed Henry Whetcroft, Notary Public.

Official- Jos Scott to be marshal for the Eastern Dist of Va.

Money was appropriated by Sen & Hse of Reps for satisfying annuities to: Isaac Van Wart, Paul Paulding, David Williams, Jos De Bealeau, Jos Traversie, Jas McKensie, Jos Brussels, Eliz Bergen, chldrn of Alexr Trueman & Col Johnson.

In Chancery-Patrick Sim, of Montg Co, Md, praying the benefit of the "Act for Relief of Sundry Insolvent Debtors".   -Saml H Howard, Reg CC.

Nails for sale at my store bet the Pres' Hse & 6 Bldgs.   -Saml McIntire

MAR 30, 1801
Died: Lavater, at Zurich, Jan 2d, of wounds recd a yr ago.

Official: Wm Gardner of NH, Comr of Loans for NH
Jos Whipple, coll of the Dist of Portsmouth, in NH.
Edw Livingston, atty for Dist of New York.
John Swartwout, marshal of Dist of New York.
John Smith, marshal of the Easter Dist of Pa; vice Mr Shee who declined.
Genrl Saml Smith, sec of the Navy.

WED APR 1, 1801
Builders-Wm Lovering, Gay St nr Union Tavern, Gtwn, & Wm Dyer, I St, North of New War Ofc, Wash.

Correction-Genrl Smith is not Sec of the Navy; Genrl Dearborn has undertaken the discharge of those duties, Mr Stoddert having rsgnd.

Committee for the improvement of F St North, Wash City: Capt Jas Hoban, Mr John Kearney & Capt Clotworthy Stephenson.

FRI APR 3, 1801
Died: Orono, Chief of the Penobscot tribe of Indians, age 113, at Old Town on Penobscot River.

Died: Pierre Henry Louis, Mar 26 at Balt, agent of French Republic.

Land for sale: desiring to move to the western country, my dwelling plantation, 600 acs, in AA Co, Md, nr Saml Thomas, merchant, & saw mills; hse 40 X 28.
                                    -Philemon Dorsey.

John Woodside is a clk in the ofc of the Comptroller of the U S Treas; he was there on Jan 20th when the Treas ofc was on fire.

MON APR 6, 1801
Stolen out of my stable, bay mare. -Pennell Corbit, Cantwell's Bridge, Dela.

Witnesses to the fire on Jan 20th at the Treas Ofc: Lawson Pearson, John Coyle, Henry Kramer, Saml Roe, Thos Waterman, Basil Wood & Jonathan Freeman

WED APR 8, 1801
Ladies with letters remaining in the Post Office, April 1, 1801.

Mrs Eliza Arthur	Mrs J Bath	Mrs Nancy Bailenger
Flora Conner	Mrs Kath. Dexter	Eliza Dempsey
Mrs Susannah Foulk	Mrs Jane Fulton	Miss Prudence Fuller
Miss Polly Fuller	Mrs Mary Fenwick	Rachel Grove
Mrs Mary Jones	Mary Kennaday	Elenor P Lewis
Miss Abigal Monday	Sarah Norton	Miss Maria O Connor
Celia Pye	Miss Ann Stuart	Margaret Twedy
Mrs S Tompkins	Mrs Walbergh	

Official-Geo Dent, to be marshal of the District of Potomac.

Elizur Goodrich of Conn, resigned his seat in 7th Cong of U S.

FRI APR 10, 1801
For sale: 2 brick hses, 40 X 20, King & Columbia Sts, Alex; 2 brick hses, 25 X 36, Pa Ave, Wash; abt 8,000 acs of land in Ky. -N Voss, Wash.

For sale-se corner of sq 973, nr the Navy Yd.   -Thos Tingey, Wash.

To be sold in Bladensburgh, 20 & 30 slaves.   -Wm Steuart.

For sale: 400 acs, opposite Washington Anthony Addison, at Barnaby-3 miles from Dyer's Ferry.

MON APR 13, 1801
Mrd: Mr D. English, one of the proprietors of the museum, to Miss Sally Threlkeld, both of Gtwn, Apr 7, by Rev S B Balch.

For sale or rent: 3 story brick hse, sq 881. Terms apply to Jos Wheat, on premises, or subscriber   -Notley Maddox.

Found-a bank note of considerable value.   -Josias M Speake.

Will exchange lots in Wash for tract of land nr the mkt.
    -Alexander Young, Wash.

Reps in Congress elected for Md: Genrl Saml Smith; Jos H Nicholson; John Archer-881 votes [29 votes to John Carlisle]; Richd Sprigg vice John C Thomas; Genrl Heister, Mr Plater & Mr Campbell

WED APR 15, 1801
Ran away-Jack, abt 23 yrs, mulatto, from Colmore Duvall, lvng in PG CO, Md.

Jos Clay, apptd 5th Crct Crt U S has declined his appointment.

FRI APR 17, 1801
Official: Walter Jones, Jr, apptd atty for district of Potomac.

Balt, Md, Apr 15. The hse of & occupied by Col Rogers, in Mkt St, was burnt & reduced to a pile of ruins. All barely escaped.

Mr Pichon, Charge Des Affaires of French Rep, has mv'd from the city to Gtwn, which place letters shd be addressed.

Orphans Crt of Wash Co, will commence its session at the hse of Mr Wm Rhodes, Wash. - John Hewitt, Reg.

In Chancery-Edw Moore, debtor of Calvert Co, prays the benefit of an "Act for Relief of Sundry Insolvent Debtors". -Saml H Howard, Reg CC.

Appointments made by John Adams-date of commission, Dec 12, 1800:
David Hopkins, marshal of Dist of Md.
Wm Clark, Chief Justice in & over Indiana Terr
Henry Vanderburgh, 2d Judge, Indiana Terr. John Griffin, 3d Judge, do.
Jos Hamilton Davies, Atty for Ky Dist.
John Marshall, comr with Oliver Wolcott & Chas Lee, [In rm of Timothy Pickering] to adjust claims with State of Ga.
John Jay, Chief Justice of the U S-Dec 19, 1800.
Saml Dexter, Sec of the Treas-Jan 1, 1801.
Saml Bradford, marshal of the Mass Dist-Dec 22, 1800.
Aquila Giles, marshal of the Dist of NY-Dec 22, 1800.
Wm Cranch, comr of Wash City-Jan 8, 1801.
Solomon Sibley, mbr of the Leg Cncl of the NW Terr-Dec 23, 1800.
John Ellis, Adam Bingamin, Alex'r Montgomery, John Stampley & Flood McGrew; mbrs of the Leg Cncl of the Miss Terr-Dec 30, 1800.
John Marshall, Chief Justice of the Supreme Crt of the U S-Jan 31, 1801.
Roger Griswold, Sec of War-Feb 3, 1801.
Arthur St Clair, Gov of the NW Terr-Feb 3, 1801.
Robt Hays, marshal of the Tenn Dist-Feb 20, 1801.
<u>Circuit Judges of the U S:</u>
First Crct: John Lowell, of Mass, Chief Judge-Feb 20, 1801.
Benj Bourne of R I; & Jeremiah Smith of NH, Judges of same Crct-Feb 20.
2d Crct: Egbert Benson, of NY, Chief Judge-Feb 20, 1801.
Oliver Wolcott, of Conn, & Saml Hitchcock, of Vt, Judges of same Dist, do.
3d Crct: Jared Ingersoll, of Pa, Chief Judge-Feb 20, 1801.
Richd Bassett, of Delaware; & Wm Griffith, of NJ, Judges of Pa-Feb 20.
4th Crct: Chas Lee, of Va, Chief Judge-Feb 20, 1801.
Philip Barton Key of Md; & Geo Keith Taylor of Va, Judges-Feb 20, 1801.
5th Crct: Thos Bee, of SC, Chief Judge-Feb 24, 1801.
John Sitgreaves, of NC; & Jos Clay Jr, of Ga, Judges-Feb 24, 1801.
6th Crct: Wm McClung, of Ky, Judge-Feb 24, 1801.

District Judges: John Davis, vice Mr Lowell-Feb 20, 1801.
Ray Greene, vice Mr Bourne, do.
Jacob Read, vice Judge Bee, Feb 24, 1801.
Wm H Hill, Judge of NC Dist, vice Mr Sitgreaves-Feb 24, 1801.
Circuit Judges to succeed those who declined:
Wm Tilghman, Chief Judge of the 3d Crct, vice Mr Ingersol-Mar 3, 1801.
Philip Barton Key, Chief Judge of 4th Crct, vice Mr Lee-Mar 3, 1801.
Chas Magill, Judge of 4th Crct, vice Mr Key, promoted-Mar 3, 1801.
Crct Crt for the Dist of Col.:
Thos Johnson, of Md, Chief Judge-Mar 3, 1801.
Jas Marshall & Wm Cranch, assist Judges-Mar 3, 1801.
Harrison Grey Otis, Atty for the Dist of Mass-Feb 20, 1801.
Edw S Loe Livermore, Atty for Dist of NH, vice Mr Smith-no date.
John Wilkes Kittera, Atty for Western Dist of Pa-no date.

MON APR 20, 1801
Ran away-Dick, negro, abt 19; has belonged to Mr Richardson Stuart of Balt; left me bet Alex & Gtwn.   -Andrew Erwin, Wilks Co, NC.

Died: Dr Herschell, Astronomer, in Eng, discoverer of new planet, Georgium Sidus. [Apr 27-Report unfounded]

Wm Stillman, of Va, has obtained a patent for a machine, cld "The Veneering Plough"-cutting doves in cabinet ware.

Patent obtained by Saml Hamlin, in Prov, R I,-capstan & crank fire engines.

Philadelphia, Apr 11. Civil actions against Peter Miercken, John Dunlap, Jos B McKean, Joshua Bosly Bond, Jas Simmons & Geo Willing; for riot & assault on the editor of the Aurora, on May 15th, 1799.

WED APR 22, 1801
Died: Son of Mr Josiah Adkins, of West Simsbury, Conn, abt 14 yrs of age; drowned by the late rains.

FRI APR 24, 1801
Alexandria-election of mbrs of Hse of Reps: Richd Brent, Rpblcn-125 votes, Leven Powell, Fed-64 votes. Hse of Dels for Fairfax Co: Nicholas Fitzhugh-142 votes, Henry Rose-111 votes, Edw Dulin-67 votes.

For sale: sheathing copper, bolts & nails. -Wilsons & Maris, 105 Mkt St, Balt, Md.

Robt W Peacock, has remv'd to Mr Voss' hse nr Pa Ave.

Charlotte Hall School, St Mary's Co, Md. Apply for VP in said school, 250 pds per annum.   -Neale H Shaw, Reg.

Mon Apr 27, 1801
Committed to the goal of Wash Co, DC; negroes; Robert-prop of Richard Sanford, Orange Co, Va. John Butler, says he is a free man. Andrew, prop of Mr Edw Gantt, of Berkeley Co, Va. John Peters, prop of Mrs Rormdell, of Calvert Co, Md. -Daniel C Brent, marshal of DC.

New mbrs of the Americ Philosophical Soc-Phil, Apr 17, 1801:
Thos T Hewson of Phil; Jos Joaquin De Ferrer of Cadiz; Francisco Peyrolon Sec of the Royal Soc; De Amigos De Pais, of Valencia. -Jos Clay Sec.

New medicinal store, John Ott, at shop formerly occupied by Dr J Reintzel in Gtwn.

Wed Apr 29, 1801
List of Officers apptd by Pres Adams on Feb 16 & Mar 3, 1801.
Cavalry: Alexander McComb, Jr-2d Lt.
1st Regt of Artl & Engneers-Lts:

Jared Brooks	Robt Gray	Lewis Landais
Wm A Murray	Jos Cross	Peter Lamkin
John B Barnes	A R Armistead	Geo Armistead
Chas Hunt	Enos Noland	Clarence Mulford
John F Powell	H W Bissell	Kilian V Renssalaer
Henry Tilton [declines]	Enoch Humphrey	Prescott Barron, *Surg's Mate*

2d Regt of Artl & Eng
Jonathan Williams, Maj
Loyd Beal, Capt — John Lillie, Capt — Josiah Dunham, Capt
Lieuts:

Thos Brindley [declines]	Wm Wilson	Moses Swett
John Walbach	Jas Wilson	Lewis Howard
Augustus Hunt	Pearson Titcomb	John Grange
Saml Seaton	Waters Clark	Wm Cocks
John Heiskell	Geo Peter	Nathan Parks
Jesse Lull	Augustus Strong	Saml Welch

Stephen Thomas, *Surg's Mate*
1st Regt of Infty-1st Lts:

Geo Kirkland	Wm Swan	Sylvest G Whipple
Ninian Pinckney	Jas Ashman [declines]	

2d Lts: T W Williams	Benj Wallace	Wm Carson
Horatio Stark	Simon Owens	Jos C Cooper
Robt G Barde	Richard Skinner	Ambrose Whitlock
D Armistead	Van Bennet	Chas Blake, *Surg's Mate*

Ebenezer Lawrance, *Surg's Mate*
2d Regt of Infty-2d Lts:

John Brahan	Wm Elliott	Levi Alexander
Danl Hughes	Robt Bell	Uriah Blue
John Duer-[declines]	John Hinson [do]	Jos Miller
W H Woolridge	John H Douglass & Edw Reynolds, *Surg s Mates*	

3d Regt of Infty-1st Lts:
Saml Erwine	W Potter-[declines]	John W Brownson
Saml W Magaw	Philip S Schuyler	E W Wheeler.
2d Lts: John Williams	Alex. Cooper	Thos Lee
Daniel Baker	Henry B Brevoort	John Hylton
Henry R Graham	Benj Wilkinson	Jas Smyth Jr
Reuben Everitt, *Surg s Mate*		

4th Regt of Infty-2d Lts:
Wm Gardiner-[declines]	J Wilkinson Jr	G W Harwood
Wilkinson Jones	Jas Cunningham	Richd Buck
Edmund P Gaines	Henry Hopkins	Benj Nowland [declines]

Cadets in Svc of U S:
Henry B Jackson	Saml Gates	Silas Clark
Wm Gates	Jos Provaux	J B Wilkinson
Simon Levy	Josiah Taylor	Ambose Porter

FRI MAY 1, 1801
John Milledge, elected a mbr of Congress from Ga, vice Jas Jones, decd.

Norfolk, Apr 22. U S ship *President,* at anchor in Eliz Rvr-Thos Truxton, Sr ofcr; writes of seamen being impressed by the French.

Wayne's Gaz U S: Writ of Capias was srv'd on the editor of this Gaz, at the suit of the Hon Dr Michl Leib, & $5,000 bail demanded & given; the editor is to appear in the Supreme Crt.

MON MAY 4, 1801
Reps to Congress for Va: Philip Rootes Thompson, vice J Nicholas, declnd. John Talliaferro, Jr, vice Gen Lee, declnd. Saml J Cabell, for dist of Albemarle, etc. John Smith, for dist of Frederick, etc.

Wm Bainbridge, esq, is cmder of the U S *Geo Wash,* now in Algiers.

Thos Munroe is postmaster, in post-ofc in Wash City.

Application at next crt of Wash Co, for licence to keep a ferry over the Potomac. -John Andrey, Philip Alexander, Wm Washington.

WED MAY 6, 1801
New Rpblcn Leg of R I:

Governor	Arthur Fenner	*Lt Gov*	Saml J Potter
Atty Genrl	Jas Burrill Jr	*Genrl Treas*	Henry Sherburne
Sec	Saml Eddy		
Senators	John Innes Clark	Jos Rice	Saml Elam
	Beriah Waite	Thos Hoxsie	Nicholas Taylor
	Job Watson	John Harrie	Timothy Wilmarth
	Wm Waterman		

Stephen Girard, owner of brig, *Sally*, of Phil, was naturalized a citizen of Pa in 1777, has since then resided in the U S.

Indiana Terr. Contonment, Wilkinson-Ville, Mar 14, 1801. My Duty to report that yesterday a dreadful tornado visited our camp. Killed-1 Sgt. Wounded: [Blank] *Cap Lukens-badly; Lt Webster; Lt Layborne; Lt Shiras; Lt Hookes' leg broken & badly wounded. [Signed] Ferdinand L Claiborne. [*as written]

Abstract-Americ vessels captured by British cruisers, Since Jan 1, 1800:

Vessel	Port	Owner
Gadsen	Charleston	Frederick Kohn
Genet	Boston	Nathan'l Fellowes
Brig *Polly*	Phil	John L Clark
Schnr *Susanna*	Balt	Jonathan Harrison
Cutter *Crocodile*	NY	Scott & Seamen
Charlotte	NY	Henry A & John G Costor
Brig *Sally*	Phil	Stephen Girard
Brig *Ruby*	Phil	Chandler Price
Schnr *Geo*	Balt	Wm Patterson
Maria	Balt	Jas Biays
Sloop *Little Charlotte*	Bristol R I	Chas D'Wolfe
Schnr *Aurora*	NY	R Johnson & Co
Ship *Eliz*	Boston	J Codman
Brig *Sea Nymph*	Phil	Louis A Tarrascon
Brig *Gracy*	Balt	Rogers & Owings
Schnr *Rover*	Balt	Rogers & Owings

Lisbon, Jun 27, 1800. Vessels captured by the British as reported by Thos Bulkely to Timothy Pickering, esq, Sec of State: Brig *Peacock*, David Crafts mstr, prop o/Eben Parsons, o/Boston-captured by the *Guernsey*, Paul Bienvenu, mstr.
Brig *King Solomon*, Jas Hewett, mstr, prop of Benj Hill of Newport, R I.
Brig *Susannah*, J V Spencer, mstr, prop of Blacklock, Bower & Wm Milligan of Charleston, captured by the privateer of *Guernsey*, Paul Bienvenu, mstr & La Bouch privateer of Gibraltar [owned by Jews in Lisbon].
Brig *Hind*, Danl Ropes Jr, mstr, prop of Jos White & Wm Orne of Salem.
-captured by the B M frig *Anson*, P C Durham, Cmder
Brig *Sea Nymph*, Jas McKiver, mstr, prop of Lewis A Tarascon of Phil-captured by the armed ship *Barwel*, John Toole, mstr.

FRI MAY 8, 1801
Geo Andrews has remv'd to 9th & E Sts, where he manufactures all kinds of ornaments for chimney pieces, etc. [Washington]

Thos McKean Thomson apptd Sec of Pa; in place of A J Dallas, rsgnd.

MON MAY 11, 1801
Richd Dinmore has remv'd his groc store from Gtwn to sq 119.

Auction & Commission Store. Auctioneers in PG Co, Md & Wash are Robt Camp & Co, nr Pa Av, Washington City.

WED MAY 13, 1801
Mrd: Miss Carroll, d/o Chas Carrol, esq, of Carolton, to Robt Goodloe Harper, esq, May 7, by Rt Rev Bishop Carrol.

Died: Matthias A Hersmon, ntv of Germany, age 125 yrs by most accounts; on Apr 18, on Patterson's Crk, Hampshire Co; had 3 wives in Ger & 1 in this country. -Winchester, May 6.

Proposals for bldg the Marine Barrack in Wash. -Wm Marbury.

Phil May 8. Sentence of the Mayor's Crt in the case against *Owen Foulke, John Melbeck, *Edw Shoemaker, John Coxe, *Abraham Singer, Wm Lewis & John Morrell for a riot & assault against the editor of the Aurora. Melbeck & Coxe- $100 ea & costs. Lewis & Morrell, one cent ea & costs. *Fined $120 ea & costs.

FRI MAY 15, 1801
For sale: Sloop, *Lively*. -H & T Moore, auctioneers.

Appointments by the Pres of the U S: Albert Gallatin, Sec of the Treas; Henry Potter, Judge of the 5th Crct; John Monroe, of Va, Atty for Western Dist of Va; Thos Sumter Jr, Sec of the Leg to the French Rpblcn; Geo Gilpin, Judge of the Orphans Crt of Alexandria Co.

Geo Dent has rsgnd the ofc of marshal for Potomac.

New Books at Rapine, Conrad & Co, 4th B St & N J Ave, Washington:
Nocturnal Visit by Maria Regina Roche.
De Valcourt by Mrs Bennett.
Rash Vows by Madame De Genlis.
The Farmer's Boy by Robt Broomfield.

Geo Hembold Jr is publishing a sketch of Mr Jefferson's life; engraving will be executed by Mr David Edwin. Phil, May 6. -Geo Helmbold, Jr.

MON MAY 18, 1801
Jos Habersham, Postmaster Genrl. Genrl PO, Wash City.

Life of Wm Cowper, author of "The Task", poet: born at Berkhamstead, in Buckinghamshire, his fr being the incumbent of the living of that place; our poet is descended from the 1st Earl Cowper, Lord Chancellor of Eng, his grfr being one of the chldrn of that nobleman. Wm resided in Huntingdon a few yrs & became a friend of Rev Mr Unwin. When the Rev died he accompanied his widow to Olney; in Olney he produced his earliest works.

May 17th Cmdor Dale took leave of the Pres & proceeded to Hampton to take command of the squadron.

Winthrop Sargent, Gov of Miss Terr, arvd at Boston from Natches.

WED MAY 20, 1801
U S ship, *Portsmouth*, sold at Balt, $31,150, to Jeremiah Yellot, of Balt.

Christopher Ellery, Rpblcn, chosen Senator in R I.

FRI MAY 22, 1801
Notice: all persons indebted to est of Bennett Fenwick, late of Wash, decd, are to make payment. -Jas B Heard, Atty. Mary Ann Fenwick, excx.

In Chancery-Jas A Magruder, of PG Co, Md, prays for benefit of "Act for Relief of Sundry Insolvent Debtors".   -Saml H Howard, Reg CC

In Chancery-Benani H Wade, of PG Co, Md, trader, prays for benefit of "Act for Relief of Sundry Insolvent Debtors". -Saml H Howard, Reg CC

In Chancery-Wm Allein, of Calvert Co, Md, trader, prays for benefit of "Act for Relief of Sundry Insolvent Debtors". -Saml H Howard, Reg CC

MON MAY 25, 1801
Persons wishing a pew in the NJ Av Chr, apply to Rev Andrew T McCormick.
   -John T Frost, Register.

London, Apr 18. Passports are made out at the foreign ofc for M M Jos Buonaparte, Dr Gayot & Maret.

WED MAY 27, 1801
Reward-$5, for strayed or stolen horse.   -Robt Cherry, NJ Av, Wash

Deserted-the following soldiers:
Isaac Davis, age 19 yrs, farmer, born in Pr Wm Co, Va;
Jas Nelson, age 22 yrs, farmer, ntv of Pr Wm Co, Va;
Jas Henning, age 21 yrs, hse carpenter, born in Berkeley Co, Va.
Richd S Blackburn, Capt 1st Regt Artl & Eng, Cmndng. Dumfries, Pr Wm Co, Va.

Liverpool, Mar 4, 1801. The annexed vessels have lately been seized in this port for having tobacco on board with the view of smuggling. Restored-*Columbus*, John Dishon, Balt; *Rose*, Reuben Jones, NY; *Peggy*, W Latimer, NY; *Warren*, J Parker, NY. Under seizure: *Perseverence*, D Sterling; *Citizen*, C Blakeman.

FRI MAY 29, 1801
Appointments by the Pres of U S:
S Bishop, Coll of New Haven, Conn; David L Barnes, Judge of R I Dist; Reuben Etting, marshal, Dist of Md. By Sec of the Navy: Woodbury Langdon, Navy agent at Portsmouth, NH; Wm Hunter, Navy Agent at Savannah, Ga vice Ebenezer Jackson, rsgnd.

Died: Mrs Bingham, May 11, at Bermuda; consort of Wm Bingham, of Phil. [Retired there for her health]

For sale or rent: hse occupied by Mr John Dempsey, lot 6 sq-fronts on E Capt St.
-Saml N Smallwood, Wash.

Notice-gentlemen of Militia formerly commanded by Capt Lewis Williamson, are to return the arms & accoutrements belonging to the State of Md.
-Saml N Smallwood, 1st Lt

For rent: store lately in the tenure of Dr Galasspy & Co. Pa Ave. Nr the Capitol.
-Josias W King

In Chancery-Barton Wathen, of Chas Co, Md, prays for benefit of "Act for Relief of Sundry Insolvent Debtors". -Saml H Howard, Reg CC

MON JUN 1, 1801
Died: Wm Winton, esq, May 29, at Detroit of erisypelas; late Maj in Cavalry of U S.

Consuls have granted an annuity of 600 Francs to wid of Geo Saunier.

Capt De Vaisseau, killed board frig *Africaine*.

Ran away, Apr 26, from pilot boat at St Mary's, Jas Tatton, age abt 19 yrs.
-John Welsh.

NY: Hurricane killed Jacob Pownall at Ellis Island on May 25.

WED JUN 3, 1801
Marshal's sale: Crct Crt of Wash Co, DC, all the right, title & int of Walter Queen to land *"Enclosure"*, 3 miles from Wash, abt 188acs; to satisfy debt due to Eliz Doyle, for the use of John Darnall. -Daniel C Brent, marshal.

Jas Lyon, having comtemplated establishing a library in Wash, unable to do so, relinquishes the pursuit to Richd Dinmore.

Jas Lyon, of Gtwn in Dist of Col, he being declared bankrupt, is required to surrender himself to the comrs in Jul at the hse of Jos Semmes, Gtwn.
-John C Dent-clk/commission.

In Chancery-Benjamin Boyd, of PG co, Md, trader, prays the benefit of "Act for Relief of Sundry Insolvent debtors". -Saml H Howard, Reg CC

John Duskins, waggoning, missing 2 wks from his family; it is supposed he was murdered by a negro who is now in the goal; other reports have seen him nr Balt.
-His wife, Ann Duskins, Wash City.

State of Health compels me to quit present business. -Jas Thompson.

FRI JUN 5, 1801
In Chancery-Richard T Cheseldine, of Montg Co, Md, trader, prays for the benefit of "Act for Relief of Sundry Insolvent debtors".
-Saml H Howard, Reg CC

In Chancery-Chas Wayman, ctzn of U S & this state, prays for the benefit of "Act for Relief of Sundry Insolvent debtors". -Saml H Howard, Reg C C

U S ship, *Trumbull*, sold at auction at NY for $26,500; purchased by Messrs Robinson & Harshorne, merchants of NY.

MON JUN 8, 1801
Reports are circulating injurious to my character; decision will be obtained in a crt of Law. -Thadey Hogan, Wash City.

WED JUN 10, 1801
Died: Fredk Augustus Muhlenberg, Jun 4, at Lancaster, Rec-Genrl o/land ofc.

Jun 5, the National brig, *Scammel*, J H Jones, Cmder, arvd at Balt, Md.

FRI JUN 12, 1801
Died: John Wilkes Kiterra, at Lancaster, late a mbr of Hse of Reps of U S.

For sale: 9 lots in sq 693, on each a 2 story brick hse, 6 fronting on NJ Av, 3 on E St So. Also 1 lot in sq 802, 3d St. -Moffett & Nesmith, New Ave.

MON JUN 15, 1801
Wm Baker, apptd marshal of Potomac Dist, by Pres of U S.

Wm Lee of Mass, apptd by the Pres of the U S, Commercial Agent of the U S for Port of Bourdeaux, in Republic of France.

Life of Mozart-born in Salsburg in 1756; [fr a musician of considerable merit,] 1769 apptd Maitre De Concert; died in 1791 at age 35 yrs.

Gov of Md has issued a proclamation, declaring the following as duly elected Reps in Congress: Saml Smith, Richd Sprigg Jr, Danl Heister, John Archer, Thos Plater, Jos H Nicholson, John Campbell & John Dennis

WED JUN 17, 1801
Mrd: Mr Jos Hall, age 99, to Miss Patience Gulick, age 60, at South Amboy, on May 25th.

Died: Mrs Altie Van Doren, age 95 yrs, May 17, at Middlebush, Somerset Co, NJ, wid of Mr Christopher Van Doren.

Died: Mrs Nichols, age 95 yrs, at Elizabeth-Town, NJ.

Wash Assoc & U S Ins Co. -J Stickney, Sec'ry Pro Tem.

FRI JUN 19, 1801
Mbrs of Fed Lodge No. 15 to meet in Wash.-Chas McCalley-Sec.

MON JUN 22, 1801
Official: Agent with Cherokees & Military Agent in Tenn; Col Return J Meigs in place of Capt Lewis & Col Hendley.

Died: Christopher Ludwick, baker General in Rev War.

Died: John Smith, at NY, late Lt Col Com of 1st Legion in svc of the U S.

Apptd by the Pres of the U S: Danl Marsh, Coll of Perth Amboy; Jas Linn, Supervisor of NJ. Com'rs to treat with svr'l nations of Indians east of the Miss: Gen Wm R Davie; Gen Jas Wilkinson & Col Benj Hawkins.

WED JUN 24, 1801
In chancery-Clement Chamberlain, of Montgomery Co, Md, praying the benefit of "Act of relief for sundry insolvent debtors".
                                            -Saml H Howard, Reg CC

I wish to employ labourers to work on the streets of Wash.-Middleton Belt.

Brohawn & Boys have taken Mr N Young's Wharf for a lumber yd.

FRI JUN 26, 1801
The Pres has recd from Dr Waterhouse, some new vaccine or cow-pox matter, which he has given to Dr Gannt of Gtwn.

Gaz of the U S-Law case. Levi Hollingsworth v Wm Duane. Crct Crt of the U S for the Eastern Dist of Pa 3d Crct; held at Phil on May 18, 1801. Case-libel on the plntf, in the Aurora, a paper published by the dfndnt. Jurors:

Priestly Blackiston-[foreman]	Joshua Byron	John Stelle Jr
Philip S Bunting	Dominic Joyce	Geo Barclay
Richd Jones	Joshua Edwards	Geo Peter
Jas Stokes	Richd Tittermary	Richd Humphreys

Witnesses: Owen Mullen, brought up in Ireland & was abt 38 yrs old; he knew the dfndnt in Ire-that he, dfndnt, lived with his widow mthr in the town of

Clenmell, in the Province of Munster. Witness left Ire in 1785. Witness: Gavin Hamilton, born in Canada. Much discussion as to where dfndnt was born. Dfndnt told some he was born on Lake Champlain in 1760 & he left with his mthr in 1771 for Ireland & he arvd in Phil from India in 1795. Witness, Thos Hickey, knew the dfndnt in Clenmel in Ire; when he, Hickey, was 17 yrs of age; Hickey came to Americ in 1794. Jury returned a verdict that the dfndnt was not a ctzn of the U S, but an alien & subject to the King of Great Britain.

MON JUN 29, 1801
Capt Thos Williams has arrv'd at Salem, Mass, from Algeziras.

The *Warren*, Sloop of War, sold in Boston for abt $18,400 to Nathan'l Fellowes.

WED JUL 1, 1801
4th of July celebration at hse of Mr Richard Charles, NJ Av & Capitol Hill, at the Sign of the Ship.

FRI JUL 3, 1801
Died: Wm Jones, age 61 yrs, of Halifax, at his seat nr Raleigh, NC, a firm Republican.

Official appointments by the Pres of the U S:
Geo Maxwell, Atty for Dist of NJ.
John E Caldwell, Commercial Agent for the City of Santo Domingo.
Edw Jones, Commercial Agent for Guadaloupe.
Peter Muhlenberg, Supervisor for the Dist of Pa.
Jas Irwin, Coll & Inspec of Mass Dist.

MON JUL 6, 1801
Reward-$100 for letter sent from Louisville, Ga, to Abraham Baldwin, Wash, containing $1000, prop of this Univ, robbed of its contents.
                                             -Josiah Meigs, Pres. Univ of Ga.

New York, Jul 2. Jul 1 Geo Clinton, esq, Gov elect of NY, took the oath prescribed by the Constitution, to entering upon the duties of his ofc.

Jas Logan [from Proud's History of Pa]: grson of Robt Logan of Scotland, who was s/o Patrick Logan of Scotland, remv'd into Ire & resided in Lurgan, where Jas was born. Jas remv'd to Pa with Wm Penn, in his latter voyage to America, age 25; many yrs in public affairs; retired to Stanton, his country seat, nr Germantown, nr Phil. Died Oct 31, 1751, age abt 77 yrs. A Quaker, he had svrl chldrn, who survived him; eldest son, Wm, many yrs a mbr of Govnrs cncl.

WED JUL 8, 1801
Ladies with ltrs in Wash Post ofc, Jul 1, 1801.
| Nancy Ballenger | Mrs B Courme | Mrs Doulery & Co |
| Jane Douglass | Mrs Langley | Mrs Wilde at Mr Andrews |

Robt Ware Peacock, Atty at Law, mv'd his ofc to F St sq 290.

Sale of non residents land for taxes; Act of Ky Assembly, we purchased, at Frankfort in Nov last, for a company, these tracts:

Name Listed	Acs:	County & Water Course:	Prchsd:
Philips & Young	100000	Scott & Franklin, Eagle Crk	whole
Jas Steele	30000	Hardin, Green Rvr	whole
Saml Sackett	3000	Bourbon Licking	whole
Richd Johnson	2000	Jefferson, Floyd's Fork	whole
Saml Pearl	500	Mason, Farrows Crk	whole
Andrew Byrn	500	Mason	whole
Alex Stewart	500	Campbell	whole
Dubartis Shepherd	3000	Clarke, Ky Rvr	2900 acs
John Archer	2000	Harrison, Wms Rvr	whole
John Donnell	1400	Licking	whole
Same	2000	Clarke	1999 acs
Same	2644	Mason	2600 acs
Same	1231	Mason	650 acs
Lawrence Slaughter	3750	Mason	3500 acs
Adam Banks	100	Mason	40 acs
Richd Johnson	200	Mason	150 acs
Eliz James	1000	Mason	150 acs
Ridgley & Nathans	3000	Franklin	2900 acs
J P Harrison	663	Shelby	39 acs

-C Bank, Thos Bodley, Agents for the Company.

Columbian Library-kept in an apartment of the Columbian Acad, David Wiley, principal of acad is librarian. Directors: Stephen B Balch, John Templeman, David English, John Threlkeld, Thos Turner & Chas D Green.

Crct Crt of Wash Co, DC, Jul 2. John Chancey, guilty of larceny-publicly whipped; Chas Houreman, guilty of larceny, publicly whipped & burnt in the hand; Saml Baker, guilty of larceny-burnt in the hand; John Peden & Saml Morris, guilty of larceny, pardoned by Pres of U S.

FRI JUL 10, 1801
In Chancery-Thos K Beale & wife, v Wm King & Wm Hammond.
Bill is to forclose or have a sale on mortgages executed by the dfndnts who executed their several deeds to Jos Clark, decd, of these tracts,
Champeon Forrest, Addition to Champeon, Forrest Hammonds Search, Support, Chance, Portland Lapland, Remnant & Support; Clark devised all his est to his wife, who after his death mrd Thos K Beale. Wm King resides out of the state.
Apply by Nov next.   -Saml H Howard, Reg CC

MON JUL 13, 1801
Appointments by Pres of U S: Wm C C Claiborne, Gov of Miss Terr; Joel Lewis, marshal for Delaware Dist.

Geo Prescot, esq, is apptd Gov of Lucia; Geo Nugent, esq, of Jamaica.

WED JUL 15, 1801
Alexander Paulovits was born Dec 23, 1777, mrd Oct 9, 1793, Maria Louisa Eliz Alexiowna, of Baden-born Jan 4, 1779.   -The Emperor Alexander.

FRI JUL 17, 1801
Slaves committed to Wash Co prison: Will, age 26 yrs, says he is prop of Jesse Robinet; Debby Williams, age 22 yrs, alias Parker, says she prop of Mr Pinckney, Old Town, Balt.   -Danl Carroll Brent, Mrshl-DC.

MON JUL 20, 1801
Land sale: 2 tracts, together 92 acs, in DC. -Geo Frank.

Intending on leaving the city in Oct next, disposing of my furn, 2 negro men, riding horses, etc.   -Benj Grayson Orr.

For sale: scow, at Dyer's Ferry. -John L Naylor or Benj More, NJ Av, Wash.

Meeting at Mr Rhode's Hotel, of subscribers to a mkt, to be built on Pa Av Edw Eno to collect subscriptions; Wm Brent apptd Treas; Jas Hoban & Clotwerthy Stephenson, to engage contractors.   -W Thornton.

Died: John Hempstead, age 106 yrs, April last, in Stephentown; ntv of NY.

Died: Mr H Mackenzie, May 8, at Edinburgh, of fall from his horse. Compt of Taxes for Scotland.

For rent: the hse I occupy, sq 142, Aug 1.   -Nicholas King.

For sale or lease for 10 yrs, farm, Culpepper Co, Va, on Flat Run, 750 acs. Also *"Reverson"*- 250 acs, adj above, with dwlg hse, 60 X 40. Terms apply to Robt Brooke Voss, esq, who lives adjoining the prem. -Nicholas Voss, F St, or W. I. Voss, Navy Yd, Wash.

WED JUL 22, 1801
Strayed from the plantation of H J Stier, esq, nr Balt, a black cow.
                    -J M Vanhorne.

Appointments: David Gelston Coll for the Dist of NY. Chas Pinckney, esq, Minister Pleni of the U S to Crt of Madrid; Robt Smith, esq, Sec of Navy.

FRI JUL 24, 1801
Apptd by the Pres: Hermanus H Wendell, marshall for Albany Dist.

MON JUL 27, 1801
Died: Alexander Wilcocks, at Phil, Recorder of Phil.

Appoint'd by the Pres: Edw Jones, of DC, to be Commercial Agent-Guadaloupe. Thos Aborn, of R I, Comm Agent-Cayenne. Geo W Erving, of Mass, Consul-London. Peter Dobell, of Pa, Comm Agent-Havre. Fulwar Skipwith, of Va, Comm Agent-Paris. John C Murray, of NY, Consul-Glasgow. Jos Peelis, Consul-Malta. Etienne Cathalan, Comm Agent-Marseilles. Daniel Clark, of New Orleans, Consul for that port.

WED JUL 29, 1801
The merchants of New Haven, remonstrate against the removal of Elizur Goodrich, esq, from ofc of Collector for New Haven Dist & the appointment of Saml Bishop, esq, who will be 78 yrs old in Nov Signed by-Jeremiah Atwater, Elias Shipman, Abraham Bradley, Abel Burnett. -Isaac Beers, Pres of Bank, & Chamber of Commerce in New Haven. [Shipman is Pres of New-Haven Ins Co.]

The U S ship of War, *Herald*, sold at auction in Boston for $14,100 to Mr. De Wolfe, of R I, the purchaser.

FRI JUL 31, 1801
English Hse of Commons: indemnity bill-Sir Francis Burdett presented petitions from Jasper Moore, John Roberts, John Belcher, Thos Evans, John Perrott & Thos Goodluck; severally apprehended by warrant of the Duke of Portland, complaining of cruelty on the part of Aris, Gov of the Coldbath-Fields prison.

MON AUG 3, 1801
Died: Matthias Howman, age 100 yrs, Jul 18, nr Winchester-Va.

Died: Mr Vaneman, age 91 yrs, in Wilmington, Del.

For sale: hse frames & lumber. John Conner, Somerset Co, nr Princess Ann, Md.
-Thos Munroe, Wash City.

Phil, Jul 25. Convention of delegates from Abolition Socs in different parts of the U S; Richd Hartshorn, Pres; Othniel Alsop, Sec.

Official appointments: Saml Osgood-supervisor for dist of NY.
Silas Lee, atty for dist of Maine vice Danl Davis apptd Judge by State of Mass. Geo Blake, atty for Dist of Mass. Benj Jarvis, coll Penobscott. Malachi Jones, srvyor Currituck, NC. Jacob Lewis of Mass to be Consul at Calcutta. Saml Duncan, coll at Michillimakinac.

Harrisburg, Pa paper states the removal by the Post-Master-Genrl, of Gottlieb Yungman, post-mstr at Reading & apptd John Walter.

WED AUG 5, 1801
Commission of bankruptcy filed against Robt Morris, of Phil.

Fri Aug 7, 1801

Windsor [Vt] Gaz: in Shutesbury, Mass, there is now living Ephram Pratt, born Nov 1, 1687 in East Sudbury, Mass; s/o John Pratt, who landed & settled in Plymouth in 1620; Mr E Pratt mrd Martha Wheelock & had 6 sons & 2 dghts; 4 sons are living, eldest is 90, youngest 82 yrs; was visited by grchldrn of the 6th generation; his wife died at age 98 yrs.

Official Appointments: Alex'r Wollcott, coll-Middletown, Conn vice Chauncey Whittelsey. Ephraim Kirby, supervisor-Conn vice John Chester.

Reward-$50, for 2 villains who robbed me at my hse of abt $400; a suspect is O'Riley, schoolmaster, lately living in this neighbourhood. -Harrison Pelly, Montgomery Co, Md. [nr Seneca]

Mon Aug 10, 1801

List of Americ seamen in Kingston, Jamaica, on board British Navy, or have been on board & discharged or dead. [followed by name of-ship]
John Altinson, his wife & chldrn are in Charleston, SC-*Calypso*
Jas Alexander, of Plymouth, Mass-*Surprize*
Saml McAverhill, of New Bedford, Mass, died in Kingston Hosp.
Somer Adams, of Boston, dischgd in May from *Abergavenny*.
Isaac Bavington, of Bath, Wilcasset, Maine Dist-*Bourdelais*
John Bevan, of Norfolk, Va, dschgd-Naval Hosp, Feb 27, 1801.
Wm Brown, of Balt, taken from brig *Mercury* to the *Thunderer*
Wm Brackman, of Burlington Co, NJ, dschgd Apr 24, 1801
Jas Blund, of Phil, dschgd Apr 24, 1801-*La Ciene*
Jas Brown, of Hartford, Vt, dschgd Jun 9, 1801-*Lowstaffe*
Daniel Caldwell, of Hartford, Conn, has wife & 7 chldn-*Nimrod*
Jas Conwell, of Alex, Va-*Merlin*. Peter Cook, of Balt-*Surprize*
John Chamberlain, of NY-*Surprize*
Saml Caswell, of Marlehead, Mass-*La Ciene*
John Choate, of Mass, dschgd Apr 1801-*Crescent*
John Kerr, of Boston, 16 yrs, taken from schr *Edw & Edmund-Lark*
David Cairnes, of NY-*Topaze*
Jas Calbert, of Pr Wm Co, Va-*La Magician*
Wm Cornell, of Phil, dschgd May 6-*La Ciene*
Ezra Crocker, of Barnstable, Mass, dschgd Jun 10-*Lowstaffe*
Chas Dudley, Americ Citizen-*Bonnetta*
Abraham Day, of Gtwn, Mass-*Lark*
John Davis, resid unknown-*Brunswick*
Daniel Done, of Brookfield Co, of Worcester, Mass-*Echo*
Saml Dunham, of Deer Island, Penobscot, Maine Dist-*Nimrod*
Christopher Davis, of Portland, Maine Dist-*Surprize*
Philip David, of Newport, Dela-*La Neriade*
John Elsdune, of Boston, Mass-*Thunderer*
Enoch Edwards, of NJ-unknown
Thos Edwards, of Phil-*Apollo*
Jas Elmes, has wife & chldrn in Phil-*Tisiphone*

David Eldridge, of Chatham, Cape Cod, dschgd Jun 11, 1801-*Lowstaffe*
Wm Floyd, of Balt, run-away-*Meleager*
Jacob Fleetwood, of Broadhills, Cape Henlopen-unknown
Wm Ford, of Md-*Echo*
Warren Foster, of East Hadem-*Tisiphone*
John Fitzpatrick, of NY-*Lenegenuer Acustra*
Nicholas Freeman, of Phil, mrd to Cath Weaver, by Rev Mr Schmiddt, Minister of Lutheran Chr-*Sans Pareil*
John Fosset, of Phil-*York*
Saml Follet, a citizen-*La Ciene*
Thos Fleming, of Talbot Co, Md, dschgd Apr 24, 1801-*Tisiphone*
Peter Forrester, of PG Co, Md, dschgd Jun 11, 1801-*Lowstaffe*
Jas Golding, of NY-*La Legere*
Jos Goodwin, of Cherry Alley, Phil-*Arah*
Barney Galey, has wife & chldrn at Balt-*Ratler*
John Gardiner, of Springfield, Conn-*La Ciene*
Stephen Griffin, Newbury-Port, Mass-*Surprize*
John Green, ntv of NY-*Amphion*
Thos Graham, of Wilmington, Pa-*Echo*
Geo Hall, Germantown, [mulatto man]-*Neriade*
Benj Haincock, of Chester, Pa-*Sans Pareil*
Wm Hill, of Portsmouth, NH-*Topaze*
Leavin Heatly, of Balt, dschgd Apr 23, 1801-*Circe*
Thos Hunter, of Dinwiddie Va, dschgd Apr 24, 1801-*La Ciene*
Wm Halliday, of NY, dschgd from the *Arab*
John Hamilton, fr lives in Hartford, Conn-*Bourdelon*
Stephen Howell, of NY, his mthr lives in Balt-*Juno*
David Holbrook, of Darby, Conn-*Albiciere*
Jas Junior, late boatswain of Balt Sloop of War, [Dead]-*Carnatic*
John Johnson, of Phil, [black man]-*Thunderer*
John Jennet, of Whochum, Bedford Co, Mass-*Crescent*
Abraham Jennet, in Naval Hosp, Port Royal, sent from-*Brunswick*
Jas Jones, of Lanesborough, Mass-*Quebeck*
Jas Jackson, of West Chester, has wife & child in NY-*Arab*
Simon Jorden, of nr Portland, Maine-*Volage*
Reuben James, dschgd Apr 25, 1801-*Cierce*
Levy James, board same vessel
Henry Johnson, of Phil, dschgd Apr 25, 1801-*Juno*
Wm Mosely Keeling, of Pr Ann Co, dschgd from-*Carnatic*
John Ketman, mrd in Phil, fmly resid 14 Plumb St-*Lowstaffe*
Liborn Lockwood, of Greenwich, Conn, dschgd from-*Arab*
Benj Littlefield, of Kennebeck, Maine Dist, Mass-*Sans Pareil*
Jas Low, of Charleston, SC-*Echo*
Henry Lively, of Balt, dschgd-*Cierce*
John Leonard, of Phil, dschgd Apr 22, 1801-*Thunderer*
Martin Lawrence, of Boston, dschgd Jun 10, 1801-*Lowstaffe*
John Mulbrean, of Phil, dschgd May 12, 1801-*Surprize*
Maj McDonald, of Dorchester, Md, dschgd Apr 14, 1801-*Crescent*

Geo McKenney, of Hill's Twn, Kennebeck, Mass-left the *Bonetta*
Thos Moore, of Pa-*Echo or Cierce*
Jonathan Martin, of Balt, dschgd Apr 22, 1801-*Cierce*
Saml Martin, b in Ga, svd time in Balt to Jas Stone, a shoemkr on board-*Bonetta*
Wm Nevan, of Scituate, Mass-*Thunderer*
Geo North, dschgd from-*Cierce*
John Petis, of Brattleborough, Dist of Maine-*Quebeck*
Peter Paine, of Cape Ann, Mass-*La Amiable*
John Polt, of New London, Conn-unknown
John Pitt, of Lyme, Conn-*Tisiphone*
John Parker, of NY, son of Peter Parker-*Bonetta*
Geo Peal, of New-Castle, Del.-*Abergavenny*
John Pouselding, of Beverly, Mass-*Cierce*
Lewis Paterson, of Phil, dschgd Apr 23-*Tisiphone*
Wm Praw, of Newport, R I, has wife & 2 chldrn, dschgd Jun 4, 1801-*La Volage*
Wm Reed, of SC-*Meleager*
John Peirce, of Wareham, Plymouth Co, Mass-*Trent*
Archibald Richardson, of Patuxent, Md, dschgd Apr 23-*Ceirce*
Benj Reynold, ntv of Phil, dschgd Apr 24, from-*La Ceine*
Wm Randall, of New Windsor, NY-*La Ceine*
Stanford Stodderd, of New London, run away from-*Arab*
Fancis Sampson, of Cape Ann, run away from-*Arab*
Jas Shields, of Balt, dschgd Apr last-*Cierce*
Lederisic Staler, of New London-*Stork*
Jas Stewart, of Salem, Mass-*Arab*
John Sewall, of Providence, R I-*Arab*
Wm Stanford, of Caroline Co, Md-*Sans Pareil*
Wm Scrivern, of Queen Anne's Co, Md-*Sans Pareil*
Stephen Stitwell, of Long Island-*Surprize*
Timothy Sharler, of Middletown, Conn-*Bourdelais*
John Stafford, of Charleston, Mass, dschgd Jun 17-*Lowstaffe*
Israel Smith, of Roxbury, Mass, dschgd Jun 17-*Lowstaffe*
Wm Thompson, of Phil, run away from-*Merlin*
David Tyler, of Balt, dschgd Apr 22-*Cierce*
Wm Wakefield, of Balt,-*Thunderer*
Robt Walker, of Balt, died on board-*Carnatic*
Wm Wickham, of Phil-*Arab*/ John Wilson, of Norfolk, Va -*Thunderer*
John Williams, of Alex, Va, dschgd Apr 14-*Crescent*
John Wade, of Phil, late mate of schr of *Edw & Edmund-Lark*
Isaac Wartman, State Unkn -*Bourdelais*
Thos Wilson, of Balt, Md-*La Ciene*
Benj Wetheral, of Wellfleet, Mass, dschgd Jun 9-*Lowstaffe*
Wm Brinton, of Boston, mthr living nr the Boston Stone with a Mr Chambers - *Lowstaffe*
John Brookes, has a protection from Isaac Holmes, of Charleston, SC Aug 9, 1796, & was dschgd Jun 15 -*Lowstaffe*
Saml Brown, mulatto man, born at NY, dschgd Jun 15, 1801-*Lowstaffe*
Daniel McLarty, of Balt-*Bonetta*

Died: Brig Genrl Benedict Arnold, in England.

Ltr that follows is from Nt'l intel-dated Aug 7, 1801]
Abstract of ltr from Wm Savage, esq, Agent of U S, dated Kingston, Jul 6, 1801. A number of Americ seamen have lately been liberated from svr'l ships of war on this station, a proper respect is paid to my signature. -Wm Savage

Reward-$50 for horses stolen at Hagers-Town, Md; thieves are known in Balt & Gtwn & known by the names of Thos Waters & Rowland Rogers. -John Pearson, Darby, Delaware Co, Pa.

WED AUG 12, 1801
Highest prices given for empty bottles, Gilbert Docker, grocer, Capitol Hill, NJ Av, Wash.

Merchants & ctzns of the U S, resident at Cape-Francois:

Lewden & Duhamet	S Lacoste	B Casting	Earle Dodge
Atwood W Dodge	Sim Hillen	Chas Tracy	R Stevenson
Wm Knox Jr	John N D'arcy	R Moore	J Suckley & Co
Thos Asbury	Jas Williams	F Low	Wm F Carty
Humphrey Taylor	Jona. S Smith	Peter Dorey	John Mayor
Frederick Tracy	S G Albert		

FRI AUG 14, 1801
Bottled porter-bottling cellar, Bridge St, opposite the PO.-R C Stanley, Gtwn.

Slaves committed to goal at Wash Co, DC: Solomon Johnston, age 33 yrs, says he belongs to Capt Johnston, of Balt. John Paine, age 26 yrs, says he belongs to Col Martin Pickett, of Fauquier Crt Hse, Va. Mark, alias Thos Gordon, age 40 yrs, says he belongs to David Allison, of Falmouth, Va. Ben Cole, age 22 yrs, says he is a free man & resid of Fells Point, Balt. -Daniel C Brent, mrshl of DC.

MON AUG 17, 1801
Died: Jonathan Edwards, DD, at Schenectady, NY, Pres o/college of that place.

Supreme Crt of the U S-Chief Justice marshal. Silas Talbot, Capt of the U S ship of War the *Constitution* v Hans Frederic, seaman, claimant of the ship, *Amelia*, her tackle, apparel & furniture. Decree of the Crct Crt of NY was correct in reversing the decree of the Dist Crt, but not correct in decreeing the restoration of the *Amelia* without paying salvage. [This case is covered in 2 & 1/3d pages of the Nat'l Intell]

Admirality case, Norfolk, Va-Aug 3, 1801 before Hon Cirus Griffin, Judge. Saml Barron, his ofcrs & crew v the schr *Success*. The said schr *Success*, her guns, tackle, furn & apparel, to be forfeited for being employed in the slave trade, in violation of the Act of Cong; & the same of said Saml Barron, Cmder of the ship of war cld the *Chesapeake*; schnr *Success* was owned by Saml W Green of Providence, R I & was commanded by Paul Brownell; proceeds from sale of the schr *Success* to be pd to Wm Pennock, agent for said libellants. -Seth Foster, clk.

Died: John Steymets, age 62 yrs, at Schenectady, NY.

WED AUG 19, 1801
Strayed from Amos Wilkinson, tinner, a black horse, Wash City.

Circulating library. Hugh Somerville, at his store & resid, so side of Pa Ave, nr the Hotel Bridge, Wash

Louisville, Warren Co, Ga. Grievance-the appointment of Thos Gibbons to the ofc of Dist Judge for the Dist of Ga.

Smith Co, Tenn, Jul 20, 1801. Jul 4th anniv celebration at the plantation of Wm Sanders, esq, Col of the Regt of Smith Co; Capt Grant Allen, Pres; Maj Andrew Greer, VP; volunteers: Capt Wm Alexander, Dr R D Berry & Maj T Dixon.

Cncl of appointment of NY-apptd: Edw Livingston-Mayor; John Stagg Jr, Sheriff of NYC; Elisha Jenkins, Compt of State, vice John V Henry, remv'd; Thos Tillotson, Sec of State, vice David Hale, remv'd.

FRI AUG 21, 1801
Died: Dr Richd Bailey, physn of Port of NY, at Staten Island of malignant fever.

For sale: land where I now reside, 1130 acs, on Mountain Run, Culpeper Co, Va; also, tract of nrly 700 acs, nr Fredericksburg, *"Sutherland's"* tract of land. Price may be known of Mr D Grinnan, of Fredericksburg, or my son, living with Mr Stone, of Fredericksburg.   -R Slaughter, jun. Culpeper, Va.

Principal ofcrs of the Government of the United States.
Supreme Exec. Thos Jefferson, Pres;   Aaron Burr, VP & Pres of Senate.
Dept of State: Jas Madison, Sec;   Jacob Wagner, Chief clk.
Dept of Treas:
Albert Gallatin, Sec;   John Steele, Comptroller
Richd Harrison, Auditor;   Wm Miller, Comr of Revenue
Saml Meredith, Treas;   Jos Nourse, Register.
War Dept:
Henry Dearborn, Sec;   Wm Simmons, Accountant;
Wm Irvine, Super of Military Store
Israel Whelen, Purveyor of Public Supplies;
Navy Dept: Robt Smith, Sec;   Thos Turner, Accountant.
Judiciary-Supreme Crt: John Marshall, Chief Justice
Assoc Justices:
Wm Cushing of Mass;   Wm Patterson of NJ;
Saml Chase of Md;   Bushrod Washington of Va

Alfred Moore of NC; Levi Lincoln o/Mass, Atty Genrl;
Elias B Caldwell of Wash City, clk. 1st Crct: John Lowell of Mass, Chief Judge; Benj Bourne of R I & Jerem Smith of NH, Judges.
2d Crct: Egbert Benson of NY, Chief Judge; Oliver Wolcott of Conn & Saml Hitchcock of Vt, judges.
3d Crct: Wm Tilghman of Pa, Chief Judge; Richd Basset of Dela & Wm Griffith of NJ, Judges.
4th Crct: Philip Barton Key of Md, Chief Judge; Go. Keith Taylor of Va & Chas Magill of Va, Judges.
5th Crct: Dominick A Hall of SC, Chief Judge; Henry Potter, N C Judge & one appointment vacant.

Dist ofcrs. Judge Atty Marshal

	Judge	Atty	Marshal
Maine	David Sewall	Silas Lee	Isaac Parker
Mass	John Pickering	John S Sherbourne	Bradbury Cilley
Mass	John Davis	Geo Blake	Saml Bradford
R I	David L Barnes	David Howell	Wm Peck
Conn	Richd Law	Pierpont Edwards	Philip B Bradley
Vt	Elijah Paine	David Fay	John Willard
NY	John Sloss Hobart	Edw Livingston	John Swartwout
NJ	Robt Morris	Geo Maxwell	Thos Lowry
Pa	Richd Peters	Alexder J Dallas	John Smith
	Jas Hamilton	Presley Carr Lane	
Del	Gunning Bedford	Geo Read Jr	Joel Lewis
Md	Jas Winchester	Zebulon Hollingsworth	Reuben Etting
Va	Cyrus Griffin	John Monroe	John Scott
	Thos Nelson		
Potomac	Walter Jones	Wm Baker	
Ky	Harry Innes	John H Daviess	Jos Crockette
NC	John Sitgreaves	Benj Woods	John S West
SC	Thos Bee	Thos Parker	Chas B Cochran
Ga	Chas Jackson	Ambrose Gordon	vacant
Tenn	John McNairy	Thos Gray	Robt Hays
D C	Wm Kilty	John T Mason	Jas Marshall
	Danl Carroll Brent	Wm Cranch	

John Hewitt Reg of wills-Wash Co   Cleon Moore for Alex Co.
Wm H Dorsey, Judge of orphans Crt for Wash.
Geo Gilpin, Judge of orphans Crt for Alexandria.

Commissioners of Loans:

NH	Wm Gardner	R I	Jabez Bowen
Mass	Thos Perkins	NJ	Jas Ewing
Conn	Wm Imlay	Pa	Stephen Maylan
NY	Matthew Clarkson	Md	Benj Howard
Dela	John Stockton	Ga	Richd Wylley
Va	John Hopkins	SC	John Neufville
NC	Sherwood Haywood		

Ministers-Resident in Foreign Countries:
Rufus King, Min Pleni-London;   Robt R Livingston, do.-Paris.
Thos Sumter Jr, Sec of Legation;   Chas Pinckney, Min Pleni-Madrid
John Graham-Sec of Legation.
Consuls & Commerc Agents in Gr Britain & Its Dependencies:
Geo W Erving-London, managing claims for spoliations.
David Lenox, Agent for protecting Americ seamen in Gr Britain.
Elias Vanderhorst, Cnsl-Bristol. Robt W Fox-Falmouth;
Jas Maury-Liverpool; Jos Wilson-Dublin; Thos Auldji, Vice Cnsl at Poole;
Geo Knox, Cnsl at Kingston Upon Hull; John C Murray-Glasgow;
Jas Holmes-Belfast; John Church-Cork;Harry Grant-Leith;
Jacob Lewis-Calcutta, India; Benj H Phillips-Curacao; John Gavino-Gibraltar;
Nicholas Rousselet-Demarara & Effequibo; John Elmslie Jr-Cape of Good Hope;
Jos Peelis, Malta.
Commercial Agents To the French Rpblc & her Dominions:
Fulwar Skipwith-Paris   Jas Blake-Antwerp
Wm Lee-Bordeaux   Peter Dobell-Havre De Grace
Edw Jones-Island of Guadaloupe
Mr De La Motte, vice Commerc Agent, Havre De Grace
Thos Aborn-Commerc Agent-Cayenne
Wm Buchanan-Isle of France & Bourbon
Etienne Cathalan-Commerc Agent-Marseilles
Thos F Gantt-do-Nantz   Francis L Taney-do-Ostend
Tobias Lear-Genrl Commerc Agent-St Domingo-resident at the Cape
John E Caldwell-Commerc Agent for city of St Domingo
Bartholomew Dandridge, Cnsl for Sthrn Dept excluding Petit Goave
Robt Ritchie-do-for Port Au Prince.
Consuls to Kingdom of Spain & Its Dominions:
Moses Young-Madrid   Jos Yznardi Jr-Cadiz
Robt Montgomery-Alicant   Wm Kirkpatrick-Malaga
Lewis Meagher O'Brien-St Andero   Augustus Madan-La Guira
Danl Clark-New Orleans   John Morton-Havana
Wm E Huling-vice Cnsl-N Orleans   Wm Willis-Barcelona
Josiah Blakely-St Jago, Cuba   John Culnan-Teneriffe
Consuls to Kingdom of Portugal & Its Dominions:
Thos Buckley,at Lisbon   John Street at Fayal
Consuls to the Batavian Rpblc:
Sylvanus Bourne, Amsterdam   Jos Forman, Rotterdam
Consuls to the Kingdom of Denmark & Its Dominions.
Hans Rodolpho Saabye, Copenhagen Henry Cooper, Santa Cruz
Prussia: Frederick W Lutze, at Stettin
Germany: Jos Pitcairn, Hamburg John Lamson, Trieste
Frederick J Wichelhausen, Bremen Philip Marck, Franconia.
Kingdom of Sweden:
Elias Backman, Gottemberg
Italian States:
Thos Appleton, Leghorn   John Matthiew, Naples
John Baptiste Sartori-Rome   Fredk H Walloston, Genoa

To the Barbary Powers:
Richd O'Brien, Algiers Jas Leander Cathcart, Tripoli
Wm Eaton, Tunis Jas Simpson, Morocco

Ministers, Cnsls & Commissaries of Foreign Powers Resident in the U S:
Gr Britain: Edw Thornton, Charge Des Affaires
Thos Barclay, Cnsl Genrl for Eastern States.
Phineas Bond, Cnsl Genrl for the Middle & Southern States.
Thos McDonough, Cnsl for NH, Mass, R I & Conn.
John Breese, vice-Cnsl, R I. Gabriel Wood, Baltimore.
Benj Moodie, Cnsl for North & South Carolina & Ga.
John Wallace, vice Cnsl for Ga.
From the French Rpblc:
Louis Andre Pichon, Chg Des Affaires & Commissary Genrl cf Commercial Relations.
Citizen Ofter, vice Comm of Commercial Relations for Va.
Chas Francois Liot, do for Pa & Delaware. Louis Arcambal, temp, do, for Md.
Marc Antoine Alexis Giraud, do for NH, Mass, R I & Conn.
From the Kingdom of Spain:
Chevalier De Yrujo, Minister Plenipotentiary
Thos Stoughton, temporary, Cnsl Genrl.
Antonio Argote Villalobus, Cnsl for Va & Ky.
Jean Baptista Barnabeau, Cnsl for Md.
Diego Morphy, Cnsl for North & So Carolina
Felipi Fatio, Cnsl for Pa.
Don Manuel Rengel, for Ga.
Ivan Stoughton, for NH, Mass, Conn, R I & Vt.
Joses Wiseman, vice Cnsl at Newport.
From the Kingdom of Portugal: Richd Codman, V-Cnsl, Mass.
John Abram, vice Cnsl-NY
Jas F Vercnock, vice Cnsl, S C
Richd Codman, vice Cnsl, Mass.
From the Batavian Rpblc: R G Van Polanen, Minister Resident
Adrian Valck, Cnsl for Md & Va
Jan Rosmen Graves for S C & Ga.
J H C Heineken, Commercial Agent, Pa.
From Prussia: Johann Ernst Christian Schultz,-Cnsl, Balt.
From Sweden: Richd Soderstrom, Cnsl Genrl.
Jos Winthrop, V-Cnsl, Charlesotn, SC
Jonathan Swift, Columbia & Ports on the Potomac.
Chas F Deyen, V-Cnsl for NH, Mass & R I.
Henry Gahn, V-Cnsl for NY & Conn.
John Cowper, V-C, Norfolk & all Ports in Va except those on Potomac.
John Baritz, V-C for NC Peter Collin, V-C for Md.

North-Western Terr: Arthur St Clair, Gov   Chas Willing Byrd, Sec
                     John Cleves Symmes,   Wm McMillan,
                     Chief Justice   Atty, for Ohio District
                     Jas Findlaye, Mrshl   Jos Gilman, Judge

	Jonathan Meigs Jr, Judge	
Mississippi Terr:	Wm C C Claiborne, Gov	John Steele, Sec
	Seth Lewis, Chief Justice	Peter Bryan Bruin, 2d Judge
	Danl Tilton, 3d Judge	
Indiana Terr:	Wm H Harrison, Gov	John Gibson, Sec.
	Wm Clark, Chief Justice	Henry Vanderburgh, 2d Judge
	John Griffin, 3d Judge	

Receivers of Public Money for Lands:
Jas Findlay, Cincinnati;   Elijah Backus, Marietta;
Zaccheus Biggs, Steubenville;   Saml Findley, Chilicothe.
Registers of the Land ofc of the U S:
David Hoge, Steubenville;   Peregrine Foster, Marietta;
Israel Ludlow, Cincinnati;   Thos Worthington, Chilicothe.

MON AUG 24, 1801
Died: Gen Gunn, very suddenly, at Louisville, Ga.

Frederick-Town, Aug 4, 1801. Meeting in support of Rpblcn candidates; David Shriver & Roger Nelson- [Electors who are to elect the Senate of this state]. Signed by fellow ctzns & friends:

		Geo Burkhart
Adam Keller	Saml Davall	John Runsberg
John Hoffman	Henry Kuhn	Henry Crouise
Law Brengle	Abraham Shriver	Danl Clarke Jr
John Gantt.		

WED AUG 26, 1801
Died: Gen Jos McDowell, in NC, late a mbr of Fed hse of Reps

Biographical notices of Thos Erskine. 3d son of the late Earl of Buchan & youngest bro to the present Earl; went to sea with the late Sir John Lindsay, nphw of the Great Earl of Mansfield; Mr E was abt 26 yrs of age when he commenced his course of legal study; he mrd & Mrs E accompanied him to Minorca; was called to the bar in Trinity Term 1778.

FRI AUG 28, 1801
Alexander Kaminsky & _____ Kleirschmidt guilty of forging & uttering notes of hand in sum of $18,300; guilty-14 yrs hard labor on the rds. -Balt, Md.

Richard Ricker apptd to ofc of Assist Atty-Genrl of NY, vice Cadwallader D Colden, remv'd.

New-York paper: the late Robt Randal, who died on Jun 5th last, at his seat nr this city, age 50 yrs; has left by his will upwards of thirty thousand pds for establishing an asylum for the infirm & disbaled seamen, to be called the "Sailor's Snug Harbor".

Mon Aug 31, 1801
Navy Dept: Pensions pd Jan 1 & Jul 1, party must produce to Sec of Navy a certificate from the Cmder of the ship on board of which he became incapacitated; a Marine-from the Commanding Officer. Signed-Benj Stoddert by order, Ar. Thomas, P clk-Navy Dept.

The remonstrance of the merchants of New Haven, on appointment of Saml Bishop, Collector of that port, has recd public attention.

Wed Sep 2, 1801
For sale: all Geo Walker's right to lots in Wash City 4 & 5 in sq 1019, lot 1 sq 1044, lots 3, 4, 5, 6, 11, 12, 13, 14 sq 963, & interest in others; to satisfy debt due Overton Carr, for use of Henry Roger.
-Daniel C Brent, marshal. Wash City.

In Chancery-Jas Ray v Thos Law, Jas Piercy & others. Bill is to procure a title to lots in Wash City; Piercy mortgaged said lots, May 15, 1800, to cmplnts and has fled the State of Md & gone to parts unknown.
-Saml H Howard, Reg C C.

Public sale, part of the rl est of Abraham Young, decd; a lot in DC with 2 story brick hse. -Henry Whetcroft, trustee.

Fri Sep 4, 1801
For sale: 7,000 acs, Albemarle Co, Va, in heart of this est the tcwn of Warren & a large dwelling hse. 2583 acs in Albemarle Co, part of land cld *Green Mountain*. 2100 acs in Buckingham Co, Va. 2100 acs in Kanawha Co, cld *Green Bottom*. -Wilson Cary Nicholas. Warren, Va.

Mon Sep 7, 1801
To be sold, 15 negroes & stock, to satisfy mortage made to Jekyll & Skelton Jones. -Wm Claughton, Hierom Opie & Saml Beachum, comrs. Chancery-Crt of Northumberland, Va: "*Mount Sion*", prop of Catesby Jones, decd, together with the mill, to be sold, to satisfy deed of mortage made to Walter Jones for payment of money, by the said Catesby; reserving to the widow her dower in the said land & mill.

Wed Sep 9, 1801
Electors of the Senate of Md: *Balt City*, Jas H McCullock; *Balt Co*, Tobias E Stansbury & John T Worthington. *Montg Co*, Upton Beall & Thos Davis, Fed candidates. *PG Co,* Allen B Duckett & Leonard Covington, Rpblcns.

Reward-$20, ran away, Tom, abt 40 yrs of age.-John Stevens, Wash City.

Augustus B Woodward, of Potowmac Dist, Aug 31, deposited in this ofc a book which he claims as author, "*Considerations on the Substance of the Sun*". Witness: Geo Deneale, clk of Dist of Potowmac.

FRI SEP 11, 1801
Murder on the Ohio river: Bennett Rogers was killed by negro man, Jack Neal; Ralph Elliott, jumped from the boat and drowned; Rogers had stayed at Mr Clark's hse in Wash City & Elliott was helping him in transporting 6 negroes to Tenn; Rogers spoke of sisters in Tenn; Neall to be hung, Sep 19. Bodies of Rodgers [2 Splgs] & Elliott were found by the people of Galiopolis.

For sale: lot 4 sq 490-Wash City.-Wm Clark

Frederick-town, Md: Result of election for electors: Roger Nelson-1769 votes, David Schriver-1764 votes [Rpblcns] & Richd Potts-1539 votes, Francis B Sappington, 1534 votes [Fed]. *Nottingham Dist, Md*: Capt Leonard Covington-256 & Allen B Duckett-251, Maj Edw H Calvert-87, Dr Wm Marshall-85. *Cecil Co, Md*: Messrs Gilpin & Sheridine, Rpblcn candidates, are elected. *Harford Co, Md*: Wm Smithson & John Montgomery-elected.

Christopher Williams was arrested in Balt for privateering under British colours, against Americ commerce. Unable to obtain securities for $2,000, he was committed to jail.

Common law is law of the U S: case of Isaac Williams, tried before this crt on an indictment for having on Feb 27, 1797, at Guadaloupe, accepted from the French Rpblc a commission & instructions to commit acts of hostility against the King of Gr Britain; said Wms then a ctzn o/the U S; Wms said he came to the U S in 1796 & did not stay 6 mos; jury found him guilty-$1,000 fine & 4 mos imprisonment.

MON SEP 14, 1801
For sale: the sloop, *Ann & Mary*, built in 1800. -John T Frost

Md Election. Electors of the Senate chosen: AA Co-John F Mercer & Edw Hall; Wash Co-Saml Ringgold & H Schebly; Kent Co-J Parker & B Chambers; Annapolis City-Gabriel Duval.

WED SEP 16, 1801
Saml Meredith, Treas of U S, to resign this month or next.

Farming Soc of Ireland. Rt Hon John Foster-Pres. Committee:
Marquis of Sligo	Rev Richd Wynne	Sir Edw O'Brien
Geo Grierson	Owen Wynne, esq	Jas Harvey
Richd Reynell	Rt Hon D Latouche	Ross Mahon
Chas P Doyne	John Garnet	Robt St George
S Garnet Jr	Rev Dr Beaufort	Ger. O'Farrel
Henry Stewart	John Hamilton	

Rt Hon D Latouche & Co.
Treas-Mr C Mills, No 44, Cuffee St, Dublin, Sec & Agent.

FRI SEP 18, 1801
Crct Crt of Wash Co, DC. sale of some hsehld furn & billard table, to satisfy a debt due by Robt M'Munn to Jos Caldwell. Also, hsehld furn, to satisfy debts due by Frederick Conrad to Jos Riddle & Jas Dall, assignees of Thos Vowell to Jas McDonald, & to Jas Smith, assignee of Ebenezer Parkins.
-Daniel C Brent, marshal of DC.

MON SEP 21, 1801
Md election-electors. Caroline Co-Wm Whiteby & Solomon Brown, Rpblcns. Talbot Co-JB Robins & EK Wilson, Fed. Worcester Co-Geo Robinson & Levin Winder, Fed. Dorchester Co-Moses Lecompte & WB Martin, Fed.

Died: Dr David Jackson, Sep 18, in Phil.

Mbrs of Cong for Ky. North Dist: John Fowler-7175, Wm Garrard-2048, Philemon Thomas-1351. So Dist: Thos T Davis-8902, John Pope-2401. Fowler & Davis are re-elected.

Died: Robt Yates, age 65 yrs, in Albany, formerly Chief Justice of NY.

Sup Crt of Pa. prosecution of Andrew Brown & Saml Relf, editors of Phil Gaz, for a libel on character of Alexander Jas Dallas. Dfndnts pleaded guilty; sentence-each fined $300, costs of prosecution & to keep the peace & be in good behavior for 1 yr & sum of $1000 & 2 sureties of $1000 each.

NY-Meeting of aliens at Lovett's Hotel, John Lovett-chrman, Walter Morton, sec: petition to Congress for a repeal of "The Naturalization Act of 1798". Committee chosen: Robt Swanton, John Thomson, Hugh R Murray, Walter Morton, Henry Herford, John Wood, Thos Boston Campbell, Alexander Cuthill.

Carlisle, Pa.-credit shd be given to Fredk Antes & Sebastian Shade, esqs, agents for Pa & Md, for removing obstructions in the Susquehanna river bed to render safe navigation.

WED SEP 23, 1801
Agricultural Soc of Providence: Pres Jabez Bowen, of Prov; VP Saml Elam of Newport; Treas Geo Champlin of Newport; Sec Olney Winsor [not given]; Corr Sec Thos Arnold of Providence. Also voted: Danl Lyman, Nicholas Taylor, Jos Cundell, Christopher G Champlin, Arthur Robbin, Wm Hunter, all of New-Port Co. Moses Brown, Aza Arnold, Jos Jenckes, Jas Brown, Hosea Humphrey, John Inne Clark-all of Providence Co. Saml J Potter, Peter Phillips, Elisha R Potter, Danl E Updike, Wm Marchant-all of Washington Co. Ray Greene, Christ. Greene [s/o Christopher], Jas Rhodes-all of Kent Co. Wm Bradford, Benj Bour, John T Child, Josiah Humphrey, Joshua Bickwall-all of Bristol Co.

The Bank of the U S is determined to establish a branch bank in Wash City. Jas Davidson, Jr, of Phil, appointed cashier.

Died: Dr Hall, visiting physician for Port of Phil, at Lazaretto, nr Phil.

FRI SEP 25, 1801
Reward-$10 for return of my apprentice boy, Geo W Brown, age abt 17 yrs, had my permission to go home but overstayed the time allowed.
-John Minchin, NJ Av, Wash.

Winthrop Sargent, late Gov of Mississippi Terr, has published a pamphlet vindicating his official conduct.

Commission of Bankruptcy has been issued against Isaac Smith of Harwich, resident in Boston, Mass; trader; to appear at ofc of Nathan Goodale, esq, in Tremont St, Boston. -John Heard, Sec'ry.

Election of Md Senators at Annapolis; Rpblcn tkt carried the entire majority; Western Shore: Walter Bowie, John Johnston, Richd Harwood, Wm Smith, Jas H McCulloch, John T Worthington, Saml Ringgold, John Tyler, Richd Mackal. Eastern Shore: Henry Hollinsworth, Robt Wright, Wm Whitely, Wm Polk, Wm Hayward, Jas Brown. Unsuccessful Fed tkt: Chas Carroll, Jas McHenry, Chas Ridgely of Hampton, Thos Johnson, John Thomas, Henry H Chapman, Wm Marshall, Richd Wotton, Elia Williams, Wm Matthews, Chas Goldsborough, Jas Holyday, Nicholas Hammond, Wm Richardson, Littleton Dennis.

Bag of feathers mislaid Dec last. Jas Mitchell recd same from Messrs McCulloch & Birkhead at Balt; bag of feathers were directed to Saml H Smith, Wash; he was to deliver same to Mr English, Gtwn. Mr M did not deliver. Info wanted respecting the residence of Mr Mitchell. -Saml H Smith, Washington City.

Elizur Goodrich has been apptd Prof of Law at Yale College.

MON SEP 28, 1801
Ltr to Jos Blyth, Paul Trapier, Erasmus Rathmahler, Savage Smith, Robt Grant, Saml Wragg & John Shackelford, esqs, dated-Gtwn, SC, Apr 15, 1801, Regarding: Proposed canal to be cut thru North Island.-[Col]-Ch. Senf

For rent: 4 lge brick hses on Capitol Hill. -Daniel Carrol, of Dud'n.

Run away, David Butler, negro, abt 30 to 35 yrs of age, committed to Wash jail.
-Daniel C Brent, marshal of DC.

WED SEP 30, 1801
Wash Co, DC. Lewin Talburtt, of Wash Co, made application for ltrs of adm on est of Jas Robinson, decd. -John Hewitt, Reg.

Lots for sale, Washington City, by Power of Atty: lots 12 & 13, sq 407-Mr John Aikin will show the prem. Public auction at Mr Thos Yates vendue store, Wash. -Saml Vincent, North Gay St, Balt. For particulars inquire of Alex'r McCormick, merchant, nr the Capitol.

Fri Oct 2, 1801

Died: Col Frederick Antes, at Lancaster, Pa; Whig & Rpblcn.

Died: Mrs Swanks, age 24 yrs, in Wash, leaves an only dght & a tender & affectionate husband, sincerely to lament a loss which he must severely feel. Rev Mr Foxall delivered an oration adapted to the occasion.

Died: John Hoofnagle, age 92 yrs 6 mos 3 days, at Lancaster.

Sheriff's Sale. Genrl Crt for Western Shore of Md: sq 74 in Wash City & lots 7, 8, 9, sq 38; furn etc, prop of Isaac Polock, to satisfy judgment of Abraham Vanloghen against him. -Notley Maddox, late Sheriff of PG co, Md.

Orphans Crt of Wash Co, DC. For sale at *Rock Hill*, late resid of Gustavus Scott, esq, decd: number of negroes, furn, etc. at farm, "*Strawberry-Vale*", Va, negroes, horses & cows of said Gustavus Scott.
                    -Elias B Caldwell-adm.

For sale: billiard table. -Jasper De Carnap, NJ Av, Wash.

Mon Oct 5, 1801

Fredericksburg, Sep 22-Lightning hit the hse of Col Minor injuring his dght age 16 or 17, a child abt 3 or 4, Col & Mrs Minor; his 5 other chldrn were uninjured.

To be sold: at dwlg place of Mary Jackson, PG co, nr Caldwin's Tavern; 6 negroes & other prop of Fielding Belt, late of PG co, Md, decd.
                    -Tobias Belt & Beal Duvall, adms.

Lancaster, Sep 30. Andres Ellicott, esq, is apptd sec of the land ofc vice Tench Coxe, esq, rsgnd.

Wed Oct 7, 1801

Balt City, Md: Election of Delegates in Leg of Md-Rpblcn tkt, John Scott & Thos Dixon, elected without opposition.

Died: Dr Jas Church, proprietor of the cough drops, pills & botanical teas, in NY, Oct 1.

Ladies with ltrs in the Post-ofc, Wash City, Oct 1, 1801:
Mrs Lucy Addison	Nancy Bury	Eliz & Daniel Brussit
Juliet Bellybreaker	Mrs B Courne	Sarah Caspeder
Mrs Dobbin	Miss R Pollock	Mary Palmatary
Ann Shaw	Emily Thompson	Priscilla Yearts

Fri Oct 9, 1801

John Oakley apptd Coll of Port of Gtwn, in place of Genrl Jas M Lingan, rsgnd.

Died: Seth Paine, esq, printer, Sep 18, editor of Charleston City Gaz; ntv of Dedham, Mass.

Alexandria & Norfolk Packet. Tristram Butler has now a new safe sailing sloop, *"George"*, for passengers; lying at Ricket's Wharf; apply to Newton & Co.

Bankruptcy is awarded Geo W Kirkland, late of Wash Co, DC.
-Elias B Caldwell, clk to comrs.

Thos Munroe is postmstr in Washington City.

Md Election. Rpblcn Tkt for hse of Delegates:

Frederick Co	Roger Nelson	David Shriver	Thos Hawkins
	Henry Kemp		
PG Co	Mr Bowie	Mr Wood	Mr Carr
	Mr Van Horne		
Montgomery Co	Robt P Magruder	Tho S Davis	Hezekial Veatch
	Elinelech Swearingen		
Calvert Co	Walter Mackall	Rezin Estep	Wm Carcaud
	Wm Holland		
Balt Co	N R Moore	T E Stansbury	A Lemmon
	Thos Love		

MON OCT 12, 1801
Directors of U S Branch ofc of Discount & Deposit at Wash City:
Trastram Dalton, Thos Tingey, Thos Peter, all of Wash City;
John T Mason, Jos Carleton, Wm H Dorsey, John Dunlap, all of Gtwn;
Wm Oxley, John C Vowell, of Alexandria; Jas Davidson Jr, of Phil, cashier.

Capt John Striker is apptd Naval Agent for Balt vice Archibald Campbell.

For sale: Sloop of War, *"Maryland"* at Mr Henry Wilson's Wharf, Fells Point.
-Joshua Dorsey, esq.

WED OCT 14, 1801
Delegates to represent Annapolis, Md: Allen Quinn, & Richd Ridgely; Wash Co: Messrs Cellers, Smith, Tilghman, & Ott; St Mary's Co: W Hebb, Wilfred Neale, Ralph Neale & L W Barber.

Col David Hall, Rpblcn candidate, elected Gov of Delaware.

Col Benj Talmadge, Federal, chosen a mbr of Congress, at Conn.

FRI OCT 16, 1801
Reward-$3 for bay horse that strayed from me nr Barry's Wharf, Wash City.
-Mark Crowley.

Mon Oct 19, 1801

Appointments by the Gov of Pa: Saml Bryan, Compt-Genrl vice John Donaldson, rsgnd; Geo Duffield, Register Genrl vice Saml Bryan.

Wm Whann is apptd cashier in the bank of Columbia.

Archibald Roane is elected Gov of Tennessee.

Md Election [all Rpblcns]

Caroline Co	Robt Orrell	Thos Mason	Wm Douglass
	John Tillotson		
Talbot Co	Thos S Denny	Wm Rose	Edw Lloyd
	Nichs Martin Sr.		
Queen Ann's Co	Chas Frazier	Jos Thompson	Stephen Lowry.
	Saml Burgess		
Kent Co	Jas Houston	Benj Hanson	John Thomas
	Alex'r Stuart		
Harford Co	John Montgomery	Dr Elijah Davis	Jas Lytle
	John Forwood Jr		

Pa City Elec. Reps elected: Saml Wetherill, Hugh Ferguson, Jas Gamble, Robt Porter, Philip Odenheimer. Pa Co: Wm Penrose, Elisha Gordon, John Goodman Jr, Jacob Holgate, Jas Engle & Geo Ingles.

Wed Oct 21, 1801

Died: Maj Griffith John McCree, at Smithville, nr Wilmington, Oct 3, Coll of Wilmington Port.

Died: Gen Mathew Locke, age 71, at his seat nr Salisbury, Rowan Co, Sep 7. Sep 9th he was buried at Thyatyra.

Reward-$20 for strayed or stolen horse in Wash. -Jas Mathers, nr the Capitol.

Slaves committed to the Wash Co jail: John Maynard, age 29, mulatto, formerly prop of David McMechen, esq, of Balt, who sold him to Mr White, to a Mr Bingham & Mr Sargeant from Ga. Jim Wilmer, negro, age abt 26 yrs, says he was formerly prop of Mr Cumberland Dugan, of Balt, who sold him to White, Bingham & Sargeant from Ga. Harles, age 25 yrs, says he belongs to Mr Tubman, of Benedict, St Mary's Co, Md. -Danl Carroll Brent, marshal of DC.

Fri Oct 23, 1801

Ltr from ofcr on U S frig, Phil, dated Gibraltar, Jul 15, 1801. Lt Maley, formerly commanded the U S schnr, *Experiment*, is prisoner of the Spaniards at Algesiras-[the ofcr was mate o/ship belonging to Phil., Capt Flinn, Cmder.]

Jonathan Bayard Smith has been elected Mayor of Phil City.

Stockholders of Bank of Columbia-I was yesterday srvd notice that I cld no longer be employed as cashier. The President of the bank will reply to my ltr at the next meeting of the directors. I have srvd for 7 & 1/2 yrs. -Saml Hanson of Saml.

MON OCT 26, 1801
Case of John Brown, bankrupt. He is to surrender himself to the comrs, at Rhodes Tavern, Wash City. -John C Dent, Sec to the Commissioners.

Case of Chas Love, bankrupt, late of Wash Co, DC, merchant, is to appear at the hse of Wm Rhodes, Wash City. -John C Dent, clk to comrs, Wash.

Isaac Vanhorne is elected mbr of Cong, Pa vice Peter Muhlenburg rsgnd.

WED OCT 28, 1801
Died: The late Prof John Millar, of Milbeugh, Sep 30; born in 1735; Prof of Law at Glasgow Univ

Vt Election: Isaac Tichenor-Gov; Paul Brigham-Lt Gov; Benj Swan-Treas; Amos Marsh-Spkr; Roswell Hopkins, Sec. Judges of the Co Crt of Windham Co: Saml Knight-Chief Judge; Benj Burt & Jason Duncanside-Judges.

FRI OCT 30, 1801
For sale: hsehold furn at the hse of Col Habersham, Gtwn. -Jereimiah Connor, auctioneer, Washington City.

Circulating library has been mv'd to the hse of John D Brashiers, bet Pres' & Mkt sq hse. Conducted under the care of John McDonald. -Hugh Somerville.

MON NOV 2, 1801
Improvement-Sheets of sheet copper produced at the manufactury of Col Paul Revere & Son, at Stoughton, were lodged at ofcs in this town; they have erected works where copper for sheathing ships, *cold rolled,* is produced. The frig, *Boston,* was bolted & spiked with bolts & spikes from this manufactory.
-Boston Paper.

David Jackson, Druggist & Apothecary, has remv'd from Chestnut to 26 So 3d St, Phil, Pa.

J B Dumoutet, jeweller of Phil, will open at the hse of J W Lytton, High & Bridge Sts, Gtwn, DC.

Deed of trust from Amariah Frost & Esther, his wife, dated Aug 1800, sale of lot 17 sq 634, Wash City. -John G Ladd

WED NOV 4, 1801
Apptd by the Pres: Gideon Grainger, postmaster, v Jos Habersham, rsgnd.

Reward-$10 for Nell, negro woman, age 38 yrs, ranaway from nr Piscataway, PG Co, Md. -Nicholas Young.

FRI NOV 6, 1801
In Chancery, Oct 31, 1801. Ratify sale made by Henry Whetcroft; lot of ground in Wash City, prop of Abraham Young, decd, sum $1150, subject to the right of dower. -Saml H Howard, Reg. CC

Just published in Boston: *The History of Land Titles in Massachusetts*, by Jas Sullivan, Atty Genrl of that State. [400 Pgs; Price $3. Net proceeds for the Historical Society].

WED NOV 11, 1801
For sale: lot in Wash City, sq 886, Delaware Ave. Apply to Messrs Kurrack & Percival in Phil, or Benj Burch on NJ Av, Wash City.

Public Sale by order of Orphans' Crt of Wash Co, DC. The late dwelling of Jas Robinson, decd, abt 1 mile from Eastern Branch Ferry; & his prsnl prop.
 -Lewis Talburtt, adm, Wash.

For sale: 2,500 acs in Northumberland Co, Va, late the resid of Presley Thornton. -Richd Peters, Jr, 85 Walnut St-Phil.

Criminals escaped from Wash Co prison: Francis Higdon, age abt 26 yrs, has relations in Chas & St Mary's Co, Md. Jas Scully, age abt 40 yrs. Harry, negro, age abt 23 yrs; may have gone to Port Tobacco where his master, Lanty Maddox, resides. -Danl C Brent, Mrshl of DC.

Partnership between Baily Washington & Jos Dowson is mutually dissolved. The former will settle any accounts.

For rent: hse of Mrs Washington adjoining to Gen Dearborne. -Apply to Mr Law, Capitol Hill.

Died: Robt Smith, age 73 yrs, Bishop of SC, at Charleston, SC

FRI NOV 13, 1801
Died: Dr Wm Shippen, age 90 yrs, at Phil.

Augustus Von Kotzebue has written a sketch of his life & literary career; he was born May 30, 1761.

Crt Martial of Capt Geo Little: case principally for pillage, with other allegations; said Capt Little was acquitted Sep 7, 1801, signed by: S Nicholson, Pres; Silas Talbot, Stephen Decatur, Alex'r Murray, Edw Prebble, John Mullowny, Thos Robinson, Hugh G Campbell, Cyrus Talbot. Geo Blake, acting as Judge Advocate. Rt Smith, Sec of the Navy, approves of the sentence of acquittal.

John F Mercer, Rpblcn, is elected Gov of Md.

Mon Nov 16, 1801
Rev Mr Ralph, principal of Charlotte Hall School, rsgnd.

Wed Nov 18, 1801
Died: Mrs Mary Harris, Nov 7, w/o Theophilus Harris, merchant of Alexandria. Wife, mthr, & friend.

Died: Mr Jasper De Carnap, age 50 yrs, Nov 12, resid of Wash. He leaves his widow & 5 chldrn; he was born Feb 16, 1751. Funeral at St Paul's Chr, NJ Av, by Rev Mr M'Cormick.

Josiah Meigs is President of the Univ of Georgia.

Fri Nov 20, 1801
Burlington, Vt, Oct 29. Printing ofc of Messrs. Chipman & Fessenden, at Vergennes, was consumed by fire on Nov 17.

Mon Nov 23, 1801
Revenue Cutter, *John Jay*, sold in NY for $7,400 to Mr Crowninshield of Salem.

Lexington, Ky. Col Jas Smith, a missionary sent by the Presby Chr of Ky to the Indians has returned.

Branch Bank in Wash City: Pres-Josep Carleton, of Gtwn; Teller-Jos Saul of Norfolk; Bkkpr-Geo Boyd, of Gtwn.

Chas Richter, hair dresser from Balt, has taken a hse in Wash, opposite Mr Tunicliff's Hotel.

Wed Nov 25, 1801
For sale-assort of dry goods. Jas Hewitt & Co-hse adjoining the one occupied by Mr John Jacks, in F St.

Died: Mr Weld Gardner, merchant, s/o the late Saml Gardner, esq, at Salem.
By his death the following legacies become due, given by Mr Geo Gardner, decd, bro of Mr W Gardner, in 1773. Liberal legacies to the Marine Soc, Harvard College & the poor are itemized-[*Legacies were bequeathed by Geo Gardner, provided Mr Weld Gardner died w/out any male heirs; as his bro, Henry Gardner, is living & undoubtedly a male heir, are not these legacies null & void?] *as written in the nwspr.

Raleigh, NC, Nov 10. Abraham Swaine, late of Nantucket, mariner, was indicted for having on Jan 25 last, on the High Seas, turned pirate. He ran away from the schnr *Fidelity*, Fordam Pease mstr, belonging to Messrs McCandless of Balt; he took $1000-really $11,000 was said to be the amt.

Died: Hon Andreas E Van Braam, esq, age 57 yrs, at Amsterdam, Holland; late Pres of the Dutch East India Co & Ambassador to the Crt of Pekin.

Alexander & John Kearnes, fr & son, of Ky, lately apprehended at Salisbury, & Nathan Baggot, of Johnson Co were charged with counterfeiting. Kearnes was acquitted. Both Kearnes were to pay $5 & crt costs; sentenced to 2 yrs imprisonment at Hillsborough. [Appears to be Raleigh, NC court.]

FRI NOV 27, 1801
Notice: I intend to petition the Crt of DC, for permission to keep a ferry across the Eastern Branch at Hamilton's Point, nr Ninian Willets' over nr hospital sq, where Mr Holt lives. -John B Kerby.

Chas McLaughlin, a contractor for carrying the mails, recd the mails at his hse from the City Post ofc; he explains why north mail went south & south mail went north-by the Post Master in Gtwn or in Wash City. [Ltr to Mr Smith, Gtwn, Nov 25, 1801]

MON NOV 30, 1801
To rent: hse lately occupied by Saml Meredith, esq, Treas, on the river, West of Pres' hse. -Francis Deakins, Gtwn.

Ltr: To Robt Purviance, Coll of Balt, from Tobias Lear, Gen Com Agent of the US in the Island of St Domingo-dated Cape Francois, Nov 9, 1801. Rgrd: Late insurrection & tranquility now restored.

WED DEC 2, 1801
New store-dry goods, Pa Ave. -Sharpless & Smith.

FRI DEC 4, 1801
Chas Varden & Thos Carpenter, mutually agreed to dissolve their partnership. -Wash City, Capitol Hill.

Mr Geo Atwood, Editor of the American, a passenger in the schnr *Nelly*, Capt Chase, arvd yesterday from Cape Francois.-Balt American

Mrshl's sale; Crct Crt of Wash Co, DC; Thos K Beale, adm of Jos Clarke, use of Stephen Wilson's adm, against Wm King. To be sold: all right, title, etc of Wm King to lot 13 sq 104, occupied by Mr John Brown. -Danl C Brent, mrshl-DC.

Public Sale, "*Blue Plains, & Addison's Good Will,*", nr 500-acs. Also, at Mr McLaughlin's Tavern, Gtwn, 200 acs nr Wash. 563 acs in Montg Co, Md where Mrs Lynn formerly lived. Apply-Wm Bayly. -Walter Mackall.

MON DEC 7, 1801
Died: Col Philip Pendleton, age 52, Bath, Va.

Savannah, Nov 17. Nov 2d at Louisville, the Senate chose Hon Wm Barnett-Pres; Wm Robertson-Sec; Hse of Reps re-elected David Meriwether, -Spkr; Hines Holt, esq-clk. Ofcrs elected: Judges: Matthew McAllister, Geo Walton & Thos P Carnes. Gov Tatnall, Brig-Genrl. Wm Bulloch, esq, Atty-Genrl. Solicitors: P Van Allen & R Walker, esq. Treas: Edwin Mounger; Sec-Horatio Marbury; Dr W Cocke-health ofcr; Geo Throop, esq,-hbr mstr-Savannah

Died: Hon Ephraim Ramsay, Nov 18, at Silverbluff, Edgefield Dist, age 35 yrs, an Assoc Judge of SC

WED DEC 9, 1801
Indian prisoner, lately returned from captivity, now in Ky. Nancy Mason, d/o Geo Mason & Mary his wife, formerly Mary Butler, was born in Md, 5 miles from Gtwn; her fr, mthr, & 2 sisters were killed abt 12 yrs ago by the Shawanese Indians on the Ohio Rvr; her bro Jas & herself were prisoners; her fr had 15 negroes with him & 9 were killed; her fr had a bro, Isaac, owner of iron-works in Beeson town, Pa, & her mthr had 3 bros, Saml, Jas, & Nace Butler. Friends of this woman, who needs assistance, can apply to Judge McClung, of town of Wash, in Ky, or to Henry Innes, nr Frankfort.

FRI DEC 11, 1801
Jonesborough, Tenn. Dr Wm Dixon, elected Rep to Congress from Tenn.

Claims against est of Jasper De Carnap, late of Wash, decd. -Eliz De Carnap, admx. Henry Ingle, adm.

MON DEC 14, 1801
Ltr from Mr John Owen, Supercargo of the brig *Friendship* of NY, to his owner, dated Puerto Del Principe, Nov 4, 1801; Mr Alex'r Richards. Arv'd at Nuevitas on Oct 18; brought to by a Spanish privateer & plundered; they have robbed of yours abt $13,000; Mr Geo Richds, abt $3,000; Mr Collins, abt $3,000; of your bro, Mr N Richds, abt $700; some things of Mr Van Beuren, Capt Bulls & others, abt $300.

For sale, svt, abt 25, as butler. Apply at Stelle's Hotel. -Skelton Jones.

Committed to the prison in Wash Co, as run-aways: Lucy Watson, black woman, says she comes from Alexandria & is a free woman having srvd her time with Mr Edw Harper, of Alex, abt 25 yrs of age. Ergbert Loveless, black man, age abt 35 yrs, shows a cert of Mr Maddox, shrf of PG Co, having been sold out of his prison for his fees, no owner. -D C Brent, Mrshl, DC

To let-2 story brick hse, NJ Ave. Inquire of John Fownes on premises.

Boarding & Lodging, nr Treas Dept, Wash. -Chas Rogers.

WED DEC 16, 1801
Died: Gen Wm Darke, age 69 yrs, Nov 25, of Berkely Co, Va.

Elegant stoves at D Crawley's, 28 Nassau St. NY.

Public sale of hse & lot occupied by Capt Tingey, nr the Navy Yd.
                              -John Traver, Auctioneer.

Ltr to Andrew Sterett, Lt & Cmder of the U S schnr, *Enterprise*, dated Washington, Dec 1, 1801 & signed by Th Jefferson. Rgrd: the late engagement with the Tripolitan Cruiser captured by you.

FRI DEC 18, 1801
Last notice to creditors of Chas Love; cert of discharge will be given; declared bankrupt. -Uriah Forrest, Crct Ct of DC.

Supreme Crt of the U S. Thu, Dec 10, 1801. Thos Swann, esq, of Dist of Col, & John R Smith, esq, of Pa, admitted as counsellors of this crt.

John March, stationer, High St, Gtwn.
John Byrne has groc store in Prince, Water St, Alexandria, Va.

Hse of Reps: Petitions & memorials of the following were referred:
Polly Cumming	Peter Harvey	Ephraim Davis
Jos Eaker	Jos Goss	John Slesman of Balt
Godfrey Haga of Balt		Henry Mumbower

Sarah Fletcher & Jane Ingraham, widows & relicts of Patrick Fletcher, late Cmder of the U S frig, *Insurgent*
Jos Ingraham, late a Lt on board the U S brig of War, *Pickering*.

Mmbrs of the Hse o/Reps:
NH	Saml Tenney	Abiel Foster	Geo B Upham
	Jos Pierce		
R I	Jos Stanton Jr	Thos Tillinghast	
Conn	Saml W Dana	Roger Griswold	John Davenport
	Elias Perkins	John C Smith	Benj Tallmage
	Calvin Goddard		
Mass	John Bacon	Phanuel Bishop	Wm Eustis
	Wm Shepard	Jos B Varnum	Lemuel Williams
	Mannasseh Cutler	Richd Cutts	Joshiah Smith
	Ebenezer Mattoon	Seth Hastings	Peleg Wadsworth
	Nathan Read		
Vt	Lewis R Morris	Israel Smith	
NY	Theodorus Baily	Lucas Elmendorf	Thos Morris
	Philip Van Cortlandt	John Smith	John P Van Ness
	David Thomas	Benj Walker	Saml L Mitchell
	Killian K Van Ransselaer		
NJ	John Condie	Ebenezer Elmer	Jas Mott
	Henry Southard	Wm Helms	

Pa	Thos Boude	Robt Brown	Andrew Gregg
	Jos Heister	Jos Hemphill	Wm Hoge
	Michl Leib	John Smilie	John Stewart
	Wm Jones	Isaac Van Horn	Henry Woods
	John A Hanna		
Dela	Jas A Bayard		
Md	John Campbell	John Dennis	Danl Heister
	Thos Plater	Saml Smith	Richd Sprigg
	Jos H Nicholson	John Archer	
Va	Richd Brent	Saml J Cabell	Thos Claiborne
	John Clopton	John Dawson	Wm B Giles
	David Holmes	Geo Jackson	Anthony New
	John Randolph Jr	John Smith	John Taliaferro Jr
	Abram Trigg	John Trigg	Philip R Thompson
	Mathew Clay	Edwin Gray	Thos Newton Jr
	John Stratton		
NC	Nath'l Macon	Wm B Grove	Archibald Henderson
	Jas Holland	Chas Johnson	Richd Stanford
	Willis Alston	John Stanley	Wm H Hill
	Robt Williams		
SC	Wm Butler	Benj Huger	Thos Lowndes
	Thos Moore	Thos Sumter	John Rutledge
Ga	John Milledge	Benj Taliaferro	
Ky	Thos T Davis	John Fowler	
Tenn	Wm Dickson		
NW Terr	Paul Fearing		

WED DEC 23, 1801

Dry goods for sale at my store on E Capt St.-Wm E Mack.

Public sale, at Union Tavern, Gtwn; brick hse formerly occupied as a tavern by Mr Semmes.

-Philip B Key, Wm Thornton.

Notice to creditors of Jas Lyon; cert of discharge will be given; declared bankrupt. -Uriah Forrest, clk Crct Crt of DC.

Mrs Pick opened a millinery at Mr Kirtz's, nr Union Tavern.

MON DEC 28, 1801

Dr Tongue informs residents of Wash that he practices physick & particularly surgery. He resides on Pa Av, Wash.

Died: Mr Thos Harris, age 106 yrs, in Mifflin Co, Pa.

John Goulding, broker & commission merch, offers his svcs in Gtwn next to the Post Ofc.

Wed Dec 30, 1801

Michael Roberts is opening his store, on High St, in Gtwn. Also for sale at the above store-wines etc, Edgar Patterson.

Regimental orders. Regt Crt Martial of the 121st Regt Pa Militia, commanded by Lt Col Geo Thomas, held at hse of Maj John Light, Sep 26, 1801, by order of said Geo Thomas. Maj Wm P Atlee, Pres; Capt Adam Messencope, Capt Geo Matter, Capt Jos Nagle, Lt Wm Cornman, mbrs. Capt John Leonard declaring that he would never wear the blue & red cockade; Leonard is guilty of refusing to obey orders; unfit to hold a commission in the Militia of Pa.

Treas Dept, Dec 1801. Act passed Feb 18, 1801, regulating the grants of land for refugees from the British Provinces of Canada & Nova Scotia; priority of location determined by lot agreeably to the following schedule: [Priority of half sections of 320 acs:] Numbers assigned per name:
1-24-95 Thos Faulkner
33-112 Lt Wm Maxwell
2-135 Benj Thompson
39-41-94 Atwood Fales
3-13-83-93 Jonathan Eddy
43-50-55-67 heirs of John Dodge
4-97 John Halsted
45-106 Jos Levittre
5-35-40-44-69-81-134 John Allen
46-80 Seth Noble
6-Ambrose Cole
7-31-88 John McGown
48-71-91 Lewis F Delesdernier
8-14-27-58-87-98-103 Martha Walker, wid/o Thos Walker
49-82-128 Martin Brooks
132-John Forrreyre
129-Jos Cone
9-51 Jos Bindon
52-96-101 Eben. Gardner
10-Danl Earle Jr
53-John D Mercier
11-26-36-38-57-63-90 John Edgar
56-Edw Chinn
12-15-17-42-60-68-114 Seth Harding
59-102 Jacob Vander Heyden
100-Jas Cole
61-64-120 Wm How
16-22-115 Lt Col Bradford
62-76-99 David Gay
18-25-126 John Starr
66-Adam Johnson
19-122-130-131 Parker Clark

70-John D Mercier
20-23-109-118 Col Jas Livingston
73-107 Jas Crawford
21-65-116 Noah Miller
74-86-104 Joshua Lamb
28-34-54-72-110-125-127 P Francis Cazeau
29-111 Isaac Danks
77-113 John Livingston
30-37 Jas Price
78-79 Maj B Von Heer
32-92-119 Edw Faulkner
47-105 Martha Bogart, relict of A Bogart, & formerly relict of D Tucker.
85-89-121 Jonas C Minot
108-John Paskel
75 David Jenks
117-widow & heirs of Col Jeremiah Duggan
133-Saml Fales-only 1/4th of a Section or 160 acs.
84-123-124 heirs of Simeon Chester
[Note: This list was 1 thru 135 with the respective number prior to the person's name; many had more than one number on this list]

The National Intelligencer and Washington Advertiser
Washington, DC 1802

MON JAN 4, 1802
Peter Mills, nr Treas ofc. Persons wishing to have their lands located can apply at the Wash City Tavern for locating the Canada & Nova-Scotia refugee lands. Priority of location of half sections of 320 acs. [There are 135 names, many were repeated. This is a list of each name]:

Benj Thompson	Jonathan Eddy	Thos Faulkner
John Allen	Ambrose Coke	John Halsteda
Jos Bindon	Daniel Earle Jr	John McGown
Seth Harding	Lt Col Bradford	John Edgar
Parker Clark	Col Jas Livingston	John Starr
P Francis Cazeau	Isaac Danks	Noah Miller
Lt Wm Maxwell	Atwood Sales	Jas Price
John Dodge-heirs	Jos Levittre	John D Mercer
Lewis F Delesdernier	Martin Brooks	Edw Chinn
Ebenezer Gardiner	Jacob Vander Heyden	Wm How
Adam Johnson	Jas Crawford	David Guy
David Jenks	David Gay	Joshua Lamb
Simeon Chester-heirs	John Paskell	Maj B Von Heer
John Forrreyre	Jonas C Minot	Jos Cone

Col Jeremiah Duggan-widow & heirs
Martha Walker wid of Thos Walker
Martha Bogart-relict of A. Bogart & formerly relict of D.Tucker
[Dec 30, 1801 listing included numbers given to each of the above]
-Treasury Dept.

WED JAN 6, 1802
In chancery-Richd Spencer v Eliz & Jos Middleton. Bill is to obtain a decree to sell hse & lot in Annapolis City, prop of Jos Middleton, decd, for debt due cmplnt. Jos M. resides out of state in Wash, DC.
-Samuel H Howard, Reg CC

Hse o/Reps: Petition of Saml Dexter, late Sec of War; in his official character had rented a hse in Wash City which was consumed by fire; he had been fined in his prsnl capacity by the owner of the hse for the loss he had occurred.

FRI JAN 8, 1802
Ofcrs of Americ Philosophical Soc: Pres-Thos Jefferson; VPs-Robt Patterson, Caspar Wister, Benj Smith Barton;
Secs: John Redman Coxe, Adam Seybert, Thos C James, Jos Clay;
Counsellors: Jas Woodhouse, John Bleakly, B H Latrobe, Saml Duffield;
Curators: C W Peale, John R Smith, Robt Leslie;
Treas-John Vaughan. Meeting-Phil, Jan 1, 1802

Ladies with ltrs in the Wash Post Ofc, Jan 1, 1802.

Mary Betton	Hetta Benkson	Lucy Deaton	Sarah Jacques
Emily Thompson	Eliz McCoy	Mgt H Scott	Mrs John Kane
Jane Isabella Thompson	Mrs Tidyman	Miss F Williams	Mrs S Wragg
& [Dr Philip Tidyman]			

MON JAN 11, 1802

Reward-$50: ran away, mulatto, Cyrus, age abt 21 yrs, apprentis with millwright; he stole at Popes Crk, est of Daniel McCarty, esq, in Westmoreland, a horse & saddle made by Jas Smock, Fredericksburg; his wife belongs to Gen Lee of Stratford. -John Rose, Virginia Leeds.

WED JAN 13, 1802

Reward-$20: ran away, Jos, negro, age abt 40 yrs, from Edmund Jenings, living in Loudoun Co, Va, nr Waterford.

Meeting held at City Tavern, Phil City, Jan 4. Subject-indemnities for French spoliations. Committee: Jos Ball-chrmn, Thos Fitzsimons, Chas Pettit, Jas S Cox, Stephen Girard, Henry Pratt, John Craig. -Stephen Kingston, sec'ry.

Hse o/Reps: Memorial of Saml Dexter-Treasury to adjust & pay whatever shd be decided due on the destruction of the hse of J Hodgson occupied as a War ofc.

FRI JAN 15, 1802

Partnership bet Robt Clarke & John Tutt, painters & glaziers, is dissolved by mutual consent. -Washington.

MON JAN 18, 1802

Crct Crt of Wash Co, DC. Marshal's sale. John Henry & Henry Pratt, against lands & tenements of Robt Morris, lot 2 sq 706.
-Danl C Brent, Mrsh'l of DC.

Chariot for sale at Mr Dunlap's, oppo Mr McLaughlin's Htl, Gtwn, DC.

For sale: tract of land, 400 acs in PG Co, Md on Oxen Run. Apply to Wm Cooke of Balt Town, Mr Jas F Leileh of Manchester, Va, Mr John Addison at Geesborough, nr Wash, or to Philip B Baker, in Wash City, atty for J Addison.

WED JAN 20, 1802

Lodging from Greenleaf's Point, where Judge Symmes now lodges.
-Saml Speake, Washington.

Balt American-Jan 1, 1802. A mammoth cheese was presented to Pres Jefferson; made by the hands of Messrs John Leland & Darius Brown; cheese was made Jul 20, 1801 & weighs 1235 lbs. Signed: Danl Brown, Hezekiah Mason, Jana. Richardson, John Waterman & John Wells Jr. -Cheshire, Mass.

FRI JAN 22, 1802
Mrs Smith & Mrs Wiley have remv'd their brdg school to a 3 story brick hse, nrly opposite the bank in Gtwn

Alexandria Co, DC. Jan Term 1802-Rgrd: Grievances on lotteries, road conditions, slave purchasers coming from various parts, etc.
-John Potts, foreman.

Hse o/Reps: Petition of J C Symmes, to accept his release & relinquishment to the U S, of all his claim to land n w of the Ohio, on certain proposed terms; referred to committee.

MON JAN 25, 1802
For sale $6,666.66, land on Acquia Creek, Stafford Co, Va, abt 500 acs.
-V Peyton.

Hse o/Reps: compensation to Wm Kilty, Chief Judge of the Crt of Columbia is adequate & recommend he withdraw his memorial

WED JAN 27, 1802
Stray cow came to my hse. Owner apply to Jos Parsons.

Geo Jacobs brought before me a stray mare. -Wm Thornton, Wash City, DC.

FRI JAN 29, 1802
Ltr from Cmdor Dale to Sec of Navy, dated Oct 26, 1801, Straits of Gibraltar. Loss of cutter belonging to the frig *President* & loss of 10 men: Lt John M Claggett; Midshipman; Elias Willis, Coxswain; John Street, Seamen-John Evans, John Miles, Jacob Dodge, Wm Smith, Thos Bragg, Wm Maybrook, Jos Dickson. Saved-Geo Hammell swam to shore.

Americ Merchant Ships convoyed thru the Straits of Gibraltar on Oct 26, 1801, by the U S ship, President: Appolo-Capt Huston, owned by Saml Smith & Co of Balt.; Salacia-Capt Wm Doak of NY; Superior-Capt Smith, owned by J Murehead of Charleston; Ann-Capt Anthony Y'Nooky of Charleston; Bulture-Capt Wm Lowring, owned by Capt Wm Lowring.

Ranaway, negro , Timothy Farmer, age abt 24 yrs. Nr Liberty Town, Frederick Co, Md.   -Daniel Root, Jr

Business formerly carried on by Dr Wm Rogers, is continued by Dr Wm H Grayham.   -Wash city

MON FEB 1, 1802
Public auction of rl est of & at the mansion of late Maj Richard Chew, 1,220 acs in A A Co, on Chesapeake Bay & forms mouth of Herring Bay, 20 miles from Annapolis; apply to Dr Richard Chew who resides thereon or to Mr Philemon L Chew living within a few miles.   -J Wilkinson, Trustee.

WED FEB 3, 1802
Partnership dissolved bet Wm Doughty & Jas C King by mutual consent; King will continue lumber bus on his wharf nr Rock Crk Bridge.

Phil, Jan 27. High Crt of Errors & Appeals': Case of negro, Flora, plntf n error v execs of Jos Graisberry, decd, dfndnts; favour of dfndnts-slavery legally existed before the adoption of the present Constitution & was not abolished thereby & that the negro, Flora, was a slave.

Died: Wm Hamilton, esq, R A, [artist]. Attended the Royal Acad. This day, striken with severe fever. -London Paper-No date.

FRI FEB 5, 1802
The Pres apptd John Beckley, librarian of the 2 hses of Congress.

T M Forman, [Horse-ranger] invites Osborne Sprigg, to race his horse, [Le Boo], over the Havre De Grace Course, 4 mile heats. Forman lives 44 miles from Havre De Grace.

Meeting of the ctzns of Phil on Jan 30th, at hse of Jas Kerr. Re: repeal of the law establishing the Judiciary System enacted Nov 17, 1800. Matthew Lawler, esq, Mayor of Phil-chrmn; Mathew Carey-sec; Committee: Jonathan Bayard Smith, Mahlon Dickerson & John L Leib.

MON FEB 8, 1802
Just published: "Reflections on Gov't, Philosophy, & Education", by Jas Ogilvie, instructor at Stevensburg Acad.

WED FEB 10, 1802
Copartnership dissolved bet Alex. Cochran & Alex. McCormick; those indebted are to pay the latter who will continue the business.

My wife Eleanor Dunlavy left my bed & brd of her own accord; do not give her credit; being I am now confined within the prison of Wash Co for debts I am unable to pay. -Chas Dunlavy.

Committed to Wash jail, negro, Charlotte, abt 19 yrs of age, says she is prop of Lewis St John, nr Battle Town, Frederick Co, Va. -Danl C Brent, mrsh'l, DC.

FRI FEB 12, 1802
Land for sale belonging to est of Judger Mercer, decd, Loudon Co, Va, on Goose Creek, 4,500 acs. Apply to John T Brooke, Fredericksburg, or to Jas M Garnett, Laytons, Adms.

John Hasket, esq, apptd by the British Gov't, Capt-Genrl & Governor in Chief of the Bahama Islands in America.

MON FEB 15, 1802
For sale: My hse & lot on High St, Gtwn. Apply to Wm Waters, Gtwn.
-John Waters.

Navy Dept, Jul 14, 1800. Capt Patrick Fletcher, of the Insurgent, Baltimore. Ltr instructing him to search for the privateers bet the West Indian Islands & our coast. -Signed, Benj Stoddert.

Navy Dept, Aug 15, 1800. Lt Benj Hillar, of the *Pickering*, New Castle, Dela. Ltr instructing him to take under your convoy the ship, Florida. Join our squadron on the Guadaloupe Station, rendezvousing at St Kitts. Cargo to be delivered to David M Clarkson, our agent at St Kitts. You will fall in with Capt Decatur. -Signed, Benj Stoddert.

New York, Feb 9. Ambrose Spencer is apptd Atty Genrl, vacated by Mr Hoffman. Genrl Armstrong has rsgnd his seat in the U S Senate.

Leg. of NY-Thos Storm is Spkr; Assembly-Chamber, Jan 30, 1802.

Ltr from the Atty Genrl, Wash, Jan 25, 1802, to Henry Dearborn, esq, Sec of War. Rgrd: Potts, Wilson & North, under firm of Geo North & Co having previously purchased of Gen'rl Lee, on May 7, 1800, to convey to the U S for $42,000, 230 acs of land & right of digging ore, U S rent of $1,000 per annum to said Lee-on a good title to the premises. May 8th, Lee executed to the U S his deed of the premises; same yr North & Co conveyed by deed 221 acs with their right of digging ore from friend's ore bank. 3000 acs was mortgaged Jun 1794 to secure payment of $8,000. The U S title is encumbered. -Levi Lincoln

WED FEB 17, 1802
Last Monday Geo Walker paid up Overton Carr in full of all demands; Mr Baker's advertisement was an oversight.

Hse o/Reps: Relief of Lyon Lehman was returned to the hse with amendments by the Senate.

Died: John Vining, at Dover, Delaware.

FRI FEB 19, 1802
Public auction-PG Co, Md, Orphans' Crt: all prop of Mary Lamar, decd.
-John Lamar, adm.

Meeting in NY, Signed-Geo Clinton Jr, chrmn; G V Ludlow, sec, Feb 12, 1802.

MON FEB 22, 1802
Died: Saml Philips, Lt Gov of Mass.

Creditors of Mr Wm Baily are to meet at Mr Semmes's Tavern in Gtwn on Mar 18. -Walter Mackall, trustee

De Witt Clinton, chosen Senator of the U S, vice Gen Armstrong, rsgnd.

WED FEB 24, 1802
A. F. Dallas has resigned his ofc of Recorder of Phil City.

Judges in Va, 1787:	Edmond Pendleton	Geo Wythe
John Blair	Paul Carrington	Peter Lyons
Wm Fleming	Henry Tazewell	Richd Cary
Jas Henry	John Tyler	

FRI FEB 26, 1802
For sale-3 or 400 acs of land, in centre of my est in Marlborough; Va side of Patowmac. Mr Wm Hay, present tenant, will show the premises.
-John F Mercer, Annapolis.

Public sale: farm on Tom's Crk, nr Emmittsburg, Frederick Co, Md, abt 280 acs. -John M Bayard.

John Kean, esq, Dauphin Co, Pa, writes to John A Hanna, Rep in Cong of Pa; desires to know the state of the iron business in Pa.

After the fall of Charleston in 1780, the first action was of Fishing Creek; the gallant Capt Rooke commanded a squadron of Tarleton's Legion, fell & the whole force was beaten & dispersed.

MON MAR 1, 1802
Farm for sale in PG Co, Md, abt 400 acs, prop of late Richd Beall, decd. Apply to Saml N Smallwood, Wash Navy Yd, or to Azel Beall or Richd Walker, excs, living nr premises.

WED MAR 3, 1802
Died: Field Marshall Count Lascy, at Vienna, Nov 24.

Sale at auction: lot 14 in sq 846, Wash.   -Azariah Gatton.

FRI MAR 5, 1802
Farming land for sale; abt 1000 acs, whereon Dr John Dorr resides in Pr Wm Co, Va; also adjacent land, late the prop of Mr Thos Swann, of Alexandria; also reversionary interest in Piedmont tract, below Short Hill Mtn, Loudon Co, Va.
-Ferdinando Fairfax, Charlestown

Ltr from Evan Jones, esq, to sec of State, dated New Orleans, Aug 10, 1801. Rgrd: Need for a hospital for Americ ctzns, especially seamen & boatmen from the Ohio.

Ltr from E M Bay, esq, to sec of State, dated Charleston, Nov 4, 1801. Rgrd: proper accommodations for the poor & infirm seamen & boat-men from New Orleans.

MON MAR 8, 1802
Committed to jail of Wash Co, DC, slaves: Sarah Ann Owens, negro age 23 yrs, says she belongs to Wm Foote, of Alex; also, Peggy, mulatto woman, age abt 35 yrs, says she belongs to Joshua Power, nr Port Tobacco, Md.
-D C Brent-mrshl.

Cape Francois-an Americ gentleman named Lanchester was killed at Charleston. [Massacred by the negroes]

WED MAR 10, 1802
Rev'd Jeremiah Moore, Lewis Richards, Adam Freeman, & Wm Parkinson, ministers of the Baptist denomination, having met pursuant to appointment in Wash, constituted a church, "The Baptist Chr, Wash City."

Premium of $300 for best original plan of a college-So Carolina. Gov John Drayton, Daniel Huger, priv sec, Charleston.

List of Americ Vessels at Cape Francois on Feb 12, 1802:

Ship	Capt	City	Ship	Capt	City
Hannah	Moore	Phil	*Success*	King	Charleston
Ann	Terry	NY	*Traveller*	Billaps	Belt
Brig Mentor	Girard	Phil	*Dolphin*	Johnston	Savannah
Augusta	Davis	Boston	*Mary*	Tarris	Phil
Lear	Low	Balt	*Julia*	Holt	Phil
Nymph	Woodman	Boston	*Gen Warren*	Bowman	Savannah
Hannah	Goddrich	Boston	*Sally*	Howland	NY
Hope	Lee	NY	*Amphitrite*	Spence	Phil
Constellation	Fuller	NC	*Venilia*	Haurton	Balt
Schnr Nelly	Rodger	Balt	*Fanny*	Thompson	Balt
Peggy	Allen	Phil	*Lydia*	Brown	Phil
Rover	Veawck	Phil	*Harmony*	Levering	Alexandria
Alexander	Russel	Phil	*Eliza Ann*	Ross	Norfolk
Talbot	Sorenson	Balt	*Intrepid*	Alderson	NC
Concord	Sharp	Phil	*Cath.*	Cloutman	Boston
Little Tom Butler	Powers	Phil	*Active*	Calvert	Phil
Sloop Friendship	Busher	Phil	*Spartan*	Furlong	Balt
America	Craig	Phil			

FRI MAR 12, 1802
Looking glasses for sale. -Mr Chas Varden, Capitol Hill, Wash.

Gennessee, for sale, all my mills, hses & improved farms, in Ontario & Steuben Cos, NY; public auction at Powell's Hotel, Geneva. -Charls. Williamson. Bath, Mar 1, 1802.

For sale: frame hse & lot 5 sq 347, 11th St, Wash. -Anthony Jones.

For sale: hse & lot in Liberty St, Berkley Co, Va, newly finished by & for resid of late Thos Palmer, decd. Apply to Jas Davidson, esq, cashier of Branch Bank, City of Wash.

MON MAR 15, 1802
Partnership dissolved bet Capt Naylor & Basil Talbert in the Eastern Branch Ferry & public hse connected therewith.

Annapolis-in council: All debtors are to be published in the newspaper 3 times a wk for 3 wks.   -Ninian Pinkney, clk.

WED MAR 17, 1802
High Crt of Admiralty in Eng has given sentences of restitution in favor of following vessels & their cargoes, detained & carried in by British Cruisers, for attempting to enter blockaded port of Havre, France: [Ship, Master] *Edwin*, Robt Follanche; *Five Sisters*, J Lunt; *Lucy*, S Toppoen; *John*, John Chester; *Sophia*, F Driscoll; *Sophia*, Isaac Hands; *Georgia*, J Landon; *Juno*, J D Lawrence.

Died: Narsworthy Hunter, Mar 11, age 45 yrs, late a delegate from Miss Terr. Sat noon-interred in Presby Grave Yd in Gtwn.

Bankruptcy is awarded against Thos Waterman, late of Wash City & Co, merchant.   -John Hewitt, clk of Commissions.

FRI MAR 19, 1802
Arabian horse, the Dey of Algiers, arrv'd at Boston to John Mason, esq, by Col Swan, of Mass, now in Europe; he will stay at Mason's farm in Montg Co, Md; horse brought from Arabia in 1798, [4 yrs old], by late Grand Bailiff Fromm, of Prussia; Lt Gen Frederick Baron of Diemar purchased the horse after the death of Fromm & sent him to Hamburgh to Col Swan, thence to America. No more than 50 mares will be recd this season.   -Chas C Jones, Gtwn, Feb 26, 1802.

MON MAR 22, 1802
Thos Holt has a variety of garden seeds, shrubs & trees for sale at his garden, Eastern Branch

Fire broke out in Boston in the store of Jos Ripley & 11 stores were consumed.

WED MAR 24, 1802
Died: Notley Young, Mar 23, one of the oldest & most respectable inhabitants of DC.

Arrv'd: Arthur St Clair, Gov of NW Terr, in Wash.

Died: John Sitgreaves, Mar 4, Dist Judge for SC.

Fri Mar 26, 1802
In chancery, State of Md: Eliz Retallick, v Johanna Casenave, Peter Casenave & Edw Dudley. Suit is to obtain a decree for conveyance of part of lot 66 in Annapolis. Peter Casenave, fr of Johanna & Peter, by bond of Jun 1793, agreed to convey said lot to Dudley-100 pds; Peter, the fr, has died leaving Johanna & Peter his heirs at law & they are minors residing out of Md, Dudley also resides out of Md. Dudley assigned his right & title to Simon Retallick, decd, who by his will devised same to cmplnt. -S H Howard, Reg CC

Walter Bowie-elected Rep of U S vice Richard Sprigg, resigned.

Mon Mar 29, 1802
Orphans Crt of Wash Co, DC. Mar 29, 1802. Gustavus Scott, late of Wash Co, decd. -Elias B Caldwell, adm.

Creditors of Ezekiel King, bankrupt, appear Aug 3.
 -Uriah Forrest, clk of Crct of DC

Wed Mar 31, 1802
John Stickney, of Wash City, DC, merchant, has been declared bankrupt.
 -Gwinn Harris, clk to Commissioners.

Fri Apr 2, 1802
Public auction at Rhodes Tavern: 2 story brick hses in 14th St, sq 253, at present under let for $205 per annum to respectable tenants: David Rawn, Wm James, & R W Peacock; also on Pa Ave, leased to Mr Henry Burford, forever @ $60 per annum & one to John Gardner, @ $72 per annum. -Loring & Forrest, auctioneers. -Wm Lovell

Partnership bet Wm Moffat & Ebenezer Nesmith, housewrights; dissolved by mutual consent. Payments to the latter, Wash.

Mon Apr 5, 1802
Command of squadron destined for the Mediterranean was given to Cmdor Richard V Morris, v Capt Truxton, retired.

Public sale-all prsnl prop of Lewis Williamson, decd, at dwelling hse of Cath. Williamson, admx, Wash City. -Orphans Crt o/PG Co, Md.

New invention: improved saw mill, patent obtained-Moses Coates, West Brandywine Bridge, Pa.

Wed Apr 7, 1802
To rent: 2 story brick hse on F St; formerly occupied by Mr Dexter, lately by Mr John Brown. Enquire of Clement Dorsey, esq, Gtwn, or Wm Dyer.

Act passed for the relief of Isaac Zane, his heirs & assigns, in fee simple, 3 sections of land, of 1 sq mile ea, within the NW Terr. Signed: Nathl Macon, A Burr & apprv'd Th. Jefferson, Apr 3, 1802.

For sale, land: abt 1500 acs, *"Hicks's Niche"* on the Potowmac. Terms apply to Henry O'Riely, of Gtwn or John Gordon, Font Hill, Northumberland Co, Va

Funeral svc for late Notley Young, esq, at RCC in Gtwn-Wed.

FRI APR 9, 1802
For sale: at vendue, at Mr Semmes's Tavern, Gtwn, land cld *Scotland & Barbadoes*, 206 acs, on Eastern Branch; Mr Henry Smith lives on the premises. Same time-the shore & lot at High & Bridge Sts occupied by Mr Jas Doyle & the sq where Mr Bayly now lives, adjoining to Col Deaking & Mr Chas Lownde.
-Walter Mackall

Reward-$20 for runaway, Henry, negro, age abt 25 yrs. Chas Co nr Port Tobacco. -Edw Hamilton

MON APR 12, 1802
Mail stages have extended the Gtwn & Port Tobacco line to Leonardtwn, Md; leaves Indian King Tavern, Gtwn & Thompson's Inn, Leonardtown; meets at Pye's Tavern, Port Tobacco. Each passenger-20lbs of baggage.
-Jos Semmes, Jas Thompson.

Ladies with ltrs in the Wash Post Ofc, Apr 1, 1802.

Sarah Beckitt	Esther Carey	Eleanor Davice
Eliz Fisher	Ann G Grose	Miss Frances D Henley
Mrs Hadgessin	Julian & Nancy Leary	Isabella McCashlen
Mrs Spiers	Mrs Dehlah Stewart	Peggy Taylor
Mrs Emily Thompson	Mary Wilson	

WED APR 14, 1802
Committed to Wash Co, DC jail: Jesse, negro, says he belonged to Peyton Wayal of Ga. -Daniel C Brent, Marshal of DC.

Notice: Public is cautioned against sale of my hse on sq 432, Pa Ave, advertised by Saml Baker; Baker has not complied with the contract advertised.
-John Harrison.

Mail Pilot leaves Columbian Inn, Gtwn & Mr Wm Tunnicliff's, Wash City, for Balt, Phil & NY. -J H Barney.

FRI APR 16, 1802
Reward-3 cents, peck of potatoes & sweepings of the jail for securing Wm O'Conner, Irishman, born in Co of Tipperara, absconded from the Wash Co jail; his fmly resides in Balt. -Robt McClan-gaoler.

Mon Apr 18, 1802

For rent or sale-my bldgs on F St, lot 2 sq 289. -Jas H Blake, Colchester, Va.

Ltr from Rufus King, esq, to sec of State, dated Feb 18, 1802. The Sieur Chas Godfrey Paleske & Mr Johann Ernst Christian Schultz, have returned the Exequaturs which they recd, recognizing them as cns'ls of his Majesty, King of Prussia in the U S; their functions as such have ceased. -Signed, Jas Madison.

Notice: Persons having claims against Mr Notley Young, decd; render them to Robt Brent, Wash City. -Benj Young, Nichols Young, Robt Brent, excs.

In Chancerty, State of Md: Mark Pringle, v Nathaniel Washington & Mgt his wife, *Henderson Sim Butler & *Susannah Greenfield Butler his wife, & *John Trueman Hawkins. Obtain a decree for recording a deed executed Aug 29, 1774, by *Geo Frazier Hawkins, formerly of PG Co decd, for conveying to Wm Russel of Balt Co & his heirs; land cld "*Caledonia*"- Frederick Co, 3200 acs. *Reside in DC.   -S H Howard, Reg CC

Wed Apr 21, 1802

Died: Most noble Francis, Duke of Bedford, age 37 yrs, Mar 2, Woburn, Gr Britain, succeeded by his bro Lord John Russell.

An act for the relief of Thos K Jones. The collector for the port of Boston & Charlestown is to issue to T K Jones-the debentures for the drawback of the duties on wine imported by Jones in the ship, Juno, Capt Thos Dingley. Approved-Thos Jefferson, Apr 14, 1802.

Died: Aedanus Burke, age 59 yrs, May 30 at Charleston, SC; ntv o/Galway, Ire.

An act for the relief of Paolo Paoly, a subject of his Danish Majesty, the sum of $7,040.55-the damages & cost of suit, awarded by the Crct Crt of Pa, in favor of Paoly, owner of the schnr, *Amphitheatre*, against Wm Maley, Cmder of the armed vessel, the *Experiment*, belonging to the U S; for capture of said schnr.
-Approved, Thos Jefferson, Aug 14, 1802.

Sundry items were robbed from my hse; reward. -David Agilvie.

Public sale of dwelling hse of Anthony Addison, 20 negroes, land cld *Barnaby Manor*, 1000 acs, late the prop of said Addison. Taken by suit of Wm Stewart, & one of Nath'l Washington, for use of Geo Hawkins. -Thos MacGill, sheriff.

City Hotel, Broadway New-York, will open May 1; hotel is well known.
                        -John Lovett.

Fri Apr 23, 1802

Imported horse, Driver, will stand the ensuing season at Wash City; 7 yrs old on Apr 28 last; Driver was got by Lord Edgmont's running horse, in Eng; bred by

Lord Offery; [Long line continued----] purchased by my relative, Isaac Pickering, esq, of Foxleafe, Hampshire, Eng. -Chas Duvall

MON APR 26, 1802

Stonington, Conn-Apr 12. Reps to the Genrl Assembly; Ephraim Kirby-221 votes for Gov; David Trumbull-abt 221 for Lt Gov Persons to stand in numination for mbrs of Congress:

Asa Spalding	Saml W Dana	Amos Palmer
Latham Hull	Elisha Hyde	Elias Perkins
Aaron Olmstead	Nath'l Palmer	Elijah Munsell
Rufus Hitchcock	John Welch	Elijah Boardman
Taylor Shearman	Roswell Judson	Danl Tidden
Saml W Johnson	Roger Griswold	Thos Lyman
Joshua Stow	John T Peters	Epaph Chamrion
Saml Whittlesey	Hezekiah Huntingdon.	

Note: John Allen, Fed-2 votes; John Chester, Fed-3 votes.

Died: Dr John Moore, age 71 yrs, Feb 21, at Richmond, Surrey, Eng; fr of Maj-Gen Moore, who returned to Eng from srvg in Egypt.

Norwalk, Conn, Apr 14. Wm M Betts & Dr Phineas Miller were chosen reps to the Genrl Assembly for the ensuing session.

For sale: abt 240 acs, prop of Robt Buchan, decd, in PG Co, Md, also stock & furniture. -Jas Buchan, acting heir.

Sen & Hse of Reps: Relief of Lewis Tousard, late Lt Col Commandant of 2d Regt of Artl & Eng; sum of $675.55. Final settlement other than pay due him by the paymaster. -Nathl Macon, Spkr of Hse of Reps, Abraham Baldwin, Pres-Sen Pro Temp.

WED APR 28, 1802

For sale: frame hse on north F St, lot 3 sq 253, Wash. -Jas R Dermott.

For sale-land in Westmoreland Co, Va, 275 acs. -Peter Rust, Richmond Co.

For sale: 3 tracts of land in Chas Co, Md, total abt 199 acs, also 2 negroes.
-Mathias Redmond.

FRI APR 30, 1802

Thos Rose is opening a school nr Capt Hill, May 9.

Patrick Edwards has opened a school at Mr Doyne's brdg hse, nr the Pres' hse, Wash City.

MON MAY 3, 1802

Reward-6 cents for Mary Cochlin, indented srvt girl, may have gone to Balt.
-David Ogilvie.

WED MAY 5, 1802

Francis Maurice, Prof of French language, music & dancing, proposes to open his dancing acad at Mr Villard's Spring Garden, Wash.

Mr Jas McHenry, esq, former sec of War, rsgnd that ofc abt May 1800; in April preceeding, Mrs Ariana French leased a hse to him for one yr to begin Jun 1st; an award was made bet the parties; Mr McHenry shd pay Mrs French $208.95; for his not occupying the hse.

FRI MAY 7, 1802

Died: Richard Howell, at Trenton, late Gov of NJ.

Characters who wld be proper to fill the ofc of cnclrs, Wash City: Danl Carroll of Dud'n, Benj Moore, Tristram Dalton, Jas Hoban, Richd Forrest, Nichs King, Robt W Peacock, Robt Brent, Wm M Duncanson, Augustus B Woodward & Cornelius Cunningham -[Signed: A Washingtonian].

Richmond, May 1, 1802. Dr John Adams-75 votes, elected a Delegate to rep this city in next Genrl Assembly of Va; Mr Jas Rind- 52 votes & Mr Geo Hay -48.

MON MAY 10, 1802

Treaty of friendship, limits & accomodation bet the U S & the Chactaw Nation of Indians. Jas Wilson of Md, Brig-Genrl U S Army; Benj Hawkins of NC & Andrew Pickens of SC, Com'rs, Jan 3, 1786 at Hopewell on the Keowe. Names & seals affixed at Ft Adams on the Miss, Dec 17, 1801. Witnesses present:

Alex'r Macomb	Sec to the Commission,
John McKee	Dep Super & agent;
Henry Gaither	Lt Col Commandant;
John H Brull	Maj 2d Regt Infty;
B Shaumburgh	Capt 2d Regt Infty;
J Jones	Assist Q M Genrl;
Benj Wilkinson	Lt & Paymstr 3d U S Regt;
Lt J B Walback	Aid-De-Camp
J Wilson	Lt 3d Regt Infty
Saml Jeton	Lt 2d Regt A & E
John J Carmichaels	Surg 3d Regt U S Army.

Approved at Wash City, May 4, 1802. Th Jefferson, Pres.; Jas Madison, Sec of State. *Names & Seals affixed at Chickasaw Bluffs, Oct 24, 1801: Jas Wilkinson, Benj Hawkins, Andrew Pickens; Witnesses: Saml Mitchel-agent to the Chickasaws; Malcom X Megee, interpreter; Wm R Bootes, Capt of 3d Regt & Aid-De-Camp; J B Walbach, Lt & Aid-De-Camp; J Wilson, Lt 3d Regt. [*May 12th, 1802 paper]

Some time since, Daniel Marsh, esq, Coll of Port of Amboy, in a sudden gale, [is supposed], that his boat upset & he & his son-in-law drowned; he sailed out in a skift to transact business in the line of his official duty; Mr Marsh's body was found Thu -Newark, May 4.

WED MAY 12, 1802
An insane person, Horatio Seney, of Church-Hill, Queen Anne's Co, Md, died after a fast of 40 days. [Extract of a ltr from Chester Town, Md, Apr 28, 1802.

Saml Cabot, esq, has been instructed by the Pres to repair to London for duties before the Brd of Com'rs.   -Boston, May 4, 1802.

FRI MAY 14, 1802
Inhabitants of Wash who do not pay their taxes by first Monday in June next; will be deprived of their right to vote.   -Washington Boyd, Coll of Wash Co.

MON MAY 17, 1802
Died: John Lowell, at Roxbury, Mass, Chief Judge of U S Crct Crt for 1st Crct.

Justices of the Peace for Terr of Columbia, apprv'd by the Senate, Apr 27, 1802.

Wash County:

Danl Reintzel	Danl Carrol	Cornelius Cunningham
Thos Peter	Robt Brent	Thos Addison
Abraham Boyd	Benj More	John Mason
Wm Thornton	Jos Sprigg Belt	Thos Corcoran
Anthony Reintzel	Isaac Pierce	John Oakley

Alexandria Co:

Geo Gilpin	Francis Peyton	Chas Alexander
Geo Taylor	Jonah Thompson	Cuthbert Powell
Abraham Saw [Faw]	John Herbert	Dick Alex. Smith
Jacob Houghman	Elisha Cullen	Peter Wise
Geo Slacum	Presley Gunnell	John Dundas

WED MAY 19, 1802
In chancery: John Weems against John Weems Jr, Sarah Weems, Wilhelmina Gannt, Henry Gantt, Philip Barton Key & Chas Lowndes. To obtain partial relief against a bond executed by cmplnt to said John Weems Jr for 250 pds & a bond to Philip B Key for 500 pds. Bonds executed by cmplnt, to secure a bal to Amelia Weems, one of his fr's reps, due from him, as exec to his fr; cmplnt has a suit against him by Danl Kent; said bal is not due from him bec he was entitled to a contribution from said Amelia, for money pd by him to recover "Loch Eden" by suit brought against him by Wm Loch Chew. Some of the dfndnts reside out of state.   -Saml H Howard, Reg CC.

Mrd: John P Vanness, esq, mbr of Cong from NY State, to Miss Marcia Burns, of Wash, DC.

Rhode Island election for Gov, Lt Gov & Senators. *Arthur Fenner & Wm Greene; *Saml J Potter & Geo Brown; *Waterman Tibbits & Isaac Johnson; *Benj Howland & Isaac Baily; *Thos Hoxsie & Jonathan Maxson; *Paul Mumford & Wm Tew; *Nehemiah Knight & Elisha Barlett; *Timothy Wilmarth & Darius Smith; *Wm Waterman & Chas Wheaton. *Rec'd majority of votes.

FRI MAY 21, 1802

Address from the ctzns of the U S in Cape Francois to Tobias Lear, Genrl Commercial agent of the U S for St Domingo Island; Signed-Jas Williams, Thos C Earle, Unite Dodge, Josiah Lewden-Committee. Signed: Geo Attwood, R S Duhamel, John N Darcey, Robt Stephenson, Wm Dawson, Chas Watt, Robt Moore, Frederick Tracey, Thos Asbury, Chas Tracy, Wm Knox Jr, Sol G Albers, John Grochan, David Olivier, Christopher Deshon, Wm Nott, Wm F Carty, C Langford, Robt Smart, Edw Boden, Benj Houston, Geo McCandless. Tobias Lear responded Apr 16, 1802, Cape Francois.

To be sold: in Nottingham, PG Co, Md, for benefit of creditors of Ignatius Boone; land & dwelling hse, now a tavern, 14 acs, 7 or 8 negroes, horses, all his hselhld furn & billard table.   -Robt Bowie, trustee

Lost: certificate from Allen Quinn, esq, Justice of Peace for Annapolis, stating that Jas Prout, a black man, was free. -Jas Prout.

Connecticut election: for Gov-Jonathan Trumbull & Ephraim Kirby; Lt- Gov: John Treadwell & David Trumbull; Assistants: Wm Williams, Oliver Ellsworth, Jos P Cock, Wm Hillhouse, Roger Newbery, Thos Seymour, Aaron Austin, David Daggett, Nath'l Smith, Jonathan Brace, John Allen, Chauncey Goodrich. Treas-Andrew Kingsbury. Sec-Saml Wylls. Votes for treas & sec not counted.

MON MAY 24, 1802

John Adamson offers lots for sale in Camden, SC; where he lives.

Groceries & wines for sale; B. G. Orr, Jefferson St.

WED MAY 26, 1802

Died: Mrs Martha Washington, wid of late Gen Geo Washington, at Mt Vernon, May 20.

In chancery: Honore Martin v Ann Casenove, Nicholas Young, & Joana & Peter Casenove. Ratify sales made by John Hewitt, trustee, in Wash City: lot 4 sq 599-$126; lot 6 sq 610-$106.   -A C Hanson, Chan

We, residents of Chester Co, Pa, are witnesses to Moses Coates' new sawmill invention: Francis Garnder, Isaac Coates, Wm Baily, John Fleming & Thos C Vickers.

In chancery: Geo Beall against Eleanor Hopkins, John Hopkins & Barbara his wife, Alex'r Hopkins & Rosanna his wife, Thos & Jas Hopkins. Obtain a decree to record a deed executed on Jan 22, 1801 by dfndnt; convey to cmplnt part of a tract cld "*I was not Thinking of It*", 171 1/2 acs, also tract cld "*Hopkins Choice*", 53 acs; also tract cld "*Evans's Look Out*", 23 acs, all in Montg Co, Md. Dfndts resid in Wash Co, Pa.   -Saml H Howard, Reg CC

FRI MAY 28, 1802

Reward-$10 for Priscilla, negro, age abt 45 yrs. I bought her from John Stephens, Wash City; she lvd with Mrs Martin Huger nr Great Falls, of the Potomac for some time.   -John Sasseer, nr Nottingham.

Died: Rt Hon Lloyd Lord Kenyon, Chf Justice of King's Bench; at Bath; succeeded by his only remaining son, Geo, now Lord Kenyon. London

MON MAY 31, 1802

Appointments by the Pres & confirmed by the Senate: Albert Gallatin, of Pa, sec of Treas, vice Saml Dexter rsgnd; Robt Smith, sec of Navy, vice Benj Stoddert, resigned;
Thos Tudor Tucker, of SC, Treas, vice Saml Meredith, rsgn'd.
Gideon Granger, of Conn, Post Mstr-Genrl, v Jos Habersham, do.
Silas Lee, o/Mass, Atty for Dist o/Maine, v Danl Davies, apptd to State ofc;
David L Barnes, of R I, Judge of R I Dist Crt, v Benj Bourne, promtd
David Howell, of R I, Atty for Dist of R I, v David L Barnes, do.
Jas Nicholson, of NY, Comr of loans for NY, vice Matthew Clarkson, rsgn'd;
Henry Potter, of NC, Judge of 5th Crct, vice John Sitgreaves, dcln'd
Wm Stephens, of Ga, Judge of Dist Crt of Ga, vice Jos Clay, rsgn'd.
Wm Kilty, of Columbia, Chief Judge of Crct Crt of Dist of Col, vice Thos Johnston, dcln'd.
John Oakley, of Columbia, Coll & Inspec of Revenue for Dist of Gtwn, vice Matthew Lingan, resigned
Malachi Jones, of NC, Srvyr of Port of Curratuck, v Saml Jasper, decd;
Joel Lewis, of Dela, mrsh'l of Dela Dist, v Robt Hamilton, term expired
Jas Alger, of Ga, comr of loans in Ga, vice Richd Wylley, decd.
Wm C C Claiborne, o/Tenn, Gov of Miss Terr, v Winthrop Serjeant, term expired
John Graham, of Ky, sec of Leg to Madrid
Thos Sumter, of SC, sec of Leg to Paris
Jonas Clark, of Mass, inspec of rev for port of Kennebank
Jonathan Russel, of R I, Coll for Dist of Bristol
Wm McMillan, of NW Terr, atty for Dist of Ohio
Jas Findlaye, of NW Terr, mrsh'l of Dist of Ohio.
David Duncan, of NW Terr, Coll for Dist of Michillimackinac.
Wm Chribbs, of Indiana Terr, Coll of Dist & inspec of Rev of Port of Massac
Walter Jones Jr, of Columbia, Atty, for Dist of Potomac
Wm Baker, of Columbia, mrsh'l for Dist of Potomac.
Jas Wilkinson, Benj Hawkins, Andrew Pickens, Com'rs to treat with the Cherokees, Chickasaws, Choctaws & Creeks;
Wm Richardson Davie, of NC, comr to hold a treaty bet NC & Tuscaroras;
John S Sherbourne, of NH, atty for Dist of NH, vice Edw St Loe Livermore, nominated Feb 18, but not appointed;
Geo Blake, of Mass, atty for Dist of Mass, v Harrison G Otis, nom. Feb 18;
Saml Bishop, of Conn, Coll of Dist of New Haven, v Elizur Goodrich, nominated Feb 18;

Hermanus H Wendell, of NY, mrsh'l of Dist of Albany, vice Jas Dole, nominated Feb 21, but not apptd;
Geo Maxwell, of NJ, atty for Dist of NJ, vice Fredk Frelinghuysen, nominated Mar 2, not apptd;
Alex'r Jas Dallas, of Pa, atty for Eastern Dist of Pa, v John W Kitter, nominated Feb 18;
Jas Hamilton, of Pa, atty for Western Dist of Pa, vice Thos Dancan, nominated Mar 3, not apptd;
Presley Garlaue, of Pa, mrsh'l. for Western Dist of Pa, vice Hugh Barclay, nominated Mar 3, not apptd;
John Munroe, of Va, atty for Western Dist of Va, vice Saml Blackburn, nominated Feb 21, not apptd;
Andrew Moore, of Va, mrsh'l for Western Dist of Va, vice Rob. Grattan, nominated Feb 21, not apptd;
John Thompson Mason, of Columbia, atty for Dist of Columbia, vice Thos Swan, nominated Feb 28, not apptd;
Daniel Carrol Brent, of Columbia, mrsh'l of D C, vice Jas L Lingan, nominated Feb 28, not apptd;
Geo Gilpin, of Columbia, Judge of orphan's Crt for Alex. Co, Columbia, vice John Herbert, nominated Mar 2, not apptd;
John Hewitt, of Columbia, rgstr of wills, for Wash Co, Columbia, vice John Peter, nominated Mar 2, not apptd;
Wm Gardner, of NH, former comr of loans, to be comr of loans for NH vice John Pierce, rmv'd;
Jos Whipple, of NH, former Coll of Dist of Portsmouth, to be Coll of that dist, vice Thos Martin, rmv'd;
Jos Scott of Va, mrsh'l of Eastern Dist of Va, v David M Randolph-rmv'd.
John Smith, of Pa, mrsh'l. of eastern dist of Pa, vice John Hall do;
Jos Crocket, of Ky, mrsh'l. of dist of Ky, vice Sam. McDowell, rmv'd;
David Fay, of Vt, atty for dist of Vt, vice A. Marsh, rmv'd;
John Willard of Vt, mrsh'l of dist of Vt, vice Jabez G Fitch, rmv'd; Daniel Marsh, of NJ, Coll & inspec of Rev in Perth-Amboy, vice Andrew Bell, rmv'd;
Jas Lynn, of NJ, super. for dist of NJ, v A Dunham, rmv'd;
Mount Edw Chisman, of Va, Coll & inspec for Hampton Dist, vice _____ Kirby, rmv'd;
Isaac Smith, of Va, Coll for Cherrystone Dist, v Nath'l Wilkins, rmv'd;
Thos De Mattos Johnson, of Ga, Coll for Savannah Dist, v Jas Powell, rmv'd;
Josiah Hook, of Mass, Coll for Penobscot Dist & inspec of that port, vice John Lee, rmv'd;
Ruben Etting, of Md, mrsh'l of Md Dist, vice David Hopkins, do;
John Heard, of NJ, mrsh'l of NJ Dist, vice Thos Lowry, do;
Edw Livingston, of NY, atty for NY Dist, vice Richard Harrison, do
John Swartwowt, of NY, mrsh'l of NY Dist, vice Aquilla Giles, do.
Ephraim Kirby, of Conn, super. for Conn Dist, vice I Chester, do;
Alex. Wolcot, of Conn, Coll for Middleton Dist, v Chancey Whittlesey, rmv'd;
Saml Olgood, of NY, super for NY Dist, vice Nicholas Fish, do;
David Gelston, of NY, Coll of NY Dist, vice Joshua Sands, rmv d;

Peter Muhlenberg, of Pa, super. of Pa Dist, vice Henry Mill, do
Chas Pinckney, of SC, Minister Pleni at Crt of Madrid, vice David Humphreys, recalled on account of long absence from the U S.

WED JUN 2, 1802
Appointments made, subsequent to the commencement of the session, & confirmed by the Senate: David Latimer, Mbr of Leg Cncl of Miss. Terr, v Adam Bingamon, dclnd;
John Taylor, of NY, comr. to hold a treaty with the Seneca & other Indians;
Timothy Bloodworth, of NC, Coll for Wilmington, NC Dist, vice Griffith McRee, decd;
John Slocum, of R I, srvy of Port of New Port, R I, vice Daniel Lyman;
John Cress, Jr, of R I, srvy of Port of Pawcatuck, vice Geo Stillman; Nath'l Folsome, of NJ, Naval Ofcr for Portsmouth, NH, Dist, vice Edw St Loe Livermore
Edw Harris, of NC, Judge of 5th Crct, v Henry Potter, accepted ofc of Dist Judge;
Mickael McClary, of NH, mrsh'l of Dist of NH, vice Bradley Cilley, Commission expired;
Walter Nichols, o/R I, Naval Ofcr o/New Port, vice Robt Groke, decd;
Silas Crane, of NJ, Coll of Little Egg Harbour, vice Wm Watson, super-seded for non-attendance on his duties;
Jas L Shannonhouse, of NC, srvyr & inspec of port of Newbegun-Creek, NC, vice Frederick Sawyer, who had rmv'd thence;
Thos Worthington, of NW Terr, super of N W Dist;
David Duncan, of Indiana Terr, inspec of port of Michillimackinac;
Peter Gansevoert, of NY, Military agent, for the Northern Dept;
Wm Linnard, of Pa, Military agent for Middle Dept;
Abrahm D Abrahams of Ga, to be Military agent, for Southern Dept;
Benj Gheny, of NC, srvyr & inspec o/port o/Beauford, NC, v late John Easton,
John Heard, NJ, Coll of port of Perth Amboy, vice Daniel Marsh, decd.
Foreign agents:
Tobias Lear, Island of St Domingo, vice Edw Stevens, rsgnd;
John E Caldwell, of NJ, St Domingo, v Jas Blake, of Pa, apptd to Antwerp;
Theodore Peters, of France, vice-agent at Boudeax;
Bartholomew Dandridge, of Va, Port Republic at St Domingo;
Edw Jones, of Columbia, to Island of Gaudaloupe;
Thos Aburn, of R I, to Cayene;
John I Murray, of NY, to Port of Glasgow in Gr Britain;
Jos Pulis, of Malta, cns'l for same;
Thos Hewes, of Mass, to Port of Batavia, Java;
Jacob Lewis, of Mass, to Port of Calcutta, Bengal;
Francis L Taney, of Md, agent for Offend, vice John Mitchel, nom., not apt'd;
Chas D Coxe, of Pa, to Dunkirk, vice John Hooe, nmntd, not apptd;
Peter Dobell, of Pa, agent at Havre, vice John M Forbes, nom., not apt'd;
Thos T Gantt, of Md, agent at Nantes, vice John H Waldo, nom., not apt'd;
Wm Patterson, of NY, agent at L'orient, v Turell Tufts, nominated, not apptd;
Wm Lee, of Mass, agent at Bourdeaux, vice Isaac Cox Barret, nom., not apt'd;

Wm Buchanan, of Md, agent for Isles of France & Bourbon, vice Geo Stacy, nominated, not apt'd;
Fulwar Skipwith, cns'l to agent at Paris, v J C Mountflorence, nom., not apt'd;
The Sieur Etienne Cathalan, of France, cns'l to agent at Marseilles, vice Wm Lee, nominated, not apt'd;
Jos Isnardi, Sr, of Spain, former cns'l at Cadiz, same, vice Henry Preble, nominated, not apt'd;
Sieur De La Motte, of France, vice cns'l to vice agent at Havre;
Geo W Erwin, of Mass, cns'l at London, v Saml Williams, remv'd;
Robt C Gardiner, of R I, to Gottenburg; Wm Stewart, of Pa, to Smyrna;
Jas L Cathcart, cns'l at Tripoli, to cns'l at Algiers, v Richard O'Brien, rsgn,d;
Wm Jarvis, of Mass, to Lisbon, vice John Binkeley;
Geo W McElvoy, to Tenerisse, vice John Culman who has abandoned the place
Henry Molier, of Md, cns'l at Corunna;
Wm Riggin, of Md, cns'l at Trieste, vice John Lamson;
Jos Barnes, cns'l for Island of Sicily;
John M Forbes, of Mass, cns'l at Hamburg, vice Jos Pitcairn;
John Appleton, of Mass, agent at Calais;
Robt Young, of Columbia, agent at Havanna, v John Marton, resgnd.

Notice: to all persons trespassing on my land, formerly cld *"Elton Head Manor"*, now denominated *"Charles's Gift"*, for fowling, fishing & hunting, to my prejudice, & I am determined to enforce the laws of the country for infringing this prohibition.   -Nicholas Sewall, St Mary's Co, Md

FRI JUN 4, 1802
Died: Edanus Burke, age 59, Mar 30; ntv of Galway in Ire. Taken from the Charleston City Gaz.

Bankruptcy has been awarded & issued against Alexander Cochran, late of Wash Co, DC, merchant.   -Thos Herty, sec.

Appointment: Oliver Barnett, mrshl of NJ, v John Heard, apptd Coll of the customs for the district of Perth-Amboy.

Mrd: Jun 1, in Wash, by Rev Mr Balch, Mr Benjamin *Hensey, of DC & Miss Sally Jackson, dght of John Jackson, of Va. *Very light print.

Died: Mrs Hannah Moore, age 111 yrs, May 25, Effinghman Co, Va.

MON JUN 7, 1802
Albany Register-the late election: Rpblcns- John Smith, Saml Mitchell, Philip Van Courtlandt, Andrew McCord, Isaac Bloom, Beriah Palmer, Thos Sammons, Erastus Root, John Patterson, Oliver Phelps; Federalists: Henry W Livingston, Joshua Sands, Conrad E Elmendorf, Geo Tibbets, Caylor Griswold. Note-Mr McCord was opposed by Gen Hathorn.

Wanted immediately, a pressman, Wm Duane's Printing Ofc-Wash.

WED JUN 9, 1802
Died: Dr Darwin, Apr 18, in Eng, while writing in his study, at the prior nr Derby.

Ctzns elected for Wash City Cncl:

Danl Carrol	Geo Blagden	Jas Barry	Wm Brent
Benj Moore	Jas Hoban	Nicholas King	S H Smith
Wm Prout	Thos Peter	John Hewitt	A B Woodward

Others who recd votes:

Geo Hadfield	Jos Hodgson	Thos Tingey	Henry Ingle
C Conynham	G Coombs	Thos Herty	Geo Andrews
Peter Lenox	John Kearney	Wm Duncanson	

Federal misrepresentation: Case of the pension of Col Touifard; he arvd in America in Mar 1777; recommended to Congress by Silas Dean; Jun 1777 he recd a Brevet Commission, as Lt from Gen Washington; in 1778 he lost an arm at R I; entered into svc with the French Gov't; returned in 1794 to America. [Article is on his pensions.]

For sale: dwelling hse of Wm Brown, in PG Co, Md, & 100 acs.

FRI JUN 11, 1802
Reward-$50 for apprehending the criminals who broke the jail of this place & escaped Jun 6: Daniel Hienesey, Irishman, abt 35 to 40 yrs of age; Chas Houfman, Dutchman, abt 50 yrs of age; Thos Naylor, born in Va, age abt 19 or 20 yrs; Wm Pickeron, Englishman, age abt 25 yrs; Mille, negro woman, born in Va, age abt 25 to 30 yrs. -Robt McClan, goaler, Wash City.

Appointments by the Pres. Genrl Com'rs of bankruptcy-Columbia Dist: Wm Thornton, John M Gantt, Tristram Dalton & Sam Hanson. R I Dist: Constant Tabor, Saml Vernon, Ths Peckham & Paul M Mumford. Ky Dist: John Rowan, Danl Weisger, John Inston, Jas Morrison, John A Seitz & John Bradford.

MON JUN 14, 1802
For sale: mahogany sawed into different sizes to accommodate purshasers. Fairfax St, nr the Mkt, Alex. -Ralph Douglas, Ben. Adamson, cabinet-maker & joiner.

Leg of NH-at Concord Jun 3: John Prentice elected spkr over Jim Langdon by 20 votes.

WED JUN 16, 1802
Orphan's Crt of Wash Co, DC. Jun 8, 1802. John A Burford & Hugh Deneley, applied for ltrs of adm on est of Wm Clarke, late of the frig, *President*, seaman, decd. -John Hewitt, rg

Fri Jun 18, 1802

Genrl Commissioners of bankruptcy appointed by the President:

NH	Nicholas Gilman	Henry S Langdon	John Goddard
	John McClentock		
NY	John Broome	Wm Edgar	Jonathan Pearsee Jr
	Nathan Landford	Jaines Fairlie	Abraham G Lansing
	Geo Merchant	Danl D Tompkins	Nicholas N Quackenbush
Pa	Alex. J Dallas	Jos Clay	Mahlon Dickerson
	Thos Cumpston	John W Vancleve	John Sergeant
Va	Geo Hay	Wm Duvall	Geo W Smith
	Archibald Theveatt	Thos B Robertson	John McRae
	Benj Hatcher	Thos Burchett	

Raleigh, Jun 8. the Fed Dist Crt for this state opened & adjourned by the marshal on Jun 1st; Jun 2d the newly apptd Judge, Edw Harris, esq, of Newbern, arrv'd. Judge Hall of SC has not been heard from.

Mon Jun 21, 1802

Died: wife of Thos Claiborne, esq, Mbr of Congress, Jun 4th in Brunswick Co, Va; [Exemplary in all connubial & maternal duties].

Thos Jefferson, Pres of the U S: the ctzn, Jos Marie Lequinio Kerblay, having produced to me his commssion, I recognize him as a Commissary of Commercial Relations of the French Rpblc for State of R I, to reside at Newport. Jun 15, 1802. Also-ctzn Sotin, I recognize as Commissary of Comerc Relations of the French Rpblc for the State of Ga, to reside at Savannah.

Ran away, Wm Jones, abt 15 yrs of age, bound to the cabinet & chair business. -Wm Worthington, sr, living in Wash City.

For sale: 2 story brick hse on N St, sq 700, adjoining premises of Mr R Frazer. -Thos Herty or Jas Vansandt, NJ Ave.

Wed Jun 23, 1802

Reward-$20 for negro, Bill, age abt 20 yrs. PG Co, nr Queen Ann, Md.
                                                    -Francis M Hall

First Chamber of the Wash City Cncl chose John T Frost, 2d Chmbr chose Thos Herty as their respective secrataries.

For sale: 2 large brick dwellings on the water side, presently occupied by Chas Beatty & his son C A Beatty, Gtwn.

Fri Jun 25, 1802

The Leg of Miss Terr apptd Thos M Green as Delegate to Congress to supply the vacancy occasioned by Mr Hunter's death.

Died: Mr Joshua Morsell, age 19 yrs, in Gtwn, Jun 22, student o/law, y/s/o Jas Morsell, o/Calvert Co, Md; buried in Presby Burying Ground in Gtwn on Jun 24.

Crct Crt of DC: sale of framed hse, lot 17 sq 377, prop of Thady Hogan, to satisfy debts due Robt Brown. -D C Brent, Marshal.

MON JUN 28, 1802
Reward-$15 for stolen bay horse.   -Jas Mathers, Jr, Wash City.

In 1796 a question of laying a duty on carriages was brght forward at Va; Aty o/U S-Va filed a bill in Crct Crt against Danl Lawrence Hylton for not paying same.

WED JUN 30, 1802
Tribute to Gilbert Wakefield, B A, who died age 46 yrs on Sep 9; born at Nottingham, Feb 22, 1756, son of a Parochial Clergy; mrd Miss Watson in 1779, she being the niece of the rector of Stockport. [English Publication] -J Aikin, Stoke Newington, Sep 18, 1801.

FRI JUL 2, 1802
Orphans Crt of Wash Co, DC. Jul 1802 Prsnl est of Collen Williamson, late of Wash Co, decd. -Mgt Williamson, excx.

WED JUL 7, 1802
Ladies with ltrs in the Post Ofc Jun 30, 1802:
Lucy Addison	Eliza Abraham	Rachel Morgan
Miss Jane Wilmore	Miss Nicholson c/o A Gatlatin	

FRI JUL 9, 1802
Genrl Commissioners of bankrupt-apptd by the President:
Conn: Hezekiah Huntington, Jonathan Bull, Jos Hart, John Dodd Henry W Edwards, Elihu Munson, Jehosaphat Starr, John Nichols, Elisha Hyde, Jonathan Frisbie, Nichol Fosdick, Jacob DeWitt.
Dela: French McMullen, Jas Brobson, John Warner, Isaac H Starr.
Va: Geo Tucker.
Dist of SC: Wm Moultrie, John Blake, Theodore Guillard, Dominic A Hall, Banjamin Cudworth.
Wm White of Va, Srvyr & Inspec of Rev for Port of East Rvr;
Griffin Greene, of NW Terr, Coll of Customs for Marietta Dist;
Jas Clarke, of NC, Srvry & Inspec of Rev, Tombstone Port, Edenton Dist;
Wm Lee, esq, of Gtwn, Maj of 1st Leg of Militia of DC;
John P Van Ness, esq, of Wash, Maj of same legion;
Francis Peyton, of Alex, Lt Col, Cmmdnt o/2d Leg of Militia of DC; Henry Rose & John McKinny, Majors.

Ltr from Ralph Spence Philips, Augusta, Jun 19. Rgrd: duel between Genrl Jas Jackson & Col Rob't Watkins at Louisville on Jun 16; Jackson was wounded & called for his bro, Abraham.

In Chancery: Baily E Clark, v Wm Johnston. Bill is to obtain a decree for money alledged due from dfndnt to cmplnt; dfndnt has interest in lot 6 & part of lot 23, in Bladensburg, PG Co & he resides out of state. -Saml H Howard, reg

Orations were delivered in Alexandria by Col C Simms & A W Grayson at celebration of Jul 4th.

Mon Jul 12, 1802

Died: Jas Rivington, in NY, known as printer to King of Gr Britain for Colony of NY previous to the Revolution; at advanced age.

Uriah Forrest, Wash Co, has been declared bankrupt. -John C Dent, sec. to the Commissioners.

I, Nicholas Whelan, of Wash City, have obtained a Power of Atty from my fr, Patrick Whelan, now in city of Galway, Ire, to pay all his debts. -Nicholas Whelan.

John Curan, living in Gtwn, had his mare stray or was stolen.

Wed Jul 14, 1802

Partnership of Ralph Charleton & Andrew Armstrong is dissolved; business will be carried on by Ralph Charleton.

For sale: farm in King Geo Co, Va, 535 acs, 2 story framed dwelling hse; for terms of sale apply to Wm P Flood, living on the premises or to Francis Whiting, who in a short time will be a resid of Berkley Co.

Died: Gen Daniel Morgan, Jul 6, age 66 yrs; after a long & severe illness. -Winchester, Va.

Ctzns celebrated the 4th of Jul in Boston; apptd J Bowdoin-Pres; Chas Jarvis, Nath'l Fellows & Saml Brown, esqs, VPs; Toasts volunteers: Benj Austin Jr, Jarvis, Fellows & Brown.

Fri Jul 16, 1802

Genrl Commissioners of bankruptcy, apptd by the President:
Norfolk, Va: Littleton W Tazewell, Richard E Lee, Moses Myers & Thos Blanchard.
NJ: Thos Ward, Phineas Manning, John Cobb, Isaiah Skinn, Abraham Brown, Anthony F Taylor.
Mass: Jonathan L Austin, Thos Dawes Jr, Saml Brown ,Jos Blake, Saml A Otis, Thos Edwards, Josiah Smith, Ralph Cress, Jos Markwan & Joshua Carter.

For sale: deed of trust from Anthony Addison to Wm Brent: 300 acs, *"Chichester,* with *Addition Re-Surveyed",* opposite Wash. Land has ferry landing, cld *"Dyer's Ferry,"* now in occupation of Capt Naylor. -Wm Brent.

Senate of the U S. Seats of the present mbrs of the Senate will be vacated Mar 4th of yr designated: 1803-Anderson, Chipman, Th Foster, Hillhouse, Howard, S T Mason, J Mason, G Morris, Ogden, Ross & White. 1804-Baldwin, Brown, Cocke, Dayton, Ellery, D Foster, Franklin, Nicholas, Olcott, Sumpter & Wells. 1805-Breckenridge, Bradley, Cothoun, Clinton, Jackson, Logan, Shease, Stone, Tracy & Wright.

MON JUL 19, 1802
Ofcrs of 1st Leg of Militia in DC; apptd by the Pres.
Cavalry: Wm Brent-Capt; Nich Voss-1st Lt; Wash Boyd- 2d Lt; Henry O'Reily-Cornet. Artl: John Davidson-Capt; Edgar Patterson-1st Lt; Benj Birch-2d Lt. Grenadiers: Thos Corcoran-Capt; John Jack-Lt; Otho Sprigg-Ensign. Light Infty: Wm O Sprigg-Capt; John Hewitt-Lt; Leonard Holliday Johns-Ensign. Capts of Infty: Benj More; Henry Whetcroft; Alex. Kerr; Thos G Addison; John Reintzell; Washington Bowie; Walter Smith; Jos S Belt. Lts of Infty: Joel Brown; Peter Lenox; Saml N Smallwood; John B Kerby; Robt Peter; Richard Johns; Thos Robertson; Abner Cloud. Ensigns of Infty: Patrick Simms; Baily Washington; Griffith Coombs; Henry Queen; Henry H Young; Nicholas Hedges; Daniel Renner; Anthony Holmead. Frederick May-Surg; John Ott-Surg's Mate.
Ofcrs of 2d Leg of Militia in DC; apptd by the Pres.
Cvlry: Walter Jones, Jr-Capt; Saml Croudson-1st Lt; Jacob Griger-2d Lt; Wm H Lyles-Cornet. Riflemen: Alex r Smith-Capt; John Johnston-Lt; Wm Harper Jr-Ensign. Artl: John Lougdon-Capt; Patrick Burns-1st Lt; Ferdinand Marsteller-2d Lt. Light Inf: Amos Alexander-Capt; Geo Wise-Lt; John Hoof-Ensign. Capts of Infty: Josiah Saxen; Adam Lynn; Lewis Summers; Geo N Lyles; Clement Sewell; Presly Gunnell; John Cohogen; Chas McKnight. Lts of Infty: Jos Ingle; Jas D Wescott; John A Stewart; Leonard Cook; Robt Stewart; Lawrence Hoof Jr; Thos Darne Jr; Benj Hersy. Ensigns of Infty: Jas S Scott; Thos Moore; Jas A Sutton; Jas McGuire; Wm Turner; John Darne; Henry Talbert; Daniel McDougall.
-Wm D Bealle-Adjut. Chas A Beatty-Qrtrmstr.

Died: Mrs Chapone, at Hadley, in Middlesex, Dec 25, 1801, age 75 yrs; writer; maiden name Mulso. -from an Eng Publication.

Marshal's sale of prop of Uriah Forrest: lots 11, 12, 13, 29, & 30 sq 105. Lots 8, 9, 10 sq 119 in Wash City; lot on Fayette St in Gtwn. Also a chariot, horses & sundry items. Sold to satisfy an execution in favour of Wm Thornton, Alexander White & Tristram Dalton. Sale at Mr McLaughlin's Tavern in Gtwn & dwelling hse of Uriah Forrest, nr Gtwn.   -D C Brent, marshal.

WED JUL 21, 1802
Phil, Pa, Health-Ofc, Jul 16. Died: *John Edwards, Jul 4, of malignant fever; John Crossley, biscuit baker, Jul 4, of same; Saml Thompson, Jul 14; Henry Miller, a boy, Jul 6; John Joint, a boy, Jul 14; Wm Brown Jr, Jul 14; John Whistler, a boy, Jul 13; Jas Essicks, mulatto boy, Jul 12. [*John Edwards was a ship carpenter].   -Cornelis Comegys, Pres.

Apptd by Pres: Joshua Wingate Jr-Brigade Maj & Inspec in Militia of DC.

Reward-$10 for runaway, John Hawkins, dk mulatto, age 25 yrs; belonging to est of Benjamin White, decd. -Mary White, lvng on Montg. Rd, PG Co, Md.

FRI JUL 23, 1802
In chancery: Jacob Meitard Sr, v., John Coppenheffer, Mary Whetmore, Eliz Whetmore, Mich'l Whetmore, Cath.Whetmore, Geo Whetmore, Nicholas Whetmore, Susan Whetmore, & Mgt Whetmore. Bill states that Mich'l Whetmore gave a bond of conveyance to Coppenheffer for 8 acs in Frederick Co, Md, #6, confiscated & sold by State of Md, & part of tract, *"Long Acre,"* being part of *"Tasker's Chance"*. Coppenheffer pd the purchase money assigned the said bond to the cmplnt & prays conveyance of aforesaid land to the cmplnt & his heirs. The cmplnt states that dfndnts, Mary, Eliz Michael, Cath, Geo, Nicholas, Susan & Mgt Whetmore, are heirs at law of aforesaid Mich'l Whetmore, decd; they are all minors residing out of Md. -Saml H Howard, R C C

MON JUL 26, 1802
Health Ofc-Balt-[Rgrd: Malignant fever]-Died: John Kelly, Jul 7,Thames St-Fell's Point; Jos Hopkins, Jul 7, Bowly's wharf; Joshua Cole, appr to Thos Jewitt, currier, Jul 12, Cumberland Row; John Wilson, Jul 19, at his bro's on East St, John lived at Fell's Point nr Wilson's wharf; Chas Frederick Lanberger, a baker in Light St, dangerously ill. Wife of Jas Smith is now ill. Nich's Willis, sickened, now well. We suggest vigilance, without alarm.
-Ashton Alexander, Pres.

WED JUL 28, 1802
Americ Philosophical Soc-Jan 15, 1802. elected mbrs: Thos Cooper of Northumberland, Pa., Jarvis Roebuck, M D, St Croix, Wm Barnwell, M D, of Phil, Pa., Wm Roxburgh, M D, of Clacutta, Don Carlos Martinez de Yrujo, Mnstr Pleni for his Catholic Mjsty. Those mbrs elected on Jul 16, 1802: Chevalier Don Valentine de Forronda, cns'l Genrl of his Cath Mjsty; Peter Blicher Olfen, Danish Ambass. to the U S; Ctzn Letomme, late cns'l Genrl of French Rpblc, nr the U S; Jas Mease, MD, Phil; Philip Gyng Physick, MD, Phil; Wm Stephen Jacobs, MD Phil; John Garnett, of Brunswick, NJ; Philip Ross Roume, mbr of the French Nat'l Institute; John Garuch, MD, Phil.
                                            -Adam Seybert & Jos Clay, secs.

Tristram Dalton, apptd postmaster at Gtwn, Potomak.

Timothy Upham, of this town, was inoculated in Jun 1801 by D Wraxall in the London Small Pox Hospital; Danl Walden, s/o J W Walden, of this town was inoculated in Aug last for the Kine Pox & again in NYC; [town is Portsmouth]. at Pepperelboro, Maine, 8 young gentlemen were inoculated, viz Alex'r Jenkins, Thos Shamson, R C Shannon, Wm Dennet, David Warren, Tristram Storer, Seth Storer & R H Green; they were tested in Dr R C Shannon's Hospital in May & Jun last, w/out being affected with small-pox.

Dr Thos Baldwin delivered a sermon at Boston on May 26, 1802.

Died: Genrl Lewis Littlepage, age 44 yrs, at Fredericksburgh, on Mon last; was apptd First Confid Sec in the Cncl of Stanislaus Augustus, late King of Poland in Mar 1785; remained in that ofc until the subversion of that unhappy empire.

Kine Pox-Jul 2d. I inoculated Chas & Robt Yeaton, Geo Manent, Peter M Loud & John Rinalde, all of Portsmouth, with fresh matter from Mr Jackson West; it is now 15 days & they are in perfect health. [Elisha Low & Benj Sherburne, Health Ofcrs, attest to the above.] -L Spalding, Portsmouth, Jul 16, 1802.

FRI JUL 30, 1802
Appointments by the Pres, Jul 30, 1802:
Henry Warren of Mass-Coll of Customs for Dist of Marblehead vice Saml R Gerry, also Inspec of Rev for same; Wm Lyman of Mass, Coll for Dist of Newburyport vice. Dudley A Tyng; Wm R Lee, Coll of Salem & Beverly vice Jos Hiller; Peter Muhlenberg of Pa, Coll of Pa; vice Geo Latimer; Tench Coxe, of Pa, supervisor of the Dist of Pa; John Page, of Va, Coll of Customs for dist of Petersburg; vice Wm Heath.

Brd of Health, Balt, Md. Ashton Alexander-Pres; Adam Fonerden-sec.

Reward-$100 for the villain, Notly, alias John Smith, age 35 yrs, mulatto, cld be heading for Phil where he has a wife & 3 chldrn. He hurt me in a most dreadful way, kicks & bites & said, "Now old fellow you die!" -Geo Beall of Patrick, living in PG Co, Md, 6 miles below the Federal City.

Boston, Jul 20. Ltr dated Buenos Arres, May 5, from Capt of an Americ Ship, [chartered in this country to take freight to Europe] to his owners in this town. The iron I bought for ballast was taken out of my ship, by an order from this Gov't...I have experienced unjust treatment... Ltr from ctzns of the U S to Chas Pinckney, Mnstr Pleni to Crt of Madrid. Buenos Ayres, Apr 22, 1802. The departure of Don Francisco Del Pino, s/o the vice King here, this month, goes charged with instructions that are unjust & hostile to us... Mr Titus Welles will deliver this ltr. Signed: Thos O'Reilly, Titus Welles, Jos Russell, Robt Gray, Wm Todd Jr, Silas Atkins, Job W Hall, Wm Allen, Titus Conklin, Danl McPherson, Jona. Williams, C Eloridg, Henry Davidson, Isaac Isaacs, Josiah Gould, Josiah Roberts, Leonard Jarvis 3d, Moses Griffin, Danl Olney, John Ansley, Jona. Russell & John Grant.

MON AUG 2, 1802
Partnerhsip bet Andrew Way Jr & Jos Gross [Groff], is mutually dissolved. Payments to Way Jr; printers & bkbinders, of Wash City.

WED AUG 4, 1802
Ofcrs of the 1st Legion of Militia of D C are to meet on Mon at Rhodes's Hotel.
-Wm D Beall, Adjt.

Rpblcn ctzns of Dela. will support Caesar A Rodney as Rep to Cong.

New York, Jul 27. Treaty with the Seneca Indians to give up their claim to a small tract of land at Black Rock, on Lake Erie, for a fort, has failed. Judge Taylor of Albany-Comr for U S. Hon Mr L'Hommdieu of Suffolk; Oliver Phelps of Ontario & Chas D Cooper of Albany-comrs on the part of this state.

FRI AUG 6, 1802
Duel bet Dewitt Clinton & John Swartwout ended after Mr S. was wounded twice in the left leg. -NY, Jul 31, 1802. Acc't signed by W S Smith.

Orphans Crt of Wash Co, DC. Deborah Stewart apptd excx of Walter Stewart, late of Phil, Pa, decd; but Blair McClenachan, Francis West & Wm Tilghman, are also named excs in said will & are summoned to appear. -John Hewitt, reg.

MON AUG 9, 1802
Rpblcn citizens of Phil will support Jos Clay, Rep in Cong.

WED AUG 11, 1802
Killed: French Genrl Destaing in a duel with Genrl Regnier.

Public sale: decree of Chancellor of Md, at Rhodes's Tavern in Wash. lots 23 thru 27 sq 105; when purchased, trustee will convey all the right & est of Jas M Lingan, Ann Casenave, Nicholas Young, Johanna & Peter Casenave, parties to the said decree, to the purchasers. -John Hewitt, trustee.

Died: Mr Dandridge, American Consul, Jul 17.

MON AUG 16, 1802
Potomack Company declared a dividend on the capital stock, 3%; by order of the board, Jos Carleton, Treas.

WED AUG 18, 1802
Wm Widgery, esq, comr of bankruptcy; apposed the adoption of the Constitution; he is a director in a Maine Bank.

Damages sustained by Caleb S Riggs, from a libel published against him sometime ago by Mr David Denniston, Ed. of the Americ Ctzn, brought in a verdict of $500.

In chancery, State of Md: Chas Carroll of Carrollton, Nicholas Carroll, Daniel Carroll of Duddington, Wm Smith, Abraham Vanbibber & Isaac Vanbibber. v Anne Ogle, Rebecca Dulany, *John Tasker Carter, *Robt Mitchell, *Priscilla Mitchell, *Spencer Ball, *Betsey Landon Ball, *John Jas Maund, *Harriot Lucy Maund, *John Chenn, *Sarah Fairfax Chenn, *Harriot Peck, *John Carter Peck, *Emanuel Peck, *Hugh Quinlan, *Tasker Carter Quinlan, *Thos Jones, *Frances Tasker Jones, *Thos Jones the Younger, *Sarah Jackall Jones, *Eliz Jones, Jane Jones, Sophia Carter, Julia Carter, Ann Lowndes, Francis Lowndes, Benj

Stoddert, Benj Stoddert the Younger, Eliz, Ann, Harriot, Richard, Wm, Rebecca & Christopher Stoddert, Chas Lowndes, Levi Gantt, Harriot Gantt, & Benj Lowndes. Bill is to obtain an indenture of bargain & sale from Benj Tasker, decd, the ancestor of dfndnt, whose heirs at law they are stated to be, to Daniel Dulany & Co, for land cld *"Piney Groves;"* indenture dated Jul 2, 1751-not recorded. The said conveyance was for the use of Daniel Dulany, Chas Carroll s/o Daniel, Dr Chas Carroll of Annap, Chas Carroll of Annap, & Benj Tasker Jr & their heirs, in equal fifth parts, tennants in common, not as joint tenants; Benj Tasker the bargainer died intestate, leaving 4 dghts his only chldrn, of whom Anne Ogle & Rebecca Dulany are two; Frances Carter & Eliz Lowndes, the other 2 dghts are dead, other dfndnts are by marriage or descent, their reps & heirs at law. Rebecca Dulany resides in R I; [* reside in Va, also Geo Carter lives in Va] dfndnts: Chas Lowndes, Francis Lowndes, Benj Stoddert, Benj Stoddert the Younger, Eliz, Ann, Harriot, Richard, Wm, Rebecca & Chris. Stoddert, reside in Gtwn, DC. -Saml H Howard, Reg CC

Agriculture-vineyards in Pa & Ky: at Pottsgrove, Montgomery Co- Dr Seraphin; at Norristown-Mr Swaine; at Spring Mill-Mr Legaux; nr Phil on Ridge Rd-Mr Montmollin; Mr Peter Kuhn of Phil-a proprietor; Dr Jas Mease is 1st Americ to establish a vineyd in Pa-Cherry Alley, Phil.

Frankfort Genealogical Manuel: Napoleon Bonaparte, b Aug 16, 1767; wife Jesephe, wid of Gen Beauharnois; her first name Lapagerie; b in Marinique, 1762; mrd Dec 1796. Step chldrn: Eugene Beauharnois, Cecile Beauharnois, mrd Jan 4, 1802 to Louis Bonaparte, bro of her step fr. Bros & sisters: Jos; Lucien, a widower with out chldrn; Louis mrd to Cecile Beauharnois; Maria mrd in 1797, in Italy, to Genrl Leclerc; Caroline, mrd in 1800 to Genrl Murat; Jerome, Guide Marin; Adela, mrd in 1800 to Genrl Ciaccioche. Parents: Chas Bonaparte, b at Ajaccio, in 1739, first a lwyr, then in the Army; his widow, Letitia Raniolini, celebrated for her beauty. Uncle by the fr's side-Napoleon, late Canon at Miniato at Tedescho, in Tuscany. -Alley, Phil.

Proposals by A Davis & J Dixon, for reprinting by subscription, scarce & valuable work, the "Debates" & preceedings of the convention of Va-a copious index. -John Dixon.

FRI AUG 20, 1802
Stop the thief-black man, Wm Jackson, stole $50 belonging to Jas Maitland; I hired him from Maj McCow in Va. -John Harrison, Pa Av, Wash.

Reward-$20 for runaway, John Corran, indented appr to the book printing bus.; age 18 yrs; he was 2 yrs in the bus., as compositor he was slow, as pressman, he displayed much improvement. -Warner & Hanna, Balt, Md.

Parents & guardians of Mr Patrick Edwards's pupils consider it their duty to declare their perfect approbation of the progress made by his pupils. Signers of ltr to Nat'l Intell, Aug 13, 1802: -C Harrison, Thos H Gillis, David Shoemaker, Jas Davidson Jr, Jos Saul, Andrew Way Jr.

Notice-Committed to jail: negro, Jas, age abt 50 yrs, says he was set free by John Wilson, St Mary's Co. Rebecca, says she was sold by Joshua Poor, who lives nr Port Tobacco, to a person in Ga. -Robt McClan, jailer, Washington.

Post Masters who have been dismissed: Wm Hobby of Augusta, Ga-because he was the editor of a newspaper; Mr John Tryon, of Lebanon, NY-his situation was inconvenient-he lived on the Post Rd from Berkshire to Albany nr the Mass. Line; Augustus Davis, printer of a newspaper who divided the business bet himself & his son; Benj Lowndes of Bladensburg-his hse was some distance from the Post Rd & quite remote; Col Ezra Taylor of Desden-on petition of the inhabitants of New Milford, a neighboring town-bec he lived at one crnr of Dresden; Mr Frederic Wolcott of Litchfield, Conn-Col Tallmage was in ofc when his appointment was forwarded & did not resign in time. Note-Thos Perrin Smith of Md was apptd by the late Post-Mstr Genrl.

"*The History of Helvetia,*" written by Francis Hare Naylor; issued from the London Press; progress of the Federative Rpblcs from the middle of the 15th century. [Short extraction in the paper]

In chancery, State of Md: Alexander Clagett & Richd Henderson, v Chas Vance & Mazy his wife, & Mangery Beall. Bill to obtain sale of 2 tracts of land cld: "*Azadia*" & "*Gleaning*" for payment of a debt due from Isaac Beal decd to Saml Beall decd. Isaac Beall was indebted to David Ross, Richd Henderson & said Saml Beall, to secure payment whereof, he on Jan 9, 1775 executed a bond to them for conveyance of aforesaid land, intended merely to secure the debt. Isaac Beall, died with out paying debt, & his will devised the land to his chldrn, Ann, Alex. & Mazy Beall, tenants in common after the death of Margery his wife; Ann & Alex'r have since died intestate, under age, no issue, Mazy mrd Chas Vance & resides in Va. Saml Beall also died intestate & Alex'r Clagett adm'd his est, debt due was from instance of Isaac Beall & his heirs pd by your cmplnt, Clagett, out of est of said Saml Beall. -S H Howard, Reg CC.

Mon Aug 23, 1802

Bio. anecdotes of Mr Robt Bloomfield, author of the Farmer's Boy, Rural Tales, etc; abridged from a ltr from his bro, Geo. Robt, younger child of Geo Bloomfield, tailor from Honington; his fr died when he was under a yr old; his mthr was a schl mistress & was widowed w. 6 small chldrn. Robt was sent to Mr Rodwell of Ixworth to improve his writing; his mthr mrd again when he was 7 yrs old to John Glover & they had another fmly; Robt was 11 when the late Mr Austin, of Sappiston took him; Robt mrd Mary Anne Church of Woolwich on Dec 13, 1799; he is a lady's shoemkr & works for Davies, Lombard St; is bet 33 & 34 yrs of age; has 2 dghts & a son.

Wash Troop of Cavalry, to meet at Mr Rhodes's Hotel. -N Lufborough, Adjut.

For sale: 406 acs in Frederick Co, Va; dwlg hse, adj tract of 77 2/3 acs; tract nrby same acs; tract where I live-512 acs & dwelling hse. -Wm a Booth, Shanandoah Co, Va. [Intending to move to the State of Ky].

WED AUG 25, 1802
Duel-Augusta, Ga, Aug 11-bet L Van Allen, esq, Solicitor Genrl & W H Crawford, esq, Atty, on Jul 31 on bank of Savannah River; Van Allen died the next day.

Died: Dr Allison,-Sr Pstr of Presby Chr in Balt, Aug 21, Balt; after a long & severe illness.

Meeting of Little River Road Co, called at hse of Mrs McCable in Leesburg, Va. -Wm Hartshorne, John T Ricketts, Israel Lacey, Burr Power.

FRI AUG 27, 1802
Orphans Crt of PG Co, Md. Aug 10, 1802. Prsnl est of John Stamp, late of PG Co, decd.   -F W Wood.

To be sold: 500 acs in PG Co, Md; small tenement thereon. -Hedwich Hollyday.

MON AUG 30, 1802
Jas McGuirk, sentenced to be executed on Aug 28, for murder of his wife, has been respited by Pres of U S until Oct 23 next.

WED SEP 1, 1802
Wash City-ordered to repair to Wash without delay. *Lts:*

Isaac Chauncey	Stephen Decatur	John H Dent
Thos Robinson Jr	Saml Evans	Geo G Lee
P C Wederstrandt	Chas Gordon	Henry Van Dyke

Midshipmen:

Jas T Leonard	Richd Thomas	Abner Woodruff
Robt L Tilghman	John Trippe	Jos Bainbridge
Alex'r O Harrison	John M P Gardner	Geo H Geddes
Jas Higinbotham	Geo W Spotswood	Chas L Ridgely
Wm P Smith	Saml Angue	John Shattuck
O A Page	Edw Bennett	Chas Moore
Sloss H Grenell	Lewis Warrington	Allen J Green
John B Nicholson	Daniel S Dexter	P C Blake
Francis Wise	John O Creighton	Jas Renshaw
Johnston Blakely	Alexander Laws	Alfred Hazard
Archibald K Kearny	Wm F Nicholls	Wm Lewis
Henry P Casey	Wm H Allen	Edw Giles
Sewel Handy	Sidney Smith	Jos Nicholson
Drury M Allen	John Davis	Wm S Butler
Louis Alexis	J R Leaycraft	Wm Sim
	John Downes	

FRI SEP 3, 1802
Saml Thacher chosen Rep to Cong for Eastern Dist of Mass.

MON SEP 6, 1802
Marietta, Aug 10. Meeting of a County Convention of Wash Co on Aug 4, 1802. Present-Paul Fearing & R J Meigs for town of Marietta; Col Nath'l Cushing for Bellprie; Simeon Deming for Waterford; John Roberson & Mr Bureau for Gallipolis; Col Alex'r Oliver & Capt Abel Mathews for Adams; Ephram True & Allen Putman for Salem; Maj Jona. Cass & John McEntire for Newton; Philip Whitten & Luther Dana for Newport; Geo Ewing & Jesiah True for Ames. Subj-Admission of the ctzns of the NW Terr into a State Government.
-J Pierce, chrmn.

London Gaz, Whitehall, Jul 6, 1802. The King has apptd: Rt Hon Robt Stewart [Viscount Castlereagh]; his Grace Wm Henry Cavendish, Duke of Portland, Knight of the Most Noble order of the Garter. Rt Hon Robt Banks Jenkinson [cld Lord Hawkesbury,] Rt Hon Robt Thos Baron Hobart & Rt Hon Baron Pelham, Principal secs of State. Rt Hon Henry Addington, Chancelor of his Maj's Exhequer. His Grace Jas Duke of Montrose, Knight of the Most Ancient order of the Thistle. Rt Hon Sylvester Baron Glenbervie [that part cld Ireland,] Rt Hon Wm Dundas, Rt Hon Thos Wallace, Rt Hon Chas John Baron Arden [that part cld Ireland,] & Edw Golding to be comrs for Affairs of India.

Committed to jail of Wash Co, DC: negro, Cate, says she belongs to Jas Koath, esq, of Alexandria; Davy, age 35 yrs, negro, ship carpenter, formerly the prop of Jas Clagett of Gtwn.   -Robt McClan, jailor.

WED SEP 8, 1802
Mbrs of Co of Artl of 1st Legion of Militia of DC to meet at hse of Mr Lewis Morin, innkpr, Wash.   -Edgar Patterson, Capt.

Americ Review. Collection has been made from political writings of John Dickinson, esq, late Pres of the State of Dela & of Pa.

Visit to the vineyards: to Mr Croussillat of Phil; to Mr Dance, north of this place; nrby that of Mr Thunn; nr Phil City -Stephen Gerard, Frenchman. -Nigneron

For sale: At Mr Dougherty's Tavern, Bladensburg, lot of ground lately occupied by Mr Horatio Ross-abt 3 acs with brick hse; also the late prop of Maj David Ross, stone hse, 3 acs.   -Wm Steuart.

Duel bet Mr Richard Thweatt & Mr Edwin Fort, Sep 2, ended in the death of Mr Fort. -Petersburg

We are informed that Mr C P Wayne, late prop of this Gaz, has purchased of the Hon Bushrod Washington, the copy right of the history of the late Genrl Washington. -Gaz U States.

Portsmouth, Aug 30, 1802-Rockingham. Meeting for 5 mbrs to rep this state in Cong of the U S; Jos Pierce has rsgnd; John Langdon, moderator. Nahum Parker-316 votes; Saml Hunt-121 votes; Parker to fill vacancy of Mr Pierce. Take their seats in Mar next: Saml Hunt, Col Clement Storer, Thos Cogswell, Jona. Smith, Nahum Parker, Moody Bedel, Nichs Gilman, Saml Tenney, Silas Betton, Clifton Clagett, David Hough. -[Geo Wentworth, Twn clk.]

Ebenezer Matton declines being a candidate at the next election for mbrs of Cong.

FRI SEP 10, 1802
Duel in Savannah bet Wm Hunter & David B Mitchell; Mr Hunter died.

Strayed or stolen, 2 horses, from the Commons of Wash City. Mr Wm Holmes, Wash. -Lawrence Posey, Allens Fresh, Chas Co, Md.

Merchants of Phil write to Geo Latimer, late Coll of that Port; Subj-his zeal for unremitted svc. -John Clement Stocker, Abijah Dawes & Danl Smith, Aug 10.

MON SEP 13, 1802
Providence, R I-Sep 4. Town Meeting Tue last; following Fedr'l men were chosen to rep this town in the Gen'rl Assembly: John Dorrance, Ephraim Bowen Jr, John Carlile & Geo R Burrill. Chas Lippitt having declined re-elec. Reps to Cong-Thos Tillinghast & Elisha R Potter had 282 votes; Jos Stanton Jr & Nehemiah Knight, Democs, 78 votes.

Jas Wilson, esq, apptd postmaster in Worcestor, Mass, in rm of Isaac Thomas, esq, removed.

Stolen or strayed, gelding. -Patrick Donoughue, NJ Av, Wash.

WED SEP 15, 1802
Died: Rev Dr John Ewing, at Norristown, Pa, late Provost of Pa Un.

Newport-Sep 4. Rpblcns re-elected deputies to the Gen Assembly: Constant Taber, John Gardiner, Nath'l Hazard, Thos G Pitman, Jos Boss Jr & Paul M Mumford.

Phil Co, Sep 8, 1802. Eulogy on Maj Genrl Hand; a firm prop during the Rev War... loving & beloved...paternal attentions & filial affection.

Orphans Crt of Calvert Co, Md. Sep 10, 1802. Prsnl est of John W Simmons, late of Calvert Co, decd. -Ben Williams, adm. Sarah Simmons, admx.

FRI SEP 17, 1802
Marshal's sale: at McLaughlin's Tavern, Gtwn, lot 50, at present occupied by Jeremiah Conner, esq. Also 2 tracts adj each other-lying & being in Wash Co, cld *Scotland & Barbadoes,* 206 acs, presently occupied by Mr Henry Smith.
-Daniel C Brent, Marshal of DC.

Dover, Dela, Sep 4, 1802. Address of the Committee of Correspondence of Kent Co, to free electors of Kent Co. Signed: Wm McKee, John Fisher, John Torbert, Abraham Pierce, Andrew Gray & John Hamm.

MON SEP 20, 1802
Just published & for sale by publisher, at his conveyancing ofc Pres' sq, Wash. Vol 2 of his Digest of the Laws of the U S.
-Uriah Forrest, clk of Crct Crt of DC

WED SEP 22, 1802
Meeting of Militia of the 1st City Dist at Tunicliff's Tavern. -Saml. N Smallwood, Capt in 1st Legion.

Orphans Crt of PG Co, Md. Sep 10, 1802. Prsnl est of Jas Bonifant, late o/PG Co, decd. -Wm Townshend, adm. Joanna Bonifant, admx.

Thos Moore, Montg Co, Md, intends to publish a pamphlet for the constuction of refrigerators. We have seen this machine alluded to at the mkt: Wm Rhodes, John H Barney, David English, Chas McLaughlin.

Reward-$50 for 2 negro men: Sam, [age 21 yrs] & Luke; ran away from Caleb Weeks. Reward from Elijah Bell, King St, Alex.

City Gaz. Messrs Freneau & Williams. Ltr from Arthur Simkins, Chas Goodwin, Richd Johnson & Leroy Hammond, dated Aug 16, 1802. Subj-The election of 1800; refers to a ltr of Mr John Bee Holmes.

Halifax, Sep 6. Ltr from Brig Genrl Jos Riddick to his Excellency Gov Benj Williams, dated Gates Co, Jun 31, 1802. Rgrd: Intended insurrection by negroes at Currituck, Camden, Pasquotank & Perquimans Counties.

Phil Gaz Ofc, Sep 16, 1802. Ltr from Saml Relf to John Clement Stocker, Abijah Dawes & Danl Smith; a reply to their ltr dated same. Rgrd: documents recd from the Phil Gaz from the above 3 men.

FRI SEP 24, 1802
Gov't of the U S. Supreme Executive
Thos Jefferson, Pres.   Aaron Burr, V P
Dept of State: Jas Madison-sec;   Jacob Wagner, Chief clk;
Dept of Treas:
    Albert Gallatin-sec   Thos T Tucker-Treas
    Jos Nourse- Register   Wm Miller-Comr of the Rev
    Richd Harrison-Auditor   John Steele- Compt
War Dept: Henry Dearborn- sec;
    Wm Simmons-Acc't of Military Stores.
Navy Dept: Robt Smith- sec;   Thos Turner-Acc't.
Post Ofc: G Granger-P M;   Genrl Abraham Bradley-Assist.

Judiciary.

Supreme Crt.
Wm Cushing of Mass;
Saml Chase of Md;
Alfred Moore of NC;
Elias B Caldwell of Wash City-clk.

John Marshal-Chief Justice;
Wm Paterson of NJ;
Bushrod Washington of Va;
Levi Lincoln of Mass-Atty Genrl

District	Judge	Atty	Marshal
Maine	David Sewall	Silas Lee	Isaac Parker
NH	John Pickering	John S Sherbourne	Mich'l McClary
Mass	John Davis	Geo Blake	Saml Bradford
R I	David L Barnes	David Howell	Wm Peck
Conn	Richd Law	Pierpont Edwards	Jos Wilcox
Vt	Elijah Paine	David Fay	John Willard
NY	John Sloss	Hobart E Livingston	John Swartwout
NJ	Robt Morris	Geo Maxwell	Oliver Barnett
Pa	Richd Peters	Alex'r J Dallas	John Smith
Dela	Gunning Bedford	Geo Read Jr	Joel Lewis
Md	Jas Winchester	Zebalon Hollingsworth	Reuben Etting
Va	Cyrus Griffin	John Monroe	Andrew Moore
	Thos Nelson	Jos Scott.	
Potomac dist	Walter Jones	Wm Baker	
Ky	Harry Innes	Jos H Daviess	Jos Crockett
NC	Henry Potter	Benj Woods	John S West
SC	Thos Bee	Thos Parker	Chas B Cochran
Ga	Wm Stephens	David B Mitchell	Benj Wall
Tenn	John McNai_y	Wm P Anderson	Robt Hays

Com'rs of Loans:
Wm Gardner-NH;   Thos Perkins-Mass;   Jabez Bowen-R I;
Wm Imlay-Conn;   Jas Nicholson-NY;   Jas Ewing- NJ;
Stephen Mcylan-Pa;   John Stockton- Dela;
Benj Howard-Md;   John Hopkins-Va;
Sher. Haywood-NC;   John Neusville- SC;   Jas Alger-Ga;
Dist of Columbia: Wm Kilty-Chief Judge;
Judges. Wm Cranch & Jas Alger
John Thomson Mason, Atty.
Danl Carroll Brent, Mrshl   John Hewett, Reg of wills
Cleon Moore, Reg of wills-Alexandria
Wm H Dorsey, Judge of the Orphans Crt for Washington
Geo Gilpin, Judge of the Orphans Crt for Alexandria.

Ministers in Foreign Countries:
Rufus King-London;   Robt R Livingston-Paris;
Thos Sumter Jr-sec of Legation   Chas Pinckney-Madrid;
John Graham-sec of Legation.
Consuls & Commercial age nts:
Gr Britain: Geo W Erving-London;   Elias Vanderhorst-Bristol;
Robt W Fox-Falmouth;   Jas Maury-Liverpool;
Jos Wilson-Dublin;   Thos Auldji-vice cns'l at Poole;

Geo Knox cns'l at Kingston upon Hull:
John C Murray-Glasgow; Jas Holmes-Belfast;
John Church-Cork; Harry Grant-Leith
Jacob Lewis-Calcutta, India; Benj H Philips-Curracoa;
John Gavino-Gibraltar;
W P Gardner-Demarara, Effequibo;
John Elmslie Jr-Capt of Good Hope; Jos Pulis-Malta;
David Easton-Martinico.

Commercial agents to French Rpblc & her Dominions:
Fulwar Skipwith, Paris   Isaac Cox Barnett, Antwerp
Peter Dobell, Havre De Grace   Wm Lee, Bordeaux
Edw Jones, Guadaloupe Island   John Appleton, Calais
Thos Aborn, Cayenne   Jas Anderson, Cette
Mr De La Motte, V C, Havre De Grace   Etienne Cathalan, Marseilles
Thos T Gantt, Nantz   Francis L Taney, Ostend
Wm Buchanan, Isles of France & Bourbon

Consuls to Kingdom of Spain & Its Dominions:
Moses Young, Madrid   Jos Yznardi Jr, Cadiz
Robt Montgomery, Alicant   Wm Kirkpatrick, Malaga
Lewis Mengher O'Brien, St Andero   Wm Willis, Barcelona
Henry Molier, Coruuna   Geo Wash. McElroy, Tenerisse
Augustin Madan, La Guira   Danl Clark, New Orleans
Josiah Blakely, St Jago, Cuba   Wm E Huling, V C at N. Orleans
vacant, cns'l at Havana

To Kingdom of Portugal & Its Dominions:
Wm Jarvis, Lisbon   John Street, Fayal

Batavian Rpblc:
Sylvanus Bourne, cns'l Genrl Amsterdam
Thos Hewes, Batavia   Jos Forman, Rotterdam

Denmark & Its Dominions:
Hans Rodolph Saabye, Copenhagen   Henry Cooper, Santa Cruz
Prussia: Frederick W Lutze, Stettin
Germany: John M Forbes, Hamburg   Fredr'k J Wichelhausen, Bremen
Philip Marck, Franconia   Wm Riggin, Trieste
Sweden: Robt C Gardner, Gottenberg
Italian States: John Matthiew, Naples   John Baptiste Sartori, Rome
Frederick H Walloston, Genoa   Jos Barnes, Island of Sicily
Barbary Powers: Jas Cathcart, Algiers   Wm Eaton, Tunis
Jas Simpson, Morocco

Ministers-cns'ls & Commissaries o/Foreign Powers Reside in the U S:
Edw Thornton, Chg Des Affaires
Thos Barcley, cns'l Gen-Eastern States
Phineas Bond, C G for middle & Southern States
Thos McDonough, cns'l for NH, Mass, R I & Conn.
John Breese, VC, for R I.   Gabriel Wood, Balt.
Benj Moodie, cns'l for North & So Carolina
John Wallace, VC, Ga.

From the French Rpblc:
Louis Andre Pichon, Chg De Affaires & Commissary Genrl of Commercial Relations.
Ctzn Oster, VC of Commerc Rel for Va.
Chas Francois Liot, for Pa & Dela.
Louis Arcambal, Temporary, V C for Md.
Marc Antoine Alexis Giraud, for NH, Mass, R I & Conn.
Chevalier De Yrujo, Minister Pleni.
Thos Stoughton, Temporary, cns'l Genrl.
Antonio Argote Villalobus, cns'l for Va & Ky.
Diego Morphy, cns'l for North & So Carolina.
Felipi Fatio, cns'l for Pa.
Jean Baptiste Barnabeu, cns'l for Md.
Don Manuel Rengel, for Ga.
Ivan Stoughton, NH, Mass, Conn, R I & Vt
Joses Wiseman, VC at Newport.
Kingdom of Portugal:
John Abram, V C at NY
Jas F Vercnock, VC for So C.
Richd Codman, VC for Mass.
From Batavian Rpblc:
Andrian Valch, cns'l for Md & Va.
Jan Rosinen Graves, cns'l for So C & Ga.
J H C Heineken, Commerc agent, Pa.
Prussia: Johann Ernst Christian Schultz, cns'l, Balt.
Denmark:
Peter Blecker Olsen, Mnstr Resident & cns'l Genrl.
Jacob Eberhard August Steinmeitz, VC for So C.
Wm Scarbrough, do, for Ga.
Erich Bollman, do for Pa.   John Boutz, do, for No C.
Peter Collin, do for Md.   Jona. Swift, do for Dist of Col.
John Spendler, do for NY & Conn. Jos Winthrop, do for So C.
Sweden: Richd Soderstrom, cns'l Genrl.
Jos Winthrop, VC, Charleston, So C.
Jona Swift, Columbia & Ports on the Potomac.
Chas E Deyen, VC for NH, Mass & R I.
Henry Gahn, VC for NY & Conn.
John Cowper, VC, Norfolk & all Ports in Va, except those on Potomac.
John Baritz, VC for No C.   Peter Collin, VC for Md.

North Western Terr:
    Arthur St Clair, Gov   Chas Willing Byrd, sec
Dist of Ohio:
    Jas Findlaye, Mrshl   Wm McMillan, Atty
    John Cleves Symmes, Chf Justice   Jos Gilman, Judge
    Return Jonathan Meigs Jr, Judge

Miss Terr:
    Wm C C Claiborne, Gov
    Seth Lewis, Chief Justice
    Danl Tilton, 3d Judge
    John Steele, sec
    Peter Bryan Bruin, 2d Judge

Indiana Terr:
    Wm H Harrison, Gov
    Wm Clark, Chief Justice
    Henry Vanderburgh, 2d Judge
    John Gibson, sec.
    John Griffin, 3d Judge

Receiver of Public Money for lands:
    Jas Findley, Cincinnati
    Zaccheus Biggs, Steubenville
    Elijah Backus, Marietta
    Saml Findley, Chilicothe

Registers of the land Ofc of the U S:
    Thos Worthington, Chilicothe
    Israel Ludlow, Cincinnati
    Jos Wood, Marietta
    David Hoge, Steubenville

1-Mathew Lyon, a mbr of Congress, was fined & imprisoned, for a publication under the Sedition Law before the law had existence. 2-Adams, a Boston printer of the Chronicle, was imprisoned. 3-Frothingham, printer at NY, also imprisoned. 4-Luther Baldwin was fined & imprisoned by a sentence of Judge Washington, in Jersey. [Past cases from the Aurora]

Litchfield, Sept 8. at the Supreme Crt last wk: Maj S Wetmore of Winchester, was found guilty of wickedly & maliciously intending & contriving to defame & bring into contemp the laws & gov't of this state; fine was $100 & costs of prosecution. [Connecticut]

Duel bet Genrl Richd Dobbs Spaight & John Stanly, of Newbern, Sep 5; resulted in the death of Mr Spaight on Sep 6; Dr Edw Pasteur made the arrangements for the time & place of said duel.

MON SEP 27, 1802

Died: Mr John Fownes, merchant, Sep 24, at his dwelling in NJ Av, Wash

Died: Genrl Jacob Morgan, Sep 17, age 61 yrs, at his place at Point No Point, Phil. At age 15 he was an ensign in the Army in western parts of Pa, srvd as adjut of the regt until the peace of 1763. Rose to be 1st Maj of Regt of Militia, commanded by Col Dickinson. He was in arms until the Americ Indep; he retired a 2d time. He has long been Brig Genrl of Phil.

Lewis Deblois, Gtwn, offers for sale: Russia sheetings, India Cottons, etc at his store on Stewart or Lownde's wharf, Gtwn.

Order of Montg Co Crt. [Md] For sale, all the right, title & est of Jos Simmes, decd, land cld the *"Second Addition to Culvers Chance"*, 300 acs, lying on North West Stream, Montg Co, Md, now in possession of his widow, Cath. Simmes. -Daniel Rentzel, Adam King, John Threlkeld, comrs.

WED SEP 29, 1802
For sale: my residence on Capitol Hill, furniture, etc -Wm King; intending to remove from Wash City.

Orphans Crt of Wash Co, DC-sale of prsnl est of late Notley Young, esq, at his farms in Wash Co-stock, farming utensils, etc; at his plantation in the *Forrest of Queen Ann,* except his slaves, prsnl prop. -Benj Young, Nich Young, Robt Brent-excs.

Ltrs from Genrl Washington to Arthur Young, esq, F R S; printed lately in London. Copies of these ltrs are in the Nat'l Intell of Sep 27th thru Oct 4th, 1802.

FRI OCT 1, 1802
Stolen: a small trunk containing $100. -Wm Herron, living at Mr Reinhart's, nr the War Ofc.

MON OCT 4, 1802
Died: Mr Daniel Clarke, Sr, age 69 yrs, Sep 30, of PG Co, Md; husband & parent; left but one child to mourn his death.

Died: Mr Wm Johnson, age 21 yrs, Oct 1, in Wash; remains were interred at Rock Creek Chr.

WED OCT 6, 1802
NH Reps in Cong: Federal-Tenny, Hunt, Hough, Bettan, Clagget; Rpblcn-Parker, Storer, Smith, Bedel, Cogswell.

FRI OCT 8, 1802
For rent: 2 brick hses in Wash, Pa Av, now occupied by Sharpless & Smith as a Dry Good Store. Apply to Renner & Bussard, High St. -John R Bussard, Gtwn.

Md Election-Balt: Jas Purviance & Thos Dixon, Rpblcns, elected by a majority.

Night school opening at present schl rm on G St, Wash city.
-Patrick Edwards.

MON OCT 11, 1802
For sale: land where I now live, King Geo Co, Va, 1110 acs; store, dwelling hse, kitchen, etc. Terms apply to Daniel C Brent & Mr Jeremiah Booth, Wash City, or to John Murphy, on the premises. -Lewis Waugh.

Return of the polls in Balt Co, Md: elected-N R Moore, Tobias E Stansbury, Thos Love & Alex'r Lemmon as Reps in the Genrl Assembly of Md. Also on tkt: Chas Ridgley of Wm, Edw D Bussay, Abraham Van Bibber, Francis Snowden & Saml Peters.

Wed Oct 13, 1802

Crct Crt of DC-In chancery. Valentine Peyton, against Mary Cook, widow & relict of Jos Cook, decd, Alexander Stedman & Julia Cook, Jos Wilson & Robt Brown, adms of Jos Cooke, decd. Bill is to foreclose a mortgage of 2 lots in Wash, given by Jos Cook, decd, to Jas R Dermott; Dermott assigned to Francis Deakins, decd, Deakins assigned to the cmplnt, Valentine Peyton. Dfndnts reside in Pa. -Uriah Forrest-clk.

Intending to decline his business, sale at lower prices on crockery ware, wines, brandies, etc   -Carre De St Gemme.

Frederick Co, Md-Rpblcns elected: D Shriver, R Nelson, T Hawkins & H Kemp. Federal tkt-not elected: John Ritchie, John Fisher, John Mesler & H Spalding.

Fri Oct 15, 1802

Mrd: Thos Fenwick, esq, of St Mary's Co, Md, to Miss Nelly Young, y/d/o late Notley Young, esq, decd, Oct 12, in Wash, by Rev Mr Plunket.

For sale: lot 10 sq 256 in Wash, Pa Av, dwelling hse; deed of trust from Owen Roberts to Jas Keith, trustee.

College of NJ commencement was held at Princeton, Sep 29. Bach of Arts Degree was conferred on: David Allen, Thos H Ellis, Richard H Henderson, Jacob Parker, Caleb B Upshire-all of Va;
Robt L Armstrong, Isaac Browne, Enoch A Green, Robt Manning, Wm Mc Illvain, Wm Mc Kissock, Henry Mills-all of NJ;
Jas Dill, Chas Lindsey, Vanbrunt Magaw-all of NY;
Geo Emlin, Alexander Johnston, John Purdon-all of Pa;
Robt Habersham-of Ga;   Micajah G Lewis-of Tenn;
Hext. Mc Call, John Middleton, Wm Washington-all of SC;
Geo Strawbridge-of Dela.
Dr of Divinity: Rev Hezekiah Ripley-of Conn; Rev Robt Belfour-of Glasgow, Scot; Rev Matthias Burnet-of Norfolk, Conn; Rev John Kirkland-of Boston.
Alumni were admitted to a 2d Degree in the Arts: Lewis Morris, Frederick Nash, Wm Alston, John Alston-all of SC;
Eliezer Burnet, Elias Riggs -of NJ;
Clement Early, John Y Forsyth-of Ga;
Thos Miller-of Va;   Isaac Meason-of Pa.

Mon Oct 18, 1802

Pa election-select council. Rpblcns:-Sl. Wetherill Sr-1903 votes, Stephen Girard-1902, Mathew Carey-1893, Geo Bartram-1891, Leonard Keehmle-1887. Fed Tkt:-Saml M Fox-1603 votes, Saml Coates-1593, John Miller Jr-1584, John Connelly-1507, Edw Pennington-1598 votes.

Wed Oct 20, 1802

In jail at Wash Co-runaways: Geo alias Moses, says he belongs to Mrs Julian of Fredericksburg, Va; & Will, who says he belongs to Mrs Mary Southen of St

Mary's Co, nr Benedick, says he's been a runaway upwards 2 yrs.
-Robt Mc Clan, jailor

Ladies with ltrs in Wash Post Ofc, Oct 1, 1802:
Eliza Abraham	Maria Bailey	Cath Belt
Miss Anne Ballard	Mrs Anne Carr	Mrs Sarah Cox
Mrs Priscilla Donaldson	Martha Gordon	Rebecca Hopkins
Hannah Hoggins	Flora Johnson	Mrs Eliza Moore
Penelope Pallatson	Miss Nancy Smith	Mrs Jane Smith
Mrs Eliz Stewart	Mrs Wilson.	

Reward-$10: escaped from Wash jail, Bill Stevens, negroe, age abt 30 yrs; brought from Pa 2 yrs ago & employed by Wm Lane on Rock Crk as a waggoner & is said to be a free man. -Robt Mc Clan, jailor.

In chancery, Wash Co, DC: Chas Lowndes, John Templeman, Jas Maccubin Lingan, Thos Davis, John Weems & Edw Gantt, cmplnts, against, Francis Deakins, John Hewitt, assignee of Uriah Forrest, Benj Stoddert, Jos E Rowles, Thos Sim Lee, John Laird, Jos Forrest, Thos Law, Isaac Polock, John Murdock, Wm O'Niel, David Polock, Elisha Janney, Jacob Hoffman, Jonah Thompson, John Scott, Gustavus Hall Scott, Mary Scott, Eliz Rankin & Robt Rankin her hsbnd, Cath Scott, Juliana Scott, Wm Scott & Robt Jas Scott, chldrn & heirs of Gustavus Scott, decd, late of Wash Co, *Saml Blodget Jr, *Thos L Moore, *Jas Ried, *Hudson & York, *John Ried, *Wm Vaughan, +Harrison & Sterrett, +Chas Carroll of Carrollton, +Jas McHenry, +Chas Wallace, +John Muir, +Wm Stewart, +Lucia Deblock, +Alex McDonald & Co, +Jos Hardy, +Thos Chas Clarke, +Benj Clark, chldrn & heirs of Thos Clarke, +Martha Clarke, +Chas Thos Clark & +Ann Maria Clark, decd, late of Gtwn Jos Cavacheche, Dominic Lynch, Farris & Stocker, ^Alex J Miller, ^Richard W Ashton, ^Henry Lawrence, ^Clement Lawrence, ^Jas C Nielson & ^Pierce L Tanner, dfndnts. Bill is to obtain a decree for the sale of the bridge over Potomac Rvr built by & belonging to Gtwn Bridge Co to raise money to pay a large sum of money due from the said company to sundry persons. [*Reside in Phil, Pa.] [+Reside in Md] Jos Covacheche & Dominic Lynch reside in NYC, Farris & Stocker reside in Mass. [^Reside out of DC, but where is not known.]
-Uriah Forrest, clk.

Fri Oct 22, 1802
Honorary Medal-Congress voted to Cmdor Truxton on Mar 24, 1800; engagement in the *Constellation* with the French Man of War, *La Vengeance.* Inscription on the medal: Patrie Patres Filio Digno & beneath: Thomas Truston. The design for the medal & likeness were by Mr Archibald Robertson, of Wash city, & the die engraved by Mr R Scott, of the Phil Mint.

For sale: late the prop of John Fitzgerald, decd, on the premises, in Alexandria Town, parcels of land, a warehse, half of Wales's Brewery, [& other tracts].
-Thos Digges, Jas Keith, acting excs- Alexandria.

Mon Oct 25, 1802
For sale or rent: brick hse on crnr of Falls & Frederick St, Gtwn, lately occupied by Mr Pichon. -Geo Thompson, Gtwn.

Leg of Conn convened at New Haven on Oct 14th; Elizur Goodrich-spkr; Timothy Pitkin & Jonathan O Mosely, clks.

Wed Oct 27, 1802
Died: Capt Gerdas Hall, age 67 yrs, Oct 24, in Wash, formerly clk in Treas Dept.

Ltr from Robt Lawson, Richmond, Oct 16, 1802 to J T Callender: Subj-in Americ Rev I fought for my country...Mr Jefferson, the Pres, sent me $30 for I wished to return to Ky... [Lawson disagrees with J T Callander's writing]

Fri Oct 29, 1802
Jas McGirk was executed Oct 28, for the murder of his wife.

Orphans Crt of Wash Co, DC. Oct 29, 1802. Prsnl est of John Fownes, late of Wash Co, decd. -Sarah Fownes, admx. [sale at decd hse, NJ Av, quantity of slops & shoes]

Conn Election-mbrs chosen as reps in 8th Cong of U S: Hon John C Smith
Roger Griswold	Benj Talmage	Saml W Dana
Elias Perkins	Calvin Goddard	John Davenport

Fri Nov 1, 1802
Vt election: Isaac Tichenor is elected Gov; Paul Brigham-Lt Gov; John Swan-Treas. Counsellors:

Jonas Galusha	Saml Safford	Beriah Loomis
Eliakim Spooner	Jas Witherell	Stephen Williams
Noah Chittenden	John White	Elisha Ellis
Solomon Miller	Wm Chaberlain	John Strong

For sale: 170,038 acs, "*The Great Bent of the Kenawha*" in Va, on the Great Kenawha Rvr, Montg Co. Enquire of John Beckley, esq, clk to hse of Reps, Wash City.

So Carolina Elec: elected at Charleston: Rpblcns:
Thos Bennett	John C Paiolean	Langdon Cheves
Basil Lanneau	Henry Middleton	John Drayton
John Horlbeck Jr.	Federalist:	John Dawson Jr
Thos Pinckney	Jas Lowndes	Keatin L Simons
Thos Simons	Henry Deas	Thos Corbett Jr. (Doubtful).
Thos Somerfall.		

John Blake was elected Senator w/out opposition. The following, all Rpblcns, are elected for Christ Chr Parish: Chas Jas Air, Anthony V Toomer & Jos Alston.

WED NOV 3, 1802
To let. 2 story frame hse nr the bank; enquire of Jos Saul, Ofc of Discount & Deposit, Wash.

Thos Paine arrv'd at Balt from France on Oct 30th.

FRI NOV 5, 1802
Public sale: prsnl prop of Jasper De Carnap, late of Wash, decd; hsehld furn & a 13 yr old negro girl. -Henry Ingle, adm. Eliz De Carnap, admx.

In chancery, U S, Wash Co, DC. U S, cmplnt against Saml Jackson of Va, Wm Shannon & Joshua B Bond of Phil, Frederick Shaffer & Philip Fitzhugh, of Md. Bill is to foreclose all & every equity of redemption which the dfndnts may have in over 4 acs with bldgs, in Gtwn, part of a tract cld *The Rock of Dunbarton*; to satisfy to U S the sum of $5750 + int, from Jun 3, 1797, & costs. Saml Jackson, Jun 3, 1797 mortgaged to Wm Shannon; Shannon assigned same to Oliver Wolcott-then sec of Treas, Feb 21, 1800; Jackson mortgaged same to Shannon on May 13, 1800; Jackson by indenture conveyed to Philip Fitzhugh, who by indenture of Apr 13, 1801, conveyed to Joshua B Bond & Frederick Shaffer. S Jackson resides in Westmoreland Co, Va; Fitzhugh resides in PG Co, Md; Shaffer resides in Balt City, Md. -Uriah Forrest, clk.

Maria Franklin, age 38, was executed at Swabmunchen, nr Augsburgh; she set fire to the town of Swabmunchen, 15 times, bet. Jan 15, 1798 & Nov 2, 1801.

MON NOV 8, 1802
Wash City. Appointments: Judges of Sup Crt-Jona. Robison, Royal Tyler, Stephen Jacob. Sec of State-David Wing. Judges for Rutland Co-Theophilus Harrington, Ebenezer Wilson, Jas Witherill. Appointments by the hse: Abel Spencer, Spkr; David Wing Jr, sec; Jas Eliot, clk.

WED NOV 10, 1802
Biog: Dr Erasmus Darwin, 7th child & 4th son of Robt Darwin, born at Elston, nr Newark, Nottinghamshire on Dec 12, 1731; 1757 mrd Miss Mary Howard, d/o Chas Howard & his wife, Eliz Foley who died in 1770. By Mary he had 5 chldrn, 2 who died in infancy; eldest son, Chas, died at age 20 yrs; 2d son, Erasmus, in 1799, in dead of night, threw himself into the Derwent & drowned; 3d son, Robt, physician at Shrewsbury, mrd d/o late Mr Wedgewood. Dr Darwin, the subject, mrd the relict of Col Sacheverel Pole, in 1780; he died at age 71 yrs, Apr 18, 1802, leaving his widow & 6 chldrn by his 2d marriage; besides these there are 2 natural dghts, Miss Parkers, at school in Ashbourne.

Wash City: Appointments by the Mayor. <u>Trustees of the poor:</u>

Jos Hodgson	John Kearney	Griffith Coombes.
Benj Burch-<u>Overseer of the Poor.</u>		
<u>Wood Corders:</u>	Middleton Belt	Nathaniel Bresears
John Doyne	Zacharia Gatton	John Howard

FRI NOV 12, 1802
Hartford, Oct 23. Persons to stand in nomination for assistants in May next:
Federal:

Oliver Ellsworth	Nath Smith	David Daggett
C Goodrich	Wm Hillhouse	Th Seymour
Wm Edmonds	Jona. Brace	Aaron Austin
Jos P Cook	John Chester	Elizur Goodrich
R Newberry	S T Hosmer	Shubael Abbe
Simeon Baldwin	Math. Griswold	John Allen
E Whittlesey	Jona. Barns	

Rpblcn:

Ephm Kirby	Elisha Hyde	S W Johnson
E Devotion	Marvin Wait	Amos Palmer
R Hitchcock	Jabez Fitch	John Welch
W Bradley	J T Peter	Timothy Skinner
Danl Tilden	S Whittlesey	Elijah Munson
Joshua Stow	Isaac Spencer	Eben. Barnard
Wm Hart		

Choice of Gov for Md: John F Mercer-53 votes; Jas Murray-21 votes; W V Murray-1 vote.

Saml J Potter, present Lt-Gov of R I, is elected Senator in the Cong of the U S, vice Theodore Foster, who declined a nomination.

MON NOV 15, 1802
Orphans Crt of Wash Co, DC. Nov 10, 1802. John A Burford has ltrs of adm on est of John Bennett, late of the Boston frig, decd, claiming same as creditor.
-John Hewitt, Rgrd

Gabriel Duval, apptd by the Pres, Comptroller of the Treas, vice John Steele, rsgnd.

First five elected in the Leg of Md for the Council:
F Digges, A B Ducket, Edw Hall, R Gheislin & D Davids.
Not-elected: Th Buchanan, Abraham Shaff, John Davidson, S Rideout & John Gibson.

WED NOV 17, 1802
Marietta, Oct 26. Return of the election for Delegates to the Terr Convention.

Wash Co:	Benj Ives Gilman	Genrl Putnam	Ephraim Cutler
	John McIntire	R J Meigs	Griffin Green
	Wm Skinner	Wm Wells	

Following recd votes for mbrs of the Assembly:

			W Rufus
	Putnam Ephraim	Cutler G Greene	W Wells
Ross Co:	Mr Tiffin	Massie Worthington	Baldwin Grubb
Hamilton Co:	Mr Darlington	Jeremiah Morrow	John Paul
	Chas W Byrd	John Wilson	Wm Goforth

	Mr Kitchel	John W Browne	John Smith
	John Riley		
Adams Co:	Jos Darlington	Israel Donaldson	Thos Kicker
Jefferson Co:	Bazaleal Walls	Jennings Bare	Rudolph Bare
Belmont Co:	Elijah Wood	Jas Caldwell	
Fairfield Co:	Emanuel Carpenter	Henry Abram	

Reward-$20 for strayed or stolen horse; formerly owned by Col Simpson & Capt Gassaway, Montg Co, Md. -Clotworthy Stephenson.

Committed to Wash jail: negro, abt 22 yrs of age, John Turner or Jas Gaskins; says he belongs to Maj Thos Parker of Frederick Co, Va, nr Snigger's Gap. Also, negro woman, Cath Prout, says she's a free woman, that her mthr was freed by Thos Rutland, nr South River, Md.   -Robt McClan, jailor.

Col Thos Wynns is elected to Congress in the Dist of Edenton, NC; vice Chas Johnson, esq, decd.

FRI NOV 19, 1802

Mr Christie, of Harford, elected in Sen. of Md, vice Wm Smith, rsgnd. Mr Covington, of PG, vice Walter Bowie, & Mr Faucet, of Worcester, vice Mr Polk.

Died: Hon John Mathews, age 58 yrs, Nov 16, in Charleston, formerly Govnr of SC.

Notice: I shall petition legislature of U S, to relieve me from debts which by losses in trade I'm unable to pay.   -Wm Taylor.

Ranaway from Saml A McCoskey, living in Carlisle, Pa, negro Geo Moor, age abt 20 yrs, a waiter; $20 reward.

Partnership bet Henry Ingle & Enoch Pelton, dissoved by mutual consent; cabinet bus. on NJ Av cont'd by Henry Ingle.

To rent: hse now in tenure of Dr Bullus, bet Six & Seven Bldgs. -Joel Brown.

MON NOV 22, 1802

Mail robbery-$100 reward; 6 miles from Shelbyville; all mail for Green-Rvr Co, Nashville, Natchez & New Orleans, forcibly taken from the rider.
                    -Isaac E Gano, P M, Frankfort K.

John Milledge has been elected Gov of the State of Ga.

Tribute to valor. Silver urn presented by underwriters of Lloyd's Coffee-hse, London, thru our Mnstr, Mr King. "To Capt. Thomas Truxtun, of the American frigate *Constellation;* as a mark of their sense of his services, and admiration of his gallant conduct in taking the French frigate, of 44 guns, in the West Indies, in Feb, 1799."

Division orders, Savannah, Oct 25, 1802. Crt Martial, Maj Shad was President for the trial of Lt Stackhouse on charges by Lt Col Mitchell; found him guilty of unofficerlike conduct; disobedience of orders on Sep 30; same on Oct 11th. Fined $180 [6 mos pay when in actual svc] -Maj Gen Jackson, Charleston, Aid-De-Camp.

WED NOV 24, 1802

Died: John Ewing Colhoun, age 53 yrs, Oct 26, at his seat in Pendleton Dist, SC, Senator from SC.

Died: Wm Holmes, of Md, midshipman, age 18 yrs, Sep 21, board the U S frig *Adams* under command of Capt Campbell, in the Mediterranean; leaving his mthr & sisters; he was an only son.

For cash. at the stone hse, prop of Mr Robt Peter, nr the county wharf, kitchen articles, 3 large paintings, remainder of furniture offered at Mt Vernon sale .

FRI NOV 26, 1802 NOV

Invention has been lately made by Mr Henry Greathead of Eng, of a Life Boat.

Wm Lovell has established the "Union Tavern & Washington Hotel"; pavement all the way, 30 rms, coffee rm, all newspapers.

MON NOV 29, 1802

Mary Ann Pic is opening a millinery goods store.

Managers of the City Dancing Assemblies: W W Burrows, Wm Simmons, John Bullus, Thos Munroe, Joshua Wingate Jr, Wm Brent, Robt F How & C W Goldsborough.

Witnesses to the "Life Boat" [See Nov 26]: Richd Wilson, ship owner of *Scarborough;* Capt Gilfred Lowson Reed, an elder bro of the Trinity hse; Mr Thos Hinderwell, ship owner of Scarborough; Mr Saml Plumb of Lower Shadwell; Sir Cuthbert Heron, Baronet of So Shields; Mr Wm Masterman, ship owner, of So Shields.

WED DEC 1, 1802

Strayed away, bay colt, from Robt McMahian, NJ Av

John Baptist Ashe, Rpblcn, is elected Govnr of NC over Wm Polk & Jos Taylor.

Mrd: at Paris, M Talleyrand & Madame Grant, with impediments.

FRI DEC 3, 1802

Lottery for completing St Augustines' Chr, Phil. -M Carr, sec. Tickets from: Patrick Byrne, Mat. McConnell, Geo Taylor, all Chesnut St, Phil, Pa.

Beaufort, [P R] Nov 5. Ceremonies on opening of Beaufort College; Col Edw Barnwell, Mstr of Beaufort Lodge; plate buried was engraved-"Beaufort College. Founded Nov 4, 1802. Col Thos Talbied, Chief Architect, Jas A Agnew, Del'r". Blessing by Dr Finlay; Stephen Elliott, esq, sec of the Brd of trustees. Federal coin was placed under the plate which was covered by another stone.

MON DEC 6, 1802
Reply of the Fed mbrs of the Leg of NJ to Rpblcn mbrs was signed:
Trenton, Nov 24, 1802

Ephraim Martin	John Outwater	Peter D Vroom
Saml Hough	Thos Clark	Eben. Newton
Peter Ward	Thos Blanch	Isaac Kipp
Simon Wyckoff	Gershem Dunn	Jos Falkinburge
John Combs	Erkuries Beatty	Wm Coxe
Fred. Frelinghuysen	John Lacy	Benj Vancleve
Abel Clement	Wm Pearson	Saml W Harrison
Saml French	Stephen Burrowes	Jas Van Duyn
Wm McEowen	Wm Stockton	

Partnership bet Thos Brohawn & Stanley Byus is dissolved by mutual consent; make payments to Byus.

Richd Sprigg is apptd one of the Judges of the Genrl Crt of Md, vice Gabriel Duval, rsgnd.

Marshal's sale: brick hse & lot , Pa Av, nr Gtwn, part of property known as Six Bldgs. Lots 7 & 8 in sq 38 as laid out by Isaac Pollock. Numerous other lots in favor of Abraham Van Logan use of John T Mason, against goods & chattels of Isaac Pollock. The unimproved prop is also seized under 3 other writs of Feiri Facias in favor of: Geo Magruder & Patrick Magruder, use of John H Stone & Walter Dorsey; -Thos Turner & Saml Turner & Saml Brooke, against good & chattels of Isaac Pollock.   -Daniel C Brent-marshall D C.

WED DEC 8, 1802
For sale: Late the resid & prop of Presly Thornton, esq, 2,500 acs, Northumberland Co, Va; brick 2 story mansion. -Richd Peters Jr.
Louisville, Nov 13, 1802. Jas Bozeman writes to Isaac Benedix, post mstr, Savannah that E Divene was robbed by 2 negroes of the mail, nr Augusta.

Trenton, Nov 29. John Lambert, VP, has apptd Jos Bloomfield, late Gov, to be a mstr in chancery; & Wm S Pennington, mstr examiner & clk of said Crt.

Hse o/Reps: New mbrs took their seats; Saml Hunt from NH; Saml Thatcher from Mass; David Merriwether from Ga v Mr Taliaferro, rsgnd; Thos Winn of NC; Thos M Greene, Delegate from the Miss Terr in rm of N Hunter, decd.

Fri Dec 10, 1802
Richard Wilson & Nathaniel Segul petitioned Congress to be liberated from imprisonment in Wash Co, DC. [debtors]

Wm Bell, then my clk, absconded with $1,850 in bank notes; he is 30 yrs of age; left Norfolk Nov 23 for Balt. -Edw Johnston, Norfolk, Va-Nov 27.

New York, Dec 3, 1802. Mbrs of the NY Acad of the Fine Arts: Edw Livingston, chrmn; Robt J Livingston, treas; Dr Peter Irving, sec. Directors: Col W S Smith, Dr Jos Brown, John B Prevost, Wm Cutting, Wm M Seton, Stephen Van Ransaeler.

Mon Dec 13, 1802
Jas Garrard, esq, is Gov of the Commonwealth of Ky.

Died: Col John B Ashe, age 55 yrs, at his seat nr Halifax, Nov 27; ntv of NC; ofcr in Amer Rev

Died: Wm Clark, Nov 11, at St Vincennes, 1st Judge of Ind Ter.

Hse o/Reps. Petitions: 1-of Wm Douglass of Maine-remission of duties; 2-of John Hillary Baker-reimbursement of certain drawback duties; 3-of Gibert Combs-assistance to conduct research [Mode of ascertaining the longitude.]

Wed Dec 15, 1802
In chancery. Levin Mackall, Walter Mackall & Richd Mackall, excs of Benj Mackall, in behalf of themselves & other creditors of Leonard Holliday, late of PG Co, decd. v Richd Johns, Leonard Johns, Eliz Holliday, Mgt Holliday, Washington Bowie & Sarah his wife, Acquila Beall & Grace his wife, heirs at law of Anne Bradley Coxe, late of PG Co, decd, & of the said Leonard Holliday. Bill is against dfndnts Richd Johns, Leonard Johns, Eliz Holliday, Mgt Holliday, Mgt Bowie late Mgt Chew, Sarah Peter late Sarah Johns, Grace Beall late Grace Holliday, the grchldrn of said Leonard Holliday, decd, & against Walter Brooke Coxe & Anne Bradley Coxe his wife, which Anne was d/o said Leonard Holliday, & entitled jointly with his said grchldrn, & in proportions directed by act of descents, to his rl est; which bill has abated, as to the death of said Anne; & to make Wash Bowie, David Peter & Aquila Beall parties to original bill. Walter Brooke Coxe & his wife Anne Bradley Coxe, died without issue & without devising her interest in the rl est of her said fr; her interest devolved on Richard & Leonard Johns, Eliz & Mgt Holliday, Mgt Bowie, Sarah Peter & Grace Beall, her nphs & nieces, & on Wash Bowie, David Peter, & Aquilla Beall, who have respectively intermrd with the 3 last named dfndnts. Mgt Holliday is a minor; all dfndnts reside in DC. -S H Howard-Reg CC

Cong of U S-Hse of Reps: 1-Petition of Elisha Frizell, of Salem, NY, praying he be allowed arrears of pension due him-wounds recd while a soldier in Mass Line; referred to committee. 2-Petiton of Jas Stille, Capt in U S Regt of Artl, late Commanding Ofcr of Garrison of West Point, praying to be indemnified for the costs & damages of a suit against him in NY, for trespass committed by part of his company on Jul 4, 1800, without his knowledge or consent-referred to committee. 3-Petition of Abraham Millen, adm & resid leg of Wm Millen, presented Feb 9, 1798, referred to committee. 4-Petition of Jos McLellan & Hugh McLellan, John Taber & Danl Taber, of Portland, Maine, praying a remission of the duties of impost & tonnage, in case of ship Eliza, said owner omitted to take the oath by time prescribed by law, referred to committee.

FRI DEC 17, 1802
Rev Wm Parkinson chosen as Chaplain of Hse of Reps.

MON DEC 20, 1802
John Page, of Rosewell, elected Gov of Va, succeeds Mr Munroe.

Hse o/Reps: Petition of Jas Dohertie & others, ctzn of the Miss Terr-praying that a tract of vacant land in said terr., may be granted to Amos Hubband & Ebenezer Smith as tenants in common.

Ltr from Cncl of State to Jas Monroe. Richmond, Va. Dec 7, 1802. Rgrd: Acknowledgement of his value as a man & as a ctzn. Signed: John Guerrent, Alex. Mcrae, Wm Foushee, Alx. Stuart & S Tyler.

WED DEC 22, 1802
Reward-$200 for negro, Edward, eloped from Petersburgh in Nov, 1801, age abt 20 yrs, blacksmith, worked for Mr David Alexander of said place; Mr Thos Armstead, of Norfolk, lost a fellow about the same time. Deliver to Mr Wm Twitty, of Petersburgh. -Thos Tabb, nr Halifax Town, NC.

Ltr from Andrew Morris, Capt of the brig *Franklin*, to Jas Leander Cathcart, cns'l of the U S; dated Tripoli, Jul 22, 1802. Subj-the *Franklin*, belonging to Messrs Summerl & Brown of Phil was boarded by a Tripoline Corsair that sailed from this place abt May 20th; only myself & 3 seamen are captives; the brig was left in charge of their agents.

High Crt of Chancery of Va-Richmond Dist. Thom. Ellgey, plntf, & Wm Lane, dfndnt. Sale of land in Loudoun Co, Va, 475 3/4 acs. -Hugh Steuart, Francis Adams, John Keene-comrs.

MON DEC 27, 1802
Hse o/Reps: Petition of Thos Shubrick, of SC, praying to be released from a contract made by him in 1799 for supplying timber.

In chancery-ratify sales made by Wm Stewart, Allegany Co, Md, tracts: "*Suck*"-212 acs, L497; "*Additon to the Spring Bottom*"- 96 acs, L216; "*Workmans Desire*"-76 acs, L225; "*Johnsons Fancy*"- 50 acs, L112 10. Lot 8 sq 664, & lot 8 sq east of sq 664 in Wash City, L241 17 6. -Saml H Howard, Reg Cur Can.

WED DEC 29, 1802

Mr John Gardiner, of Wash, has obtained a patent for erecting dry docks to repair ships.

Committed to Wash jail: negro, Nancy, says she formerly belonged to John Childs of Fairfax Co, Va; negro, Rachel & her child, John, 18 mos of age, says she formerly was prop of Jas Wilson, of Calvert Co, Md. -Robt McClan, jailor.

For rent: hse & farm now occupied by Wm Walter Williams, on rd leading from Alex to Leesburg. -Har. Lane, Montg Co, Md.

Stevens Thompson Mason, has been re-elected a Sen. of U S from Va.

FRI DEC 31, 1802

Timothy Caldwell is declining brickmaking business & has for sale-2 sheds & kilns n e of the War Dept.

State of Ohio; in Convention; begun & held at Chillicothe, Nov 1, 1802. Done in convention Nov 29, 1802; laid before Congress Dec 23d. Signed: Edw Tiffin, Pres & Rep, Ross Co.

Adams Co:	Jos Darlinton	Israel Donalson	Thos Kirker
Belmont Co:	Jas Caldwell	Elijah Woods	
Clermont Co:	Philip Gatch	Jas Sargent	
Fairfield Co:	Henry Abrams	Emanuel Carpenter	
Jefferson Co:	Rudolph Bear	Geo Humphrey	John Milligan
	Nathan Updegraff	Bazaleel Wells	
Hamilton Co:	John W Browne	Chas Willing Byrd	Francis Dunlavy
	Wm Goforth	John Kitchen	John Wilson
	Jeremiah Morrow	John Paul	John Reily
	John Smith		
Ross Co:	Mich'l Baldwin	Jas Grubb	Nath'l Maffie
	T Worthington		
Trumbull Co:	David Abbot	Saml Huntington.	
Washington Co:	Ephraim Cutler	Benj Ives Gilman	John McIntire
	Rufus Putnam.		

-Thos Scott, sec.

The National Intelligencer and Washington Advertiser

Washington, DC 1803

WED JAN 5, 1803

Cong. U S-Hse of Reps: petition of John Miles, & other gun makers of Phil city, praying that additional duties be imposed on imports of same from foreign countries.

Saml Blodget, praying relief, in case of judgment recovered against him in Supr Crt of Pa, for prop in Wash, from suit of possessors of a prize tkt in a lottery authorized for improvement of said city in 1793, & of which Blodget was apptd an acting mgr & superintendent.

Meeting of the inhabitants of Wash City & Co to be held Fri next. Signed: Danl Carroll of Dudn; Wm Thornton, Abraham Boyd, Corn. Coningham, Isaac Peirce, Benj More, Thos Corcoran & Robt Brent.

FRI JAN 7, 1803

Public sale: Sundry furn & looking glasses-David English intending to remove from Gtwn in a short time.

Mr Geo Hay gave Mr Jas Thompson Callender a beating on Dec 20th, as result of a publication in the recorder of some wks past; Mr C applied to Mr John Foster, Mayor of Wash, for a warrant to bring Mr Hay before him. Hay & Callender are ctzns of Richmond.

Ladies with ltrs in the Wash Post ofc on Jan 1, 1803.

Elzey Burroughs	Miss Peggy Cattenhead	Mrs Cook
Betty Jones	Miss Mgt Eastwood	Mrs M Jones
Mrs Ann Kelly	Miss Mgt McClean	Miss Martha Nicholls
Mrs Nicholls	Mrs Susannah Nicholls	Mrs Rebecca Reeder

MON JAN 10, 1803

For sale: bet 2 & 3000 acs of land, Loudoun Co, Va, part of *Goose Creek* tract, purchased of late Col Chas Carter.-Jos Jones, Loudoun, Va.

WED JAN 12, 1803

Hse of Reps: Resolved that a monument be erected to the memory of Genrl Jos Warner, slain on Bunker's Hill-Referred to committee. Resolved that a monument be erected to the memory of Gen'rl Hugh Mercer, who was slain at Princeton on Jan 3, 1777. Monument to Genrl Francis Nash, slain in the Battle of Germantown; monuments also for Genrl Richd Butler, Genrl Nath'l Woodhull & Genr'ls Wooster, Harkimer, Davidson & Skriven.

Affidavits for Lewis R Morris, regarding recontre bet Mr Rutledge & Mr Ellery-at Piscataway on Dec 28, 1802. Jos M Simmes, of same, PG Co, Md; Nathaniel Clagett, of same place, sworn before Wm Marshall, Jan 18, 1803, J P.

Fri Jan 14, 1803

Simeon Rouse & John Lamb, Inventer & Patentee, ctzns of NY State; machine for extracting fresh water from salt water.

Orphans Crt of Calvert Co, Md. Jan 8, 1803. Prsnl est of Robt Gover, late of Calvert Co, decd.   -Mary Gover, excx.

Mon Jan 17, 1803

Hse of Reps: 1-Petition of Memucan Hunt & others to Genrl Assembly of NC. 2-Memorial of Wm R Miller & Wm H Bordman, of Boston, Mass, merchants, respectively sole owners of the ships, *Gov Strong & Mary*, requesting new certs of registry. 3-Pet of Jas Anderson & others, manufacturers of cork in NYC, for additional duty on imported cork. 4-Pet of Wm Burrit, of Salem, Wash Co, NY, praying an augmentation of pension heretofore allowed him because of wound & injuries recd while a soldier in Conn Line of Continental Army, Rev War, which rendered him incapable of obtaining a livelihood by labour. 5-Pet of Alexander McNish, of Salem, Wash Co, NY, Ensign in Col John Williams's Regt of Militia, in actual svc of U S, Rev War, to the like effect. 6-Pet of Albin Gordon, of Va, he is old & infirm, because of a wound he recd whilst a soldier in Continental Army, Rev War, on pension for $60 per annum & has a large family to support. 7-Pet of Bernard Glenn, Lt in Col Crocket's Regt of Va State Troop during Rev War, allow him to locate & survey on north side of Ohio River & obtain a patent for acres of land in a military land warrant granted to him by Va State, in lieu of land in Ky. 8-Pet of Thos Shubrick, of SC, relief in case of a contract bet him & a Navy Agent of U S, 1799, for cutting of timber, prop of the petitioner. 9-Pet of Adam Koch, to receive the bounty of land due for his svcs as a pvt soldier in 6th Pa Regt on Continental Establishment, Rev War, hitherto refused, in consequence of another person, of same name, who belonged to Capt Bartholomew Von Heer's Troop of Light Dragoons, having already recd his grant of land. 10-Pet of Roger Alden, agent for Holland land Co in NW Pa, relief in case of stamps-$190. 11-Pet of Saml Frazer, of Harford Co, Md, to receive bounty of land for svcs as pvt soldier in Continental Army, Rev War, said land has been granted to Wm Thomas, without knowledge of Frazer. 12-Pet of Sarah Peters, of Wash, DC, wid of Alexander A. Peters, decd, pension for svcs of her hsbnd who died at Fort Johnston, NC, Nov last, while a surgeon's mate in USA. All referred to com.

Reward-$50 for Rynar, negro woman, abt 25 or 30 yrs; raised by Mr Debut & sold at that estate to Mr Robertson, he sold her to Mr Ben Sothern, who sold her to me. -John S Sims, Union Crthse, SC.

Wed Jan 19, 1803

Americ Philosophical Soc, Jan 7, 1803. Ofcrs: Pres, Thos Jefferson; VPs: Robt Patterson, Caspar Wister, Benj Smith Barton; Secs: Adam Seybert, John R Coxe, Thos C James, Thos T Hewsom; Cnslrs for 3 yrs: Jonathan Williams, Andrew Ellicot, Saml Magaw, Nicholas Collin; Cnslr for 2 yrs, Tench Coxe; Curators: Chas W Peale, Robt Leslie, Wm S Jacobs; Treas, John Vaughan.

For sale-Crt of Chancery of Md-"*Harrison's Security*", Anne Arundel Co, 419 1/2 acs, Mr Wm Davidson lately resided; also lots in Wash City having been mortgaged by Wm Davidson to Wm Campbell, which have been asgnd to Thos Snowden. -Henry H Chapman, Th Harris Jr-trusts.

FRI JAN 21, 1803
Wanted: boys to learn boot & shoemkg business -John Crookshank, Gtwn.

Hse of Reps: 1-Petition of John Minor, of NC, bro & adm of Reuben Minor, decd, refrd to committee. 2-Pet of Matthew Patterson & others, inhabitants & settlers on French Broad River, within original boundaries of SC, stating inconveniences since where they reside is now considered part of Ga. 3-Pet of Geo Mason, of SC, presented on Jan 28th last, referred to Committee of Claims. 4-Pet of Richd Baker & others, praying that a post road be est'd from Fredericksburg, Va, to Paris-referred. 5-Pet. of Hugh Alexander & others, inhabitants of Ky, praying relief in case of judgments obtained against them in the Dist Crt of the U S, for Ky, for balances due from them for duties on spirits distilled & on stills; balances were pd to John Jamieson, then Acting Deputy Mrshl for said dist, who has since absconded to place unknown. 6-The Spkr had a ltr from Thos Martin, late Maj of the 1st U S Regt, stating his claim to the pay of a Capt in the Cont'l Army, after the capitulation of York-Town, Va, to the end of the Rev War; he has recd the comp of a Lt, only-referred to committee. 7-Petition of Seth Chapin, Lt in the Cont'l Army, during the Rev War, praying for comp for svcs, in observing the movements & stations of the enemy on R I, some time in the yr 1779-referred to claims. 8-Pet of Jos Pannill & others, inhabitants of the Miss Terr. praying that land they located & settled subsequent to Oct 27, 1795, may be confirmed to the petitioners. 9-Pet of Francis L Slaughter, praying to be on list of pensioners, from wound recd whilst a sldr in Col White's Regt of Cavalry, Rev War, rendered him incapable of obtaining a livelihood by labour. 10-also of Abraham Stout, Lt of Infty in Cont'l Army & of Saml Kikendall, Capt of the NJ Militia, svc during the Rev War. All referred to Committee of Claims.

MON JAN 24, 1803
Re-elected: Saml White, Sen of U S, for Delaware State.

Committee of Portsmouth, NH; subj-fire & need for assistance. John Langdon, Danl Humphreys, Jas Sheafe, Nath'l Adams, John Goddard. Phil, Jan 19.

Rev B Alliston, Principal of the Bordentown, NJ, Acad & in connection with Mr John J Hawkins, has made a discoverty of making paper from husks of indian corn. Patent has been obtained.

WED JAN 26, 1803
Little River Turnpike Rd Co: Pres-Jas Keith; Dirct'rs: J T Ricketts, Leven Powell, Geo Gilpin. -Alexandria.

Matter of John Jack-bankrupt; persons indebted to said bankrupt, make payments to Richard Forrest, assignee.

Fri Jan 28, 1803

Mississippi Legislature. Reps of the people of the Miss Terr respond to Wm C C Claiborne, Gov of Miss Terr; Re: numerous blessings to the public, etc. Signed, Roger Dixon, Spkr, Rep Chamber, Dec 13, 1802; Attest, Sam S Mahan, clk.

In Chancery-Wash Co, DC. Chas Minisie, John Fry & Samuel Spalding complts. v, Geo Walker, dfndnt. Bill to obtain a decree for sale of sundry lots in Wash; Geo Walker is indebted to cmplnts for sum of $5000, bond dated Dec 31, 1798; Walker does not reside in U S. -Uriah Forrest, clk.

In Chancery-Wash Co, DC. Jas Barry, cmplnt, v Chas Ross, John Simpson, John Craig, Jas Crawford, Wm Rusk, Wm Read, Matthew Pearce, Geo Plumstead. Barry, Ross & Simpson, of Pa, were tenants in common of 3 lots in Wash; Barry sold his int to Ross & Simpson; bal remains due Barry; Ross & Simpson have since declared bankrupt; they executed a deed to Craig, Rusk, Crawford, Read, Pearce & Plumstead, all of Pa. Bill is to make said lots liable for debt due by Ross & Simpson to Barry.-Uriah Forrest, clk.-Wash.

Mon Jan 31, 1803

In Chancery-Wash Co, DC. Thos Law, cmplnt, v Jas Piercy Jr, Jas Ray, Saml Treat, Jas Piercy Sr, & Amariah Frost. Bill is to foreclose the equity of redemption of prop resting in said dfndnt Jas Piercy, Jr., who in order to defraud his creditors, ran away from Wash Co & now resides in Portsmouth, Va; Saml Treat also resides there; Jas Ray resides in Annapolis city, Md, probably in jail; Jas Piercy, Sen, resides & always has in Great Britain & Amariah Frost resides in Wash City. -Uriah Forrest, clk.

Wed Feb 2, 1803

In Chancery. Patrick Murdock, v Thos Beall of Samuel, *Peter Devicman, & *Jos Forrest. Bill is to obtain a conveyance of part of tract cld "*Walnut Bottom*", Allegany Co, Md, which Thos Beall contracted for with Devicman, Feb 26, 1795. [*Reside out of Md] -Saml H Howard, Reg C C.

Fri Feb 4, 1803

Treaty bet U S & Creek Nation of Indians was signed nr Ft Wilkinson on Oconee River, Jun 16, 1802, by: Jas Wilkinson, of Md, Brig Genrl U S Army; Benj Hawkins, of NC; Andrew Pickins, of SC, Com'rs Pleni of U S. The mark "X" of 43 Indians. Interpr's: Timothy Barnard, Alex. Cornells, Jos Islands. Alex'r Macomb Jr, Sec to Com'rs. Wm R Bootes, Capt 2d Regt Infantry, J Blackburn, Lt Com Comp D, John B Barnes, Lt U S A, Wm Hill, Adj C D. -Th Jefferson, Pres, Jas Madison, Sec of State.

Creditors of Richd Willson are to meet at the new jail, on business of consequence to them. -Richard Wilson [2 splgs]

Ranaway-Wm Howington, abt 20 yrs of age, apprentice boy. 1 cent reward.
-Nathaniel E Magruder.

Leg of Pa. Crt of Impeachment, Wed Jan 26, against Alexander Addison; mbrs who declared him guilty: Wm Findley, Jas Gamble, Jas Harris, Jonas Hartzell, John Heister, John Kean, Presley Carrland, Christian Lower, Wm McArthur, Aaron Lyle, Thos Mewhorter, Thos Morton, John Pearson, John Porter, Wm Reed John Richards Wm Rodman John Steele Robt Whitehill, Saml Maclay, Spkr. Declared him not guilty: Matthias Barton Jas Ewing, Thos Johnston & John Jones. Addison convicted; ltr from same dated Lancaster, Jan 26, 1803, regarding sentence etc. Judge Addison is remv'd from his ofc & disqualified from holding same in any Crt of law within Pa.

MON FEB 7, 1803

In Chancery-Wash Co, DC. Ninion Magruder, cmplnt, v Ann Seyle, John Seyle, Geo Seyle, Jacob Seyle, Lewis Seyle, *Saml Seyle, Susannah Edmundson, *Polly & *Geo Adams, *Cath & *Peter Montz, *Betsey & *Jacob Steiner, *Barbara, *Daniel & *Lewis Hauer, *Peggy & *John Stover, *Henry, *Polly & *Adam Hauer, dfndnts. [*Do not reside in DC or within reach of process of this Crt]. Bill is to obtain a decree to foreclose property which dfndnts are clmnts.
-Uriah Forrest, clk.

Treaty bet the U S & Chocktaw Nation of Indians was concluded & signed at Ft Confederation on the Tombighy Rvr, Oct 17th past; convention made by Brig Genrl Jas Wilkinson, of Md; Signed: Jas Wilkinson; witnesses: Silas Dinsmore, agent to the Choctaws. Interpreters: John Pitchleynn, Turner Brashears, Peter H Naisalis, John Long. -Th Jefferson, Jas Madison, Wash City, Jan 20, 1803.

WED FEB 9, 1803

Joshua B Bond, of Phil, Merchant, no longer authorized to act for the subscribers on any subject whatsoever.-Henry Pratt, Thos W Francis, John Miller Jr, John Ashley, Jacob Baker, Trust of Aggregate Fund created by Jas Greenleaf, Edw Fox, Robt Morris & John Nicholson. [Feb 9, 1801 & Feb 10, 1802-2 ltrs o/atty]

Hse of Reps: Griffin Taylor, of Va, presented a petition to this hse on Jan 19, 1801; he has leave to withdraw his said petition & documents

Americ Mercury. Festival at New Haven on Mar 9th next to celebrate the elect of Jefferson. Oration will be by Pierpont Edwards; Mgrs: P Edwards, Saml Bishop, John Heyleger, John R Throop, Levi Ives, Peter Johnson, Obadiah Hotckhiss Jr, Elijah Munson. Wm Powell, Dir Rpblcn Meeting, New Haven, Jan 17, 1803.

Memorial of sundry gun manufacturers of Lancaster, Pa, was presented to hse of Reps on Feb 4th. Signed: Jacob Dickert, Peter Conter, Atram Henry, John Graeff, Henry DeHulf, Jacob & John Haeffer, Benj Hatz, Abraham Pieper & Christopher Gumpp, Jan 28, 1803.

Capt Benj Cushing, late mstr of the brig, *Argo,* appeared before Wm Harris, Notary & J Peace, Suffolk Co, Mass, on Jan 13, 1803. Subj: Cushing's trip to Isl o/Guadaloupe, Nov 27th last & the fate of 6 negroes on board.

Fri Feb 11, 1803

Hse of Reps-petitions referred to committee: 1-Amey Dardin, of Mecklenburg Co, Va, wid of & relict of David Dardin, decd, compensation for loss of horse, Romulus, prop of decd, which was impressed into svc of Southern Army under Maj Gen Greene, by order of Jas Gunn, Capt in Regt of Continental Cavalry, Jul, 1781. 2-Pet of Jona. Hastings, Deputy postmstr of Boston, Mass-praying reimbursement of expences incured in the suit against him by Wm Briggs of Maine; referred to Committee of Claims. 3-Eliphalet Ladd of NH, has right to withdraw his said petition. 4-Pet of Jas Miller & others, settlers on Mad Rvr, Ohio; right to purchase small portion of land; referred to com. 5-John Skinner of NC has right to withdraw his petition. 6-Pet of Jos Darlington & others, legal reps of Geo Wilson, decd, was read & considered. 7-Pet of John Whitney, of Mass, a refugee from Nova Scotia; relief of prop loss during the Rev War; was presented.

New jail in Wash City is completed. Cost $2,577, iron grated doors or a kitchen is not included-cost abt $300. -Geo Hadfield, city of Wash, Jan 18, 1803.

Mon Feb 14, 1803

Elisha Riggs, Bridge St, Gtwn, dry goods for sale.

Dover, Jan 23. Geo Clark, Wm Whann, Wm Poole, Philip Lewis Adam Williamson & Abraham Staats differ on resolutions adopted by the Hse o/Reps in their last session.   -Wilmington Mirror

Theodorus Bailey, Rpblcn, elected Sntr from NY, in rm of Gov Morris, a Fed.

Wed Feb 16, 1803

Notice: I forwarn any person from buying a note, signed by me to Thos McNally, for I have a claim against same.   -Richd Delphey.

Directors elected in Wash for the ofc of Discount & Deposit: Jos Carlton, Abraham Hewes, Wm H Dorsey, Wm Miller Jr, Thos Beall of Geo, Wm Newton, Thos Munroe, John T Mason, Tristram Dalton, John Dunlap, Thos Tingey, Wm Brent & Alex'r Henderson.

Committed to Wash jail, negro, Wat, age abt 23 yrs; says he is prop of Dr Parrow, of Lower Marlboro.   -Robt McClan, jailor.

Fri Feb 18, 1803

John Mackal Gant, esq, apptd Chief Justice of 1st Dist of Md; vice, Hon Richard Sprigg, esq, apptd Judge of Genrl Crt.

Mon Feb 21, 1803

For sale: 550 acs, Fairfax Co, Va, where I live. -Thos Pollard.

For sale: Light coach, Peter Humrukhausen, coach maker, Hagers Town, or to Daniel Heister, Capitol Hill, Wash.

For sale: lot on G St; to satisfy a debt due to me by Henry Dunlap of Gtwn.
-Alexander McCormick.

People of Indiana Terr are determined to suspend the 6th Article bet the U S & the Terr. Signed, Wm Henry Harrison, Pres & Dele at Knox Co. John Rise Jones, Sec'y. [Article VI: No slavery in said Terr; fugitives from any one of the original States may be lawfully claimed.] Done at Vincennes, Ind Terr, Dec 28, 1802.

Hse of Reps: Committee report that John Pickering, Dist Judge for NH,-guilty of high crimes & misdemeanors; shd be impeached.

Election of John Q Adams, as Senator from Mass, has been confirmed.

WED FEB 23, 1803
Died: Maj Thos Lansdalk, of Queen Ann, PG Co, Md, Jan 19.

Richd Lee & Co have mv'd their manufactory & wholesale store from Balt, Md, to NY; patent & family medicines. Retail sales at:

C Pierce-Portsmouth
Thomas' & Andrews-Boston
E Merriam-Brookfield
H Mahn-Dedham
Jenks & Clark-Portland
Galen H Fay-Haverhill, Mass
N Phillips-Warren, R I
Dr I Thompson-New London
Hudson & Goodwin-Hartford
J Trumbull-Norwich, Conn
Peter Van Bomel-Poughkeepsie
E Norman-Hudson
John Barker-Albany
W McLean-Utica
E Phinney-Cooperstown
Pennington & Gould-Newark
A Blauveit-Brunswick
R Games-Burlington, NJ
Wm Y Birch-Phil
J Wyeth-Harrisburgh
S Longcope-Easton
T Wilson-Norristown
Snowden & McCorkls-Greensburg
Warner & Hanna-Balt
M Bartgiss-Frederick
Gideon White-Annapolis
J Clayland-Centreville
S Curtis-Amherst,NH
Isaiah Thomas-Worcester
Cushing & Appleton-Salem
H Jones-Stockbridge
A March-Newburyport
W Wilkinson- Providence
Saml Trumbull-Stonington Pt
Dr Darling-New Haven
J Byrne-Windham
Thos Kirk-Brooklyn
John G Hurrin-Goshen
Dr Croswell-Catskill
Moffit & Co-Troy
T Walker-Rome
T B Jansen & Co-NY
S Kollock-Elizabeth Town
Sherman & Co-Trenton
Jas Wilson-Wilmington, Dela
G Dawson-Carlisle
C J Hieter & R Dickson-Lancaster
J Schneider-Reading
Dr Spangle-Yorktown
Dr S Brown-Ky
Dr Purdie-Smithfield
J Dietrick-Hagerstown
Dr Stevens-Easton
Ferson & Read-Cambridge

Rapine & Co-Washington
Dr Miller-Winchester
G Green-Fredericksburg
Ross & Douglass-Petersburgh
F Merick-Norfolk
J Alburtis-Martinsburg
R Greenhow-Williamsburg
C H S Henkle-New Mkt, Va
G Bradley-Newbern, NC
John Israel-Pittsburg, Pa

Dr Ott-Gtwn, Md
S Bishop-Alexandria
S Pleasants-Richmond
M Jones-Suffolk
Ben Johnson-Warren
I Shaw-Leesburg
R Barker-Fauquier
Jos Gales-Raleigh
C Wittich-Charleston, SC

FRI FEB 25, 1803

For sale: *"Walnut Tree Farm"*, 360 acs, 20 negroes & stock; my life estate.
-Tobias Lear, banks of Alex or Columbia.

Orphans Crt of Wash Co, DC. Feb 24, 1803. Prsnl est of John McCarty, late of Wash Co, decd. -Redmond Barry, Michael Scott, adms. Ordered by said Crt- sale of all goods & chattels & prsnl prop of decd. -Jno Hewitt, Reg.

Recommenders of Hamilton's Elixir: Chas Myers, Hempstead Hill nr Balt, Md; Luther Martin, esq, Atty Genrl of Md; Mr Alijah Henly, Bridge St, Balt, Md; Mrs Eliz Jones, So Howard St.

MON FEB 28, 1803

Bankruptcy awarded against Frederick Conrad, merchant & trader, of Wash Co, DC.   -J C Dent, Sec to Com'rs.

Died: Thos Wignell, at Phil, manager of the theatre, of Phil.

A ltr was written on Sep 5, 1793 by Sec of War, to Constant Freeman directing him not to concur in any measures from the expence of the U S for invading the Creek Country.

WED MAR 2, 1803

Bankruptcy awarded against Robt McMunn, merchant & trader, of Wash Co, DC.
-J C Dent, Sec to comrs.

F A Wagler, piano, violin, etc, instructor, has remv'd to the hse of Mr Robt Clarke, formerly occupied by the French nuns.

Lost or stolen: Bank note of Balt, $250, issued to John Thomas, dated Sep 10, 1800, maybe.   -Pontius D Stelle.

FRI MAR 4, 1803

Claims against est of Barnaby Davis to be made to W M H P Tuckfield, adm.

Natchez, Jan 15, 1803. On Wed last at this port, the ship *Mary*, Capt Darling from Boston, Mass was the first Americ ship that has attempted to ascend the Miss thus far. Also arvd on the same day, schnr *Bee*, Capt Brag, at same port.

Lands for sale: Properties of late Gen Geo Washington-600 acs in Chas Co, Md, nr Fish Trap; 519 acs in Montg Co, Md, nr Frederick Town, nr Kittorlan; 453 acs in Jefferson Co, Va, nr Chas Town & 240 acs in Hampshire Co, nr Bath; 1600 acs in Jefferson Co on 4th Ford of Bullskin; 183 acs in Jefferson Co in Wormleys Line; 571 acs in Frederick Co nr Battle Town; 2481 acs on Ashley's & 885 acs on Chattins Run in Fauquier Co. -the Executors.

Indiana Terr, Town of Washington. An act to establish a college in the Miss Terr; Wm C C Claiborne-Pres; Wm Dunbar-VP; Felix Hughs-Sec; Col Cato West-Treas; Lottery Committee-David Latimore, Wm Dunbar & Sutton Banks; Name-Jefferson College.

MON MAR 7, 1803
In Council, Annapolis-debts due to Md to be published in the Md Gaz at Annapolis; Balt American, the Telegraphs; Nat'l Intell; Mr Smith's paper at Easton; Mr Bartgiss's paper at Frederick-Town; & Mr Grieves's paper at Hager's Town. By order, Ninian Pinkney, clk.

Sen & Hse of Reps, sums appropriated: Annuity granted to chldrn of late Col John Harding & Maj Alexander Trueman, passed May 14, 1800, sum of $600.

WED, MAR 9, 1803
Wash Co, DC-petition of Richd Wilson, insolvent debtor, confined in Wash Co jail for debt, offers all his property, rl & mixed, to pay his debts. -Uriah Forrest, clk. Same for Nathaniel Seger, insolvent debtor, as above.

Appointments by Pres of U S:
Robt E Cochran, of SC, Marshal of SC, vice Chas B Cochran, rsgnd;
Jos Wood, Nw Terr, Reg of land ofc-Marietta, vice Perigrine Foster, rsgnd;
John Lelman, of Nw Terr, Comm for persons claiming lands under John Cleves Syires, vice W Goforth, resgnd;
Danl Bissell, of Indiana Terr, Coll for Dist of Massac & Inspec of Rev for Port of Massac, vice Wm Chricles, remv'd;
David Ker, of Miss Terr, to be Judge in NW Terr, vice Danl Felton rsgnd;
Jas Anderson, of SC, Comm agent for Port of Crete, France;
Isaac Coxe Barnet, of NJ, Comm agent at Antwerp;
Aaron Vale, of NY, Comm agent of U S at L'orient, France;
Thos Loveil, of Boston, Comm agent at La Rochelle;
Levett Harris, of Pa, Consul at Rotterdan;
John Martin Baker, of NY, Cnsl for Minerca Islands, Majorca & Yvica;
Marian Lemar, of Md, Consul for Madeira Island;
Wm Patterson, of NY, Comm agent at Nantz, France;
Wm H Harrison, re-apptd Gov of Indiana Terr;
Thos T Davis, of Ky, a Judge in Indiana Terr, vice W Clarke, decd;

Jesse Spencer, of Ohio, Reg of land ofc at Chilicothe, vice Thos Worthingotn, resigned;
Isaac Illsley Jr, of Mass, Coll for Dist of Portland, vice Nathaniel T Fosdeck, remv'd;
Isaac Dayton, of NY, Surv & Inspec of Port of Hudson, vice I C Tenbroeck, remv'd;
Joel Burt, of NY, Coll & Inspec for Oswego;
Thos Dudley, of NC, Srvy for Swansborough Port, vice A Carmalt, decd;
Chas Willing Byrd, of Ohio, Judge of Ohio Dist;
Michael Baldwin, of Ohio, Atty for same;
David Zeigler, of Ohio, Marshal of Dist of Ohio;
Cato West, of Miss Terr, Sec of Terr, vice John Steele, term expired
Zachariah Stevens, of Mass, Surv & Inspec for Gloucester Port, vice Samuel Whittemore, remv'd;
Jos Story, of Mass, Naval ofcr for Salem & Beverly, vice W Pickman, remv'd;
John Heard, of NY, Inspec of Rev, Perth Amboy Port;
Wm Brewer, of NC, Srvy & Inspec-Nixenton Port, vice Hugh Knox, rsgnd;
Horebrowse Trist, Coll for Miss Dist, vice John F Carmichael.

Richmond, Va, Mar 2. Ctzn meeting on Feb 28; Robt Mitchell, Chrmn; Saml Coleman, Sec; Committee: Jos Scott, Meriwether Jones, Saml Pleasants, Benj Tate, Lewis Harvie, Wm Moseley, John H Foushee, Jacob I Cohen, Wm Price, Gervas Storrs, Jos Selden, Henry L Biscoe & Benj Hatch. Wm Lindsay to deliver an oration & Capt Myers & his Company of Artl, to assist in celebration on Mar 4th.

FRI MAR 11, 1803
Orphans Crt of PG Co, Md. Mar 10, 1803. Prsnl est of Jos Cooke, late of PG Co, decd. -Robt Brown, Thos Wilson-adms.

NY, Mar 3. Capt Wm Brooks of the ship *Sally*, arrv'd at Havanna.

MON MAR 14, 1803
Broke jail-Jas Essex, age abt 30 yrs; $50 reward.
                              -N. Smith, Sherriff, Calvert Co, Md.

Hse of Reps: Relief of Moses White, adjust & settle the claim of Moses for his additonal pay & emoluments as Aid-De-Camp to Brig Genrl Moses Hazen from Aug 1 1781 to Nov 3, 1783.

WED MAR 16, 1803
For sale: prop of late John Fitzgerald, decd, in Alexandria, Va.-Thos A Diggs & Jas Keith, acting excs of J Fitzgerald.

FRI MAR 18, 1803
Opened-a hse of entertainment on the causeway in Gtwn, at Sign of the Golden Square & Compass, cld "Mechanics Hall". -Andrew McDonald.

Supreme Crt of U S, Feb Term, 1803. Wm Marbury v Jas Madison, Sec of State of the U S. at Dec 1801 term, Wm Marbury, Dennis Marbury, Dennis Ramsay, Robt Townsend Hooe & Wm Harper, by Cnsl, Chas Lee, late Atty Genrl of the U S, mv'd the Crt for a rule to Jas Madison, to show cause why a Mandamus shd not issue commanding him to deliver to them their commissions as Justices of the Peace in the Dist of Columbia.

Mon Mar 21, 1803
Creditors of Jas Robinson, decd, late of Wash Co; distribution to creditors with vouchers. -Lewin Talburtt, adm.

Wed Mar 23, 1803
Lost-red morocco pkt bk, $140 in bank notes. -Anthony Holmead, living nr Gtwn.

Fri Mar 25, 1803
Reward-$30 for return of a mare, saddled & bridled, stolen in Wash City, nr the Navy Yard. -Ebenezer Nesmith, Wash City.

Orphans Crt of Wash Co, DC. Mar 24, 1803. Prsnl est of Jas Dennis, late of frig *Congress* in said co, decd. -Jas Anderson, adm.

Chancery [Md], sale: rl est of late Thos Clark, of Gtwn, decd; lot 13 in Gtwn; lot 4 in Gtwn; lots in Wash City; also lots in Gtwn, purchased by Clark from John M Gantt. -Jas S Morsel, trust.

To let: dwelling hse, lately occupied by Messrs Howard & Varden, N & 3d Sts, nr Barry's Wharf. Apply to Capt Jos Wheat, nr the premises or to Ephraim Mills, Duke St, Alex.

Mon Mar 28, 1803
Sale by auction-2 story brick hse & lot of Mr Jas Knight, Sq 651, Carrollsburgh, Wash; subject to a payment of L112 Md currency, to Danl Carroll of Dud'n esq & 50 acs of land nr Nanticoke River, Eastern Shore, Md; also all the hsehld furn of Jas Knight. -J Connor, auct. Gtwn.

Wed Mar 30, 1803
Caution-Forewarn all persons from trusting Eliz Tait on my acc't; I am determined not to pay any debts of her; her impropriety has occasioned a separation. -Jas Tait.

Fri Apr 1, 1803
Phil, Mar 28. Sat last the city was alarmed by a fire in a 3 story brick bldg occupied by Mr Plowman as a printing ofc; Thos Bradford Jr, Atty at Law, jumped from the 2d flr & sprained his ancle & wrist; others rescued were-Mr C P Wayne, printer & Mr Jones, cbnt-mkr.

Died: Mann Page, esq, age 54 yrs, Mar 22, at his seat in Mannsfield; widow & orphan survive. -Virginia Herald.

MON APR 4, 1803

"Wild Medley" a running horse will stand in Wash City, to be let to mares at $25 per season; purchased of Mr Stubblefield, of Gloucester Co, Va, by W Thornton. [-Meaux Thornton, Col Lewis Burwell-Jan 14, 1801; Wm Johnson, Ralph Wormeley Jr, John Wood-Mar 1803; John Taylor, esq, of Mt Airy, Wm Johnston-Mar 4, 1803-Signed statements.]

Treaty was held on Jun 30, 1802 bet the Senaca Indians & the U S at Buffaloe Creek, Ontario Co, NY; John Tayler comr apptd to hold same; sum of $1200 pd by Oliver Phelps, Isaac Bronson & Horatio Jones for tract of land cld *Little Beard's Reservation*-1280 acs. Signed: John Thomson, Jas W Stephens, Israel Chapin; & Jasper Parrish, interpreter. Seal-Feb 7, 1803: Th Jefferson, Pres; Jas Madison, Sec of State.

WED APR 6, 1803

Tan-Bark wanted; from $6 to $8 a cord. -Christian Kurtz, Thos Hyde, Baker & Daws, Gtwn.

Convention at Paris, relative to the indemnities of the Grand Duke of Tuscany was signed Dec 26, 1802 by: Philip Cobentzel, Jos Bonaparte & Count Markoff.

Inspection of State Prison report-signed on Feb 11, 1803 by: Robt Bowne, Thos Franklin, Leon. Bleecker, W Vew, John Murray Jr, Geo Warner, Thos Eddy.
                            -New York State Prison.

Judges & Justices against whom complaints have been preferred to the Hse of Reps of Pa. Alex'r Addison-rmv'd.
John McDowell, Assoc Judge of Alleg Co-not decided.
Fredk Haymaker, Justice of Crawford Co, not decided.
Saml Daird & John Creigh, Assoc Judges of Cumberland Co-acquitted.
Wm Clingan, Justice of Chester Co-admitted.
David Witmer, Justice of Lancaster Co, removal addressed.
Mich'l Brobst, Justice of Berks, do. do. do.
Jjohn Ryerson, Assoc Justice of Wayne-do. do. do.
Benj Jacobs, Assoc Judge of Chester-do. do. do.
Saml Preston & Saml C Seely, Assoc Judges of Wayne Co-not decided. Henry Work, Justice of Franklin Co-acquitted.
Jonathan Cutler, Justice of Allegany Co-not decided.
1-Petitions presented for removal of Jas Anderson, Justice of Erie Co; 2-& pet. for removal of Jacob Adams, Justice of Peace in Adams Co.

FRI APR 8, 1803

For sale: Bell Plains & Hickory Bottom, late the prop & resid of Geo Lee Waugh, decd, in Stafford Co, Va. Apply to Carey Seldon, nrby, & John Sweetman will show the Hickory Bottom tract. -Gawin Corbin Turberille, King Geo Co, Doegg.

Mon Apr 11, 1803
Citizens attached to 4th Co, commanded by Capt Geo Andrews, to meet Apr 16, armed & equipped. -J C O'Reilly, Scott.

Va Election: John Clopton, Rpblcn, re-elected a mbr of Congress from Va; in Frederick Co, Genrl Smith, Rpblcn, had 554 votes & Jos Sextion had 154 votes; at Spotsyyvania Crt Hse, John Dawson was elected a mbr of the Hse o/Reps, Genrl Brooke-State Senator, & L Stanard & D C Ker, Delegates.

Wed Apr 13, 1803
London. Execution of conspirators: Col Edw Marcus Despard, J Wood, J Francis, Thos Broughtou, J Sedgwick Wratten, J A Graham, & J MacNamara. Warrant given Feb 16, 1803, in 43d yr of our reign by his Majesty's Command. [Signed] Pelham.

Lexington, Mar 29. Mar 21st, the share holders in the Vineyard Co met at the hse of Capt John Poltlethwait, in Lex., & elected the following directors:

John Bradford	Wm MacBean	Andrew McCalla
Jas McCoun	Benj Stout	Saml Brown
Geo Anderson	John A Seitz	Thos Hart Jr
Henry Marshal	Robt Patterson	Walker Baylor

Fri Apr 15, 1803
Partnership bet Robt Miller & John Douglas, mutually dissolved.

Committed to Wash jail: Solomon, negro, runaway, says he is the prop of Gerard B Casine, of Chas Co, Md. Also negro, Kate, formerly prop of Jas Keith, of Alex; says she ran away from Geo Wall, of Carolina; age abt 18 yrs. Rob't McClan, jailor, for Danl C Brent, mrsh'l for DC.

Boston, Mass. Election: for Gov-Caleb Strong 1864 votes & Elbridge Gerry 881; for Lt Gov-Edw H Robbins 1661 votes & Jas Bowdoin 1093.

Mon Apr 18, 1803
In Chancery-petition of John Thomas, 3d, of Montg Co; praying benefit of act for relief of sundry insolvent debtors. -Saml H Howard, Reg CC

Wed Apr 20, 1803
In Chancery. Atty Genrl at relation & instance of Wm Lodge & Alexander Adams v Thos Orme & Thos Beall of Geo. Bill is to vacate a grant issued to Thos Beall of Geo, for land cld *Prospect Valley* in Montg Co, or to obtain a conveyance to the relaters included in cert of survey, cld *Hard to Come At*, for account of the profits thereof. T Orme antidated a survey; survey made to Beall, survey made for the use & benefit of Orme, then a Deputy Surveyor of Montg Co. Beall resides in DC. -Saml H Howard, Reg CC

Orphans Crt of Wash Co, DC. Apr 18, 1803. Prsnl Est of Jas Sellers & also of Andrew Rutherford, both late of Wash Co, decd.   -David Waterstone, exc.

Died: Hon Josiah Smith, age 66, Apr 1, of small pox, at Pembroke, mbr of late Congress; s/o late Rev Thos S of that place; ofcr in our Rev Army; leaves a widow & 8 chldrn.

FRI APR 22, 1803
Stone-cutters wanted to work at the Capitol. -Geo Blagden

MON APR 25, 1803
Lottery-$5000, Phil city; for finishing the navigation of the Lehigh. Tkts-$5: Geo Taylor Jr, Wm Blackburn, Edw Stow, Jas Greenworth, all of Chestnut St, Phil, Pa.

Va election for Reps in Congress.
Shenandoah Co-Genrl John Smith.
Jefferson Co-Jas Stephenson, Fed; Osborne Sprigg, Rpblcn.
Harden Co-Mr Van Meter & David Holmes.
Jas City-Burwell Bassett & Thos Griffin.
New Kent Co: John Clopton & Jas Rind.
Caroline Co: Col New & Col Taylor.
In Brunswick Dist the candidates are: Col Thos Claiborne & Dr Richd Field

WED APR 27, 1803
Died: Mrs Ann Fenton Brent, w/o Daniel Carroll Brent, of Wash, Apr 25.

Ltr from Jos Barrell, esq, to Sec of the Mass Agric Soc; dated *Pleasing Hill*, Jan 1, 1803; Subj-culture of potatoes.

FRI APR 29, 1803
Recommenced the lumber bus. on Tiber's Crk -Brohawn & Byus.

Vine Co, Pa, has purchased 65 acs at Spring Hill, Montg Co; Subscriptions are $20 a share; Apply to Benj Say, 152 Chestnut St [Pres]; Mgrs: Jas Mease, 109 Spruce St; Saml Hodgdon, 126 Mulberry, Sassafras;   Elisha Fisher, 36 North Front;   Elias Yarnall, 39 High St.   -Isaac W Morris, Pear St, treas.

MON MAY 2, 1803
Carpenters & labourers wanted to work on Eastern Branch of the Potomak.
-Wm Brent, Treas of Eastern Branch Bridge Co.

Elected mbrs of the Americ Philo Soc, in Phil, Apr 15:
Jean Baptiste; Jos De Lambre, a Sec of the Nat'l Institute of France;
Danl Melanderhjelm, Prof of Astronomy & mbr of the Swedish Acad;
Eric Prosperin, Univ of Upfal;   Benj Dearborn of Boston;   Francis Nichols, of Phil.

Committed to jail of Balt, Jacob, negro, abt 23 yrs of age; says he belongs to Mr Robt Hodgson, of Ga.   -Jas Wilson-Shrf.

WED MAY 4, 1803
John Willis intends commencing the practice of medicine on Pa Ave.

Ltr dated Eddyville, Mar 10, 1803. Re: murder of Chickasaw Indian in said town on Mon last; Matthew Cook, J Furguson & Reuben Cook were apprehended-M Cook escaped-2 are in jail; murder took place in the yard of Mr J W Throop.

FRI MAY 6, 1803
In Chancery-sales made by John Hewitt, as reported, Aug 20, of certain lots in Wash, prop of Peter Cassenave, decd, to be ratified; lots 23 thru 26 Sq 105-$767.51-2.   -Saml H Howard, Reg CC

MON MAY 9, 1803
Died: John F Hamtramock, esq, Apr 11, at Detroit, Col of 1st Regt, USA; ntv of Canada, joined Amerc Army in 1775, cont'd in the svc for 27 yrs.

Americ vessels left in the port of Spain, Island of Trinidad Mar 28, 1803:
Schnr *Plutis*, of & for Boston, John Adamson, Mstr;
Brig *Thos Jefferson*, of Machias for Boston, Danl Elliot, Mstr;
Brig *Peter*, of & for Newburyport, Peter Le Briton, do;
Brig *John*, of & for ditto, John Knap, do;
Brig *Alex'r & Sally*, of & for ditto, Stanwood, do;
Brig *Portland*, of & for Portland, Tucker, do;
Brig *NewHaven*, of & for do, Bunkers, Mstr;
Schnr *Emma*, of & for Marblehead, Jos Girdler, Mstr;
Schnr *Paragan*, of & for NY, B Dodge, Mstr;
Schnr *Rising Sun*, of & for NY, Henry Rippely, Mstr;
Schnr [not recollected], of & for NY, Kingstand, Mstr;
Schnr *Yeofrem*, of & for Edenton, NC, Carpenter, Mstr;
Schnr *Surecia*, of & for Yarmouth, Cither, Mstr;
Schnr *Little Tom*, of Charlestown for NY, King, Mstr;
Schnr *Eleanor's Cargo* for Messrs Brent & Thorn, of Wash City.

WED MAY 11, 1803
Died: Mrs Diana Maria Ray, w/o Jas Ray, esq, & d/o late Col Strahan of British Army, May 8, in Wash; leaves her absent husband & 2 infants.

Mrd: John C Dickson, of Wash, to Eliz Raser, of Fredericktown, by Rev Mr Knox, May 1.

Orphans Crt of Wash Co, DC. May 10, 1803. Prsnl est of Thos Rose, late of said city, decd.   -Mary Rose, admx.

Ran away-dark mulatoe French girl, abt 15 yrs of age, not long in this country.
-L Demun, from Mr Xaupi, nr the Bank.

Fri May 13, 1803

Died: Isaac Bloom, of Clinton town, in Dutchess Co; Judge of Crt of Common Pleas, mbr of Hse of Reps, elected last fall.

Died: Gen Stephens Thos Mason, May 10, at Phil, a Rep of Va in Congress of U S; in Phil for medical treatment; husband & parent.

For sale: 390 acs in Montg Co, Md, nr Mr Wm Darnes's; Henry Jones on the premises. -Ben W Jones & Henry Jones.

Mon May 16, 1803

Notice: petition of John Barber, debtor, confined in Wash jail; praying for act of relief of insolvent debtors.   -Uriah Forrest, clk.

John G Jackson, Rpblcn, is elected to Congress for Harrison, Va.

Wed May 18, 1803

Reward-$20 for Moses, negro, who left my svc. -Asil Spalding, Chas Co, nr Port Tobacco, Md.

Phil, May 14. Tue last, the remains of the late Genrl Stephens Thomson Mason, of Va, were interred in the Burial Ground of the Prot Episc Chr, in Arch St, bet 4th & 5th Sts, & deposited nr those of the late Henry Tazewell, esq, a Senator & Colleague of Genrl Mason. The procession mv'd from the hse of Mr Jas O Ellers, crnr of 4th & Spruce Sts; the Militia Legion commanded by Gen Shee was in the advance . Burial svc was by Bishop White.

Boston Election. 7 Reps were elected: Harrison G Otis, John Lowell, Jonathan Hunnewell, Saml Parkman, Wm Smith, Wm Brown & John Philips. Also on the tkt: Jas Bowdoin, David Tilden, Russel Sturgus, Nath'l Fellows, Ahial Smith & Chas Paine.

Fri May 20, 1803

Public sale of ware hse & wharf, occupied by Messrs Steuart & Beall; crnr of Frederick & Key's St in Gtwn; sale, for money due from late Francis Lewis Taney. -J Mason, Gtwn.

Raising of Va wheat by Justin Ely, esq, of West Springfield; purchased land on West Bank of Connecticut Rvr in Oct 1798; article continues on his crops & soil, etc.

Mon May 23, 1803

Proclamation by Gov John Francis Mercer, of Md; $400 reward for perpetrators of murder & robbery of Adam Wable, paper mkr, aged ctzn of Anne Arundel Co, Md, Mar 13 last.

Massachusetts Soc voted that a gold medal be presented to Hon David Humphreys for introducing the Merino breed of sheep from Spain into this country. A premium of $100 or a gold medal to Col Robt Dodge of Ipswich, for his experiments in raising forest trees from seed.   -John Avery, Sec.

Cornelius P Van Ness & Danl C Holiday, esqs, were licensed as Attys & Cnslrs at Law of the State of Md.

WED MAY 25, 1803
Scheme of a lottery for use of Holy Trinity Chr, for Religious Soc of German Roman Catholics in Phil city-1st prize is $10,000.   Com'rs: Adam Premir, Anthony Hoockey, Chas Bouman. Tkts for sale: Matthew McConnell & Geo Taylor Jr, No. 82 & 67 Chestnut St.

FRI MAY 27, 1803
Died: Wm Smith, late Provost of College of Phil, at Phil.

Ltr from Mr Simpson, Cnsl of the U S, at Tangier to Sec of State, dated Mar 28, 1803. Yesterday, Thos Beck & David Ervin late seamen belonging to the schr *Betsey* of Norfolk, Va, arrv'd here from Morocco; they will be sent to Gibraltar. On Mar 3d, John Brodie of the *Betsey* was redeemed by Mr Gwyn at Mogadore. The mate, Chas Rivers, was drowned & mstr Saml Shore died on the beach on the coast of Africa.

Died: at Boston, John Codman.

David Wily is librarian at Columbian Lib, annual dues $2.

Gov of SC notifies that Thos Lowndes, Wm Butler, Benj Huger, Wade Hampton, Richd Winn, Levi Carney, Thos Moore & John Earle, esqs, are elected Reps in the Congress of the U S from S C.

MON MAY 30, 1803
Francis Donnelly, schoolmaster, late from Phil, to open school on Monday next, nr the West Mkt. Wash City.

Wash City Cncl apptd the following ctzns Assoc Judges of Election: Alex'r McCormick, Griffith Coombes, Leonard Harbaugh, John Willis, Jos Hodgson & Joel Brown.

WED JUN 1, 1803
Wash City: Samuel N Smallwood declines being a candidate for City Council, work at Navy Yd requires his attention. Geo Blagden also declines being a candidate for Council.

Sarah Collins, living nr the Navy Yd lost a milk cow; Jas Flurty, living on Capitol Hill, lost a black horse.

Ranaway: John, negro, abt 27 yrs of age, from Jos Griffiss, living in Calvert Co, Md.

FRI JUN 3, 1803

Richd Frazer, Washington, Jun 1st; declines a nomination for the city cnsl as he is engaged in an active public station which engages the whole of his time.

Died: Sir Wm Hamilton, Apr 5, of diarrhea, at his hse in Piccadilly, age 73 yrs.
-London Paper

For sale: lot & brick hse where Mr Adam King now keeps store, on High St, Gtwn.   -Philip B Key.

Partnership of Geo Quinn & Thos Simms is dissolved with mutual consent. Payments to Geo Quinn, Wash City. [Groceries]

MON JUN 6, 1803

Died: Capt Herod, shot & scalped by Indians, while at work in his field, May 20. -Chillicothe

Chas Cotesworth Pinckney & family has arrv'd from Boston.

Dist of Col, Jun 3. Crt Martial, Maj John P Van Ness, Pres; Trial of Ensign Thos West Peyton of the 1st Bat of the 2d Legion of the Militia of DC, on charges against him by Capts Lynn, Lyles, Scott & Geiger; Peyton & Mr Jos Mandeville Jr did conduct themselves in conduct unbecoming an ofcr & gentleman; charges not supported & Peyton is acquitted & released from arrest.
-Brig Gen John Mason, Joshua Wingate Jr, Brig Maj & Inspec of Militia of D C.

WED JUN 8, 1803

Matthias Hart, gun-mkr, commenced business, in the hse lately occupied by Mr Robertson, nr Mr Hertford's Distillery, Pa Ave, Wash.

Mbrs of the Council, Wash City elected:
Wm Brent	John P Van Ness	John Hewitt
Saml H Smith	Nicholas King	Chas Minisie
Benj More	Danl Carroll	Danl Rapine
Joel Brown	Geo Hadfield	Jos Hodgson

Not elected:	Jas Hoban	Chas Jones
Henry Herford	Wm Prout	Griffith Combe
Peter Lenox	David Peter	

Pres of U S has apptd Robt Brent, Mayor of Wash, for ensuing year.

FRI JUN 10, 1803

Notice: Oath of insolvent debtor to be administered to Israel Loring.
                    -Uriah Forrest, clk.

Mon Jun 13, 1803
Ranaway-Anna Mingo, age 20 yrs, negro, from John L Jennings, Cool Springs; former prop of Saml Maddox, St Mary's Co, Md.

Freemen of Connecticut. Hartford, May 31, 1803. Persons to be supported for nomination:

Oliver Elswort	Henry Champion	C Goodrich
Wm Hilhouse	Wm Edmond	Jabez Clark
Stephen T Hosmer	Elizur Goodrich	John Chester
Aaron Austin	Roger Newbury	Simeon Baldwin
Shubael Abbe	Mathew Griswold	David Daggett
Nath'l Smith	Jonathan Brace	Jonathan Barnes
	Jos Walker	John Allen

Ltr regarding trial for defamation, at Norfolk Co Crt in Eng; Col Wm Tooke Harwood, dfndnt; Col H lost his fr early in life & was taken into Sir Edw Astley's hse [now late]; accomplished himself the same as the present Sir Jacob Astley, s/o Sir Edw; Sir Edw mrd twice. Trial was bet Sir Jacob & Col H.
-Signed-A Mechanic.

Col John Taylor, of Caroline, elected to Senate of U S, by Executive Council of Va, vice Gen Mason, decd.

Wed Jun 15, 1803
Patent made out & signed by the Pres., to Gurdon F Saltonstall, of Fayetteville, NC: invention of new principle in ginning cotton.

To let: for 1 or 2 yrs, the hse where I now live, F St, opposite the Bank.
-Mary Sweeny, Wash City.

Fri Jun 17, 1803
Strayed or stolen at Wash, a bay horse; was formerly owned by Col Simpson & Capt Gassaway-Montg Co, Md.   -Clotworthy Stephenson.

Brattleborough, Jun 6. Gen Martin Chittenden is elected to rep the N W Dist of this state in next Congress; he had 400 votes over Col Hay.

Mon Jun 20, 1803
Committed to jail of Balt, runaway, John Philip Worm, German, abt 23 yrs of age, baker, says he belongs to Messrs Blair & Valkman, living in Lombard St, Phil. -Jas Wilson, sheriff.

PG Co, Upper Marlboro, Apr 13, 1803. Meeting of Rpblcn ctzns: Thos Contee, chrmn; Trueman Tyler, sec. Committee: Stephen West, Leonard Covington, Thos Ducker, Clement Dyer & John M Gantt. Support will be for: Robt Bowie, Archibald Vanhorn, Peter Wood & Stephen West, esqs.

Univ of Pa, Jun 11, 1803. Commencement held on Thu last;
Bach of Arts was conferred on: John Fox, Geo Gray Leiper, John McAllister, Abraham Shoemaker & Saml Wilcocks
Master of Arts: Edw Shippen Burd, John C Brown, David Jackson, Rev John Johnson, Hartman Kuhn, Alernon S Magaw, John S Oswald
Dr of Med: Henry Ashton, Robt Carter, Wm Dawney, Jas Hutchinson, Thos Maffie, John S Mitchell, Oliver H Spencer, Garret E Pendegraft, Franklin Scott, Como G Stephenson, John R Young, John M Walker, Thos Walmsley, Danl Wilson, Robt Holmes.
Dr of Divinity: Rev John Blair Linn, pastor of 1st Presby Chr in this city.

JUN 22, 1803
Ezekiel Dance of Chesterfield Co, Va, nr Petersburg, has horses & colts for sale.

Pblc sale: part of prsnl est of late Collen Williamson, decd.
-Mgt Williamson, admx

J Gardner instructs in arithmetic, bk-kpg, etc. Mrs Gardiner teaches needle work, tambouring, etc. President's Square, brdg & day schools, Wash City.

FRI JUN 24, 1803
Farm for sale: Jefferson Co, Va, nr Harpers Ferry, 580 acs, shown by tenant, Geo North, at Charlestown.   -Jos Nourse-Gtwn.

Jun 23d the corner stone of the Washington Theatre was laid by John P Van Ness. -Wash City.

MON JUN 27, 1803
Mrd: Mr Benjamin Waters, of Montg Co, to Miss Mary Finagan, of Wash, Jun 23, by Rev Mr Long.

Meeting was held on Jun 23d at the hse of Mr P D Stelle, Wash City, to make arrangements for 4th of Jul celebration; Committee: Robt Brent, Judge Kilty, Danl Carroll of Dud, Thos Munroe, Col Burrows, Capt Caffin, Saml H Smith, Maj Van Ness & Capt Tingey.

WED JUN 29, 1803
Ranaway at Lancaster, Pa, negro, Lester, age abt 20 yrs. Wm Barton, Lancaster.

John Bristow, mbr of the Brd of Trade, lately died at Calcutta, worth two million of pds sterling; s/o a tradesman in Devonshire, Eng; Mrs Bristow introduced eastern fashion in dress.

FRI JUL 1, 1803
Bridge across the Delaware, soon to be carried into effect; Mr Timothy Palmer, celebrated New Eng bridge bldr, presented an estimate of the cost-not over $80,000; & the fittest scite.-Phil Paper.

Reward-$5 for Edmond, negro boy.   -Richard Frazer, Wash.

Mon Jul 4, 1803
Runaway committed to Balt goal, Ellick, mulatto man, age abt 27 yrs; says he belongs to Mr John Harris Upshear, living in Essex Co, nr Holmes's Hole, Va. -Jas Wilson, Sheriff.

Guyton Morveau in 1773 experimented in fumigating with muriatic & sulphuric acids to cleanse the church at Dijon of morbid matter which arose on opening the sepulchral vaults. In England Dr Carmichal Smyth practised the same at the hospital at Winchester.

Literary Fair. New York-Jun 25. Mathew Carey, President.

Wed Jul 6, 1803
Committed as run away, negro, Ellick Thompson, abt 30 yrs of age; lately sold by Peter Becraft of Balt Co to person unknown. -Laurence Brengle, sheriff, Frederick Co, Md.

Fri Jul 8, 1803
Ladies with ltrs in the Wash Post ofc, Jul 1, 1803:

Mrs Eliza Alexander	Miss Mary Clarke c/o Saml Boots
Phebe Casey at Richd Charle's	Mgt Davis
Madame Elwis	Mrs Butler Lee
Miss Mary Mitchell [2]	Eliz Stone
Mary Santoreous	Miss Gracy Turner
Widow Wilson	

O Che Upo-Faw, on Coosau Rvr, May 30. On May 24th the Seminolies & other Chiefs in opposition with their leader arrvd. W A Bowles at their head arrv'd on the 28th. Bowles was apprehended & sent in irons under guard of Indians to Gov Tolch of Pensacola for his crimes.
-Benj Hawkins, his Excellency Gov Milledge, Ga.

Capt Walter Jones Jr delivered an address at the Fourth of July celebration in the town of Alexandria.

Mon Jul 11, 1803
Ltr to expel the slander against my son, John G Jackson, born Sep 22, 1777 in Hardy Co, Va; his mthr remv'd to Backannon in this county bec of the Indian War; I escaped to Clarksburg with my small family; my son resides there; my son was elected to Rep the Co of Harrison in Legislature of Va for 3 yrs in 1798, during the last yr he mrd; a Miss Triplett charged that he had violated a marriage promise to her & was awarded $400 damages, upon oath of her sr-in-law, Mrs Triplett.   -Geo Jackson, Harrison Co, Va. May 23, 1803.

Ranaway at Warburton, the seat of Thos A Digges; negro-Moses, abt 26 yrs of age; $10 reward.   -Thos A Digges.

Law Intelligence: Frances A Triplett v John G Jackson, alledged breach of marriage promise. Sept Term, 1802, Dist Crt of Va, Monongalia Crt hse before Archibald Stewart, Judge of Genrl Crt. Hedgman Triplett, bro of Frances, never heard any declaration to marry his sister; Mrs Williams is sister to the dfndnt; "Jury thought proper to believe her". [next article]

Publication appeared in the Wash Telegraphe of Trial bet Frances E Triplet & John G Jackson, in which Adam Hickman is a witness with a preface that he is a man of low & infamous character, we certify that he is a man of upright disposition & of unblemished character. Apr 20, 1803. Alison Clark, Thos Haymond, Micajah Barkley, Maxwell Armstrong. Benj Wilson Jr have found him punctual, fair & honorable. Wm G Payne, Morgantown, May 19th, 1803- was one of the counsel of Mr Jackson & took notes upon the trial.

WED JUL 13, 1803
Ross Co, Ohio, election for Rep to Congress: Elias Langham-459 votes; Jeremiah Morrow-400; Michael Baldwin-210; Wm McMillan-30; Republicans except for McMillian, Fed.

Phil, Jul 6. Anniversary of Nat'l Indep. *Militia* under Genrl Shee;
First Div: Maj Jonas Simons;
Troop of Horse-Capt Leiper; Rifle Corps-Huff;
Lt Infty Co-J M Irwin.
Brass Field Piece: Co of Artl-Goodman; Infty Corps-Ruth;
Infty-Lyle.
Drums & Fifes & Colors of First Div: New Infty Corps-Waterman; Infty Corps-Lloyd; Infty-Fotterall.
2d Div: Maj Thos Willis; artl w. brass field piece.
Infty-Capt Sweeney; Infty-Duane; Infty-Montgomery;
Bat Co of 80th Regt-Dazell.
Drums & Fifes, 2d Div: New Infty Corps-Capt Fox;
Rifle rangers, New Corps-Seyfert; Infty Corps-Cope;
Infty-Simington.
Brass Field Piece-Corps of Atrl-Souder; Rifle Corps-Snyder;
Troop of Horse-Lt Shaeffer. Same was celebrated at Geo Mevers's in Vine St.

FRI JUL 15, 1803
Committee of Washington Theatre is to meet at hse of Wm Levell, Pa Ave. J P Van Ness request payment of 3d installment-$10.

Tobias Lear is apptd Cnsl Genrl to the Barbary Powers & is expected, with his sec & family, in Boston to take passage in the frig *Constellation*, Cmdor Preble.

Saml Flagg, Abraham Lincoln & Francis Blake are apptd comr's of bankruptcy for the Dist of Massachusetts.

Mon Jul 18, 1803
Committed to PG goal, Jack, abt 22 yrs of age, black, says he was sold by Jos Griffiths, of Calvert Co, Md, to person from whom he escaped.
-Thos Macgill, sheriff, PG Co, Md.

Appointments to ofc- Cabinet ofcrs: Henry Dearborn of Mass; Levi Lincoln of Mass; Albert Gallatin of Pa; Robt Smith of Md; Jas Madison of Va.
Foreign Mnstrs: Mr Livingston of NY; Mr King of Mass; Mr Pinckney of SC.
Ofcrs in other depts: Gideon Granger of Conn; Abraham Bradley of New Eng; Gabriel Duval of Md; Wm Miller of Pa; Richd Harrison of Va; Jos Nouse of Pa; Thos T Tucker of SC; Wm Simmons of NY; Thos Turner of Md.

Wed Jul 20, 1803
Ranaway, Frank, negro, blacksmith, from Richard Stuart living at Popis Creek, Westmoreland Co, Va.

Jackson Douglass, insolvent debtor, confined in Wash Co goal, prays for relief.

Geo Quinn has opened an auction rm on F St, nr the Pres' Hse.

Fri Jul 22, 1803
Boston, Mass.-Americ Indep: procession escorted by the cadet co under Col Welles; Rev Mr Baldwin gave the prayer; Wm Sullivan gave the oration. Apptd-Dr Chas Jarvis-Pres; Russell Sturgis, Benj Austin Jr, & Nath'l Fellows-VP; Jacob Austis, Eben Rhoades, Thos Lewis Jr-Mrshls. Maj Arazer's Co & Capt Sohonnot's Co of Artl, under Mr Jennings, partook in the celebration.

For sale: 150 acs nr Eastern Branch Ferry. -Michael Lowe.

Mon Jul 25, 1803
For sale-tract of land nr the ft of the Blue Ridge & Short Hills in Loudon Co. Va; 2340 acs. Thos Alwood Digges, Warburton, nr Alex. Or Jas McIheney nr the premises or John Janney, mrchnt-Alex.

Runaway, negro boy, Jonathan, says he belongs to Wm Husk, nr Battletown, Va. -Laurence Brengle, Sheriff, Frederick Co.

Annapolis Gaz: 4th of Jul Anniv-salutes by Capt John Muir & Capt Richd Harwood; the 2 companies were reviewed by Gov John Mercer.

Wed Jul 27, 1803
Died: Genrl Josiah Tutuall Jr, late Gov of Ga, at Nassau, NP, Jun 6.

Com'rs apptd in Pa by Gov of Pa: Andrew Elliot, Robt Patterson & Benj Henry Latrobe; to lay down the best rte for cutting a canal, to unite the Dela & Chesapeake Bays..

FRI JUL 29, 1803

In Chancery-Md, Jul 11, 1803. Thos Johnson's creditors v his heirs' claims, viz-Patrick Magrath, Dr David Steward, Patrick Wheelen, & John Davidson, against est of said Thos Johnson, are not established to the Chancellor's satisfaction.   -Saml H Howard, Reg CC

Ltr to Thos McKean, Gov of Pa, from Thos Cooper, dated Wilkesbarre, Nov 18, 1803. Subj: Commerce.

A report on the obstructions in the Susquehannah, Dela & Lehigh-was given by Reading Howell, Frederick Antes, Wm Dean, Timothy Matlack, Saml McClay, John Adlum, Saml Boyd, Bartrain Galbreath, Thos Hulling, John Adlin & Benj Rittenhouse, 1790.

MON AUG 1, 1803

Anchor Tavern & Oyster Hse. [late the Fountain Inn]-Geo Pitt has taken the inn & solicits patronage & support.

Closing the affairs of est of late Daniel Carroll Sen. esq, of Rock Creek, Montg Co, Md. -John Carroll, Robt Brent, Wash.

WED AUG 3, 1803

For sale: painters colors of all sorts. Lewis Clephan, east of Branch Bank, F St, Wash City.

FRI AUG 5, 1803

Died: Louis, I King of Etruria, at Florence, Italy, May 27; elevated by Bonaparte in 1801.

Crct Crt of Wash Co, DC. U S v Benj More. Indicted for charging & receiving fees for performance of certain duties as Justice of Peace for Wash Co, DC. More confessed receipt of fees but said he was entitiled to them. Crt gave judgment in favor of the defendant.

Committed to goal of PG Co, Md: Richard, negro, abt 30 yrs of age; says he belongs to Genrl B Kersein nr Port Tobacco, Chas Co, Md; was hired by Mr O'Brien in Wash City.   -Thos Macgill, sheriff, PG Co, Md.

My wife, Mary Green Hardy, has absented herself from my bed & brd, without any cause whatever. I will not answer to her dealings from this date.
                    -Anthony Hardy.

MON AUG 8, 1803

The ship, *Chas Carter*, sailed from Norfolk on Jul 23d; 6 leagues from Cape Henry she was boarded by the British frig, *Boston*, Capt Douglass; Americ ctzns, Augustus Topham, Jos Hudson, Thos Hodgins & the carpenter were forced from the *Carter*; on Wed the Boston arvd in Hampton Rds. Topham swam to shore & related the above.

WED AUG 10, 1803
Ranaway at Eastern Branch Ferry, Wash: Abraham, negro, abt 28 yrs of age; formerly the prop of Dr Blake of Calvert Co, Md. -Levin Talburtt.

FRI AUG 12, 1803
Grand Jurors for Balt Co, Md:
Cornelius H Gist, Foreman;

John Brevitt	Henry Paysen	Robt Mickle
Geo Piestman	Richd Pearce	John McFaden
Jacob Site	Christopher Raborg	Jas Croxall
Thos Tenant	Wm Parks	John Fitz
Robt Stewart	Nath'l Moreton	Jacob Rogers
Nath'l Hynson	Wm Hawkins	Robt McKun
John Munmkhuysen	Henry Shoeder	Mark Pringle

Died: Rev John Young, age 40 yrs, Jul 24, of bilious fever, mbr of Associated Reformed Synod, pastor of United Congregation of Greencastle, West Conoco-Que & Great Cove, leaving a wife with 3 small chldrn & a 4th expected shortly.

Died: Isaac Story Jr, esq, of Rutland, at Marblehead, Aug 2.-Salem Reg.

MON AUG 15, 1803
Died: Mr Thos Tryon, age of 110, some of his friends say 120, at Coxsacke, NY.

P Peterson, Danish Charge D'affairs to U S has arvd at NY.

WED AUG 17, 1803
Died: Samuel Bishop, age 80 yrs, at New Haven, Coll of Port.

Trention True American of Aug 8. Tue last at Fleimington, Crt of Genrl Qrtr Sessions for this county, Judge Beavers presided; Jas J Wilson, Sr editor of this paper, entered a cmplnt in behalf of the State against Thos Coward, Garret D Wall, Peter Furman, Robt Armstrong, Enoch Green & Wm McKissick, for assault, battery & riot; only Coward was indicted-bail $200. John Vandergrist was foreman. On Wed last Thos Coward went before the Grand Jury & made cmplnt against Jas J Wilson for assault; evidence given by Garret D Wall, Enoch Green & Joshiah Fithian. Indictment not found by Grand Jury.

Died: Gen John Neville, age 72 yrs, Jul 29, at his seat on Montous' Isl.

FRI AUG 19, 1803
Orphans Crt of Wash Co, DC. Chas Hyde, made application for ltrs of admin on ests of Thos Keen, decd, a sldr in the late Capt D Britts Co of the _____ sublegion who died in 1795, & of Jonathan Coffin, decd, a soldier in Capt Kinsbury's Co.   -John Hewitt, Reg.

Peter Miller has commenced the Biscuit Bake Hse, nr the Sugar hse on NJ Ave, Wash City.

MON AUG 22, 1803
Scheme of a lottery to build a Cath Cathedral Chr in Balt City. Mgrs: Rt Rev Bishop Carroll, Rev Francis Beeston, Messrs-David Williamson, Robt Walsh, Chas Ghequiere, Patrick Bennet, Arnold Livers, Luke Tiernan, Francis Mitchell. Tkts also in the hands of Wm Brent & Jas D Barry.

Died: Mrs Lydia Story, Aug 9, in Wash, late of Charleston, nr Boston, consort of Wm Story, formerly of Boston, Mass. She leaves her sorrowful partner & 4 children.

In Chancery-Wash Co, Terr of Columbia. Chas Daight & John Blagge, & Edward W Laight, & the said Chas Laight, adm of Wm Laight, decd, cmplnts, against Geo Walker, dfndnt. Walker, on Jan 23, 1802, to secure payment of $18,820.26 to Wm & Chas Laight of NY, merchants, executed a bond for the same purpose, & the deed exhibited by the cmplnt. Bill is to foreclose any equity of redemption & obtain sale of premises. Walker does not reside in Wash but expected daily.   -Uriah Forrest, clk

WED AUG 24, 1803
Patent: Horizontal wind-mill, adapted to grinding all sorts of grain. John Baptiste Aveilhe, inventor, Havre De Grace, Md.

Geo Clymer is elected Pres of the Phil Bank.

FRI AUG 26, 1803
Info wanted of Francois Serraire, who was carried to Phil from Port of Marseilles by Capt Michel, abt 6 yrs ago, & his fr, an inhabitant of Digne in the department of Lower Alps, has not heard from him.

Died: Mr Redmond Barry, respectable ctzn, occasioned by the kick of a horse on his head.

Partnership of Wm Cherry & John Donnell, Wash City, is dissolved; conduct of Cherry such as to render measure necessary on my part.
                    -John Donnell, Wash City.

Orphans Crt of Calvert Co, Md, ltrs of adm, De Bonis Non in prsnl est of Robt Gover, late of Calvert Co, decd. Gassaway Pindell, of AA Co, A D B N, of Robt Gover, decd.

Fort St Stephens on the Rambigbee Rvr, Wash Co, Miss Terr; Jul 4th. The ctzns gathered at the hse of John McGrew, esq; Maj John Callier acted as VP; celebration of Americ Indep.

Mon Aug 29, 1803
Notice: Difference bet Mr Donnell & McIlvain will be settled in a Crt of Equity. -Wm Cherry. [See Fri Aug 26, 1803]

Wed Aug 31, 1803
5th Crct, Va Dist, May Term 1803:-Decree of said Crt to expose for public sale: *"Mt Salus"* alias *"Millthrope"*, Fairfax Co, on *Difficult & Wolf Trap Runs*, by deed 550 acs, by survey 673 acs. Capt Jas Wiley, residing nr the premises will show the land. -Chas Little, Jas Wiley, Jas Douglass.

Elected to srv in the next Congress for Ky: David Walker, John Boyle, Mathew Walton, Thos Sandford, John Fowler & G M Bedinger [all Rpblcns]

Fri Sep 2, 1803
For rent: 3-2 story brick hses in Wash City, North E St. -T H Gilliss, at the Navy ofc, Wash City.

Dist of Col. John Hand, mstr of the sloop *Hiland* of Phil, John Albright, Mate, & Mr Jos Hughes, passenger, appeared before Cleon Moore, Notary public for Alexandria, D C; sailed from Phil with rest of the crew & had on board, David Kitchell, ntv ctzn of the U S; on the 22d they fell in with the British ship, *Leander*, Capt Cain; Kitchell was impressed & not seen since. Signed: John Hand, John Albright, Jos Hughes-Alexandria, Aug 27, 1803.

Mon Sep 5, 1803
Edmund E Greenwell, adm, will make payment of distribution, among creditors of est of Robt Greenwell, of St Mary's Co, Md, decd, at Leonard town in St Mary's Co on Tue.

Lexington, Ky, Aug 16. Ctzns dined at Capt John Postlethwait's; celebrated the cession of La to the U S; John Bradford, Pres; Jas Hughes, VP.

Dr John Condit apptd Senator of U S by VP of NJ, vice Aaron Ogden-vacancy occasioned by the expiration of the time.

Wed Sep 7, 1803
Mrs Keets Brdg School nr Centre Ville, Md. Ltr giving utmost merit to Mrs Keets, Mr Paire & the young ladies. -Jas Shent, John Danes, Perry E Noel & John Thackett.

Instances of the use of "West's Rheumatic Ring", Edw West: Benj Beeler, Dec 6, 1799, Lexington; Wm Ross, Dec 4, 1799, Lexington; Azariah Higgins for his wife, Dec 6, 1799, Lexington; Thos Vaughan, Mar 15, 1800; Asa Combs, Dec 26, 1799; Jesse Williams, Dec 17, 1799, Bourbon Co; Wm N Potts, May 31, 1800. Vaughan, Combs, Potts, & Williams-Sworn before Archibald McIlvain, Justice of Peace, Jul 27, 1800. -Thos West.

Cotton Manufactors: machines will be made by Peter Eltonhead, Phil.

Orphans Crt of Wash Co, DC. Orlando Cook has applied for ltrs of adm on est of Nathan Goodall, late of Wash, decd.

Wm H Burbridge was indicted at Dist Crt of U S for NY Dist for stealing a ltr commited to his care, as clk in PO in NY, with bank notes totaling $800; prop of John D Martin, merchant in NY. He pleaded guilty & recd 30 lashes on his bare back & 6 mos imprisonment because of his youth.

Elias Perkins has rsgnd his seat of Rep in the U S.

Fri Sep 9, 1803
Eloped from my svc, Jas Stone, appr to the hse carpenter business, Irishman, age 19 yrs.   -Peter Lenox, Wash.

Frederick-town, Aug 17. Ctzn Genrl Danl Heister recommended for nomination at 4th Dist in Congress of U S. Signed: Saml Duvall, Frederick Heisley, Abraham Shriver, Jos Swearingen & Roger Nelson.

Mon Sep 12, 1803
Died: Lewis Thos Villaret Joyeuse, late Capt Genl of Martinique, at that island.

Died: Rev David Tappan, D D, Sep 10, at Cambridge, Prof of Divinity in Harvard College, age 51 yrs.

Committed to goal of Balt: Tom, negro, 19 yrs of age, says he belongs to Mr Usher Williams, of Charleston, SC. Also Wm Groce, negro, 50 yrs of age, says he belongs to Mr John Chisley of Pr Wm Co, Va. Also, Geo Fairfax, negro, 17 yrs of age, says he belongs to Mr Priestly Right, of Westmoreland Co, Va, nr Cole Carter's mill. -Jas Wilson-Shrf.

Apptd trustees of the poor, Wash City: Peter Lenox, Jos Mechlin, Griffith Coombs, Geo Blagden & Wm Pront.

Wed Sep 14, 1803
Reward-$100 for person who entered a stable nr my dwelling hse & stabbed a valuable mare.   -Nathaniel Gregory.

Died: Jas R Dormott, age 48 yrs, Sep 9, citizen of Wash, after a lingering sickness; buried with rights of the Church at St Patrick's Chr by Rev Dr Caffery.

Fri Sep 16, 1803
Stolen or strayed, milch cow, at John Dempsie, living in Wash City, nr the Navy Yard.

Phil, Sep 12. Brd of Health: Wm T Donaldson, Pres; Felix Pascalis, sec.

Hartford, Sep 7. Inhabitants are enjoying good health. Signed: Eliakim Fish, Mason F Cogswell & Leonard Bacon.

Wm McCreery nominated a Rep in Congress for Balt City, Md. Nicholas R Moore, for Balt Co, Md.

New York, Sep 9. Fire in bake hse occupied by Mr Simon Fraser, 3 Cliff St; List of the suffers:

Simon Fraser		
Safety Magee	grocer	1 Cliff St
John Vernon & Co	silversmiths	93 John St
Jas Hazlet	chr mkr	93 John St
Roderie McLeod	accountant	6 Cliff
John Carne	chr mkr	2 Cliff
Reuben Munson	comb mkr	2 Cliff
Abraham Bokee	cooper	5 Cliff
Mich'l Bloomer	pilot	8 Cliff
Sarah Taylor	widow	10 Cliff
Saml Pooley Jr		4 Cliff
Lewis Faugeres	M D	79 John
Jerusha Haviland	widow	77 John St

MON SEP 19, 1803
Died: Mr Lee Lewes, comedian, Jul 23, at Islington Spa, Eng.

For sale: plantation where I live, abt 600 acs, 4 miles from Wash, 5 miles from Alex. -Overton Carr on the premises.

Died: Comdr Barry, Sep 13, Naval Hero, first hoisted the flag of the Americ Navy in 1775.

WED SEP 21, 1803
Ch McLaughlin, Sec & Treas of Washington Jockey Club Races.

FRI SEP 23, 1803
Reward-$25 for negro, Saml Commer, abt 24 yrs of age; he signed passes as John Goodal, Henrico & is guilty of forgery.
-Edw Cox, Goochland Co, Va.

Died: Mr Woodfall, in London, Aug 1, reporter of Parliament debates.

MON SEP 26, 1803
Died: Mr Wm Woodfall, age 58 yrs, at his hse in Queen St, Westminster; vet of public literature. -From a London Paper.

Ranaway, negro, Jack, abt 25 yrs of age. -Henry Woodward, Anne Arundel Co Fork, Patuxant, Md.

WED SEP 28, 1803
Mrd: Mr Tunis Craven, merchant of Alex, to Miss Hannah Tingey, d/o Capt Thos Tingey, of Wash, Sep 25, by Rev Mr McCormick.

Apptd by the Wash Mayor-John Willis, Superintendant of Police.

FRI SEP 30, 1803
Walter Story Chandler, trustee of est of Israel Loring, insolvent debtor, to sell at public auction prop of said debtor; by order of Wm Cranch, esq, Judge of Crct Crt of DC.

MON OCT 3, 1803
Orphans Crt of Wash Co, DC. Oct 3, 1803. Will annexed, est of Jas R Dermott, late of Wash Co, decd. -Alice Dermott, adm.

For sale: 200 acs, prop of Eliz Corry, decd, late of Chas Co, Md, tract is in Mattawoman Swamp; rented for the present yr by Mr Geo Dixon, possession to purchaser on Jan 1, 1804.   -Thos Lancaster, trust.

WED OCT 5, 1803
Balt City for Congress: Nicholas R Moore-2335 votes; Wm MacCreery-2048; Geo Buchanan-208. Assembly: Thos Dixon-2077 votes; Cumberland Dagan-1525; Jas Purviance-630; Edw Alsquith-329.

FRI OCT 7, 1803
Ladies with ltrs in Wash Post Ofc Oct 1, 1803:

Mrs Sabinah Bonnau	Mrs Blount	Mary Baker	Hannah Bond
Nelly Thomas	Eliza Chandler	Elinor Davies	Mrs Mary Elicott
Ann Hand	Hillary Lannam	Eleanor Pickerell	
Caroline Clagott c/o Mr Hanson			

OCT 10, 1803
Died: Saml Adams, age 82 yrs, at his hse in Boston, late Gov of this Commonwealth, Oct 2.   -Boston Chronicle.

Boston, Oct 2d. Arv'd the trading ship, *Galen*, Capt Robt Hinckley; she left London Aug 25th; passengers: Saml Cabot & Richd Peters of Phil; Dr Nath'l Chapman of Va; Thos Elwyn of Portsmouth, NH; Mr Wm Elwyn of London; Lt Edw Wyer & Mr John P Parker, of Boston.

Mbrs of 8th Congress:
New Hamp ...... Simeon Olcott & Wm Humer.
R I .... Christopher Ellery & *Saml J Potter.
Mass............. *John Q Adams & Timothy Pickering.
Conn............. Jas Hillhouse & Uriah Tracy.
Vt .... Stephen R Bradley & *Israel Smith
NY .... Dewitt Clinton & *Theodorus Bailey.

NJ .... Jonathan Dayton & John Condit.
Pa .... Geo Logan & *Saml Maclay
Md .... Robt Wright & *Saml Smith.
Va .... Wilson C Nicholas & *John Taylor.
NC .... David Stone & Jesse Franklin.
SC .... Thos Sumter & Peirce Butler.
Ga .... Abraham Baldwin & Jas Jackson.
Ky .... John Brackinridge & John Brown.
Dela .... Saml White & Wm H Wells.
Tenn .... Wm Cocke
 Ohio .... *John Smith & *Thos Worthington.
*New Members

Hse of Reps: (*New mbrs)

NH	Saml Tenney	*Saml Hunt	*David Hough
	*Silas Bettan	*Clifton Clagget	
Mass	Wm Eustis	Saml Thatcher	*Seth Hastings
	Manasseh Cutler	Richd Cutts	*Eben. Seaver
	*Phineas Bruce	Lemuel Williams	*Wm Stedham
	Jos B Varnum	Peleg Wadsworth	Phanuel Bishop
	*Thos Dwight	*Tomson J Skinner	*Nahum Mitchell
	*Jacob Crowinshield		
R I	Jos Stanton Jr	Nehemiah Knight	
Conn	John C Smith	Roger Griswold	Benj Talmage
	Saml W Dana	Calvin Goddard	*Simeon Baldwin
	John Davenport		
Vt	*Martin Chittenden	*------ Chamberlain	*Jas Elliot
	Gideon Olin not elected		
NY	*Geo Tibbets	John Smith	Saml L Mitchell
	Philip Van Cortland	*Beriah Palmer	David Thomas
	*Andrew McCord *	Danl C Verplank	*Thos Sammons
	*Erastus Root	*John Patterson	*Oliver Phelps
	*Joshua Sands	K K Van Rensselaer	*John Cantine
	*Gaylor Griswold	*Henry W Livingston	
Dela	*Caesar A Rodney		
Pa	*Jos Clay	*Jacob Richards	Mich'l Leib
	Robt Brown	Isaac Van Horne	*Fredk Conrad
	Jos Heister	*J Anderson	*John Whitehill
	*John Rhea	John Smilie	John Stewart
	John A Hanna	*David Bard	Andrew Gregg
	*Wm Findley	*John B C Lucas	Wm Hege
Md	Jos H Nicholson	*Wm MacCreery	John Archer
	Danl Heister	John Campbell	Walter Bowie
	*John Dennis	Thos Plater	*N R Moore
Va.	John Randolph jr	John Smith	John Clopton
	*Thos M Randolph	*John W Eppes	John Dawson
	*Jos Lewis jr	Edwin Gray	David Holmes

	Anthony New	Thos Claiborne	*Walter Jones
	Thos Newton jr	Abram Trigg	John Trigg
	*Peterson Goodwyn	*Jas Stephenson	*John G Jackson
	*Thos Lewis	Matthew Clay	*Thos Griffin
	Philip R Thompson		
NC	Nathaniel Macon	Willis Allston	Richd Stanford
	*Saml D Purviance	*M Williams	*Jas Gillespie
	Thos Wynns	Jas Holland	*Wm Blackledge
	*N Alexander	*Jos Winnston	*Wm Kennedy
SC	Wm Butler	Thos Lowndes	Richd Winn
	*Levi Carney	Thos Moore	*Wade Hampton
	*John Earle	Benj Huger	
Ga	David Merriwether	Peter Early	*Saml Hammond
Ky	John Fowler	*Matthew Walton	*John Boyle
	*Thos Sandford	*G M Bedinger	*Matthew Lyon
Tenn	Wm Dickson	*Geo W Campbell	*John Rhea
Ohio	*Jeremiah Morrow		
Miss Terr	*Wm Lattimore, Del		

WED OCT 12, 1803

In Chancery-DC. Mark Stockwell & Stephen Pleasonton, against Pierce Purcell. Dfndnt mortgaged lot 3 sq 224, Wash City, to cmplnt on Nov 18, 1802, payment of $1000; no part of said money has been paid; dfndnt has remv'd to Charleston, SC, & resides there. Bill is to obtain payment. -Uriah Forrest-clk.

Knoxville, Tenn: John Sevier is elected Gov & Wm Dickson, Geo W Campbell, & John Rhea, Reps. Jos Anderson is re-elected Sen to Cong; & Daniel Smith, Sen, as of Mar 1805.

Died: Mr Wm Leatherbourow, at the hse of Wm Taylor nr the Capitol; on Oct 8th; Mr L was from Balt & leaves a widow.

FRI OCT 14, 1803

Dublin, Aug 24. Persons now in custody, charged with high treason: Felix Rourke [considered the rebel leader], agent Wm Lewis Walker; Thos Donelly: agent-Co. McNally; John Lilleen; Jas Byrne; John McKenny; Walter Clare; Lau. Begley alias Bayley; Nichs. Farrel; Mich'l Kelly; Martin Burke; agent Jas Curran; Edw Kearney; John Begg; Par. Maguire; J Doran; Owen Kirwin, agent Jas Curran. Yesterday Mr Jas Dickson of Kilmairham, tanner & Mr Bernard Doyle were taken into custody. At Dundalk in the County of Lauth, persons were apprehended by John Page & his bro, Saml.

In Chancery-Wash Co, DC. Jas Stephens, Wm O'Neale, & Wm Loughty, cmplnts, v Ann Cook admx & Thos Chas Cook, reps & heirs of Chas Cook, decd, dfndnts. Chas Cook died; his prsnl est not enough for his debts; Cook left considerable rl prop. Bill is to sell rl est necessary to pay his debts.

                    -Uriah Forrest, clk.

Mon Oct 17, 1803
In Chancery-Wash Co, DC. Chas Wadsworth, cmplnt v Owen Roberts & wife, Geo N Nyles & John Harper & Jas Keith, dfndnts. Aug 8, 1801, Roberts mortgaged to Wadsworth, prop in said bill to secure to cmplnt the repayment of money lent by him to dfndnt; Jun 1, 1802, Roberts contracted a debt with Harper & Lyles, procured a deed of trust to be executed by Roberts & wife for prop mortgaged to cmplnt, to dfndnt Jas Keith, to secure to Harper & Lyles their claim against Roberts. Bill: Foreclosure of mort & sale of prop.
-Uriah Forrest-clk.

Wed Oct 19, 1803
Luke Shannon, insolvent debtor, confined in Wash Co jail; asking for relief.
-Uriah Forrest, Ck.

Orphans Crt of Wash Co, DC. Oct 19, 1803. Prsnl est of Alexander Wilson, late of Wash Co, decd. -Eliz Wilson, admx.

State of votes in Chatham Co, Ga, Oct 3, 1803, Genrl Election:
Cong-Jos Bryan 169 votes; Matthew McAllister 69 votes
State Senate-Edw Harden 196 votes; Edw Telfair [blank];
Hse of Reps: Geo M Troup 211 votes; Jos Welsher 176 votes; Thos U P Charlton 141 votes; Jas E Houstoun 53 votes; John Love 13 votes.

Fri Oct 21, 1803
In Chancery, Oct 14, 1803. Richard Jones, v John Hill. Bill is to obtain a decree for recording a deed executed by the dfndnt on Oct 1, 1800-part of a tract cld *Blenheim Hill* nr Bladensburgh. J Hill has remv'd out of Md.
-S Howard-RCC.

For sale: negro man slave. Apply to Mgt Adams, living nr Bladensburgh.

Oct 15th Jacob Van Ness & John C Dent of Wash, were admitted by the Genrl Crt of this state, now in session at Annapolis, as cnslrs & attys.

Mon Oct 24, 1803
Hse of Reps: Petition of Lewis Prahl, of Northern Liberties of Phil City, Pa, white-smith; comp for arms nrly finished & ready for the Cont Army but were stolen by the enemy in the Rev War.

Scholars of Columbian Acad, Gtwn, exhibited public speaking:
Lewis P W Balch	Richard B Dorsey	Benj Bohrer
Thos Magruder	Geo Templeman	Wm Mecklin
Jas Corcoran	Thos Corcoran	John Traverse
Saml Magurder	Richd Polkinghorne	Benj Harbaugh
Jos Clarke	Jos Semmes	Wm Worthington
John Hyde	Henry Goszler	Chas Worthington.

Acad is under the direction of Rev David Wiley. The following recommend it to parents & guardians: Stephen B Balch, Chas H Beatty, Jas Melone, John Travers,

Elisha Riggs, John Crookshank, John Ott, Thos Corcoran & Wm H Dorsey.

Libels. Crt of Session for Rensselear Co, at Troy, last wk: Indictments against David Allen of Lansingburgh, as author in said Gaz for libel on Pres Jefferson; Jas Dole of Troy, author in said Gaz for libel on the Dist Atty; the editor of said Gaz for libel on the Chief Justice of this State; Ebenezer Foote, Dist Atty, author of pieces in the Farmer's Reg, for libel on Jas Dole. [NY Paper]

Hse of Reps: Memorial of Moses Tryon of Wethersfield, Conn, late a Capt of the U S ship of War, *Connecticut*; & of Richd Law Jr of New London, Conn, late Mstr Commandant of the Sloop of War, *Richmond*; praying they may receive the difference in the proportion of salvage.

Trial of Edw Kearney, for high treason, Dublin, Sep 1. Jul 23, 1803. He with others attacked the King's Troops. Jury:

Richd Allen, Foreman	Robt Henry French	Thos Kinder
Wm Suell Magee	Jas Walcot Fitzgerald	John Halpen
Wm Mocree	John Duncan	Godfrey Burne
Richd Davidson	Thos Conner	Wm Stanford

Witnesses: Patrick McCabe, lived in Francis St, trade: calendar man; Edw Wilson; Jas Stack, a Cpl of the 21st; Lt Collman of the 9th; Mr Richd Cowley, watch constable, proved the death of Lord Kilwarden in Vicar St Watch Hse, by a number of pike wounds.

WED OCT 26, 1803

Reward-$10 for negro, Dick, abt 20 yrs of age; seen at Fredricksburg at the races; prop of Dr Robt W Rose of this county.
                                   -Leonard Hollurry, Halifarm, Orange Co, Va.

Owen Kirvan was convicted of high treason for atrocities on Jul 23d; sentence of death was pronounced by Hon Baron George.
                                             [See Oct 14, 1803-Dublin]

Reward-$20 for Bill, mulatto, abt 18 yrs of age.   -John T Mason, Gtwn.

FRI OCT 28, 1803

Application is intended to be made at the Treas for renewal of certificates of registered debt which have been left, viz, No. 2203 & 2201, given Jas Moore & Andrew Henderson for $165.69 each; one to Chas Aurent, No. 2199-same amt; one to Chas Miller, [No #]-same amt; one to Meredith West, No. 2193, for $264.62; bearing int from Jul 1, 1781.   -Wm Calhoun

For sale: property bequeathed to me, in trust with power to sell, by the late Mr Thos Dick, of Bladensburg, viz, farm he had in his own possession, 1300 acs, north of Bladensburg; part of tract, "*Hills & Dales*" in Montg Co, 70+acs; part of "*Crawford's Adventure*" 160 acs, adj the lands of the late Richd Henderson, Bladensburg; hse & lot in Bldnsbrg where the late Mr Dick resided, 6 acs; lot 7 sq 704 in Wash. Mr John Hugh will show the land. -John Laird, trust.

Order of Orphans Crt of Chas Co, Md: public sale at hse of Elisha Jones's nr Broad Creek, sundry negroes.   -Edw Jones Jr, adm of Alexius Jones, decd.

Albany Gaz-statement of the Albany Mercantile Co up to Oct 11, 1803; John Guyler, Cashier. Signed: John Jauncey, Derick A Brade, Robt Gaskaden, Geo Wilson, Saml McElroy, Jas J Hoit (by his atty), John Jauncey, John Macauly, Saml Whiting, G Fairman, T R Austin, John Brunson, Chr. Leffingwell, Jacob Norris, Meads & Randel, John Hendrickson, Jos Fry, J P V Benthuisen, B V Benthuisen, Abm D Lansingh, W B Whiting, John Gates, John Whiting, Nathan Whiting, Nancy Tiffany [by Saml Whiting, their agent] & Isaac Leavenworth

Bankruptcy awarded against Jas McDonald, of Wash Co, DC. -Richd Forrest

Mon Oct 31, 1803
St Mary's Co Crt, Md. Application made by heirs & reps of late Geo Booth, of said co, to obtain division of his rl est. John Booth & John Keneln Booth, absent from said co, & entitled if present, to make election to take est of said G Booth, who died intestate.   -J Harris clk, St Mary's Co.

Died: Edmund Pendleton, at very advanced age, Oct 26; at Richmond. In 1776 he was a Whig & in 1798 a Rpblcn.

Daniel Roney was to collect for subscription to *"American Patriot"*; he gave written receipts & not the printed ones, issued by the proprietor; defrauding him.
                                -Saml Kennedy.

Wed Nov 2, 1803
Senate resolved to wear crape for Stevens Thomson Mason, a Senator, decd. Also for Saml Adams & Edmund Pendleton. Mr Pendleton was in Gov't svc from age 23 & died age 85 yrs.

Orphans Crt of Wash Co, DC. Oct 31, 1803. Prsnl est of Redmond Barry, late of Wash Co, decd.   -Johanna Barry, admx.

Robt Ellis, debtor, confined to Wash Co prison; oath of insolvent debtor will be administered & a trustee apptd.

Fri Nov 4, 1803
Saml McIntire has opened a groc & liquor store at the Navy Yd oppo Mr Prout's.

Widow Fownes, living on NJ Av, advertises "Genteel Boarding".

Mon Nov 7, 1803
Wines & whiskey for sale at my warehse in Water St bet Gen Mason's & Messrs Jeremiah Williams & Co. -Chas F Brodhag, Gtwn.

For sale: Dry goods in Cumberland, Allegany Co, Md, attended to by Aquila A Browne, esq, & the hse in which the store is kept; also 800 acs, same co; 1116 acs cld *"Recourse"*, Alleg Co; part of *"White Oak Point"* Harden Co, Ky; 1000 acs, Monongahala Co, Va, nr Col Francis Deakens's lands; 1800 acs in Randolph Co; titles are clear.

Hse of Reps: Petition of John F Randolph & Randolph McGillis in behalf of themselves & others for svcs of the Militia of Ga, made Feb 6, 1803-Referred to Committee of claims.

WED NOV 9, 1803

Leg of NJ has elected: Andrew Kirkpatrick, Chief Justice, & John Condit, Sen of U S.

Strayed, 2 fat steers. -Meahlon Atkinson, nr Centre Mkt-Wash.

FRI NOV 11, 1803

Hse of Reps: 1-Petition of Abraham Millen, adm & residuary leg of Wm Millen, decd, compensation for flour, corn, shorts, furnished by decd for use of Continental Army during Rev War. 2-Pet of John Thompson, of Chester Co, Pa, grant of land he is entitled to for his svcs in regt commanded by Col Byrd, on expedition against the Indians. 3-Pet of Wm Wyman, of Roxbury, Mass, Capt of regt commanded by Col John Patterson, Rev War, bal due him for recruiting 72 men at his own expense. 4-Pet of Wm Mattocks, of Danville, Vt, coll of tax for dist 12, for advertising of taxes due in newspapers etc. 5-Pet of Jas Paddock, Craftsbury, Vt, to the like effect. 6-Pet of Christopher Stock, of Va, for svcs as in Va Line of Cont Army, Rev War. 7-Pet of Wm Pancoast, of Gtwn, Wash, patent for vacant land in Wash. 8-Pets of Chas D'Wolf, Constant Taber, Wm Gardner, Simon Davis, & Saml Martin, all of R I, relief in case of certain bonds. 9-Pet of John Taggart, of Phil, Pa, refund of duties on property consumed in a fire. 10-Memorial of Zachariah Cox, for injuries sustained in 1798, at Natchez, Miss Terr, & at Nashville, Tenn, by armed men belonging to the Army. 11-Pet of Chas Vattier, ntv of France, now resid of Cinc, Ohio, for his share of lands. 12-Pet of Philip Wilson, of Phil, Pa, value of rice & claret furnished Cont'l Army in 1778. 13-Pet of Achilles Douglas, of Va, val of waggon & team, impressed in Sep 1794, by Militia of Va, under Command of Col Wm Campbell. 14-Pet of Jason Reeve, New London Co, Conn, wounds recd while a Cpl of Marines on ship-*"Trumbull"* in svc of U S, Dec 20, 1800. 15-Pet of John F Randolph & Randolph McGillis, for svcs of Militia of Ga. All referred to Committee.

MON NOV 14, 1803

Orphans Crt of PG Co, Md. Nov 14, 1803. Prsnl est of Nicholas Sansbury, late of PG Co, decd.   -Alexius Sansbury, Jos Sansbury, admrs.

Stolen: mare, saddle & bridle, off the race ground. -Mr John W Pratt, nr the Six Bldgs, Wash City.

Ranaway-bros, Wat & Ben, 19 & 18 yrs of age, negro men, from Brice J Gassaway, living in AA Co, Md. Reward-$200.

Ran away, Dick, negro, age abt 25 yrs, from Jas Thompson, at Leonard town; prop of Mr Richard Watts nr Great Mill.

WED NOV 16, 1803
Chancery of Md-sale for benefit of creditors of Robt Whitaker, decd. 500 acs with 2 dwelling hses, nr Up Marlb., Md. -Isaac Lansdale, trust.,PG Co, Md.

Meeting of the Wash Dancing Assembly, Nov 14th; Thos Tingey-Pres; Joshua Wingate-Sec; Mgrs: Danl Carrol of Dud'n; Thos Law; Wm Brent; John Willis; Lewis Harvie; Gabriel Duvall, Wm Kilty & Thos Munroe.

French Gentleman: Agricultural svcs or French teacher. Apply to De Chavla c/o Mr Duane at Wash City or at Phil.

FRI NOV 18, 1803
Deserted from board U S frig, *Essex,* Thos Williams, seaman, abt 19 yrs of age; also Richard Davison, seaman from the hosp, belonging to the frig *Congress*. -Capt John Cassin, super of Navy Yard.

Robt Bowie, esq, Nov 14, was elected Gov of Md.

MON NOV 21, 1803
A J Villard opened a Coffee & Oyster Hse on Pa Av oppo the Ctr Mkt.

Grey horse stolen from the plantation nr Upper Marlboro. -Benjamin Oden.

WED NOV 23, 1803
Hse of Reps: 1-Memorial of Thos Ketland of Phil, praying a drawback of duties on imports from Batavia, East Indies, in ship *Washington,* [owns same]; in the month of Jun, 1801. 2-Pet of John Hunter, of Fairfax Co, Va, praying liquidation & settlement of a claim for 7 mos rent of a hse-prop of John Fitzgerald, Naval ofcr of the Customs for Alexandria Dist & Port in 1799; Fitz. died insolvent in debt to the U S & his prop seized & taken for their use. Referred to Committee. 3-Pet of John Edgar of Randolph Co, Indiana Terr, reimbursement for merchandise furnished by him for the safety of the settlements bet Kaskaskias & Kahokia, from hostile Indians. 4-Pet of David Valenzin, ctzn of Venice & subject of Germany, comp for losses & injuries from the capture of an Imperial Polacre nr Valetta Port by the U S schnr, *Enterprise*-Lt Sterrett, 1802. 5-This petition & that of Peter Chas L'enfant, presented Feb 19, 1801-Referred to committee.

Henry Polkinhorn, saddler, harness, Army accoutrements & trunk mkr, has taken his 2 nphws, Wm & Richard M Hall, into partnership, at store lately occupied by Mr Conner, 2 drs from the Bank of Columbia. -Gtwn, Nov 23.

Sale by Mr John Travers at his Auction Store, High St, sundry articles.

Hse of Reps: Petition of Andrew Moore, of Va, complaining of undue election & return of Thos Lewis, to svc as mbr in this Hse;

FRI NOV 25, 1803
Bankruptcy has been awarded John Williams Lytton, of Wash Co, DC.
-Lewis Ford, Sec to Com'rs.

Double barrell gun was taken at a rm from Mrs Johnson's nr the bank-reward $5.
-W Howison.

Ranaway, Jack, negro abt 15 yrs of age; raised in Dorchester Co, Md. Info to Col John B Earle, Wash City or Wm Richard at Pendleton Crt Hse, SC.

Ltr from H Dearborn to his Execl Edw Tiffin, Gov of Ohio; War Dept Oct 31, 1803; Subj: ofcrs of the Spanish Gov't at New Orleans may refuse to give possession of the Country of La, ceded to the U S by the French Rpblc; I Am directed to assemble 500 of the Militia of Ohio........

MON NOV 28, 1803
Public sale of prsnl prop of the late Thos Dick, at his farm nr Bladensburg.
-John Laird, Exc.

WED NOV 30, 1803
For sale or rent: Rumsey's Iron works; title held by F Fairfax, Charlestown, Jefferson Co, Va.

Notice. All indebted to John Crookshank, decd, to make payment to Chas Glover, adm.

Deserted-on U S frig *Cheapeake*, Wm Orang, age abt 17 yrs, seaman; recruited from Balt a few wks ago. Reward-$8.
-Capt John Cassin, Superintendent of Navy Yard.

Ltr from Thos T Davis, esq, dated Kaskaskias, Indiana Terr, Oct 18, 1803 Subj: Travel thru Indiana.

Nov 29th Mr Merry presented to the Pres of the U S, his ltrs of credence as his Britannic Majesty's Envoy Extra. Mnstr Pleni. to the U S.

FRI DEC 2, 1803
For sale: 200 acs in Fairfax Co, Va, & dwelling hse cld *"The White Hse"* at the Long Glades. Intending to remove to Alexandria town.
-Zebulon Warner, White House.

Hse of Reps: 1-Petition of John Wood, comp for svcs rendered, prsnl injuries sustained, & advances of money, whilst a Capt of a detachment of the Militia of

NY, commanded by Col John Hathorn, in svc of U S against the Indians during Rev War & was captured, confined for considerable time by said Indians. 2-Said petition & that of Jas Gillespie, of NC, referred to committee. 3-Hse requests copies of documents relative to arrest & confinement of Zachariah Cox, by ofcrs in svc of U S, at Natchez, in 1798. 4-Pet of Alex r Summervill, case of bal of pay due for svc as 2d Lt in 8th Pa Reg of Cont'l Army during Rev; bal of pay was delivered to Moses Carson, Capt of the Co in which he srvd, who deserted to the enemy in Spring of 1777. 5-Memorial of Moses Rawlings, for difference of pay bet Lt Col & Col of a Regt of Riflemen in svc of U S during Rev War-month of Aug 1776 until Jun 1779-Referred to committee. 6-Pets of Abijah Barnum, Jos Willoughby, Daniel Smith, Jos Day, & Elihu Barnum, of Monckton, Addison Co, Vt-Barnum lost tax money in Sep 20, 1802 on way to pay same to U S for Vt Dist. 7-Memorial of Thos Doyle, late Maj of 1st Sub-Legion in svc of U S, for costs of suit in defending a prosecution against him by John Bishop, pvt soldier in 4th Sub-Legion; Bishop, at Ft Massac attempted to dessert to the Spaniards in 1795.

Mon Dec 5, 1803

Reward-$10: deserted from hospital on Nov 29, seaman, Thos Harvy, of U S frig *Congress*, age abt 30 yrs. -Capt John Cassin, Super of Navy Yard.

Hse of Reps: 1-Petition of John Gillick, s/o John Gillick, decd, settlement of a claim for pay etc, due for svcs of decd, as soldier in 2d Va Regt on Continental establishment, Rev War. 2-Pet of Thos Marshall Baker, of Upton, Worchester Co, Mass, be placed on list of pensioners, wounds recd in R I Aug 1778, while Capt of Co of Militia in svc of U S. 3-Pet of Ezekiel Scott, pay for svcs as Maj in Regt of NY State Troops, 1781, for 3 yrs. 4-Pet of Henry Glenn, of Schenectady, NY, employed during Rev War in svc of U S. All referred to Committee.

Wed Dec 7, 1803

John Hammand, Pa Ave, opposite the Ctr Mkt, has commenced the tin mkg business; Mrs Hammand, manuta-mkg business.

Ltr from Capt John Rodgers recd by the Sec of the Navy, Hon Robt Smith; dated U S frig, *NY*, Potomac, Dec 6, 1803. Subj: Destruction of the *Bashaw* of Tripoli's largest cruiser.

Fast Sailing ship *Comet*, John McNeill Mstr-constant trader, will sail for New Orleans. -Wm Taylor, No 8, Bank St, Balt, Md.

Reward-$5 for run away, John Melco, appr lad abt 16 yrs of age.
 -Daniel McDougal, Navy Yard.

Sale of land & negroes. *"Dernier Resort"*, 322 acs nr Mattawoman Crk; 460 acs where I reside nr Port Tobacco Crk; *"Hawthorn"*-400 acs; all-Chas Co, Md.
 - M I Stone.

Fri Dec 9, 1803

Louisville, Nov 12. Mon last these ofcrs were elected, viz, David Emanuel, Pres of the Senate; Wm Robertson, Sec; Hon Abraham Jackson, Spkr of the Hse of Reps; Hines Holt, clk; Thos Milledge re-elected Gov

Bankruptcy awarded to Zebulon Warner, of Wash Co, DC.

Insolvent debtor, Jacob Gross, confined in Wash Co prison for debt.
-Uriah Forrest, clk.

Mon Dec 12, 1803

Insolvent debtor, Jos Dowson, confined in Wash Co prison for debt: trustee apptd to Dowson. -Uriah Forrest, clk.

Info wanted of Wm W Thomas, of Orange Co, Va; if alive, returning home will be to his advantage; said Thomas srvd on board the frig *"United States"* in 1798 & 1799.

Wed Dec 14, 1803

Mr Venable is elected Senator of U S for Va, in rm of Col Taylor, who has declined a re-election.

Robt Whitehill, esq, re-elected Spkr of Senate of Pa, & Simon Snyder, esq, Spkr of Hse of Reps.

Jas Turner is re-elected Gov of NC, w/out opposition.

Fri Dec 16, 1803

Died: Mrs Eliz Davidson, w/o Jas Davidson, Sen., esq, cashier of ofc of Discount & Deposit of Wash; on Dec 12.

Notice: A draft was drawn by me in favor of Joshiah Foster on Houlder Hudgins, both of Matthews Co, Va; same was fraudulently obtained from me; not paying unless compelled by law. -Labret Scott, Gtwn.

Lexington, Ken, Nov 22. Circular sent by the Sec of State to the ofcrs intended to command on an expedition. Sec's ofc, Frankfort, Nov 18, 1803. Signed Harry Toulmin, Sec of State. Subj: 4 mos expedition to La.

Wm S Nicholls opened a seasonable goods store, High St, Gtwn.

Mon Dec 19, 1803

Th W Pairo has opened a new store in Gtwn, nr High St, superfine London mens' & childrens' clothing.

Message to the Hse of Reps, Nov 24, 1803, by Gov of SC, Columbia, Jas B Richardson. Subj: His duties as Gov'r to the State of SC.

WED DEC 21, 1803
Died: Wm Vans Murray, esq, late Minister from U S at the Hague; Dec 11 at his seat in Dorchester Co, Md. -Balt Paper.

Strayed-a bay horse from the Commons of Washington. Hugh Densley offers reward of $5.

Michael Roberts has an assortment of stationary for sale at his store in Gtwn.

Francis Pic will open a millenery & fancy goods store in Gtwn.

Impressed Americ seamen & others board Americ vessels:
Ed Bass, ntv of Phil, last Mar or Apr;
Robt Carter Gilliam, ntv of Suffix Co, Va, vessel-*Warren*, do time;
John Leland Wade, ntv of Bristol Co, Mass, brig-*Mahela Winsor*, do;
Wm Hall, Henry Clarke & Jas Clarke, Irishmen, not stated as ctzns of U S, Americ ship-*Industry;*
Chrstphr Tillinghast, ntv of N Kingston, R I, ship-*Sterling*, May 20;
John Roberts & John Backham, a Dane & a Swede, Americ ship-*Sheperdess*, John Bryan, mstr;
Barnabas Otis Jr, ntv of Plymouth, Mass, May 29, brig-*Hannah;*
Samuel Wilson, ntv of Md;
Andrew Sampson & Peter Thompson, ntv of Curacoa & Norway, but Americ ctzns, May 31, 1803, Americ ship-*Martha*, Henry Waddel, mstr;
Wm Brown, ctzn of U S, schnr-*Astrea*, Jun 5;
John Danl Kessler, John Anderson & Mich'l Jones, Jun 6, ship-*Wm & Jane*
Richd Rodman, Jun 7, ship-*Atlas*, Sweeny Wilson, mstr;
Denny Sweeny, ntv of Ire, Jun 7, ship-*Washington*;
Wm Ireland, ntv of Suffolk Co, NY, ship-*Alknomac*, John Gore, mstr;
Jos Simonds & Sylvester Pendleton, ntv Americans & resids of NY, Jul 7, schnr-*Recovery*;
Ephraim Vandwser, Americ ctzn & ntv of NY, schnr-*Perseverance*, Danl Coyle, mstr, Jul 18;
Josiah Hunt, ntv of Newburyport, Mass, Jul 17, Brig-*John*, Jona Titcomb-mstr.
John Whiting, ntv of Glocester Mass, Jul 17, same vessel;
Nath'l Keene, Americ ctzn, Jul 18, ship-*Md*, John Wickham, mstr;
Jos Stevens, Americ ctzn, Jul 18, schnr-P*erseverance*, Danl Coyle, mstr;
Wm Evans, Englishman, & Thos Challis, Americ Citizen, Jun 19 & 26, ship-*Joseph*, Jas Jairason, mstr;
Jas Emmerson, ntv of Lincoln Co, Mass, schnr-*Harriett*, Nath'l Knight, mstr, Schnr-*St Lucia*,---- Shipley, mstr;
Benj Elldridge & Wm Jinney, ntv of Falmouth, Mass, schnr-*Hannah* Jul 20;
Wm Whipp, ntv of New Haven, Conn, & John Simpson of Va, Jul 30, ship-*Phaeton*, ___ Boush, mstr;
Geo Arnold, ntv of Gr Britain, & J Williamson, a Swede, ship *Venus*, Lemuel Bruce, mstr;

David Kitchell, ntv of U S, Sloop-*Hiland*, John Hand, mstr, Aug 22; Oliver Harris, ntv of Boston, Aug 14, schnr-*Harriet*;
Chas Tracy, Americ ctzn, Aug 25, ship-*Marion*, Wm D Seton, mstr;
Thos Doyle, ntv of Phil, seaman of brig-*Hector*, Sep 6;
Saml Watt, Andrew Pace, John Davis, ship-*Charlotte*, Thos Hasam, mstr, Sep 11, [Watt-Americ ctzn];
Jas Matthews, Chf Mate of schnr-*Amazon*, John Murray, mstr, Sep 14;
Wm Watson, ntv of Conn, Sep 29, ship-*Ontario*, Seaman Weeks, mstr;
Thos Cook, ntv of NY, & Geo Wilson of Scotland, Oct 1, ship-*Americ Packet*, Soloman Swain, mstr;
Henry Cobb, ntv of Falmouth, Mass;
Danl Walker, ntv of Phil, ship-*Fox*;
Jesse Dillings, ntv of Wethersfield, Conn;
Richard Johnson, ntv of Middletown, Conn;
Jos Mace, ntv of Newburyport, Mass;
Saml Hill, ntv of Providence, R I;
Henry Kipps, ntv of Hamburgh & NA ctzn of U S, Americ ship-*Eagle*;
Wm Chandler, British Subject, Americ ship-*Anna*, Caleb Johnson, mstr;
Wm Fegarie, of Americ brig-*Sally*, claimed as a citizen of France;
Jos Nicholson, black, Brig-*Canton*, Oct 5.

FRI DEC 23, 1803
Gold of a high quality was found by 2 or 3 chldrn of John Reed, ntv of Hesse Cassell, Ger, in Cabarraus Co, NC.   -Raleigh, NC.

Americ vessels detained by British armed vessels for adjudication in the crt of vice admiralty at Antiqua.

Jefferson	Saml Vinnard of & bound to Portsmouth, NH;
Enterprize	Capt Harding, of & for NY;
Eliza	Allen Pendleton, of & from NY;
Leah	Jos Carre, of & for Balt;
Lucretia	Capt Buckly, of Conn;
Julian	Capt Jerkins, of Newbern, NC;
Eagle	Capt Brenan, of & for Norfolk.

For sale: Set of saw mills, on Drowning Creek, 97 miles from Geo Twn, SC.- Wm Norment, Millville, nr Lumberton, NC, or Saml D Purviance, Wash.

Notice: Persons are warned from purchasing a 2 story brick hse on north F St, which was seized on Dec 20 as prop of Frederick Betts, of Wash.
-Geo W Betz.

MON DEC 26, 1803
For sale: per will of late Patrick Henry, 1800acs in Charlotte Co, Va, poor land. Apply-Mr Randolph, Hse of Reps for terms. -Edmund Winston, exc of Patrick Henry, Buckingham Co, Va.

WED, DEC 28, 1803

Stocks issued to Jacob Trilamer of Amsterdam, for renewal, have been lost; dated-Oct 23, 1791, Nov 23, 1791, Dec 7, 1792, & Dec 5, 1792; by Reg of Treas.

-Robt Gilmor & sons

Proclamation by Pieirre Clement Laussat, Colonial Prefect & Comr of the French Gov't to the people of La; Subj-the French Rpblc resigns her dominion over La. at New Orleans, Nov 30, 1803. Signed, Laussat; Dangerot, Sec to the comr.

Rpblcns elected reps in Congress for NJ:

Henry Southard	Ebenezer Elmer	Wm Helms
Adam Boyd	Jas Sloan	Jas Mott

FRI DEC 30, 1803

Proclamation signed by the Pres of the U S on Nov 25, 1803, ratifying the treaty bet the U S & the Choctaw Nation of Indians. Signed Aug 31, 1803 at Hoe-Buck In-Too-Pa; J Wilkinson-Brig Genrl; Young Gains-interpreter; Jos Chambers-U S Factor; Jno Bowyer, Capt 2d U S Regt; Mingo Poos Coos, Alatala Hooma.

Treaty made at Vincennes in Indiana Terr bet Wm Henry Harrison, Gov of said Terr, super of Indian Affairs & Comr Pleni of U S & the Kaskaskia Tribe of Indians was signed Aug 13, 1803 in presence of Jno Rice Jones, Sec to the comr; Henry Vanderburg, a judge of the Indiana Terr; J F Rivet, Indian Missionary; Vcyo, Col of Knox Co Militia; Cornelins Lyman, Capt 9th Infty Regt; Jas Johnson of Indiana Terr; W Parke, do; Jos Barron, interpreter.

For sale: Deed of trust from the late Mr John Beall, 240 acs & dwlg hse, nr Bladensburg.   -Ben Lowndes, trust

Died: Peter Wood Jr, esq, Dec 7, Delegate from PG Co, Md, at his lodgings at Mr Stevens, Annapolis. Interment-Burying Ground, Wash City. Pallbearers: Edw H Vezey, Dr Milten, Mr Sharadine, Mr Vanhorn, Mr Calvert & Col Lyles.

The National Intelligencer and Washington Advertiser
Washington, DC 1804

JAN 2, 1804

Those indebted to the late firm of Redmond & Garret Barry of Wash, are to make payment to Garrett Barry, surviving prtnr.

Reward-$1000 for Jos Hart of Hartford City, having committed forgery on the Middletown Bank & absconded. -Elijah Hubbard, Pres, Middletown, Conn.

Treaty bet the U S & Delawares, Shawanoes, Putawatimies, Miamies, Eel Rvr, Weeas, Kickapoes, Piankashaws & Kaskaskias Indians was signed Jun 7, 1803 & confirmed by the Pres of the U S on Nov 25, 1803.

Treaty at Ft Wayne on the Miami of the Lake. Signed: Wm Henry Harrison; John Rice Jones-sec; Jno Gibson-sec Ind Ter; Tho Pasteur-Capt 1st Regt Infty; Wm Wells-interpreter; Jno Johnson-U S Factor; Hendrick Aupaumut-Chief of Muhecon; Thos Freeman. At Wash City on Dec 26, 1803: Th Jefferson, Pres; Jas Madison sec of State.

WED JAN 4, 1804

Ran away, appr boy, Robin Hood, age abt 14 yrs, joiner in Wash City. Reward-50 cents.   -Andrew Thompson, joiner, Wash.

Deserted on board frig *U S*, Robt Fagan, ntv of NJ, abt 30 yrs of age.
-Capt John Cassin, Super of Navy Yd, Wash.

FRI JAN 6, 1804

Impeachment-Jan 4, 1804-Hse o/Reps against John Pickering, Judge of the dist Crt of NH, for high crimes & misdemeanors. Names extracted: Geo Wentworth, srvyr of NH; Oct 15, 1802 the ship *Eliza*, Wm Ladd late mstr, was seized; Eliphalett Ladd; Jos Whipple, coll of Portsmouth; John S Sherburne.

MON JAN 9, 1804

S Thomee has remv'd his gilding store from Gtwn to Alexandria.

Wash Co, DC. Brought before me, a stray sorrel horse. -Alex. Soper, *Nonsuch Farm*, belonging to Mrs Young. [Wash Co, DC.]

WED JAN 11, 1804

St Geo Tucker is apptd a Judge of Crt of Appeal of Va in rm of Edmond Pendleton, decd.

Caution-a person who assumed the name of Jas Nicholson, & cld himself my bro, obtained money from 2 men of my acquaintance in NJ & Dela; for the last 4 yrs, my bro, Jas Nicholson has been but little in the U S; he sailed from Phil for Canton, where its presumed he now is.   -Jos H Nicholson.

Wash City-committee to enquire into official conduct of Saml Chase & Richd Peters are: J Randolph, Nicholson, J Clay, Early, R Griswold, Huger & Boyle.

FRI JAN 13, 1804
Wm Cowan is an agent of the Virginia Yazoo Company.

Dr John Sibley, late of Fayetteville, now of La, writes a ltr to J Gales, printer, in Raleigh. Subj: description of Louisiana.

Americ Philosophical Soc: Tho Jefferson-Pres; Robt Patterson, Casper Wistar, Benj Smith Barton-VPs; John Redman Coxe, Adam Seybert, Thos C James, Thos T Hewson-Secs; Wm White, Jona. B Smith, Peter S Duponceau & Adam Kuhn-Cnslrs; Chas W Peale, Robt Hare Jr, John Church-Curators; John Vaughan-Treas.

MON JAN 16, 1804
In Chancery-Smallwood's creditors against his heirs. Claims exhibited against est of Genrl Wm Smallwood, decd, without sufficient vouchers & not passed-not rejected either, have gone a long time without anything done on their part.
-Saml Harvey Howard, Reg CC

Orders of Genrl Wilkinson, at camp of the Americ Troops, on left bank of the Miss., nr the city of New Orleans, Dec 17, 1803, Parole Columbia. Signed: D Wadsworth, Aid-De-Camp, Pro Tem.

Deserted on board frig, *Congress*, Jan 12, Jas Manley, seaman; Garret Marten, German; & Wm Comeford. -Capt John Cassin, Super of Navy Yd, Wash.

WED JAN 18, 1804
Absconded-Cimon, black slave, abt 26 yrs of age; came from Mrs Eden's est in St Mary's Co where he was cld Peter; his bro, Harry, is slave to Miss Grace Stone & was hired in Wash City.   -M I Stone, Chas Co, Md.

FRI JAN 20, 1804
For sale: deed of trust dated Jan 8, 1798, bet Isaac Polock of the 1st part, Wm Deakins Jr, since departed of the 2d part, & Jonah Thompson & Richard Veitch of the 3d part; lot 49 on Water St, Gtwn, hse at present occupied by Mr Barney as a tavern; also lot 77 in Gtwn, part of that wharf lately occupied as a lumber yd by Mr Geo King & 2 story brick dwelling hse. Apply to Tompson & Veitch, Alexandria; John T Mason, Gtwn; or to Francis Deakins, exc & devisee of Wm Deakins Jr, decd.

Ranaway, Harry, negro, abt 25 yrs of age, from Francis I Carter, Dumfries; late the prop of Christopher Criglar or Edw March of Frederick Co, Va. Info can be given to Mr Saml Davis in Dumfries or Mr Saml Jackson in Pr Wm Co, Va.
-Francis I Carter, Wythe Co, Va.

Mon Jan 23, 1804

Hse o/Reps: Relief of John Coles, owner of the ship *Grand Turk*, in svc of the U S; for detention of said ship at Gibraltar by direction of the Americ cnsl at that port, from May 10 to Jul 4, 1801. Claim to be adjusted.

Ladies with ltrs in Wash PO, Jan 1, 1804:

Miss Renose Brown	Mrs Betsy Cook	Miss Kitty Hughesm
Mrs Mary Hammon	Fanny Johnston	Mrs Island
Mrs Sarah Lewis	Mrs Ann Macubin	Mrs Ann H Magruder
Mrs Sunday	Miss Charlotte Thornton at Col Washington's	

Wed Jan 25, 1804

Nicholas Fevrier, insolvent debtor confined in Wash Co Prison for debt.
-Uriah Forrest, clk.

Fri Jan 27, 1804

Robt P Wade, insolvent debtor confined in Wash Co Prison for debt.
-Uriah Forrest, clk.

Hse o/Reps: Petitions of Ann Alricks & Judith Crow, both of DC praying to be freed from their matrimonial obligations. Mv'd to a committee formerly apptd on petition of Marcella Stanton.

Meeting at John H Barney's Tavern, Gtwn; Danl Reintzel, Mayor, cld to the chr; Wm O Sprigg, sec; John Mason, Benj Stoddert, John T Mason, Thos S Lee, Danl Reintzel & Wm O Sprigg-committee; Subj: Building a bridge over the Potomak. John Threlkeld, John Peter, Adam King, Abner Ritchie, Thos Corcoran & Wm Stewart apptd to receive signatures.

Mon Jan 30, 1804

Reward-$10 for John Law, cabinet mkr, a boarder abt 25 yrs of age came to the hse of Mr Peter Meem in Gtwn, Potomac, & stole articles of clothing; said he srv'd his time with his cousin, John Law, of Balt; may have gone to Va. In pkt of surtout that he stole was a psalm bk with the name Ann Collingwood with her age & time of her death. -Saml Collingwood
Nicholas Hillary

Chas Bastian, insolvent debtor confined In Wash Co Prison for debt.
-Uriah Forrest, clk.

Wed Feb 1, 1804

Fire broke out in the brick store in State St, occupied by Mr Jos Pierce Jr, merchant, & Gilbert & Dean, printers; losses as occupiers & owners of goods were: John Parker, J Peirce Jr, N & R Freeman, E & N Withington and Gilbert & Dean.

Hse o/Reps: An act for the relief of Paul Coulon, as agent for the captors of the ship *Betty Cathcart* & brig *Aaron,* prizes to the French Privateer La Bellona; sum of $6,241. Nath'l Macon, Spkr; John Brown, Pres of Sen; Apprv'd, Th Jefferson-Jan 26, 1804

Address to ctzn Peter Clement Lauffat, comr of the French Gov't on Dec 29th by: Danl Clark, Geo Pollock, P F Dubourg, J Proffet & J L Lanthois, at New Orleans; Subj-Vol corps of the city of N Orleans.

FRI FEB 3, 1804
Ranaway, Harry, my sv't, age abt 21 yrs of age, black, ntv of SC. -Andrew Burnet, coll, SC dist. Deliver to my plantation nr Parker's Ferry or in Charleston.

MON FEB 6, 1804
David Hepburn, gardener at Tyber Gardens-Ctr Mkt, has garden seeds for sale, Wash.

Petersburg, Jan 27. Meeting of the ctzns convened at Edw Powell's on Jan 25; Robt Birchett, chrmn; John Baker, sec. Subj: Acquisition of La.

WED FEB 8, 1804
Madam Le Clerc, sister of First Consul & wid of Gen Le Clerc, who died at St Domingo, was mrd to M. Le Prince De Borghese, Nov 15, at Morfontaine.
-Paris Papers.

Ranaway, Billy Bundy, age 26 yrs, negro. -Lucy Brooke, Essex Co, Va.

Senate of Pa declared the seat held by Gen John Steel in that body vacant bec he accepted an appointment from the Gov as one of the comrs under the act of 1799. Incompatible with his holding a seat in the Senate.

Selim, Arabian horse, brought to this country by Capt Jas Barron, in U S frig, *Chesapeak,* last summer, will stand at my hse in Dinwiddie Co, nr the Cut Bank Bridge. -Wm Starke, Groveland, Dinwiddie Co, Va.

Notice: Persons are forewarned not to hunt on our plantations. PG Co, Md.
-B Mackall & T F Brooke

Reward-$50 for a bay mare stolen in Balt by John Smith. Info to Messrs Finley Taylor & Finley residing in Howard St, Balt, or Jas Reed, in Adams Co, Pa.

In Chancery, Feb 1, 1804. Ratify sale made by John Hewitt, trustee, for sale of rl est of Gerrard T Conner; *"Elizabeth"*-178 acs in Montgomery Co, Md, for $601.   -Saml H Howard, Reg CC

FRI FEB 10, 1804

Patent machine for boring holes in rocks under water or in any situation has been purchased from Jean Baptiste Aveilhe, original inventor, by A Lindo, Winchester, Fred Co, Va.

MON FEB 13, 1804

In Chancery, Jan 13, 1804. Abraham Saw v Abel Sargent. Bill is to obtain a decree for sale of 3 lots in town of Western Port, Allegany Co, Md. Sargent, since Oct 7, 1792 owes 500 pds, money not paid, to cmplnt.
-S H Howard-Reg C C.

Hse o/Reps: John Foster Williams & Lemuel Cox were employed to survey the harbor in the Island of Nantucket; passed Feb 16, 1803.

WED FEB 15, 1804

Appointments made by Pres Jefferson:
Jas Munroe, Mnstr Pleni of U S to Gr Britain, vice, Rufus King, rsgnd;
Tobias Lear, Consul Genr of U S for Algiers, v Jas Leander Cathcart;
John M Goetchius, of NY, cnsl for Genoa;
Isaac Coxe Barnet, of NJ, agent for Port of Havre De Grace, France, vice Peter Dobell, rsgnd;
Levitt Harris, of Pa, cnsl for St Petersburg, Russia;
Thos Rodney, of Dela, Judge of Miss Terr, vice Seth Lewis, rsgnd;
Nathan Sanford, of NY, atty for NY dist
Jared Mansfield of Conn-srvyr Genrl for nw of Ohio, v Rufus Putnam, rmv'd;
Isaac Briggs, of Md, srvyr for South Tenn;
Edw Turner, of Miss Terr, Reg of Land Ofc within same lands lying west of Pearl Rvr, Adams Co;
Chas Jones Jenkins, of SC, comr for valuation of lands & dwelling hses, enumeration of slaves for 5th Div of SC;
Tench Coxe, of Pa, Purveyor of Public Supplies, vice Israel Whelan;
Henry Warren, of Mass, coll of Customs for Plymouth, Mass;
Isaac Ilsley, of Mass, coll for Portland & Falmouth;
Saml Ward, of Mass, Naval Ofcr for Salem & Beverly;
Thos Durfee, of R I, inspec of rev & srvyr for Tiverton, R I;
Abraham Bishop, of Conn, coll for New Haven, Conn;
Saml Osgood, of NY, Naval Ofcr for NY;
Callender Irvine, of NY, inspec of rev & srvyr of Buffalo Creek, NY;
Robt Lee, of NY, coll for Niagara, NY;
Jeremiah Bennet Jr, of NJ, coll for Bridgetown, NJ, v Eli Elmer, rmv'd;
Chas Gibson, of Md, inspec of Rev & srvyr for Easton Port, Md;
Thos Dudley, of NC, srvyr of Swansboro, NC;
Brian Hellen, of NC, coll for Beauford, NC;
Jos Turner, of Ga, coll for Brunswick, Ga;
Hore Brown Trist, of Miss Terr, coll for Miss dist.
Henry Wilson, of Md, Commercial agent at Ostend, vacant;
John Cutler, of Md, coll & inspec of rev for Snowhill, Md, vice Wm Selby;

Martin Tapscott, of Va, coll & inspec of rev for Yeocomico Rvr, Va, vice, A Thompson, decd;
Peterson Gurley, of NC, srvyr & inspec of rev for Winton, Edenton dist, NC, vice Laurence Mooney, decd;
Thos F Ferebee, of NC, srvyr & inspec of rev for Indiantown, Camden, NC, vice, Thos Williams, decd.

Hse o/Reps: Memorial of Thos Tingey, Robt Brent, Thos Herty & Augustus B Woodward & others; erection of a theatre; Wash City.

FRI FEB 17, 1804
Deserted from Marine Barracks: Moses Stickney, born in Mass, age 22 yrs; Geo Simmons from Va, age 25 yrs; Geo Edoet, born-NY State, age 22 yrs. By order of Col Burrows. -J R Fenwick, Adj M Corps, Wash.

MON FEB 20, 1804
Orphans Crt of Wash Co, DC. Jas McLaughlin applied for ltrs of adm with will annexed on prsnl est of Laurence Connelly, late of U S frig, *NY*, seaman, decd.
-John Hewitt, Reg.

Died: Jos Priestley, favorite of science, advocate of civil & religious liberty, Feb 6, would be age 71 yrs on Mar 24.

WED FEB 22, 1804
In Chancery-sale made by Wm Stewart, trustee, for sale of rl est of David Ross, decd; lot 5, 54 acs, part of tract cld *The Resurvey*, on *Mackey's Luck*, Frederick Co, Md, for $523.80, to Abner Ritchie; ratify same.
-Saml H Howard, Reg CC

FRI FEB 24, 1804
Ranaway-Phil, mulatto, abt 20 yrs of age, shoemkr. Cumberland, Allegany Co, Md. -Upton Bruce

Public sale of plantation of late Benj Duvall, decd, by order from Orphan's Crt of PG Co, Md. -John Duvall, exc.

Benj Ames an insolvent debtor confined in Wash Co Prison for debt.
-Uriah Forrest, clk.

Orphans Crt of Calvert Co, Md. Prsnl est of Daniel Kent, decd, of said co.
-Jos Kent, adm-Lower Marlbro, Feb 24.

MON FEB 27, 1804
Rpblcn mbrs of Leg of NY meeting was held at Albany-Geo Clinton was nominated Gov, & Jeremiah Van Rensselaer, Lt Gov; both declined a re-election at a previous meeting. John Lansing Jr, was then nominated Gov & John Broome-Lt Gov

Phil, Feb 21. Meeting of the Medical Students in Univ of Pa, Feb 18; Prof Woodhouse to deliver oration on death of Dr Jos Priestley. -John Hoskins, chrmn. Extract of a ltr from Thos Cooper, of Northumberland to Jas Woodhouse, Feb 6, 1804, followed.

I intend to relinquish the employment of ltr carrier on Mar 31. -Edw Eno.

WED FEB 29, 1804
I will resume the business of taking likenesses at the rms lately occupied by me in the hse of Mr David Shoemaker on F St.   -St Memim.

FRI MAR 2, 1804
For sale: blacksmith's shop & tools, F St, nr Mr Rhode's Tavern.
-Geo Blount, sadler, Wash City.

Celebration at Nottingham, PG Co, Md, at Capt Boon's Tavern: Gov Bowie, Pres; Thos Contee, VP. Rgrd: Accession of Louisiana.

MON MAR 5, 1804
Patent Bark Mill: Improvement in cutting & grinding barks can be seen at Thos Benger's Bark Manufactory nr Branford Crk nr Phil.   -Jacob Worrel, Thos Worrell. [2 splgs] Frankford, Phil.

Election of ofcrs of Bank of Col. at the hse of Jos Semmes, Gtwn.
-Wm Whann, Cashier.

Public sale of land, late the prop of Robt Alexander, 545 acs, bet Alex & Gtwn, adj the land of Philip Alexander, formerly the resid of Mr Custis, decd. Apply to Geo Deneale in Alex. -Thos Swann, Edmund J Lee, Geo Deneale, comrs. [decree of Crct Crt of Col dist for Alexandria Co].

Meeting of the ctzns of Norfolk & Portsmouth, Va, in Mr Ruffaud's Long Rm, on Feb 17; Wm Newsum, chrmn; A C Jordan, clk; Subj: Acqstn of La.

Loudon Co, Va; meeting of the ctzns on accession of La; Stacy Taylor, Pres; Dr Jas Heaton, VP.

WED MAR 7, 1804
Persons having business with me as agent either for the joint or separate est of Robt Morris, John Nicholson & Jas Greenleaf, or who wish to buy prop of the Aggregate Fund in this city, apply to Capt Thos Tingey, Wm Cranch or Mr Saml Elliot Jr, during my absence. -Jas Greenleaf, Wash.

FRI MAR 9, 1804
Orphans Crt of PG Co, Md. Feb 21, 1804. Prsnl est of Ninian Willett, late of said Co, decd.   -John T Willett, exc.

Interrogatories on part of the Hse o/Reps to Wm Lewis & Alex'r Jas Dallas, into official conduct of Saml Chase & Richd Peters; were you present at the trial of John Fries for high treason in Crct Crt of Pa in 1799 & 1800? Wm Lewis, Quaker, was present; Alex'r Jas Dallas, do.

Hse o/Reps: Mr Nicholson announced to the hse the death of Genrl Danl Heister, after a long illness. He died Mar 7th & will be interred at Hagers-town where the Genrl lately resided.

Public sale of right, title, interest & est of Nicholas February, insolvent debtor, 16 3/4 acs & dwlg hse in Gtwn & furn.   -Chas Beatty, trust, Gtwn.

Boston Glass Co-manufactory in Boston, Mr John Mutzenbecher or apply to Amos A Williams, Balt, Md.

MON MAR 12, 1804
Scheme of lottery for use of German Trinity chr, 6th St, Phil. Adam Premir, Anthony Hoockey, Chas Bowman, comrs. Geo Taylor Jr, 85 So 2d St. Matthew McConnell, 82 Chestnut St.

Deposition of Philip Norborne Nicholas was taken at the hse of Geo Wythe in Richmond, before said Wythe & Jos Scott, comrs authorised by the Hse o/Reps of the U S. Rgrd: Impeachment of Saml Chase & Richd Peters.

WED MAR 14, 1804
Orphans Crt of PG Co, Md. Mar 12, 1804. Prsnl est of Wm Magruder, late of said Co, decd.   -A Covrington, PG Co.

Impeachment of Chase & Peters: deposition of Jonathan Snowden was taken; deposition of Geo Read, atty of the U S for Dela dist, residing in New Castle, age 37 yrs & upwards.

FRI MAR 16, 1804
Scheme of a lottery to build an acad in Richmond City, Va. Tkts: Robt Pollard, Dr John Brockenbrough Jr, Wm Price-Reg, Saml Pleasants Jr & Wm Prichard. Richmond, Mar 2.

MON MAR 19, 1804
Lexington, Mar 6. Ctzns convened at the hse of Capt Alex'r Shields to partake of a dinner; occasion: acquisition of Louisiana; Capt John Caruthers, Pres; John Leyburn, VP.

Died: Mrs Ann Williams, age 39 yrs, Mar 18, consort of Mr Walter Williams, of Montgomery Co, Md. Leaves her husband & 4 chldrn & other relatives.

Bolting cloths just recd from Oliver Evans of Phil; at my store in Gtwn.
                                                -Wm Morgan.

Strayed or stolen, mare & mare colt, at Bladensburgh Mill. -Greenbury Barns.

WED MAR 21, 1804

To be sold-2 lots of 320 acs, in Ohio, granted to Martha Bogert a refugee from Canada. Patents & description -Philip Van Cortlandt, Wash City.

Absconded, Adam, negro, age 23 yrs, from Alexander Scott living nr Port Tobacco, Md. Reward-$20.

Ran away-Raleigh Leister, appr, mulatto, age 19 yrs, from Wm Foxton, plaisterer, Washington. His mthr lives nr Pearcy's Tavern, Westmoreland Co, Va; his black fr lives with Rev Mr Davis, in Alex.

FRI MAR 23, 1804

Ltr & report from the agent to Pres of U S-Public lands nr Detroit. [Signed-C Jouett to the Hon Henry Dearborn, esq, sec of U S, for Dept of War. Report from Pres Jefferson]. At Sandy Creek 16 inhabitants took possession of their farms in 1792, under purchases from Jos Benack who claimed ntv right since 1780, people are Canadians. Rocky River-Tenure is derived from an Indian deed executed by the Chiefs in 1786 to Francis Pepin; Pepin sold his claim to Geo MacDougall who cnvyd 2/3ds of the tract to Meldrum & Parks, a Mercantile hse in Detroit; North Side is claimed by Gabriel Godfroy under Indian deed dated 1788, 2 families reside now on the rvr. River Huron-Indian deed dated 1794 cnvyd 4500 acs to Gabriel Godfroy. Encore or Bark Rvr-16 Canadian French hold abt 300 acs there & the farms were settled in 1792, 1794, & 1797, without any kind of authority; others purchased in 1776 by Peter F Comb from the Indians. Detroit-225 acs, 4 acs occupied by the town & Ft Lenault, rest is a common, except 24 acs which were added 20 yrs ago to a farm belonging to Wm Macomb. Gros Isle-cultivated by 10 farmers who pay annual rent to est of Wm Macomb, by whom it was purchased of the indians in 1776. Hog Island-chartered in 1765 & at that time purchased of the indians by Geo MacDougall, whose heirs in 1786 sold it to Wm Macomb.

MON MAR 26, 1804

Cont'd-ltr & report of Fri Mar 23d-lands nr Detroit- See above.
Milk Rvr-30 settlers, 20 settled in 1788-farms purchased from the Indians. Point O Tramble-Canadians, 3,759 acs was purchased by Patrick Sinclair, British Commandant at Ft Sinclair in 1765 from the Indians; he held it until 1782 when he left the country & by deed of gift, gave it to Vatiren, a Canadian, who sold it in 1784 to Meldrum & Parks.

Ltr from Capt Wm Bainbridge to Cmdor Edw Preble; dated, Tripoli, Barbary, 12th Nov 1803; Subj: Loss of U S frig, *Philadelphia*, late under my command. -Wm Bainbridge

WED MAR 28, 1804

Wanted: A teacher in the Forrest of Patuxant, 5 miles from Bladensburg. Apply to: Wm Wilson, Tilghman Henry, Jas Waring, Saml Magruder & John Hillary.

For sale: 2 pianos & some good violins. -Fr A Wagler, opposite the Roman Chapel, Gtwn.

Died: Mr Richd Frazer, Mar 25, purser of the Navy Yd in Wash, leaving an afflicted wife & family.

Late ofcrs of frig, *Philadelphia*, Capt Bainbridge, signed a ltr of highest & most sincere respect: *Lts*-David Porter, J Jones, Theodore Hunt, Ben Smith & Wm S Osborn. *Surg*-John Ridgely; *Purser*-Keith Spence; *Sailing Mstr*-Wm Knight; *Surg's Mate*- Jona. Cowdery & Nichs. Harwood; *Midshipmen*-Bernard Henry, Jas Gibbon, Ben F Reed, Wallace Wormeley, Robt Gamble, Jas Biddle, Rd B Jones, Dl. T Patterson, Wm Cutbush & Simon Smith. *Sail Mkr* - Jos Douglass; *Boatswain*-Geo Hodge; *Gunner* -Richd Stephenson; *Mdshipman*-Jas Renshaw; *Carpenter*-Wm Godby. Men quartered at the Americ Consular hse at Tripoli-the above men & *Capt's clk*-Wm Anderson; *Masters' Mate* - Minor Forentan; *ships' Steward*-Jas C Morris; *Sgt Marines*-Otis Hunt & David Irvine; *Cook*-Wm Leith; *Master at Arms*-Jas Casey; *Cpl*-Peter Williams; John Baptist, Lewis Hecksener, Frederick Lewis, Chas Mitchell, Peter Cosk, Leonard Foster & Wm James.

Celebration of the acquisition of La was held in Richmond, Va on Mar 5th; oration by Mr Jas Ogilvie. Present: Gov Page, Chanc. Wythe, Judge Nelson, Col Hitchburn of Mass, Mr Fulton of Balt, Dr W Foushee, Maj Wm Duval & Robt Mitchell. Toasts volunteers: Mr Chevallie; P N Nicholas, Henry L Bisco, Wm Thomson, Col Wilkinson, J J Cohen, S McCraw, Mr Shepard, Thos Posser & Mr McCance-an Hibernian.

Augusta Ga, Feb 25. Celebration of acquisition of La; ctzns met last Sat at Maj Durkee's Hotel; Dr Murray, chrmn; Maj Genrl Twiggs & Walter Leigh, VPs.

Gilmanton, NH, Mar 22. Dinner & ball-acquisition of La: volunteer toasts by: Gen Jos Badger; Judge Cogswell; Rev Mr Smith; John Ham; Nath'l Cogswell & Stephen Moody.

FRI MAR 30, 1804
Acts passed-8th Congress: 1-Relief of leg reps of David *Valenzin, decd; 2-Relief of heirs of John Habersham. 3-Relief of Paul Coulon. 4-Relief of John Coles. 5-Relief of Saml Corp. 6-Relief of **Moses Young. 7-Payment of $2,800 to Philip Sloan to indemnify him for his ransom from captivity among the Algerines, as interpreter to Algerine Mission. *Valenzin, decd, for value of prop captured from him in the Mediterranean by the Americ squadron in 1803. **Moses Young was the Agent of Claims at Madrid.

MON APR 2, 1804
Wm Johnson of SC apptd an Assoc Justice, vice Alfred Moore, late an Assoc Justice of the Supreme Crt of the U S, having rsgnd said ofc.
-Th Jefferson, Mar 29, 1804.

Bernard McMahon, seedsman, 129 Chestnut St, Phil, Pa.

WED APR 4, 1804
Mrd: Richd Cutts, esq, Rep from Mass, to Miss Paine, of Wash, Mar 31, by Rev Dr Gantt.

Following ofcrs have been ordered to join the ships put in commission & preparing for the Mediterranean:

Saml Barron	John Rodgers	Jas Barron
Hugh G Campbell	Isaac Chauncey	Geo Cox
Wm C Jenckes	Saml Evans	Edw Wyer
P C Wederstrandt	Chas Ludlow	Marmaduke Dove
Christopher Gadsden	Oliver H Perry	John M Gardner
Dl Murray	Geo Balfour	Edw Cutbush
P Lt Medar	Thos Triplett	Nathl Tisdall
Starling Archer	Jos W New	Alexr McWilliams
Larkin Griffin	Wm Baker	Isaac Garretson
Chas Wadsworth	Buller Cocke	Silas Butler
Thos Johnston	Geo H Geddes	Edw O'Brien
Jas S Higinbotham	Saml Angus	Dl C Sim
Geo Dabney	John Shattuck	Wm P Smith
Jno Godwin	Edw Bennett	Geo Parker
Johnston Blakeley	Winlock Clarke	Ep R Blaine
M T Woosley	Wm H Allen	Wm McIntosh
Edw Trenchard	Sloss H Grenell	John B Nicholson
Archd K Karney	Edw Giles	Orde Creighton
Sidney Smith	Benj Turner	Geo S Hackley
Noble W Glen	Wm S Butler	Jno R Leaycraft
Wm Sim	John Downes	Henry L Martin
Jas P Wilmer	Walter G Anderson	Francis Mitchell
Lewis Hunt	John Daboie	Jas Marshall
Jno R Sherwood	Di P Ramsey	Francis B Whiting
Chas Jones	And. W Stuart	Jacquelin Harvie
Rd H Wilson	Henry Thomas	Edw Winslow
Thos Shields	And W McDowell	Overton Carr
Geo A Hannah	Walter Stewart	Jas A Miller
Thos Swearingen	Jacob Hite	Wm. Walker
Eli E Danielson	John Stocton Jr	Thos Shephard
Alfred Coale	Chas W Rivers	Jos Sabb
Alex'r S Wadsworth		

Appointments: John Saml Sherburne, of NH, dist Judge of NH.
Jonathan Steele, of NH, atty for NH.
Jos McIlvaine, of NJ, atty for NJ.
Jonathan Russell, of Providence, R I, cnsl at Tunis.
Wm H Burr, of NJ, coll & inspec for Burlington, vice Moses Kempton.
Jos Winner, of NJ, coll & inspec for Great Egg Harbour, vice Alexander Freeland.

Wm Fisher, of Va, coll for So Quay.
Benj Tupper, of Ohio, receiver of public monies at Marietta.
Willyss Sillman, of Ohio, Reg of land ofc at Zanesville.
Thos Van Swearingen, of Ohio, rec of public monies at Zaneville.
Wm Bache, srvyr of Phil Port.
Chas Kilgore, of Ohio, reg of land ofc at Cincinnati.
John Willis, of Md, coll & inspec for Port of Oxford.
Merriwether Jones, of Va, comr of loans for Va.
Hore Brown Trist, of Miss Terr, coll of Miss.
Benjamin Morgan, of New Orleans, Naval ofcr of port of New Orleans.
Alexander Bailey, of Miss Terr, coll & inspec for Port of Natchez.
Wm G Garland, of New Orleans, srvyr & inspec of Port of New Orleans.
Chas Collins Jr, of R I, coll & inspec for Port of Bristol, R I.

FRI APR 6, 1804
Chas Wayman, Gtwn, advertises clover seed for sale.

Hse o/Reps: Mary Gresham has leave to withdraw her petition.

Tkt for electors of Pres & V Pres, recommended by the people of Pa:
Chas Thompson	Wm Montgomery	Matthew Lawler
Robt McMullen	Wm Brooke	Francis Swaine
Thos Long	Henry Spering	Jas Whitehill
Peter Frailey	Jos Bowman	Jas Boyd
John Bowman	Wm Brown	Jacob Hostetter
Geo Smith	Jacob Binnet	Jas Montgomery
John Hamilton	Nath'l I_ish.	

Ranaway-Harry, negro, abt 30 yrs of age, from Hiram Belt, residing nr Bladensburg. He was raised in St Mary's Co, Md.

From the Bee: Rpblcn Festival was held at Canaan [New Lebanon] on Mar 12th; oration by John King; entertainment by Mr Elam Tilden.

Hse o/Reps: Thos Coleman of NC has leave to withdraw his memorial.

MON APR 9, 1804
Crt of Impeachment: U S v John Pickering, Mar 2. Petition of Jacob S Pickering, son of John Pickering, & a ltr from Robt G Harper were submitted; Subj: John Pickering was insane for more than 2 yrs. Deposition given by Saml Tenney, of Rockingham Co, NH; depo of Ammi R Cutter of Rockingham Co, NH; depo of Joshua Brackett of Portsmouth, NH; depo of Wm Cutter of Portsmouth, Rockingham Co, NH; depo of Wm Plumer-Wash, Mar 5, 1804.

Notice: sale of frame hse lately occupied by John B Winut on L St nr the Navy Yd. -Wm Adams. Also 2 brick hses nr said place.
                                                -Levi White & Stephen Parry.

	1774	1803
Population of U S	2,486,000	5,771,412
Militia:	421,300	972,000
Seamen:	15,000	63,500

-S Blodget.

WED APR 11, 1804

Spacious crnr lot, sq 687, presented by Danl Carroll of Dud'n & Tnos Law, esqs, for bldg a hotel thereon. Subscription is now opened & may be seen in hands of: Danl C Brent, Geo Blagden, Jas Hoban, Griffith Coombs & Robt Brent.

Those who have subscribed for erection of the Mason's Lodge in Wash are to pay: Mr Alexander McCormick, Chas Jones, chrmn to the committee, or Nicholas King, sec.

Chas Shoemaker, insolvent debtor, confined in Wash Co prison for debt.
-Uriah Forrest, Ck.

Trial of John Pickering: deposition of Edw St Loe Livermire; Portsmouth, NH, Feb 15, 1804; Attest-Geo Sullivan, Justice of Peace

FRI APR 13, 1804

Ladies with ltrs in Wash Post Ofc, Apr 1, 1804:

Miss Kitty Boarman	Peggy Fornsworth	Miss Delia Forman
Mrs Hanson	Mrs Mary Holford	Mrs Eliza Hitchcock
Eliz McKennan	Harrot A Nance	Cath Mary Nicholson
Mrs Rebecca	Eliza Seymour	Miss Anne Smith
Mrs Casey Smallwood	Miss Polly Stewart	Miss Smallwood
Martha Veich	Mary Wilson	

Mass. election results:

Office	*Candidate Name*	*Votes*	*Candidate Name*	*Votes*
Governor	Caleb Strong	1980	Jas Sullivan	650
Lt Governor	Edw H Robbins	1909	Wm Heath	730
Senators	Oliver Wendell	2647	Wm Brown	1802
	John Phillips	1544	Jos Russell	1516
	Josiah Quincy	1452	Abiel Smith	1209
	Jos Bowdoin	1126	David Tilden	1136
	Benj Austin	847		

Wm C C Clairborne, Gov of Miss Terr, authorised establishment of the "Louisiana Bank"; subscriptions from: Edw Livingston, Evan Jones, J Merieult, Paul Lanusse, Wm Garland, Pierre Sauve, Jos Tricou, John Lanthois, Wm Donaldson, Nich's F Girard, John McDonnough Jr, Jerome LaChiapella, Benj Morgan, H B Trist, Mich'l Fortier & Beverly Chew.

My wife, Maying Stanton, eloped from my bed & board. I will not pay any debts by her contracted.   -Patrick Stanton, Wash.

MON APR 16, 1804
Awards in favor of Americ claimants made bet Dec 5, 1803 & Feb 19, 1804: Payable by the British Gov't.

Vessel	Master	Americ claimant
Ann	Jos Marshalk	John Carrere, Jas & Wm DePeyster
Betsey	John Helm	John Carrere & Moses Meyers
Birmingham	Wm B Forster	Jas Clarke
Commerce	Jonathan Neal	Jonathan Neal
Eagle	Henry Manning	Mr Penman & Co
Fanny	Danl Campbell	John Hollins & Richd Caton
Hector	Geo Connell	Alex'r Anderson, Geo Connell, Abraham Kintzing Jr, Manuel Jee, Henry B Blachard, Billton & Massey, Millar & Murray
London Packet	Richd Smith	Seth Barton
Maria & Eliza	Thos Clements Jr	John Skynner & Sons, Jos Hinkley
Minerva	Saml Holt	Blair McClenachan & Patrick Moore
Narcissus	D Moulton	John Cornelius Vandel Hewell
Peter Augustus	Philip Robson	John Hollingsworth & John Shallcross
Rebecca	Ebenezer Nutting	David Cargill
Sukey	Anthony Andaulle	Geo Makepeace
William	Henry Stoddard	Wm Marshall & John Whiting, Valch & Co, Thos & Saml Hellingsworth.

Thos Barclay, insolvent debtor, confined in Wash Co prison for debt.
                                    -Uriah Forrest, Ck.

Trial of John Pickering: Jos Whipple, coll of Portsmouth was sworn; Jonathan Steele, clk of the Crt, sworn; John S Sherburne, dist atty, do.

Ofcrs of the Marine Corps ordered into svc on Mediterranean Espedition: Lt Amory, Hall, Hooper & Lane.

WED APR 18, 1804
Dissolution of partnership bet Wm Ross & Robt Tilley; firm in Bladensburg; mutual consent; Tilley will continue on F St.

Partnership bet Jas Webb & Brooke, cabinet mkrs, dissolved by mutual consent; Webb will continue on Pa Av, Wash City.

Trial of J Pickering: Simeon Olcott & Wm Plumer, Senator from NH, sworn; Ebenezer Chadwick & Edw Hart, sworn; Pickering had habits of intoxication. Proposed partnership bet Jas C King & Absalom Joy is dissolved.
                                    -Absalom Joy, Gtwn.

Advertisement of Brew hse in Alexandria. -Thos Cruse, Alexandria.

FRI APR 20, 1804
For sale: land whereon Francis *Bone, an insolvent debtor resides; 125 acs & dwelling hse. John Duvall. Also, same place, deed of trust to Robt Bowie & Alexs Boone, 15 negroes. -Robt Bowie, Alexs Boone. [*as written.]

To rent: 2 two story frame dwelling hses in Mkt St; 1 story brick hse & lot in Gtwn; a frame hse in High St which I occupy.
-Andrew Kaldenbach, Gtwn.

Rpblcns meet in Albany, Feb 22d; Morgan Lewis candidate for Gvn'r; John Broome for Lt Gvn'r. Committee: John Tayler, Ezra L'Hommedieu. Robt Johnston, Caleb Hyde, John Woodworth, Sylvester Dering, Lucas Flmendorf, Alex Sheldon, Jedediah Peck, Henry Rutgers, Peter H Wendover, Benj DeWitt.

MON APR 23, 1804
Mrd: Mr Nathan Foyles to Miss Susan Davis, both of Wash, Apr 19, by Rev Mr McCormick.

Strayed or stolen, sorrel horse, Saml Speake, of Wash. He was late the prop of Rev Mr Knox, formerly of Frederick.

WED APR 25, 1804
Deserted from on board the schnr, *Victory*: Chas Young, Peter Lamb, Michael Doyle & John Steward. -Wm P Smith, Marine Barracks, Wash.

FRI APR 27, 1804
A wood skow was left at my wharf. -Griffith Combe, Wash.

Orphans Crt of Wash Co, DC. Apr 13, 1804. Prsnl est of Jas O'Brien, late of Wash Co, decd. -John O'Brien, admr.

MON APR 30, 1804
For sale or rent: hse on north F St opposite Mrs Johnson's brdg hse. Apply: Lewis Morin, Pa Av or to Morris Lambert.

For sale-deed of trust from John Kennedy, part of lot 1 sq 291 in Wash City on Pa Av & 2 story brick dwelling hse occupied by Augustus B Woodward, esq.
-Geo Thomson, John Murdock.

Mrd: Mr John Wall to Mrs Eliz Brooks, both of Wash, Apr 26, by Rev Mr Parrot.

Died: Wm Macley, late a mbr of Hse o/Reps of Pa from Dauphin Co, Apr 16 at Harrisburg.

Died: Mrs Maria Eppes, w/o John W Eppes, esq, & d/o Thos Jefferson, esq, Apr 17, at Monticello.

Notice: Public sale on the premises; all the right, title, claim & interest of Jos Boone, in lot 2 sq 1044 & 2 story framed dwelling hse, Wash City; per suit of Wilson Hunt, for use of Philip Nicklin & Robt Griffith.
-Danl C Brent, Mrshl

WED MAY 2, 1804
Died: Col Richd Barnes, of St Mary's Co, Md, Apr 29. His will declares all his negroes, bet 3 & 400, free 3 yrs after his death, provided they behave themselves well.

Meeting of the claimants in Boston, Mass, Apr 20th. Copy to be sent to Christopher Gore, esq. Signed Richd D Tucker, sec. Subj: Reparation for losses stipulated by the 7th Article of the British Treaty. Response by C Gore. Committee: Benj Pickman, Stephen Gorham & Aaron Putnam, Esqs.

Mrd: Mr Daniel Rapine, bkseller, to Miss Charlotte Osborne, both of Wash, Apr 29, by Rev Mr Balch.

Ltr from Capt Saml Lewis of the schnr *Sukey*, of Phil; dated Bermuda, Apr 8, 1804; Lewis is a ntv ctzn of the U S; Subj: his return cargo has been condemned & he was in held in custody in Burmuda.

Ranaway-Jas Gardiner, age abt 19 yrs, appr to the carpenter trade; s/o John Gardiner, tailor in Gtwn.   -Simeon Mead, carpenter, Wash.

FRI MAY 4, 1804
In Chancery-Wash Co, DC: Thos Law, cmplnt. v Richd Gridley Jr, dfndnt. Gridley is indebted to Law for a large sum of money & also bound by contract to build a 2 story brick hse in Wash City, mortgaged a lot-part of sq 770; bill is to foreclose Gridley Jr from all redemption in said lot; Gridley Jr remv'd from Wash.   -U Forrest, clk.

Strayed or stolen horse.   -David Ogilvie, Wash City.

In Chancery-Wash Co, DC: Francis Mantz, cmplnt v John Mantz, dfndnt. Antecedent to the cession of that part of DC, which was in Md, to Congress, Francis & John purchased in partnership by equal moieties, of Geo Zimmerman, 2 lots in then Hamburg, PG Co, now in Wash City. Zimmerman cnvyd the said lots to John, alone, & not to Francis. Bill is to obtain a cnvyance of cmplnt's part of said lots to him. -U Forrest, clk; John T Mason, solicitor

For sale: lot 5 sq 289, North F St; lot 13 sq 289, from F to G Sts.
-Chas McNantz.

MON MAY 7, 1804

In Chancery-Wash Co, DC. Robt S Bickley, cmplnt, v Saml Blodget Jr, Thos McEwen, Wm Davidson & Wm Smith D D of Phil, Thos Peter, Thos Munroe, Robt Brent, Benj Stoddert, Elias Boudinett Caldwell, Wm Thornton, John Stickney, Adam Lindsay, Edw Fritkey, Jas Dougherty, Francis Lowndes, of Wash Co, DC, dfndnts. Bill is to obtain a cnvyance in fee simple of lots in Wash Co, DC with Great Hotel; & to receive $21,500 with int from Dec 26, 1801 & cost of suit, all adjudged to him by Sup Crt of Pa on Dec 25, 1801, as owner of tkt 37,531 in the lottery for improvement of Wash City. Order of Wm Kilty, Chief Judge of Crct Crt of DC.   -U Forrest, clk. [See below]
In Chancery-Wash Co, DC, Oct 9, 1802. Wm Fennell, cmplnt, v dfndnts-Bill of same crt in Pa & same purpose, i e, for sum of $11,495 for tkt 12,515, from Wash lottery.

John B Duclairack, Prof of Music & Dancing, teaching both in Gtwn.

Orphans Crt of Chas Co, Md. Nov 2, 1803. Est of Jas Graham, late of Chas Co, decd.   -Gerrard Briscoe, adm.

Patent right: for painting rms to represent paper hangings. Patent purchased from John Selby, original inventor, for Wash, Va, NC, SC, Ga, Tenn, Providence of La & New Orleans. -Messrs Richd Ryland, Wm Byrne, Stocco Plaisterers, Capitol Hill, Wash City.

WED MAY 9, 1804

In 1800 when the census was taken in Wash City the inhabitants amt'd to 3,210; in 1803 the census now stated was taken, the inhabitants amt'd to 4,352. 1803: white males-1902, white females-1510, slaves-717, free blacks-223.

Sworn as attys & cnslrs in the Supreme Crt of the U S at the last term:
John Quincey Adams of Mass;   Geo W Campbell of Tenn;
Richd Raynal Keene of Md;   Geo Young of DC;
Zebulon Hollingsworth of Md; Thos R Roots of Va;
Rufus Easton of NY State

Ranaway-Edw Vidler, appr to taylor's bus., age abt 11 yrs of age; taken from Balt by his mthr & carried to Wash City; supposed to be with his fr at Mr P Miller's nr Barry's Wharf. -B Yoe & J Compton, 92 Mkt St, Balt.

FRI MAY 11, 1804

Died: Jeremiah Wadsworth, age 61 yrs of age, Col in Rev War; (many yrs a Rep from Conn in Congress of U S); May 7, at Hartford, Conn.

Ship news. Louisville, Apr 14. Arrv'd at this port on Mon last, new brig *Nanina*, Capt Saml McCutcheon from Pittsburg where she was built, prop of Tarascon brothers, Jas Berthoud & Co; also new ship *Louisiana*, Capt Jas McKeaver, on board the family of Mr Berthoud.

Mon May 14, 1804

Escaped from NY State Prison: Wm Wicket, Edmund Barns, Jos Amblet & Wm Griswold.

Notice: Decree of Crct Crt of Wash Co, DC in suit of Valentine Peyton, against Mary Cooke & Alexander Stedman & Julia his wife, Jos Wilson & Robt Brown, dfndnts, in Chancery; to be sold lot 5 sq 253, Wash City & hses.
-Danl C Bent, Mrshl

Savannah, Apr 28. Ctzns were in a state of agitation from charge to the Grand Jury delivered by Jabez Bowen Jr, Judge of the Superior Crt.
Jury of Chatham Co:

Wm Smith, Foreman;	C Gibbons	Wm Blogg
Jas McIntosh	S Shad	Wm Lewden
Jas Alger	Jas Cline	John Gibbons
Isaac Minis	W Brown	Sam Simons
Jas Belcher	John Y White	Jos Rice
Jos Machin	John Pettibone	Sampson Neyle
David Gugel	T Barnard Jr	Henry Putnam.

At meeting of the Crt hse on Apr 25th, following were present:

Genrl Mitchell	Chas Harris	John Y Noel
Thos Gibbons	Jos Welscher	Jas E Houstoun
Richd Leake	Chas Baldwin	Morris Miller
Jeremiah Cuyler	John M Barrein	Geo Allen
Wm B Bulloch	John Lawson	Richd M Stites
Fingal T Flyming	Jos Stoops	Thos Netherclift
Jas Townsend	Wm Davies, esqs;	

D B Mitchell-chrmn & Wm Davit-sec. Ctzns applaud conduct of the Grand Jury & apptd John Bolton, Edw Telfair, Saml Howard, Edw L Davies, Geo D Sweet, Richd M Stites, Jos Arnold, John I Gray, Norman McLeod, Saml H Stackhouse, Wm McAllister, Robt Mackay, Wm Stephens, Jos Clay & Jos Miller to serve on sundry committees. Bowen was charged with an attempt to excite a domestic insurrection-Signed John Pooler, J P [L S]. John P Oates, jailor, C C, Apr 26, 1804. Other names: Barack Gibbons, Richd Turner, Solomon Shad, Jas Alger, Saul Simons & Jonathan Cline.

R I elections: Arthur Fenner re-elected-Gov; Paul Mumford-Lt Gov

Wed May 16, 1804

In Chancery-Wash Co, DC-Oct 9, 1802. Geo King, John Davidson & John B Evans, cmplnts. against Anne Young the widow & Saml W Young, Eliz Young, Susanna Young, Richd Young, John Young the chldrn & heirs of Abraham Young, decd, & Wm King & Adam King all of Wash City & John Ball, Henry Pratt, John Ashley, Thos Willing, Francis John Miller Jr & Jacob Baker of Phil, dfndnts. Abraham Young, decd, late of Wash City, did in his life time; on Sep 16, 1792 sell to Wm King & Wm Prout parts of land in Wash cld *Chance*,

Hogpen Enlarged & Knock-100 1/2 acs. Wm King on Jul 20, 1794 pd his moiety of said prop to John Nicholson, late of Phil, now decd. Bill is to have the said prop sold to produce sufficient sum to pay the cmplnts. Saml W & Chas Young have since remv'd from Wash.   -Uriah Forrest-clk

In Chancery-Wash Co, DC. Jan 28, 1804. John G Ladd v Amariah Frost. Bill to foreclose a mortgage on half of lot 17 sq 634 in Wash, given by Frost to Ladd. Frost is not an inhabitant of Wash.   -Uriah Forrest, clk

Public sale-"*Dunlah*", prop of R Lee, esq, 300 acs, near Montgomery Crt hse. Mr Wm Clements, living nr the premises will show the prop. Also in Gtwn, Parts of "*Scotch Ordinary*" nr Gtwn, 73 acs. Part of tract cld "*Read's Swamp*", 467 acs, nr Piscataway. Part of land cld "*Bead's Reserve*" nr the latter tract, 310 acs.   -Jas Clerklee

Ranaway, Will, negro man, age 25 yrs, from Hector R Eskridge, Pr Wm Co, Va. Reward-$50.

Sale at auction-hse & lot on So Side of Pa Av, opposite Ctre Mkt, prop of John Harrison, tallow-chandler.   -John Travers, auct, Gtwn.

FRI MAY 18, 1804
Partnership bet Geo Quinn & Edw Fitzgerald is dissolved by mutual consent. Settle with Geo Quinn.

Decree of Crct Crt in Chancery, Wash Co, DC-sale of land in Hawkens & Beatty's Addition to Gtwn; suit of Dr Ninian Magruder, cmplnt, & Ann Seyle, Geo, Jacob, Lewis, Saml Seyle, Susanna Edmondston, Polly & Geo Adams, Peter & Cath. Mantz, Jacob & Betsey Steiner, Barbara, Daniel & Lewis Hauer, John & Peggy Stover, Henry, Polly & Adam Hauer, dfndnts.
   -Chas A Burnett, Gtwn.

Wanted: Appr to a saddler, boy abt 14.   -Geo Blount, Pa Av

Decree of Crct Crt of Wash Co, DC-sale of all right, title & int of Jonathan Jackson, decd, lots 21 & 22 in sq 75, lot 2 sq 164, part of lot 14 sq 75, Wash City; lots in Gtwn nr Jos Peck's hse, also lot on Wash St nr hse occupied by Wm A Rind, also lot crnr of Congress & West Sts; suit of Wm H Dorsey, Nicholas Hedges, Geo Craig & Adam Whann against Agnes Jackson-excx, Wm Jackson-exc; Jonathan, Matthew, Eliz & Susanna, infant heirs of Jonathan Jackson, decd, dfndnts. -Agnes Jackson, Wm Jackson, trustees

Orphans Crt of Wash Co, DC. Apr 27, 1804. Prsnl est of Richd Frazer, late of said co, decd.   -Saml T Smallwood, adm

Decree of Crct Crt of Wash Co, DC-sale of lot 5 sq 253 in Wash City with hse; suit of Valentine Peyton against Mary Cook & Alexander Stedman & Julia his wife, Jos Wilson & Robt Brown, dfndnts.   -Danl C Brent, Marshal

Stage to run from Gtwn to Bath, Berkley Co, Va, once a wk, fare-$8.
-Leonard Cokendaffer

MON MAY 21, 1804
Runaway, Milly Thomas, negro, age abt 38 yrs, committed to Balt co jail; says she did belong to Wm Briscoe, o/Chas Co, Md. -Thos Bailey, Shrf-Balt Co, Md

WED MAY 23, 1804
Brd of trustees of So Carolina College have elected Dr Jonathan Maxcey of NY, Pres; Dr John McLean of Princeton College, NJ, Prof of Math; Rev Robt Wilson of Abbeville dist, SC, First Prof; Mr Enoch Hanford of SC, 2d Prof of Languages.

List of ofcrs on board the Ketch, *Intrepid,* Lt Com. Stephen Decatur, Jr; Lts: Jas Lawrence, Jos Bainbringe, Jonathan *Thorn; Surg: Lewis Herman. Midshipmen belonging to the *Constitution*: Ralph Izard, John Rowe, Chas Morris, Alex Laws, John Davis. Thos McDonough-*Enterprize* & Thos Oakley Anderson-*Syren*. Orders were to burn the frig [late the U S frig] *Phil*, at anchor in Tripoli Harbour, Feb 16, 1804. *[Correction of May 28 from Thom to Thorn]

Ranaway-Prince, negro, age abt 22 yrs, from Robt Graham, lvng nr Dumfries, Va.

FRI MAY 25, 1804
Mary Wilson, without any cause, absented herself from me after being guilty of intemperance; she may not have credit on my account. -Richd Wilson.

Wanted: Gun-lock filers. -Mathias Hart, Wash City.

MON MAY 28, 1804
Wash Bldg Co wishes to contract for bldg materials for brick bldg adj Wm Woodward's on Pa Av Clotworthy Stevenson, Jos Huddleston & Orlando Cook.

Hse o/Reps report. Petition of Wm Dunbar of Miss Terr & of Mayor, Aldermen & assistants of the City of Natchez, Miss Terr; Subj: land the city claims without a title, while Wm Dunbar claims the former upon a Spanish Grant, dated Apr 19, 1797, by Gov Gayofo

Richd Forrest writes that he is not a candidate for the approaching election in Wash City for city cncl.

WED MAY 30, 1804
Mass election: Votes for Gvn'r: Caleb Strong-30,097 & Jas Sullivan-23,979.

Jas Hoban declines being a candidate for ensuing election for cncl in Wash City. John Hewitt & John Davidson, F St, Wash City, decline.

Fri Jun 1, 1804

Sale, Jun 11: Those lands, lots & hses in Wash, where taxes & costs have not been paid. -Geo Magruder, coll of 6th dist.

Mon Jun 4, 1804

Public auction of lot 57 at crnr of Fayette & 1st Sts next to Mr C Lowndes' facing the Roman Chapel, a 2 story frame hse. Dower in the prop will be relinquished. -Edw Noun Butler.

Crt Martial proceedings of Col Thos Butler, of 2d Regt of Infty were held at Frederick town, Md, Nov 21 until Dec 6. Disobedience of orders & neglect of duty. The Genrl will dismiss the subject. -J Wilkinson.
-Th Cushing, adj & inspec of the Army.

Wed Jun 6, 1804

Wanted: A miller-nr Winchester, Frederick Co, Va. -D Carlile

Died: on May 28, Mr John Burchan of Wash City, after a lingering illness, leaving an aged mthr & other relatives, remains were interred on May 29th at the Presby New Burying Ground in Gtwn; mbr of the Baptist chr in this place.

Crt Martial convened at Fredericktown, Md, on Nov 21; Col Thos Butler of the 2d Regt of Infty arraigned on disobedience of orders & neglect of duty. Col Berbeck, Pres; mbrs: Lt Col Freeman, Maj MacRea, Capt Read, Capt Freeman, Capt Boote, Capt Saunders, Capt Bruff, Capt Steil, Capt McClallen, Capt Beall, Lt Osborne, Lt House [Judge Advocate], all mbrs of the Crt.

Chas Love has an assortment of wine for sale at his warehse, on Jefferson St, Gtwn.

Public sale of 800 acs, Loudon Co, Va; Mr Solomon Betton now residing on it. -Chas Fenton Mercer. Also 11000 acs on Ohio Rvr in Va, below Great Kanahwa. -John Fenton Mercer, Chas Fenton Mercer.

Fri Jun 8, 1804

Order of Crt of Calvert Co, Md-sale of plantation on which Capt Walter Smith formerly resided, 1225 1/8 acs, on St Leonard's Creek; also nr the same, 667 1/2 acs; premises nr Parkers Creek, 536 1/2 acs; apply to Mr John Turner who resides nr the first two. -J Wilkinson, Jas Hughe, John Turner, comrs.

In Chancery, May 15, 1804. Naylor Davis, creditor, v his heirs. Order that sale by Trueman Tyler, trustee, for sale of rl est of Naylor Davis, decd, be ratified; part of a tract cld the *Forrest*, part of tract cld *Forrest of Sherwood*, & part of *Cool Springs*, for 1 Pound, 18 Shillings & 5 Pence per ac.
-Saml H Howard, Reg CC

Mon Jun 11, 1804

Ranaway-2 negro boys, Wm Dyson & Chas, age-15 & 16 yrs, from Osborne Belt, residing on Post Rd nr Bladensburg, PG Co, Md.

Oration on cession of La to U S; delivered May 12, 1804 in St Michael's Chr, Charleston, SC, by David Ramsay, MD.

Wed Jun 13, 1804

Wash City cncl elected Saml Harrison Smith, Pres & John Gardiner, sec of the First Chamber; Nicholas King, Pres & Thos Herty, sec, of the Second Chamber.

Mrd: Mr Wm Kean to the agreeable Miss Julia Docker, both of this city, by Rev Mr McCormick, on Jun 10.

Fri Jun 15, 1804

Persons having claims against the est of David Valenzin for supporting him during his imprisonment will send their accounts to sec of Navy.

Mon Jun 18, 1804

Wash City. Baron Homboldt, who visited this city is abt 32 yrs of age; he has traveled for the past 19 yrs & will return to Europe in a few wks.

Charges against Judge Jabez Bowen Jr. Jan last he destroyed a record of Sup Crt of Chatham Co, plea or answer of Thos Gibbons, to action instituted against him, by Oliver Bowen, decd. Apr 23 delivered a speech, tending to excite insurrection; held converse with slaves tending to inflame their minds; [& other similar charges.] His excellency John Milledge, Gov & Commander in Chief of Army & Navy of Ga, & of Militia thereof Augusta, Georgia, May 26. David Emanuel, Pres of Senate. Wm Robertson, sec. May 18th Bowen was remv'd from his ofc as Judge of Sup Crt-Ga.

Wed Jun 20, 1804

Application for renewal of lost certificates; #s 362 thru 366, dated Apr 5, 1804, in favor of John Coles of New London, signed by Jos Nourse, reg.
                                        -John McGowan

Fri Jun 22, 1804

Mississippi Soc.-Natchez, Oct 1, 1803: Those present: Isaac Briggs, W C C Claiborne, Wm Dumbar, John Henderson, Jesse Greenfield, David Lettimore, Ferdinand L Claiborne, John Girault, Benj Farar, Israel E Trask & Lewis Kerr.

Strayed bay horse-Wm Fletcher, residing opposite Branch Bank.

Mon Jun 25, 1804

Committed to Frederick Co jail, George, negro, age 14 yrs, says he belongs to Capt Newman of Gtwn. -Geo Creager-shrf. Also in same jail-Ceasa Langston, age 37 yrs, negro, says he belongs to Mr Isaac Langston of Herford Co, NC.

Also Jim, negro, & Mima, mulatto woman, say they belong to Mr Peter Larkins of Farquhar Co, Va; ages 34 & 25. —G Creager, Shrf

Notice—John Edwards is apptd by the Legionary Crt of 1st Legion of Militia of DC to collect fines. —Wm D Beall, clk

WED JUN 27, 1804
Republican tkt of electors of Pres & VP for State of Va:

Richd E Lee	*Norfolk Borough*	John Goodrich	*Isle of Wight*
Edw Pegram	*Dinwiddie*	Dr Richd Field	*Brunswick*
Thos Read	*Charlotte*	Cred Taylor	*Cumberland*
Wm H Cabell	*Amherst*	Geo Penn	*Patrick*
Geo Wythe	*Richmond City*	John Taylor	*Caroline*
Larkin Smith	*King & Queen*	John Minor	*Spotsylvania*
Wm Ellzey	*Loudoun*	Wm Dudley	*Warwick*
Wm McKinley	*Ohio*	Mann Page	*Gloucester*
John Taliaferro Jr	*King Geo*	Richd Brent	*Pr Wm*
Hugh Holmes	*Frederick*	Jas Dailey	*Hampshire*
Jas Allen	*Shenandoah*	Archibald Stuart	*Augusta*
Jas McFarlane	*Russel*	Gen John Preston	*Montgomery*

FRI JUN 29, 1804
Camden, SC—Jun 12, 1804. John McDonald, mail carrier, was committed to goal on info of John Winfield, esq, of Marlborough dist & Isaac Hawley of Fayetteville, on suspicion of fraudulently opening the mail in his custody; one ltr had the Augusta post mark & was from Seaborn Jones, esq, dated Jan 14, 1804. He appeared before Judge Brevard.

Dr Manasseh Cutler of Mass & Benj Huger from S C declined being a candidate in the next election.

MON JUL 2, 1804
Ranaway from U S frig, *U S*, Englishman, Thos Burton, Reward—$10. John Cassin, superintendant, Wash, Navy Yd.

Rpblcn mbrs of the Leg of R I have nominated Constant Taber, Jas Helm, Jas Aldrich & Benj Remington, as elegible persons for electors of Pres & VP also Jos Stanton & Nehemiah Knight for Reps in Congress.

WED JUL 4, 1804
Ladies with ltrs at Wash Post Ofc—Jul 1, 1804:

Miss Nancy H Baker	Ann Crone	Mrs Ann Carr
Peggy Dorsey	Mrs Eliza Davies	Mrs Susannah B Finch
Mgt Gibbs	Martha Gordon	Miss Hanson
Hillary Lanham	Mrs Lewis	Miss Nancy Rustan
Mrs Jane Savery	Maria Thomson	Mrs Ann H Winthrop
Eliza Thompson	Cath Wilson	Mrs Maria Ronels c/o Mr Stelle

FRI JUL 6, 1804

Raleigh, NC, Jun 25. Crct Crt for this dist; suit brought by the Earl of Coventry & others, Reps of the late Earl Grenville, against Mr Collins & Mr Allen of Edenton. In 1664 the Province of Carolina was granted by King Chas II to 8 Lords Proprietors, of whom Lord Carteret after-wards created Earl Grenville. In 1729 one of the Lords Prop surrendered parts of the Prov to the Crown. In 1744 the Crown & Grenville divided the Province & 1/8th part was allotted for Earl Grenville. In 1763 he died leaving Robt his son & heir at law. Feb 1776 Robt died & devised his estate to trustees for Lord Garteret & others. In 1796 Lord Weymouth one of the trustees died. Deposition of John Parkinson was read. Dfndnts cnsl stated that the rights of the plntfs were lost by the change of the Gov't; dfndnts were in actual possession of the land since 1787. To be cont'd at next term. Fri Jul 6, 1804

Gtwn College, annual pension is $220 per student over 12, those under 12-$200.
-Rt Rev Leonard Neale, President

Died: Deacon Aaron Phelps of & at Suffield, Jun 25.

MON JUL 9, 1804

Wash City-Cornelius Coningham apptd superintendant of police in rm of John Willis, rsgnd.

Died: Henry Crymes, of Bath Co, Va; broke his skull with a stone on Tue Apr 24; lived until Apr 26.   -Times

Orphans Crt of PG Co, Md. Jun 28, 1804. 1-Prsnl est of John Turner Willett, late of PG Co, decd. 2-Ltrs of adm De Bonis Non, on prsnl est of Ninian Willett, late of PG Co, decd. -Ninian T Willett

New York, Jun 29. Company of book sellers met last week; medals went to Jacob Johnson of Phil, Hopkins & Seymour of NYC; Isaac Collins & son & David Bliss of NYC.

Mr Phillips, bkseller of St Paul's Chr Yd, London, has given Bushrod Washington fifteen hundred guineas for the English copy right of the life of his illustrious uncle, compiled from his own manuscripts. $70,000 were given for the Americ Copy-right. Work shd appear in both countries on May 15.
-Eng. Paper

Ranaway-Wm Johnston, age abt 18 yrs, appr to printing business, from ofc of the Western Star.   -Edw Cole, Lewistown, Pa

WED JUL 11, 1804

Reward-$500 for Strother, age 22 yrs, his wife Phillis, age abt 20 or 22 yrs, negroes, from my plantation nr Chester Crt hse, SC; formerly belonged to Edw Carter, Pr Wm Co, Va.   -John Johnston, Chester C H, SC

Morgan Lewis was inducted into ofc of Gov of NY, Jul 2. Jas Kent, Sr Justice of the Sup Crt to the ofc of Chief Justice, vice Mr Lewis; Danl D Tomkins of NYC, to fill Judge Kent's place.

Phil-Jul 4th celebration. Ctzns met at Capt Vogde's Inn; Matthew Lawler, Mayor & Gen Barker presided. Others met at Kennedy's Long-Rm, Mkt St; Dr Geo Logan, Pres, Jonathan Bayard Smith & Tench Coxe, VPs; Mahlon Dickerson read the Decl of Indep.

FRI JUL 13, 1804

Land for sale. Wishing to remove to the westward; land in Montgomery Co, Md, nr Conrad Myers Ferry, 230 acs; store hse now occupied by Jesse Philips.
-Richd Jones, of Edw

Ranaway-Charles, age abt 40 yrs, negro, from Jas Kirk, living in St Mary's Co, Md, nr Point Look Out.   -Jas Kirk

Deserted from board U S Gun Boat, No. 1, Richd Hollowell, shipped in Balt, age abt 24 yrs, shoemaker. -John Lovell, mster, Navy Yard, Wash

Deserted board U S frig *U S*, Richd White, age abt 23 yrs. Reward-$10.
-John Cassin, superintendant, Navy Yard, Wash

Boston-Jul 4th Celebration at Fanueil Hall, Wash. Infty under command of Capt Jos Loring; Hon Jas Bowdoin in the chair; toasts volunteers: Dr Eustis, Dr Jarvis, B Austin Jr, G Blake, Jas Prince, Col Gardner & Maj Brazer.

Rpblcn committee, ctzns of Albany, Jun 29, 1804: Richd Lush, Henry Quackenbush, Geo Merchant, Chas D Cooper & Solomon Southwick.

MON JUL 16, 1804

Abraham B Venable is elected Pres of Bank of Virginia; W C Nicholas to coll ship at Norfolk.

Festival held at Powhatan Crt-hse at tavern of Saml Marshall; Majors Edw Mosby & Jacob Mishaun were present.

Duel bet Gen Hamilton & Col Burr on Jul 11, at NY, mortally wounded Hamilton; both men fired at the same time; Gen Hamilton's ball did not touch Col Burr; duel was political.

Mr Owen Roberts of Balt has obtained a patent for the invention of a hemp & flax break.

WED JUL 18, 1804

Genrl Hamilton died at the hse of Wm Bayard, esq, at Greenwich. Funeral from Mr Church's hse in Robinson St.   -NY

Stolen: Sorrel horse, from the commons nr Capitol Hill, Wash. -John C Dickson

Died: Col John Trigg, in Bedford Co, mbr of Congress from Va.

FRI JUL 20, 1804
Stop Thief. $50-reward for villain who stole jewelry, cash, gold seal, etc from bureau of Geo Pitt, Gtwn.

Gen Hamilton's funeral. Pall Bearers: Gen Matthew Clarkson, Oliver Wolcott, Richd Harrison, Abij. Hammond, Josiah Ogden Hoffman, Richd Varick, Wm Bayard, & Judge Lawrance. Top of the coffin was the Genr'ls hat & sword. His 4 sons followed with John B Church, Washington Morton, Mr Malcom.

In Chancery-Md, Jul 3, 1804. Alexander Contee, v Thos Johnson, John Mason, Williams Kilty & Rinaldo Johnson. Bill is to obtain a cnvyance of prop cnvyd by Rinaldo Johnson to the other dfndnts on Sep 19, 1801 in trust for payment of his debts or to vacate said deed; Rinaldo has become insolvent; John Mason & Wm Kilty reside out of Md. -Saml H Howard, Reg CC

MON JUL 23, 1804
For sale-my plantation, adj Upper Marlbro, PG Co, Md, 800 acs & dwlg hse. -David Craufurd, Upper Marlbro. [or to Nathan'l Craufurd residing 8 miles of Wash]

Pews in gallery of Prot Episc Chr for public sale. Apply to Mr Clement Smith, Treasurer at Bank of Columbia. Trustees: Chas Worthington, Wm H Dorsey, Thos Corcoran, Walter S Chandler & Walter Smith, Gtwn.

WED JUL 25, 1804
For rent. 3 story brick hse, nr Treas ofc, formerly occupied by Mr Wm Rhodes as a tavern. -Mary Ann Fenwick, Gtwn

Last will of Alexander Hamilton, of NYC. Appoint John B Church, Nicholas Fish & Nathaniel Pendleton of NYC to be excs & trustees. My dear wife Eliz, etc & my dear chldrn, etc.. Jul 9, 1804. Wit: Dominick F Blake, Graham Burrils, Thed B Vallsau. NY Surrogate's ofc, Jul 16, 1804, Silvanus Miller-Surrog.

Wash Co, DC. Petition of Thos Hayward, insolvent debtor confined in Wash Co prison for debt. -Uriah Forrest, clk

Died: Chas DeKrafft, Jul 24, srvyr & draftsman of Treas Dept.

Notice. Those who have demands against the est of John Burchan, late of Wash City, decd; apply to John Craven or Jos Stretch, excs of the estate. Wash City, Jul 21.

Absconded from my plantation in PG Co, nr Upper Marlboro, Wm Johnson, negro, age 43 yrs. Reward-$20. -Stephen West

Fri Jul 27, 1804

Runaway-Michael, negro, age abt 36 yrs, from Francis Hance, living in Calvert Co nr Hunting town, Md.

Crct Crt of DC. Ratify report of Daniel Carrol Brent, of sale made by him as trustee of prop decreed in suit of U S against Saml Jackson, Wm Shannon, Phillip Fitzhugh, Joshua B Bond & Fredk Shaff. Prop purchased by Gabriel Duvall, esq, sum of $6,600. -Uriah Forrest, clk

Mon Jul 30, 1804

Wash Co, DC. Case of insolvent debtor, Thos Galer, confined in Wash prison; trustee apptd. Also Evan Evans, same data. -Uriah Forrest, clk

Dr Jacob Hall of Harford Co, literary character, writes that the poems of Mrs Allen, consort to the Rev Mr Allen of same co, are poetic genius.
-J Hall, Christopher's Camp, Mar 24.

Wed Aug 1, 1804

Strayed or stolen-pair of bay horses. Phineas Bradley, Wash City, or Renner & Bussard, Gtwn.

Apptd by the Gov-Genrl of New Orleans: Jas Pitot, Mayor & Justice of the Crt of Pleas. Peter Petit, Chas Patton, Thos Randall & Stephen Rachery, Justices of the Crt o/Pleas. Francil Munhall, Ntry Pblc, Edw C Nicholas, clk.

Dr John Brockenbrough was apptd cashier of the Bank of Va on Wed last.
-Richmond, Jul 23

Charleston, Jul 14. Alexander McClure, esq, arvd from the East Indies in the ship *Horison* a few days ago; collected seeds of useful plants & a # of birds.

Fri Aug 3, 1804

Died: Mrs Mary Tunicliff, age 38 yrs, Jul 31, w/o Mr Wm Tunicliff on Capitol Hill; leaves her hsbnd & son; she was born in Shropshire, Eng.

Ranaway-Will, negro, from Jas Heighe, living in Calvert Co, Md.

For rent-2 or 3 small farms in PG Co, Md, nr Bladensburg.
-Leonard M Deakins

Mon Aug 6, 1804

Bank of Potomac in town of Alexandria; under direction of: Elisha Janney, Cuthbert Powell, Wm Fitzhugh, Wm Hartshorne, Thos Swann, Thos Vowell, Chas Lee, Jacob Hoffman, Jos Riddie, Jas H Hooe, Wm Hodgson, Robt Young, Phineas Janney, Jas Keith Jr & Jas Batton.

Died: Maj Genrl Wm Irvine, of cholera morbus, Jul 29, ofcr of Rev War; ntv of Ireland; educated to medical profession; died Pres of Soc of Cincinnati; hsbnd & parent; age 63 yrs.   -Philadelphia, Aug 1

Eddyville, Cumberland Rvr, Ky, Jul 1, 1804. The Barge *Experiment*, owner-Mr Jas Lyon, arrv'd here from New Orleans w/ sugar & liquors.

WED AUG 8, 1804
Crct Crt of Wash Co, DC. Aug 7, 1804. Ratify sale of Chas A Burnett made as trustee of prop decreed to be sold in suit of Ninian Magruder against Ann Seyle & others. Prop was purchased by Danl Reintzelar for $2,450.
-Uriah Forrest, clk

New York-Aug 3. Jury of inquest have found Aaron Burr guilty of the murder of Alex'r Hamilton; Wm P Van Ness, att'y at law & Nath'l Pendleton, cnslr at law, were accessarie.

FRI AUG 10, 1804
For sale: Port wine of superior quality.   -John Banks, High St, Gtwn

For sale: 200 cases of R I fresh lime.   -Michael Cleary, Gtwn

MON AUG 13, 1804
Ranaway, Davy, age abt 22 yrs, negro, from J B Hance, lvng nr Huntington, Calvert Co, Md.

WED AUG 15, 1804
Crct Crt of Wash Co, DC. Agnes Jackson & Wm Jackson, trustees for rl est of Jonathan Jackson decd; sale made by them of prop to be sold in suit of Wm H Dorsey; ratify sale made to sundry persons for $2,042. -Uriah Forrest, clk

Benj Bache, residing in Phil, some yrs age, reported that Temple Franklin, grdson of Dr Benj Franklin, was compiling works of Franklin for publication; none have appeared to this day.

FRI AUG 17, 1804
Strayed or stolen, a cow from the Commons in Wash City. Reward-$2.
-Mary Sweeny

Com rs for bldg a wharf in Wash City: Timothy Caldwell, David Shoemaker, Peter Lenox, Lewis Morin & John P Van Ness.

Meeting to organize a fire co in Wash City: Jos Stretch -chrmn; Thos H Gilliss-sec; & John Woodside, committee of 3.

Wash Boyd, coll of the Wash Co, DC, tax; returned to the board of comrs the following list of land & lots of ground in said county on which there is no prsnl property to pay the taxes:

Robt Allison	Henry Appleton	Henry Addison
John Appleton	Thos Addison	Danl Addison
Sam Blodget	Jacob Boyer	Matthias Buckley
Jas Beall of Jas	Walter Baker	Wm Budicomb
John Beall Barnes & Redgate		John B Bordly
Fielder Bowie & Wm Deakin's heirs Benj Brookes		
Raphael Boarman	John Barnett	Henry Bradford
Wm Beans	Jas Brown	Alex. Buchan
John Brice	John B Bradley	Wm Bushel
Jos Boone	Wm Boyne	John Beckley
Robt Beckley	Upton Beall	Joshua B Bond
Jos N Chiswell	Hugh Campbell	Hezekiah Clagett
John Camp	John Casey Jr	Benedict Calvert
John Campbell	Peter Casenev's heirs	Chas Carroll Jr
Richd Conway	Saml Chace	Chas Carroll of Carolton
John Craig	Dr. Jas Craig	Notley Young & Benj Oden
Cyrus Copper	Clagett & Mason	Chas Carter
Danl Carroll of Dudn	Edw Carter	John Crocker
Chas Carroll	Jas Duer	Robt Dennison
Elias Davidson		Tristram Dalton's trustees
Wm M Duncanson	Ignatius Digges	John Dennis & Sam Wilson
Robt Darnal	John Duhy	Thos Dick
Tristram Dalton	Deblois & Nicholson	Thos Dobbon
Benj Declary	Geo Ehrenzeller	John Eden
Jos Eliott	Geo Eskridge	Ebenezer Eliascn
Wm Fitzhugh	Forrest & Stoddert	A Fishers heirs
John Fay	Abraham Eaw	Joshua Gregg
Henry Gaither	Michael Gangaivare	Fredk Golden's heirs
Rev Mr Golden	Mich'l Gross	Henry Goil
Philip Gadson	Levi Green	Jas Greenleaf's assignees
Richd Gridley	Sam Galloway	Richd Graham
Sam Griffin		

Gillis, Gronevaldt, Rudolph Mees & Pieter Vander Waller, Van Vollen & Hoven [listed together]
Pieter Godfrey, Rutger Jan Schimmelpendick & Robt Danl Gromelin [do]

Jas Gilchrist	John Gowan	Valentine Hoss
Geo Holstien	Henry Hillary Jr	John Hass' devisees
John Hackett	John Hammell	David Harry
Christopher Hughs	Maximilian Heuster	Henry Hill
Martha Hall	Richd Henderson	Robt T Hooe
Jonathan Hall	Wm Hemmersly	Wm Hindman
J Hepburn	Ringold Hillary	Jos Hickman
Peter Hall	Simon Halvert	Wm Heye
Christian Hughes	Wm Johnson	Wm Jarret
Thos Johns heirs	Wm A Johnson	Thos Jennings

Ch Jenners
Henry Kontz
Ludowick Kemp
Andrew Kesler
Peter Kempt
Thos Keland

Jas Johnston Jr
Thos J Johnston Jr heirs & Robt Johnston
Henry Klinger
Frederick Kemp
Nicholas Kinson
John Kennedy

John Johnston

Christian Kemp
Laurence Kreeger
Patrick King
Karrick & Purcival.

MON AUG 20, 1804
Wash Co, DC-No prsnl prop to pay taxes-cont'd-see Aug 17:

Andrew King
Darby Lux
Wm Lane
John B Laithe
Morris Nicholsons assignees
Casper Mantz
Philip H Myers
David Merky
Benj Morris
Stephen Moylan
Ebenezer Mackie, Morris Nicholson & W Prout
Thos Pierce of Va
J Penrose
Anthony Van Manninck, Saml Porter & Jas Sterret
Henry Moscrop
Wm Prout & Danl Carrol of Dud'n & Wm King
Peter Holmead & Butler David Polock
Peter & Bayly, Francis Pratt & others
Wm Robinson
David Ross
Jas Reid
Stoddard & Templeman
Saml Snowden
Geo Swingle
Geo Stricker
Amos Smith
Jacob Snyder, Christian Flaut, Jos Flaut [listed together]
Geo Sley
Jonathan Slaters heirs
Jos Slater
Wm Simmes
Nicholas Sluby
Walter Stuart
Evan Thomas
Edw Tilghman
Richd Tilghman
Appelona Whitehair
Henry Warman
Henry Walter

John Lingenfelter
A Leitch
Abraham Lindo
A Lawson

Jas McCormick
Jacob Myer
Luther Martin
Ephraim Mills
Jas Mewburn

Cuthbert Powel
Wm Prentice

Henry Pauling

Wm Ragan
Henry Rozier
Rhodes & Higdon
Kim Streeves
Richd Snowden
Philip Sybert
Edw Skinner
Henry Stall

Mich'l Shanks heirs
Chas Stuart
Henry Slater
Alex. Shaw
Jacob Stiner Jr
Arthur Shaaff
Jos Thoms
Jas Tilghman
Ann Tarvin
Wm & E Waugh
Jos Wilson
Thos Wand

Win Lux
Edw Langley
Peter Chas L'Enfant
Francis Leck

Wm McGrath
Saml Miller
Wm McCreery
Barbara Marshal
Thos Morton Jr
Anthony Van Manninck
Edw Parkinson
Jas Piercy

Owen Roberts
John Randall
Aaron Ritenover
Matthias Ritenover
Matthew Ridley
Wm Russel
Chas Schell
Benj Spiker
Isachar & Mahlon Scolfield
John Lyles heirs
Christian Schells heirs
Geo Small

John Stuarts heirs
John Smith
Andrew Smith
John H Stare
J Strange
Francis Shicard
Jas Tomkins
Matthew Tilghman
Henry Tims
John Winters
John C Wilson
B Wigells heirs

Wm Wooten	Bazil Waring	Jas Wharton
Ambrose White	Thos Wilson	John Wilson
Nathan Walker & Jas Thomson [listed together]		Thos Williams
Wm Wilson	Levin Winder	David Williamson
Elias Youghman	Wm Yates	Abraham Young's heirs

Payment by 1st Monday in Nov next. -John Mountz, Wash Co, DC-clk.

Died; John Neusville, esq, Jul 29, at his hse in Charleston; raised a large family; age 76 yrs & 9 mos.

WED AUG 22, 1804

Runaway-Joe, negro, abt 28 yrs of age; says he belongs to Col Wm Winn, of Harford Co, NC, & absent from his master for 2 yrs. -Geo Creager, shrf, Frederick Co jail, Md

In Chancery-U S dist Crt, Wash Co. Saml Craig, cmplnt, v Robt McClann, Wm McClann, Wm King, dfndnts. Bill states that Wm King, seized in fee of part of lot 41 in Gtwn, did on Sep 10, 1793, lease the same to Robt McClann for 99 yrs; Sep 3, 1795 same was sold & reconveyed to Wm King; Wm King believing he was seized of said lot & premise sold same to Saml Craig. Craig found record of Wash Co-deed of assignment dated May 2, 1794 from Robt McClann to Wm McClann, which deed is prior to deed of Robt McClann to W King. Wm McClann does not reside in DC. -Uriah Forrest, clk.

FRI AUG 24, 1804

Wash Co, DC. Case of Chas Nevitt, confined in Wash Co prison, debtor.
-Uriah Forrest, clk.

For sale: farm on which I reside, 1000 acs, Michael Taney, Calvert Co, Md.

Runaway-Anthony-abt 28 yrs of age, negro, committed to Wash Co, Md jail.
-N Rochester, shrf of Wash Co, Md.

MON AUG 27, 1804

Died: Overton Carr, esq, Aug 22, of PG Co, Md, age 50 yrs.

Mr Christopher Perkins, of Stockton, Durham, Eng, has invented a thrashing mill; can do 20 bushels in one hr.

WED AUG 29, 1804

Ran away, Rachel, negro wench, abt 20 yrs of age. -Francis Clark

Orphans Crt of Wash Co, DC. Aug 23, 1804. Prsnl est of John B Winnsett, late of Wash Co, decd. -Mgt Winnsett, admx.

Died: Richd Jordan, age 40 yrs, Aug 13, hsbnd & parent. St Mary's Co, Md.

Fri Aug 31, 1804

Died: Mr Francis McClure, printer, on Aug 28th, after a short but severe illness; remains left the hse of Mr Orlando Cook & were buried in the Public Burial Ground east of the city; procession formed: band of music, Masonic Soc, Rev Mr McCormick, Wash Typographical Soc, Capt Strigg's Light Infty & ctzns. Wash City.

Orphans Crt of Calvert Co, Md. Aug 29, 1804. Prsnl est of Sarah Weems Allein, late of Calvert Co, decd. Jas G Wood, exc, of PG Co, Md.

Boston, Aug 21. Brig *Camillus*, Capt Kennard, in from Guadaloupe, sailed from there on Jan 16th & on the 24th was brought to by his Maj's schr *Le Clare*, Lt Sutton; Thos Carpenter, boatswain, was barbarously treated. Carpenter was born in Falmouth, Maine.

Charlotte Hall School-Geo Ralph, Principal, Charlottesville Cool Springs; wanted a French prof-salary $400 per annum.

Mon Sep 3, 1804

NC election for mbrs of Cong: [All are Rpblcns]
Jas Holland	Wm Blackledge	
Thos Wynns	Nath'l Macon	Richd Stanford
Jas Gillespie	Mr Winston	Willis Alston
*Thos Blount	*Duncan McFarland	

*New members. [Per correction of Sep 7, 1804]

Wash Co, DC-petition of Eliz Lewis, insolvent debtor, confined to Wash Co prison for debt.   -Uriah Forrest.

Wed Sep 4, 1804

Died: Mr Nauche, Pres of the Galvanic Soc, at Paris; burnt to death by a bottle of phosphorus used for experiments.

Runaway, Wm, negro, says he is the prop of John Chessey, of Va.
-Sutton J Weems, shrf, Calvert Co, Md

John Hamman, Wash City, has a stray sorrel filly.

Fri Sep 7, 1804

Died: Master John Alexander Smoot, eldest s/o Mr Alexander S Smoot, Sep 1, leaving a fond mthr & indulgent fr.

Died: Cmdor Jas Nicholson, age 69 yrs, at his seat in NY.

Proposals by John Dixon for printing by subscrip, periodical work, to be entitled the Va Magazine, or Monthly Miscellany.

Wash Co, DC. Geo Brown, insolvent debtor, confined to Wash Co prison for debt. -Uriah Forrest, clk

Crct Crt of DC. Jul 25, 1804. Report of Daniel C Brent of sale made as trustee of prop decreed to be sold in suit by Thos Law against Jas Piercey Jr, Jas Ray, Saml Treat, & Jas Piercy, Sen; prop purchased by Thos Law for $10,000. -Uriah Forrest, clk

Genrl meeting of the Union Fire Co, 2d Ward. -J H Kearney, sec.

To be sold, my quarter in Cornwallis's Neck, cattle, sheep etc; lease of plantation; nr the mkts of Dumfries, Colchester, Alexandria, Wash & Gtwn. -Raphal Boarman

Info wanted of Geo Richmond, carpenter, ntv o/Scotland, left Jamaica abt 13 yrs ago for America & not since heard of; enquiry made in Winchester Centinel May 1802. He will hear of something much to his benefit. -Geo Lind, Strasburg, Va

MON SEP 10, 1804
Jos Stanton & Nehemiah Knight, Rpblcns, re-elected Reps to Congress for R I. Mathew Lyone is re-elected for Ky.

For sale-decree of High Crt of Md, in Chancery: lot & dwlg hse in Annapolis-N E st & Scotch St; now occupied by Wm Brown. -Nicholas Brewer, trustee

WED SEP 12, 1804
Reps elected to the R I State Leg:
Constant Taber	Nath'l Hazard	Thos Peckham.
Paul M Mumford	Simeon Martin	Enoch Hazard

In Portsmouth: Robt Lawton, esq, chosen moderator;
Delegates to Genrl Assembly:
Nicholas Easton   Saml Pearse
Thos Corey Jr   Stephen Slocum
                              -Newport, R I, Aug 30

Wash Co, DC-Case of John Aiken confined in Wash Co prison for debt. -Uriah Forrest, clk

For sale: 100,000 acs in Wayne & Tallassee Cos, Ga. -John Beckley, Wash City

FRI SEP 14, 1804
More impressed seamen: ship *Independence*, Capt Jasorn, from Portland; boarded abt 4 miles from the Hook by an ofcr from the *Cambrian;* John Williams & Jas Cornish, both Americans were impressed; Cornish is a ntv of Kennebeck & Wms of NYC & resided on Cherry St.

Meeting of Delegates, New Haven, Conn-Aug 29, 1804. Wm Judd, chrmn; Henry W Edwards & Lemuel Whitman, clks.

Union Fire Co, 2d Ward, meeting at Rhodes Tavern. Richd Forrest, chrmn; Jas Hoban-Pres; Andrew Way Jr-VP; Wash Boyd-Treas; Jas H Kearney-sec. Engrs: Clothworthy Stephenson, Peter Lenox, Lewis Morin & Henry Langtey. Firemen: John Hewit, Thos Thorpe, Thos Carpenter, Henry Herford, John P Van Ness, & Jos Calvert. Laddermen: Jos Huddleston, John Aitkin, Orlando Cook, Geo Moore, Hugh Boyd, Thos Given, John Dobbin, & Chas McNantz. Centinels: David Shoemaker, Richd Forrest, John McGowan, Geo Way, Lewis Clephan, & Thos Herty. Firemen: John Payne, Edw Frethy, Benson L McCormick, Ezra Varden, Alexander Cochran, Robt Tilley, Wm James, Wm Thornton.

MON SEP 17, 1804
To be sold: estate cld "*Chichester*", 695 acs, includes Dyers Ferry; oppo Wash City. Apply to Capt Marbury of Blue Plains, Col Hanson of Navy Yd. -Anthony Addison, Barnaby, PG Co, Md.

WED SEP 19, 1804
Orphans Crt of Calvert Co, Md. Sep 18, 1804. Prsnl est of Nathan Smith, late of said co, decd.   -Theodore Hodgkin, adm

Thos W Pairo has opened a dry goods store in Wash City.

Baron Humboldt was born in Prussia, Sep 14, 1769.

Gurdon S Mumford to be Rep in Congress for counties of NY, Richmond & King. New York State, Sept 14.

Directors chosen for the Bank of Potomac-Wash City:
Jacob Hoffman	Elisha Janney	Cuthbert Powell
John G Ladd	Wm Hawthorne	Jas Patton
Jas H Hooe	Jos Riddle	Jas Keith Jr
Wm Fitzhugh	Wm Hodgson	*Thos Vowell

*Chosen President of the Bank of Potomac.

FRI SEP 21, 1804
Saml S Harwood, Montgomery Co, Md, intends to petition Genrl Assembly for an act of insolvency to release him from debts he is unable to pay.

MON SEP 24, 1804
Edw Shippen is a Chief Justice of the Supreme Crt of Pennsylvania.

In 1673 M Joliet & Marquette, 2 French Canadians, explored the Miss. to Arkansas; in 1680 M de La Sale explored the Miss. & on the lower part of Illinois he garrisoned a fort cld *Crevecour*; he sent Fr Hennepin down the Miss. until he reached the ocean. In 1682 M la sale & M Jonti went down the rvr & named the country Louisiana & built a fort in the Chickasaw Terr below the Ohio cld *Prudhomme*.

Partnership bet Nicholas Voss & Chas Glover is dissolved; settle with N Voss, under firm of Chas Glover & Co.

WED SEP 26, 1804

Decree from Crt of Chancery-sale of all rl est of Thos Clagett, esq, late of PG Co, decd; 1800acs in town o/Piscataway. -Thos Duckett, trust, PG Co, Md.

Reward-$10 for pkt bk lost bet Wash Bank & Gtwn, containing $30 in notes.
                                                                -Jas Wallis.

FRI SEP 28, 1804

Wash City-Sep 26 the Crct Crt found Jacob Ray & Philip Williams guilty of passing bank-notes knowing them to be forged.

Phil, Sep 24-Wm Barry, mariner from Norfolk, aged 19, was stabbed by several Spanish Sailors without any provocation on Sep 22; he lanquishes under his deep wounds.

Ranaway, Ann or Nan, negro girl, abt 19 yrs of age; purchased her of Mr John Brent, nr Port Tobacco.   -David Rawn, Wash City

Thos Thorpe has opened a hse for travellers in Wash City.

In Chancery, Sep 17, 1804. Chas Carroll of Carollton, against Aquila Beal & Grace his wife, Eliz Holliday & Mgt Holliday, which Grace, Eliz & Mgt are the only chldrn & co-heiress' of Leonard Holliday the younger, late of PG Co decd. Bill is to obtain a sale of rl est of said Leonard Holliday for payment of debt due to cmplnt, prsnl est is insufficient. L Holliday was indebted to C Carroll on bond dated Oct 25, 1783; all dfndnts reside in Gtwn, DC. -S H Howard-Reg C C

John McElwee has purchased Mr John Avilhe's interest in a patent wind-mill for DC; will sell rights to those wanting to erect them in said dist; info-apply to Mr Benj Perkins, President's Sq. -John McElwee, nr Seven Bldgs, Wash

MON OCT 1, 1804

Died: Francis Ambroise Didot, Jul 10, at Paris, printer, age 74 yrs.

Public sale. Last will & testament of John Emery, decd; lots 5 & 15 sq 431-lot 5 has frame hse; & part of lot 2.   -Geo Blagden

Died: Widow Mary Williams, in Wash.

WED OCT 3, 1804

Died: Dr Alex r Mitchell, Sep 28 at Bladensburgh, PG Co, Md; hsbnd & fr.

For lease, plantation late the prop of Maj John C Jones, at Lower Cedar Point, 200 acs, Chas Co, Md.   -Dorothy H Jones

John Clark Peacock-committed to jail for horse stealing; horse is in c/o Robt Sutton. -Coningham, Wash City

FRI OCT 5, 1804
Jas Elliott is re-elected a Representative for Vermont.

Reps in Congress for Balt City & Co:
N R Moore & Wm MacCreery, both Rpblcns.
Roger Nelson elected vice Danl Heister, decd.
Votes for Reps of in Md. Genrl Assembly were:

Baltimore City	*John Stephen	1542	*Andrew Ellicott	1192
	Thos Dixon	1001	Cumberland Dugan	336
Baltimore Co	Tobias E Stansbury		Alexis Lemmon	
	Moses Brown		Geo Harryman	
Frederick Co	Thos Hawkins		Danl Clarke	
	Joshua Cockey		Joal Waters	

[*-elected].

Ltr from Lt Pratt to inspec of the Army, dated Savannah, Ga, Sep 12. Extracts- Entire destruction of Ft Greene & 13 lives lost, 7 of which were soldiers; incessant high winds & storm. Men lost: Cpl Reuben Armstrong; musician- Wm Crafts; Pvts-Daniel Lacy, Jos Whitaker, Thos Moore, John Glynn, & Saml McWilliams. also lost was Capt Nicoll's son who died with Lacy who was trying to save his life; & 3 women & 2 chldrn belonging to the fort.

MON OCT 8, 1804
John A Stuart of Fairhaven, Va, applauded the trustees of Charlotte Hall School at the annual examination of pupils.

Col Simon Larned chosen a mbr of Congress for Berkshire dist, Mass.

Notice; I forewarn all persons from trusting or paying, Mary Caldwell, late w/o Timothy Caldwell, of Wash; agreement in writing of separation binds her not to contract any debts or receive any of my rents or monies. -Timothy Caldwell, Wash

Md election-Assembly.

Cecil Co	D Sheridine	E Veazy	Dr Miller	Dr Alexander
Kent Co	Jas Scott	R Hatcheson	John Moore	John Thomas
Talbot Co	Edw Lloyd	Wm Meley	P Spencer	Robt Goldsborough

State of Polls in Harford Co, Md:

*John C Bond	844	*Thos Ayres	812	*John Montgomery	733
*John Forwood	665	Jas Lytle	627	Elijah David	560
Andrew McAdow	301	Jas McComas	455		

*First 4 gentlemen are therefore constitutionally elected.

Orphans Crt of Wash Co, DC. Oct 6, 1804. Prsnl est of Mary Williams, late of Wash City, widow, decd.

-W Cranch

WED OCT 10, 1804

Orphans Crt of Wash Co, DC. Oct 9, 1804. Prsnl est of Francis McClure, late of Wash, decd.   -Orlando Cook

Crct Crt of Wash Co, DC-In Chancery. Adam King against Wm King, Walter Brookes, & Thos Contee. Bill is for cnvyance of lot 270 Wash Co, to Adam King in fee simple. Walter Brookes resides in A A Co, Md; Thos Contee resides in PG Co, Md.   -Uriah Forrest, clk

Races, Nov 13, Wash Jockey Club.   -C McLaughlin-sec & treas.
New school opened on North F St.   -J Sewell, Wash City

Died: Hore Browse Trist, Aug 29, at New Orleans, coll of port; of yellow fever.

Wash Co, DC. Petition of Mary Duffee confined in Wash Co prison for debt.
-Uriah Forrest, clk

Elisha Riggs has mv'd his store to hse formerly occupied by Mrs Pic, nr the Union Tavern.

FRI OCT 12, 1804

Life of Pres Willard, lately decd. [Boston Centinel] Pres Willard was born at Scarborough, Dec 29, 1738; s/o Rev Saml Willard, a minister, who died when his son was a minor; Pres W. recd B A Degree in 1765; 1767 elected a tutor for Greek Dept; 1772 settled in the ministry at Beverly; 1781 remv'd to Cambridge as Pres of the Univ; private life-hsbnd & parent; died Sep 25.

Apptd by the Pres:
Coll & or Inspec: Philip Greene for port of Marietta
John Brent - Nanjemoy
Edmund P Gaines - Mobile
Wilson C Nicholas - Norfolk & Portsmouth
Wm Fisher for So Quay
David Broadie of Hampton
Naval Ofcr of New Orleans: Wm G Garland
Srvyrs: Joshua Prentiss - Marblehead
Robt Carter Nicholas - New Orleans
Thos C Ferebee - Indian town
Edmund Key - Llewellesburg
Commissioners of Loans: Edw Hall for Md
Isaac Neusville for SC
Tomson J Skinner for Mass
Wm Few for NY
Justices of the Peace   Saml H Hamilton

	Saml N Smallwood
	Robt Alexander Jr
Marshal of Md:	Thos Rutter
Reg of Land Ofc:	Thos Fitzpatrick for lands West of Pearl Rvr
	Geo Hoffman at Detroit
	John Badollet at Vincennes
	Michael Jones at Kaskaskia
	Jos Chambers land E of Pearl Rvr
Judge of Miss Terr:	Ephraim Kirby
Receivers of Public Monies:	Frederick Bates at Detroit
	Elijah Backus at Kaskaskia
	Harry Toulman at Ft Stoddert
	Jos Chambers for lands East of Pearl Rvr
Com rs:	Return J Meigs & Danl Smith-for holding a treaty with the Cherokees
Atty:	Walter Jones Jr for Dist of Col
	Daniel Humphreys for NH

Wash City-trustees of the poor apptd by the Mayor: Henry Ingle, Peter Lenox, Geo Collard, John Woodside, Ebenezer Nesmith.

For sale: in Bladensburg, articles of the late John Scott, decd Oct 12.
-Richd Cramphin, exc,

Orphans Crt of PG Co, Md. Oct 1804. Ordered that Geo Newman, adm of John Murray, sell the dec'ds prsnl est. -Saml Tyler, Reg

Mon Oct 15, 1804
Died: Francois Ambroise Didot, age 74, Jul 10, at Paris, printer, born Jan 1730; leaving 2 sons, Pierre & Firmin.

Wash Co, DC. Petition of Thos Hurdle in Wash Co prison for debt.
-Uriah Forrest, clk

Reps to Congress-Pa: Jos Clay, Jacob Richards & Mich'l Leib.

Columbia, SC Sep 9. Pres of the U S apptd Dominick Augustine Hall, esq, of this state, to be dist Judge of the Territory of Orleans.

Ladies with ltrs in Wash Post ofc-Oct 1, 1804:
Sarah Clemmons	Mgt Edelin	Mary Russell
Miss Sarah Grant	Agness Gacon	Mrs Kalender
Mrs Barbara Marshall	Mrs Magrath	Mrs A C Ramsey
Mrs Charity Fording c/o Maj Forrest		

Wed Oct 17, 1804
Died: Alexander White, at Winchester, Va, formerly a Rep in Congress & comr of this city.

Sir Wm Jones was born in 1746 at his fr's resid in Wales; he was s/o the celebrated mathemetician Wm Jones; both the diciple & friend of Sir Isaac Newton; in Apr 1783 he mrd Miss Shipley, d/o the late Bishop of Stasaph & sister to Rev W D Shipley, Dean of that Diocese. In April, 1794 he was attacked with a billious complaint-died on Apr 27th, 1794.

Died: John H Stone, at Annapolis, Md, formerly Gov of Md.

A mthr & widow is looking for her son, Chas Brown, age 18 yrs, left NY in Upper Canada on Apr 13, to cross the lake in a bark canoe with Benjamin, a baker. Be living, send to editor of Albany Centinel; he may hear of his mthr something more to his advantage.

Info wanted, viz John Hamilton, s/o Jessey Hamilton; Wm Hamilton, of White Castle; & Saml Hamilton, 1st cousin of above Wm Hamilton; all ntv of Ire who came to this country some time ago & not heard from since. Write to their friends in Phil, it would relieve their anxious solicitude.

Died: Saml J Potter, Sep 26, at So Kingstown, Senator of U S from R I, age 54.

FRI OCT 19, 1804
Jul 4, 1804-Festival in St Genevieve, dist of La; ctzns partook of a dinner provided by Madame Valle, wid of late Commandant of the dist; Dr Walter Fenwick, as Pres, Rufus Easton, esq, as VP; toasts were drank & a ball was held at the hse of Madame Moreau.

MON OCT 22, 1804
Lost between the Capitol & the Branch Bank, a note in my favor, drawn by Richd Marshall, $1000, dated Oct 8, endorsed by myself, John Hedges of Thos & Saml Hamilton. Finder leave it with Saml Hamilton. -Wm B Beanes

Died: Mr T P Oldfield, age 16 yrs, in Eng, at the Grotto hse, Margate. -Times

WED OCT 24, 1804
Solomon Meyer has opened the Centre hse Inn, Wash City.

Died: Mrs Juliana Hazlehurst, w/o Isaac Hazlehurst, esq, of Phil, Jul 11 at Cloverhill, nr Mt Holly, NJ.

Saml Clark has remv'd from Alexandria to Gtwn & opened his shoe store in Gtwn, opposite Mr Cochrane's.

FRI OCT 26, 1804
Schnr, *Harriot*, John Sutton, mstr, will sail from Dunlap & Ervin's Wharf in Alexandria for Norfolk, in a few days.

Died: Jos Briggs, Sep 16, Priv sec to his excellency the Gov Genrl of La.
-New Orleans, Sep 18

Died: Mrs Rachel More, w/o Benjamin More, Oct 23. [Wash City item]

MON OCT 29, 1804
Music & Language teacher-P Mauro at Mr Semmes's Tavern, No 6, Gtwn. [Piano forte & flute]

Runaway-Elijah, negro, age 22 yrs, says he belongs to Jas Fishback, living in Culpepper Co, Va, was committed to the Frederick Co jail. Same for negro, Merryman, age abt 17 yrs, says his master's name is John Beverist who lives in Fauquier Co, Va. -Geo Creager, shrf, Frederick Co.

Ltr from New Orleans, dated Sep 8, 1804. Yellow fever prevails in this city; our friend Hore B Triste has fallen victim to the same; Gov Claiborne & his Lady were attacked by it; the troops have marched out of the city until the fever subsides.

WED OCT 31, 1804
Peter Healy has opened a new groc store in the hse nr the Capitol, lately occupied by Mr Jas D Barry. Wash.

For rent or sale-2 story frame hse, lge blacksmith's shop; enquire of Richd Jameson or Henry Holsey, on Capitol Hill, at Mr Martin's, blacksmith who works for the Capitol.   -Benj Bacon

Wm Waters has wines & cabinet ware, full line of groceries, for sale. Gtwn.

Hse o/Reps of Connecticut, Oct 17. Bill read that Jabez H Tomlinson & Agur Judson of Stradford, Hezekih Goodrich of Chatham, & Nath. Manning of Windham, esqs, Justices of the Peace, published their opinion that there is no constitution of Civil Gov't in Conn....etc.

FRI NOV 2, 1804
Vicennes, I. T., Sep 25, 1804. Meeting at the hse of Dr Walter Fenwick, in the Village of St Genivieve on Sep 2, 1804; W Fenwick-Pres & Jas Fenney-sec; Desirous that all distinction bet Americans & French-men shd be done away. Signed: Walter Fenwick, R Eastin, M Austin, F Alley, J Kindle, Wm Murphy, Jos Donnahan.   -J Finney, sec

For sale: Order of Orphans Crt of Wash Co-farm of late Notley Young, esq, adj Wash City; & a number of slaves. -Benj Young, Nichl Young, Robt Brent, excs.

About to leave this state I offer for sale hsehld furn. -Jos Saul at 2d hse in Lovell's Row, bet Bank & Treas.

Saml McIntire has mv'd his store to Pa Av opposite Mr Duane's Bk store, for sale of wines, groceries, etc.

Died: Col Francis Deakins, of Gtwn.

FRI NOV 5, 1804
Wash Co, DC. Petition of Saml McPherson confined in Wash Co prison, insolvent debtor.   -Uriah Forrest, Ck

Order of orphan's Crt of PG Co, Md-Public sale of dwelling hse of late Dr Alexander Mitchell of Bladensburg, all the prsnl est of said Mitchell. -Elias B Caldwell, adm, Georgetown.

Sale of hsehld goods at dwelling hse of late Jas Paxton, south of Six Bldg.
                                  -Saml Brook, adm

Ranaway-appr boy, Benedict Raves, age 16 yrs, shoe making bus in Wash City. -Sarah Jordan, wid of Hugh Jordan.

Stud horses wanted-apply to Thos Larkin, Mr Taylor's training groom, Wash Jockey Club.

Adam King & Co, wine store, High St, Gtwn.

WED NOV 7, 1804
Lost on rd from Balt to Wash-pkt bk containing bank bills, receipt from Bank of Alexandria for note of Mr Robt Young, Mr Saml Speake, Mr Theophilus Bowie; Mr Lund Washington; given to Wals Belt. -Jeremiah Booth, Wash

Wash Co, DC-Case of Jas Knight, insolvent debtor, confined to Wash Co jail for debt.   -Uriah Forrest, clk

Hse o/Reps-Petitions referred to committee: 1-Pet of Daniel Cotton for compensation for the injury he sustained in having his ship, *Ann Maria,* whilst in svc of U S, pressed by the Bey of Tunis to carry goods into Marseilles.
2-Pet of Moses White & Charlotte Hazen, Legal Reps of Gen Hazen, for losses of Gen Hazen, Rev War.

To rent: hse occupied by J P Van Ness. Enquire of John Little at the Treas Dept or Dr John Beatty, Gtwn. -Absalom Joy

John Worsley has opened a livery stable-S E crnr of Capt sq.

FRI NOV 9, 1804
Lindley Murray, authur of Eng Grammar; ntv of Pa; born 1745; fr rmv'd to NY; age 19 Lindley studied law; mrd early in life but no chldrn.

Message of Pres Thos Jefferson was delivered at 12 O'clock, Wash, Nov 8, 1804. Copy of same in Nov 9 newspaper.

Hse o/Reps: 1-Petition of Messrs Tyron & R Law-for a proportion of salvage which they consider to have accrued under law of 1799. 2-Pet of John McClelland, old disabled soldier of Rev War, severly wounded at Battle of Eutaw Springs in 1780. Referred to committee.

MON NOV 12, 1804
In 1621 Nova Scotia was granted by Jas I to Sir Wm Alexander.
In 1632 Md was granted by Chas I to Lord Baltimore.
In 1664 NY was granted by Chas II to Duke of York.
In 1664 NJ which the Duke of York cnvyd again to Ld Berkeley & Sir Geo Carteret.
Dela cnvyd to Wm Penn by Duke of York.
1665 Nrth & So Carolina, Ga & the Floridas-granted by Chas II to Earl of Clarendon, Duke of Albemarle, Earl of Craven, Lord Berkeley, Lord Asley, Sir Geo Carteret, Sir John Coleton & Sir Wm Berkeley.
In 1681, Pa was granted by Chas II to Wm Penn.

Boston, Nov 5. Tue a group met at Concert Hall to commemorate the birth of John Adams; Maj Gen Elliot & suite, Brig Genrl Winslow, C I Welles & Col T H Perkins were present. Volunteers: Hon Rufus King, Hon Geo Cabot, Hon Fisher Ames, Hon Josiah Quincy & Squire Seaver.

O'Brien Smith is elected a Rep in Congress from the Districts of Richland, Orangeburgh & Colleton, So C.

WED NOV 14, 1804
Harford, Nov 7. Electors chosen by the Leg of this State:
Jonathan Trumbull	John Treadwell	Oliver Elsworth
David Daggett	Joshua Huntington	Lewis B Sturges
David Smith	Asher Miller	Sylvester Gilbert

Reps of 9th Cong from Ga: Rpblcns
Peter Early	David Merriwether	Jos Bryan
Cowles Mead		

Lead Mines in Upper Louisiana: Burton was discovered by Francis Burton abt 1763; old mines-opened by Mr Ranault abt 1726; mine Ranault-discovered by Ranault abt 1724-5; mine a Maneto-opened in Oct 1799 by Americans settled on Grand Rvr; mine a La Plat discovered in Oct 1799 by an American; mine a Joe, discovered by Messrs Baker & Ally, Americ settlers in Sep 1801; mine a Lany-discovered abt 1795 by Lany; mine a La Mott-discovered by Mr Ranault abt 1723-4; mine a Robuna discovered abt 1763; mine A Gerbore-discovered by Ranault in 1745. -Moses Austin, Feb 13, 1804

For sale: thorns for hedges. Offered by Thos Main, nr Little Falls of Potomac.

For rent: Farm adj Wash City at present occupied by Thos Jenkins.
-Wm Brent

Apptd by the President:
Judge of the dist of Orleans — Dominic A Hall
Atty for the dist of Orleans — Mahlone Dickerson
Judges of the Territory of Orleans — Ephraim Kirby   John B Prevost
Sec for the Territory of Orleans — Jas Brown of Ky
Marshall for the Territory of Orleans — I J Le Breton D'ogenoir
Mbrs of Legislative Cncl —
Col Bellechaffe   John Watkins
Robt Dow   Mich'l Cantrell
Evan Jones   Gaspard Dubuys
Wm Kenner   Julien Poydras
Danl Clark   Benj Morgan
M. Bore
Mr Wikoff of Appalousa
J Romain of Attacapas

FRI NOV 16, 1804

Hse o/Reps: 1-Petition of Jos Jackson & Chas Spencer, excs of Dr Wm Carter, for his svcs in Rev War. 2-Memorial from Wm Dunbar of Miss Terr, claim to land in Natches. 3-Pet of Simeon Noys, old Rev sldr, disabled by wounds & sickness, admitted on pension list in 1792 but never recd any - needed to support his wife & 8 chldrn. 4-Pet of Susanna Taylor on behalf of the chldrn of her late hsbnd, Mr Fulton, Lt in 11th Pa Regt, for warrant for 300 acs of land. 5-Pet of John Crawford, old soldier of 1776 in Dela Regt & in sea svc, twice wounded & 3 times a prisoner, Genrl Regulation. All referred to committee.

Vermont-Electors of Pres & VP of U S:
Josiah Wright   Saml Shaw   Ezra Butler   Nath'l Niles
Wm Hunter   John Noys   [all Rpblcns]

Electors chosen by the Leg of the State of NY:
Sylvester Dering   Jas Fairlie   Cornelius Bergen
John Haring   Ezra Thompson   Maj John Wood
Conrad I Elmendorf   Albert Pawling   Isaac Sargent
Jos Ellicot   John Cramer   Stephen Miller
Abraham Banker   Mathias B Hildrith   Wm Floyd
Jonas Earl   Adam Comstock   Thos Brook
Col Henry Quackenbush   [all Rpblcns]

MON NOV 19, 1804

Baily Washington, on NJ Ave, nr the Capitol, next door to Mr Docker's Soap & Candle Manufactory, recd fine stock of goods, mens & ladies wear.

Winsor Chair Manufactory, nr Union Tavern. -Hector Sandford

Chas Peale Polk, insolvent debtor, confined to Wash Co jail for debt.
                                                    -Uriah Forrest, clk

A NY print announces the death of Genrl Philip Schuyler at Albany on Nov 10th.

WED NOV 21, 1804
Hse o/Reps: Petition of Saml Carson, an alien, praying Congress to pass a law to enable him & his heirs to hold real estate he has purchased in Alexandria, Columbia Terr. Referred to committee.

Wm Shepherd, insolvent debtor confined to Wash Co prison for debt; same for Thos Fowler.   -Uriah Forrest, clk

Genrl Thuriot, Mnstr Pleni of the Emperor of France, arrv'd at Wash.

FRI NOV 23, 1804
Hse o/Reps: Petition of Lt Wm Love of 3d Va Regt, commutation of his half pay. -Referred to committee.
[Nov 26 corr-Love was of the 3d South Carolina Regt.]

For sale: Valuable estate held in common by Messrs Josiah Collins, Nath'l Allen & heirs of Saml Dickenson, decd, cld the Lake Co; 53,000 acs in Wash, NC; 5,000 acs in Gum Neck, Tyrell Co. [Mr Nath'l Allen, is of Edenton] Company was formed in 1787. Apply to John Roulhac, atty, Plymouth, NC or Mr Stephen Cabarrus, of Edenton. -Thos Trotter, Superintendant.

Died: Capt Aaron Gregg, at New Orleans.

MON NOV 26, 1804
Appointments: Geo W Erving, of Mass, sec of Legislature at Madrid.
              Wm Brown, late of Columbia, coll of New Orleans.
              Wm Lyman, of Mass, srvyr & inspec of New Orleans.

Hse o/Reps: 1-Petition of S. G. Osgood, of NY, his purchase of Phil built ship, *Indostan*, sold in 1797 in Hamburgh, prays obtaining a new register; 2-Pet of Capt Alexander Murray, USN, he recaptured a vessel under Guadaloupe, May 1800, he was subjected to pay $13,397.58 damages, prays he may be exonerated. Both referred to committee.

Died: Gen Rewbell, Aug 6, at Paris, a Cidevant Dir of French Rpblc.

Died: Maj Wm Judd, age 63, Nov 13, at Farmington, Conn.

Printing ofc of Mr R Davison, of Warrenton, was consumed by fire.
                                                    -Raleigh, Nov 19

Orphans Crt of Wash Co, DC. Nov 25, 1804. Prsnl est of Abraham Boyd, late of said Co, decd. -Wash Boyd, adm

Order made in case of Wm Shepherd, insolvent debtor, public sale of a coache & pr of horses & his interest in part of a lot on West St, Gtwn, being the same that Richd Parrott sold to David Austin. Austin sold to Shepherd; $60 remains due to Parrott. -Robt W Peacock, trustee

WED NOV 28, 1804

Hse o/Reps: 1-Petition of Benj Emmons, as agent of 60 assocs in Vt, for land in La for settlement. 2-Pet of Timothy Phelps, of Marlboro, Vt, commissioned by Gov of NY in 1782 as shrf of Cumberland Co, NY, now a part of Vt, while on duty was attacked, lost his prsnl prop, rl est confiscated. Congress at Phil in 1782 passed resolutions for full restitution. He returned to Vt & was imprisoned for 5 mos. 3-Pet of *Geo Ball, Lt in 12 Pa Regt, wounded in 1777, never cured, praying for relief-[*Nov 30th newspaper corr.-shd be Geo Vaughan.] 4-Pet of John Devoe who srvd in Militia of NJ, wounded nr Ft Lee in 1776, praying to be put on pension list. 5-Pet of Danl Eldrige, wounded in attack at Groton, he is distressed & disabled. All referred to committee.

Ltr dated Salem, Mass, Nov 16, 1804; from Wm Bentley to John Beckley, clk's ofc of the Hse o/Reps of the U S. Subj: notice of appointment as chaplain to the Hse o/Reps in Wash is declined.

FRI NOV 30, 1804

Died: Genrl John Caldwell, Lt Gov of Ky, in Ky. Thos Posey to fill the vacancy.

Electors for Tenn: Robt Houston, of Knox Co; Richd Mitchell, of Hawkins Co; & David Deaderick, of Wash Co; all Rpblcns.

Hse o/Reps: 1-Petition of John Raynton, compensation for supplies to Lt Elliot in Calvert Co, Md, amt $55.57 in 1799. 2-Pet of Henry McFarland, of 1st Regt of U S Levie, wounded in Gen St Clair's affair with the Indians, Nov 4, 1799, praying to be provided for. 3-Pet of Mordecai Lane, old Rev sldr, praying to be provided for on pension list. All referred to committee.

Wanted to rent or purchase: large hse nr Balt, Eld Ridge, or nr Wash City. -Geo Ralph, Charlotte Hall, St Mary's Co, Md.

Stolen-bay horse. -Daniel Purnell, Long Old Fields, nr Marlborough, 8 miles from Eastern Branch Ferry.

Died: Maj Genrl Philip Schuyler, age 71 yrs, Nov 18. Remains were interred in the family vault of Hon Abraham Tenbroeck. -Albany, Nov 22

MON DEC 3, 1804

Ranaway, Fanny, mulatto, informed she is in svc of Mr Thompson in Gtwn; her mistress is Mrs Sarah Brooks. -Saml J Coolidge, Upper Marlboro, Md.

Hse o/Reps: 1-Petition of Mary Gresham, wid of Jos Gresham, liquidation of claim for svcs as sldr in Va Line-Rev Army. 2-Pet of Jas McPherson, long time prisoner with the Indians, to confirm a grant of lands made to him by the Chiefs of the Nation where he resided. 3-Memorial of Return Jonathan Meigs, salary due him as late Judge of NW Terr. All referred to committee.

Electors for North Carolina-all Rpblcns:

Peter Forney	Jos Williams	Montfort Stokes
Soloman Graves	Jos Taylor	J J Alston
Robt Cochran	Lemuel Sawyer	Jas Jones
Reading Blount	Felix Walker	Bryan Whitfield
Saml Ashe	Sen. Gideon Allston	

Genrl Assembly of the State of Conn, Oct Session, 1804. Subj: Revoking the commissions of Justice of the Peace for:
Wm Judd
A Judson
Hezekiah Goodrich
Nath'l Manning
Jabez H Tomlinson

Signed:

Luther Loomis	Walter Bradley	Hezekiah Huntington
Jas Stephens	Danl Tilden	Isaiah Loomis
Saml Hart Jr	Wm Shelton Jr	Jabez Gregory
Saml Blodget	Robt Wilson	Jas Beardslee
Arah Phelps	Aaron Arnold	Nehemiah Wilson
Saml Cook	Elizur Warner Jr	Saml Beardslee Jr
John Flyment	Sylvester Wells	Eliphalet Cooley Jr
Andrew Lyon	Amala Bradley	Saml Welles

Elections result of New Jersey:

Rpblcn Congress	Henry Southard	Ebenezer Elmer	John Lambert
	Wm Helms	Jas Sloan	Ezra Darby
Federal Congress	Aaron Ogden	Peter D'Vroom	Jas H Imlay
	Franklin Davenport	L Cadwallader	Wm Colefax
Rpblcn Electoral	Phinehas Manning	Moore Furman	Wm Rossell
	Solomon Freleigh	Alex'r Carmichael	Jacob Hufty
	Thos Newbold	Abijah Smith	

Electors Chosen-Mass. Leg:

Jas Sullivan	Eldridge	Gerry Jas Bowdoin	John Hawthorne
Thos Kittridge	Jas Warren	Josiah Deane	John Davis
Timothy Newell	Jonathan Smith Jr	John Whiting	John Bacoa
Wm Heath	John Woodman	Chas Turner	Thos Fillebrown
Edw Upham	John Farley	Jas Winthorp	

Electors chosen for Va.

Geo Penn	John Goodrich	Edw Pagram	Dr Richd Field
Thos Redd	Wm McKinley	Richd Evers Lee	Jas McFarlane
Creed Taylor	Wm H Cabell	Gen John Preston	Geo Wythe
John Taylor	Larkin Smith	John Minor	Wm Ellzey
Wm Dudley	Mann Page	John Taliaferro Jr	Richd Brent
Hugh Holmes	Jas Daily	Jas Allen	Archibald Stuart

Frigs put in commission & will soon proceed to the Mediterranean:
President   Cmdor Barron
Essex   Capt Jas Barron
Congress   Capt Rogers
Constellation Capt Campbell

WED DEC 5, 1804
Brdg hse-upper part of hse in which Mr E Riggs keeps store. -Jane White.

Annapolis, Nov 21, 1804. Ltr congratulating Wm Pinkney on his arrival in this your native city on his return from England. Signed: John Kilty, John Davidson, Burton Whetcroft, John Gassaway, John Muir & Saml H Howard.

Ranaway-Ellic, abt 23 yrs old, negro. Living in Fairfax Co, 8 miles from New Crt hse, Va.   -Hambleton Thrift

Charlotte Hall School, St Mary's Co, Md. Election for a principal to fill vacancy of Rev Mr Geo Ralph who refused to accept his appointment for the ensuing yr; salary $800.   -Neale H Shaw, Reg

Electors for R I:
Constant Taber	Jas Aldrich	Jas Helme
Benj Remington	all Rpblcns	

Electors for NH:
Levi Bartlet	Jonathan Steele	Timothy Walker
Robt Alcock	Geo Aldrich	Wm Tarlton

FRI DEC 7, 1804
Notice: Persons indebted to est of Richd Frazer, decd; payment to Saml N Smallwood, adm, Wash City.

Jas DeNeale Jr, of Dumfries, Va, invented a threshing machine. Inhabitants of Dumfries & area give testamony to same: Jno MaCrae, Jas Read, Hector Alexander, Jno Gibson, Geo Smith, Alex Henderson, Luke Cannon, David Boyle, Bernard Gallager, Wm Smith, Wm Farrow, Jos Gilbert, Thos Chapman, A Sowden.

Mon Dec 10, 1804
Peter Healy has opened a groc store in a hse nr the Capitol, lately occupied by Mr Jas D Barry. Washington.

Hse o/Reps: 1-Petitions of Nancy Flinn, whose husband accompanied Maj Trueman, killed by the Indians; & 2-John Fenton, old Rev sldr, both praying relief, were referred to committee of claims. 3-Pet of Wm A Barron of the Corps of Engineers, praying for further allowance for his expenses in the Military Acad- Referred to Com of Claims.

Electors in Md who voted for Jefferson & Clinton:
Jos Wilkinson,	John Johnson	Edw Johnson	John Tyler
Frisby Tilghman	Tobias E Stansbury	John Gilpin	Wm Gleaves
Perry Spencer.			

Those who voted for Chas Cotesworth Pinckney & Rufus King were:
John Parnham   Ephraim King Wilson

Election in Ga: Abraham Baldwin, Senator to Congress; Electors:
Edw Telfair	Jas B Maxwell	John Rutherford
David Emanuel	Henry Graybill	David Creswell

All true Rpblcns.

Wed Dec 12, 1804
Died: Col Anthony Hutchins, age 80 yrs, at his plantation, The *White Apple Village*. -Mississippi Terr.

Hse o/Reps: 1-Petition of Hannah Hobby, relict of late Marshal of dist of Maine- she may be exonerated as admx of her late hsbnd, from payment of $6000 due by him to the U S. 2-Pet of Elisha Bell & others, to be allowed 3000acs of land due his grfr, Capt Alexander Bell, for svcs during French & Indian War of 1758-9. Both referred to committee.

Runaway-Tom, age abt 21 yrs, negro, committed to Wash Co, DC jail; says he is prop of Mr Benj Berry, opposite the German Chr, Balt, Md.
                              -Jas Kinner, jailor

Meeting in Alexandria, Dec 5, 1804. Elisha C Dick, Mayor, chrmn; John Hoof, sec. Committees for the election:
John Muncaster	Wm Harper	Aaron Hewes	Andrew Jameison
Geo Gilpin	Jos Riddle	John Dundad	Edmund I Lee
John McKenny	Saml Craig	David W Scott	Abel Janney
Chas Alexander Sen	Thos Darnes	Carlyle F Whiting.	

Fri Dec 14, 1804
Senators for Va: Wm B Giles & Andrew Moore.

Electors of Pres & VP for Ky:
Isaac Shelby	Ninian Edwards	Jos Lewis	Wm Roberts
Chas Scott	Hubbard Taylor	John Coburn	Wm Irvine

Hse o/Reps: 1-Petition of Thos Ketland, drawback of duties imposed in 1801- ship, *Washington*. 2-Pet of Sarah Blagden, wid of Lt Col Blagden, Cavalry, compensation for his svcs. Both referred to committee.

Proclamation-Robt Bowie, Annapolis, Nov 28, 1804:
Chosen as Reps in Congress of U S:

District	Representative	District	Representative
1	John Campbell	2	Leonard Covington
3	Patrick Magruder	4	Roger Nelson
5	Nicholas Ruxton Moore	6	John Archer
7	Jos Hopper Nicholson	8	Chas Goldsborough

MON DEC 17, 1804

Stolen out my pasture, 2 horses, Jos Junkin, Carlisle, Pa, or apply to Wm Findley, esq, mbr of Congress in Wash City.

Mrs Eliz Burlingame, w/o Mr Burlingame, of Stutbridge, lately bec the mthr of a living son, weighing 8 lbs, on the day she was 12 yrs 6 mos 5 days of age.

Hse o/Reps: 1-Petition of Sally Lusk, for ferry & land on which she resides between Indiana Terr & Kaskaskia. 2-Pet of John Christian Topless, old sldr in Delaware Regt, wounded thru the right ft, has a wife & 6 chldn. 3-Pet of Capt Thos Campbell of 4th Pa Regt, commutation of his half pay in lieu of a pension. 4-Pet of Elisha Winters who was robbed on Miss. by Banditti, Mason's party, whose apprehension or extermination was a reward of $500 by the Gov't, one of his party shot Mason & 2 of the gang were caught & convicted, prays for allowance for his expences, time, etc, in this business. All referred to committee.

WED DEC 19, 1804

Died: Chas Augustus Stephenson, age 9 yrs, Dec 11.

"The American Gardener" - Book by John Gardener & David Hepburn, late gardener to Gov Mercer & John Mason, esq. Purchase same of J Gardener or Mrs Hepburn, $1.25.

Richmond, Va-Dec 3, 1804. Ofc of public printer vacated by the resignation of Merriwether Jones was filled by Saml Pleasants. -John Page, Spkr of hse of Delegates

Hse o/Reps: Petition of Cath Havis, of Balt Co, Md, compensation for svcs of her late hsbnd, sldr in Royal Americans Regt under Col Bouquet, 1760 & 1761.

Died: Ephraim Kirby, Oct 20, at Ft Stoddert, late of Litchfield, Conn, 1st Judge of U S dist Crt at N Orleans.

Electors of Tenn voted for Jefferson & Clinton:
David Deadrick   Geo Ridley   Wm Martin
Robt Houston   Richd Mitchell

Wash Co, DC. Petition of Walter Queen, insolvent debtor, confined in Wash Co jail for debt.   -Uriah Forrest, clk

FRI DEC 21, 1804

Sup Crt of Pa. Dec 9, 1804. Wm Duane v John Dunlap. Case is an action of trespass; violent assault committed by John Dunlap, with Peter Miercken, Jas Simmons, J B Bond, J B McKean, Geo Willing & sevr'l others on May 15, 1799; in Northampton Co. As a Military Force forced their way into the "Aurora ofc" [newspaper] where Mr Duane employed at his desk; assault then took place. Deposition: Robt Oliphant, Cashier of Norfolk Bank, dated Feb 14, 1804, before Alderman of Norfolk-Wm Vaughan. [Cont'd Dec 24: depo of John Massey-others who witnessed the assault-Jacob Cox; depo of Jacob Keighler-others there, Jacob Cox, Ed Shoemaker; depo of Bernard McMahon-related what he saw].

Hse o/Reps: 1-Memorial of Anne Ledyard, of NY State, wid & admx of Isaac Ledyard, decd, half pay for svcs of decd as hosp surg & assist srvyr in Continental Army-Rev War. 2-Pet of Wm T Smith, of Phil, certificates of funded debt be granted in lieu of 2 loan ofc certs; both referred to committee.

Orphans Crt of PG Co, Md. Dec Term, 1804. Ordered that Wm Sprigg Bowie, exc of Mgt Bowie, sell her prsnl est except the negroes. Truman Tyler, Reg of wills, PG Co, Md

Reps of Md in Cong of U S 1st thru 5th dist:

John Campbell   Leonard Covington   Patrick Magruder
Roger Nelson   Nicholas Ruxton Moore Wm MacCrerry
                              -Robt Bowie, Gov of Md

Cheap groceries & crockery ware.   -J A Xaupi, F St, Wash City

MON DEC 24, 1804
Lost: $50 notes-reward. Contact Ann Tenant, at Mr Tayloe's, NY Av

Phil Museum is the prop of C W Peale, who began it in 1785.

Hse o/Reps: 1-Petition of John Verey, fisherman from Mass., complaining of the loss of his vessel & fish, by which he lost the bounty money on salt he had taken out & praying relief. 2-Another from Ezra Weston of Mass., similar to the last presented; both referred to committee.

Supreme Crt of Pa. Duane Vs Dunlap cont'd. Called & sworn: John Massey, Jacob Keighler, Bernard McMahon.

WED DEC 26, 1804

Hse o/Reps: Petition of Capt Thos Marshal Baker, of Militia, to be placed on pension list, recd wounds in engagement with the British on R I in 1778; referred to committee.

Ranaway, Daniel, negro, blacksmith, age abt 23 yrs, lately purchased of Mr Geo Fitzhugh, of Westmoreland Co, Va; deliver to Mr Churchill Blackburn, Haywood, Wstmrlnd Co; Reward-$20.   -Wm Augustus Washington

For sale: Bk-*"The Temple of Truth"* by Rev John Hargrove, Minister of New Jerusalem Chr, Balt, Md.

Meeting of citizens of Wash; Robt Brent-chrmn, Wm R Cozen-sec.

Leg of Md has agreed to allow Wm Pinckney $12,000 for his svcs in affecting the transfer of stock in the British funds belonging to Md.

FRI DEC 28, 1804

Hse o/Reps: 1-Bill of Charlotte Hazen passed. 2-Petition of Forrest Green, of 3d Va Regt, now residing in Ga, wounded in action of Brandywine, Sep 11, 1777, be allowed a pension to support himself, his wife & 8 chldrn. 3-Pet of Abner Snow, old Militia sldr, to be indemnified his expences for wounds recd in svc of U S-Rev War; both referred to committee.

Wanted- Person to conduct a newspaper & become a partner; printing ofc ready furnished; meet with the execs of Geo Roulston, decd, in Knoxville, Tenn.

Persons indebted to est of Michael Roberts, decd, [store in Gtwn], make payment to Edgar Patterson.   -Frances Roberts -exec; Thos Cumson & Jos A Williams, excs-Gtwn.

MON DEC 31, 1804

Hse o/Reps: 1-Petition of Chas Croxail, of NJ, formerly of Col Hartley's Regt of Pa line, taken prisoner at Battle of Brandywine in 1777, 2 yrs confined on Long Island, for allowances for srving to close of war -Referred to committee. 2-Pet of Wm McClelland, raised a Md Co in 1760, compensation -rejected. 3-Pet of Peter Landais, formerly Capt of frig *Alliance,* share of prizes -rejected. 4-Pet of Cath Haines, grant of land -withdraw same.

Dr Benson, lately from Gr Britain, has taken up his residence in F St-Wash City.

The National Intelligencer and Washington Advertiser
Washington, DC 1805

WED JAN 2, 1805
Hse of Reps: Petition of Elijah Brainard, of Claremont, NH, recd a wound while in svc whose consequences he did not experience for many yrs & whose bodily tortures mitigated only by use of opium, has wife & 6 chldrn. Req a pension. Referred to committee.

Ltr from Richd O'Brien, late Consul of U S, at Algiers, to John Gavino, cnsl at Gibraltar; dated Malta, Sep 5, 1804; Subj:Transactions before Tripoli American ships attacked Tripoli Castle; we lost Lt Jas Decatur; others lost were Lt Caldwell & Mr Dorsey. Boat blew up. Sep 14, 1805-Capt Somers with Lt Wadsworth & Mr Israel, Midshipman, blown up at Tripoli. [Jan 9 paper-also Somers of Jersey; Wadsworth, of Mass & Israel, of Md.]

Hse of Reps: Petition of heirs & leg of Hannah Preston, late relict of Col Preston-died at Camp in Mar 1777, half pay for term which she survived her hsbnd-referred to committee. Petitions of Eli Elmer, Seth Bower & Jona. Moore were referred to committee.

FRI JAN 4, 1805
Rent out or lease my farm at Seneca Falls of Potomac, 18 miles from Gtwn.
-Jos Forrest, Wash City

Wash Co, DC. Case of Philip Meyer, confined to Wash Co prison, insolvent debtor, for debt.   -Uriah Forrest

In Senate of the U S.High Crt of impeachments. Wed Jan 2. The U S v Saml Chase; proceedings begin.

London, Nov 2. Sir Geo Rumbold, British resident of Hamburgh, was seized by a party of 200 French infty.

MON JAN 7, 1805
Mrd: Capt Wm Brent to Miss Kitty Johnson, Jan 6, by Rev Mr Matthews.

Hse of Reps: 1-Petition of Wm Osburn, of New Port, R I; resolved that he may withdraw his petition & documents. 2-Pet of Robt Henderson, of SC, praying that his compensation for carrying the mail to & from Fayetteville, NC & Gtwn, SC, be released from such debt of his contract as relates to a debt of the rd for reasons specified. 3-Pet of Alex'r Scott, of SC, for himself & others, relief in the case of certain negro slaves & other property, taken from ctzns of SC, on their way to the Natchez, by Cherokee Indians, in June, 1794. 4-Pet of Eliakim Morse, of Mass; referred to committee. 5-Pet of Jas Bonnell, of NJ, for renewal of settlement certificate, granted him for Military svcs as Capt of Light Infty,Continental Army, during Rev War, cert. was lost in Oct 1787; referred.

For sale: Mill seat, Frederic Co, Va, 20 acs; -Saml Kercheval, nr Stephensburg, Frederic Co, Va, or Mr Mahlon Atkinson, same neighborhood.
-Saml Kercheval

Died: Hon Peter Van Ness, esq, age 70 yrs & 21 days, Dec 21,1804; head of an ancient Dutch family, of this State. Columbia Co, NY.

WED JAN 9, 1805

Hse of Reps: Petition of Barnabas Strong, of Vt, for grant of land 6 miles sq in Indiana Terr. Referred to committee.

Orphans Crt of Calvert Co, Md. Order of sale, at late dwelling of Benjamin Ward, late of said Co, decd: negroes, stock, & furniture. -Zachariah Ward, adm Calvert Co, Md

Auction sale of lot 1, sq 377, 3 story hse, prop of John Crocker. -Thos Law, Wash

For sale: 2 slaves, man & wife.   -Henry Suttle, Gtwn

Deserted on board U S frig-*U S*, Richd Bowers & Henry Morrison, seamen. Reward $10 each.   -John Cassin

Salute to Wm H Harrison, Gov of Indiana Terr & dist of La; from the people of St Genevieve & New Bourbon; on his arrival at St Gen.
-Signed:Saml Hinch, W Fenwick & Rufus Easton

American Philosophical Soc Meeting of Jan 4, 1805. Elected:

Pres	Thos Jefferson		
VPs	Casper Wistar	Robt Patterson	Benj Smith Barton
Secs	John Redman Coxe	Adam Seybert	Thos C James
	Thos T Herson		
Cnslrs	Jas Woodhouse	Saml Duffield	Wm Shippen
	Zacheus Collins		
Curators	Chas Wilson Peale	John Church	Robt Hare Jr
Treas	John Vaughan		

-Phil, Jan 5

Died: Yten-Ti Fohi, age 101, ntv of China; died in Canada; brought to America in early youth; died while attempting to throw an iron spear weighing 600 lbs at a mark 20 ft off; death by a hemorrage.

FRI JAN 11, 1805

Geo Clinton, Jr, s/o the VP, chosen a Rep in Cong of U S, vice Dr Mitchill who resigned.

Michael Bezeler deserted from on board the U S Frig, *United States*. Reward-$10.
-John Cassin

Hse of Reps: Petition of Benj Bailey, Jas Bogert Jr, [Firm of Bailey & Bogert], Joshua Jones & John A Robertson, all of NYC, merchants; relief from late fire in NYC; petitioners have permission to withdraw their petition.

MON JAN 14, 1805
Hse of Reps: Petition of Lewis Larue, a French ctzn, at present an inhabitant of NY, for privileges of a ctzn of the U S-it was negatived.

Danl Geyer bought from me a bay horse.	-Saml Hamilton
The owner above may have him back.	-Danl Geyer

Wash Co, DC. Case of Henry Dunlap, confined to Wash Co jail, insolvent debtor, for debt. -Uriah Forrest, clk

Died: Col Jas Gillespie, a Rep from N C.

Case of Col Wm S Smith v Mr Jas Cheetham, for libel, was tried in Supreme Crt on Mon; verdict was for the plntf-$200 damages. -NY

NY, Jan 9. Crt held at City Hall, NYC, Jan 8; Wm P Van Ness, convicted of being the bearer of a challenge from the VP to the late Gen Hamilton, for aiding & abetting in the fatal duel; verdict was guilty. Trial of Nath'l Pendleton, implicated in similar charge as the second of Gen H. will take place this day; & that of Richd Riker, Dist Atty, & Robt Swartwout. Mr Woodworth, Atty-Genrl, will conduct these prosecutions.

Hse of Reps: 1-Petition of Cromwell Pearce, of Chester, Pa, claim for 2000 acs for svcs of his fr, an ofcr in expedition against the Indians; 2-Pet of David Elliott, of NJ, to be on pension list, for wounds recd in Maj Genrl St Clair's Army, on exped. against the Indians, Nov 4, 1791; 3-Pet of John Bowers, of Somerset, Mass, for bounty on his 3 schnrs, *The George, The Genrl Johnston & The Diaia;* 4-Pet of Peter Robertson, of Amherst, Hillsborough Co, NH, to be put on the pension list for wound recd at Battle of Bunker Hill, Mass, while a sldr in Col Stark's Regt. All referred to committee.

WED JAN 16, 1805
Hse of Reps: Petition of heirs of late Col J Heskin Stone, of 1st Md Regt, wounded in action of Germantown & disabling him from continuing svc in the Army, for commutation of half pay; referred.

New York, Jan 11: Trial of Nathaniel Pendleton, esq, indicted for acting as the second of Gen Hamilton in the unfortunate duel; verdict-guilty; Mr Van Ness & Mr Pendleton were found guilty, complete disfranchisement for 20 yrs.

To printers-orders for type from Wm Casson Jr & Co, London. -Chas Wirgman, 215 Mkt St, Balt, Md

Reward-$5 for strayed or stolen horse from Mr John Robertson's, PG Co, nr Piscataway, Md. -Geo N Ford, living with Jos Young, Chas Co nr dwelling of late Gen Wm Smallwood, decd.

Ranaway-Tom Danl, age abt 45 yrs, negro. Apply to Ralph Lane, Centreville, Fairfax Co, Va. Reward-$100.   -Ralph Lane

FRI JAN 18, 1805
Ranaway, John Hopewell, bet 15 & 16 yrs of age, apprentice boy. Reward-$1.
                               -Jos White, Gtwn

Hse of Reps: Petition of John Badger, of the Rev Army, disabled in svc by very severe wounds; praying relief. Referred to committee.

Eulogy was delivered by Dr Benj Smith Barton on the death of Dr Jos Priestly; Jan 3, in the Presbyterian chr in Phil.   -Philadelphia, Jan 14.

MON JAN 21, 1805
Hse of Reps: 1-Petition of Henry & Wm Stewart, of Germantown, Pa, calico printers & dyers, drawback on India good equal to same on foreign printed articles. Referred to committee. 2-Senate considered the pet of Charlotte Hazen, to allow her a pension for life, $200 per annum, Feb 4, 1803, date of her hsbnd's decease. 3-Pet of Richd Taylor, desperately wounded in the late Indian War, praying for additional allowance for his support; referred

WED JAN 23, 1805
New book store-Levrault, Schoell & Co of Paris. 61 St Patrick's Row, Balt, Md.

Meeting at Rhodes's Tavern;
Thos Munroe-Chrmn;
A Brevort Woodward-sec;
Committee:

Jas C King	David Peter	Wash. Boyd
Jos Hodgson	Benj Perkins	Jas Hoban
Lewis Clephan	Peter Lenox	Robt Brent
Danl Brent	Peter Hagner	John McGowan
John Brown	Jos Bromley	Wm Simmons
Rev Jas Lawrie	Rev Matthews	Geo Andrews
Saml H Smith	Nicholas King	John Chalmers

Jas Davidson elected Treas. [Jan 23, 1805.]

Hse of Reps: Petition of Abigail Brush, wid of Col Brush, decd, praying to be released from demand of $4000 which the U S had against the estate in his quality of coll of the Land Tax; referred to committee.

Fri Jan 25, 1805

Notice to Robt Boyes & Jas Boyes, if living, chldrn of Robt Boyes, who was s/o the late esq Boyes, of Londonderry, Rockingham Co, NH, decd; Robt the elder left Londonderry abt 30 yrs ago, mrd in Balt, Md, remv'd to Va & there died; apply to Silas Betton of Salem, NH, now in Wash City, or to Alexander Boyes, of Londonderry, may hear of some property worth their attention.

Runaway negro, Wm Blackston, age abt 27 yrs, committed to Frederick Co jail; says he is a free man.   -Geo Creager, Shrf

Hse of Reps: 1-Petition of Capt John Little of Militia of NY, relief for wound recd in the shoulder by a tomahawk during Rev War. 2-Pet of John Lowry of Col Smallwood's 1st Md Regt, increase of his pension for infirmities & advanced age. Both referred to committee.

Reward-One cent for white bound srvt girl, Matilda Edmundson, generally known as Patty, abt 13 yrs of age. Inferior to no one in the art of lying & stealing.
-T H Gillis, Washington

Mon Jan 28, 1805

An act-for relief of Charlotte Hazen, widow & relict of the late Brig-Genrl Moses Hazen: annual sum of $200 to begin Feb 4, 1803. -Apprv'd
-Th. Jefferson, Jan 23, 1805.

Oliver Evans, of Phil City, has invented improvements on merchant flour mills, obtained a patent dated Jan 7, 1791.

Deserted on board U S frig *United States*, Danl Flanagan.
-John Cassin

Hse of Reps: 1-Pet. of Bathsheba Newcomb & other legal reps of Col Preston of the Jersey Militia who died Mar 1777 of hardships & fatigue, praying commutation for his half pay; barred by the statutes of limitation; petitioners have leave to withdraw their petitions. 2-Likewise on the pet of P Pettigare who had svr'l ofcs at New Orleans, by right of purchase from Spain; reimbursement of his purchase money; he has leave to withdraw his petition. 3-Pet of Cuthbert Simms of the 1st Regt of Va Line commanded by Col Grayson; Simms was disabled by a strain recd on his marching from the southward to the northward in 1776; unable to support himself, his wife & chldrn; praying relief; referred to committee. 4- Pet of Edwin Lewis, the legal rep of Henry Mail/Mall, complaining of acts of the comrs of the Miss Terr; referred to committee.

Appointments: John P Van Ness, Lt Col Commandant of 1st Legion of Militia of the dist of Col, vice Col Brent, rsgn'd; Wm Dent Bealle, Brig Maj & inspec of Militia of said dist, vice Maj Wingate, rsgn'd; Wm O Sprigg, a Maj in 1st Legion, vice Maj Van Ness, promoted; Chas McLaughlin, Capt of Light Inf in said Legion, vice Capt Sprigg, promoted. Washington City, Jan 28.

WED JAN 30, 1805

Hse of Reps: 1-Petition of Jas Royston, old Rev sldr of 1st Regt of Artl, attached to Md Line, inability from wounds recd in svc to provide for himself & family. 2-Petition of Abraham Welebar of Warren, old Rev sldr, praying relief. Both referred to committee.

For sale: 141 acs, prop of Richd Mitchel, PG Co, Md, adj. the lands of Rev Geo Ralph, Thos Mudd & John Robertson. Apply to Matthew Walton, now at McLaughlin's, Gtwn, til Feb 15.

For sale, a family of negroes pursuant to will of Ann Digges, decd. -Thos Digges, of Warburton, nr Piscataway, or Wm Carroll, Rock Creek, Montgomery Co, Md. excs.

For sale: 2 story framed hse, 11th nr F St. -Mark Stockwell

FRI FEB 1, 1805

Died: Mrs Mary Lee, the lady of Thos Sim Lee, esq, Jan 21, wife & mthr.
-Gtwn, Columbia, Jan 22

Col F Deakins & Col Neville were commissioned by Va & Md in 1786 to lay out a rd bet upper navigation of Potowmac to nearest western navigation. Extract of a ltr from Col Deakins who died last summer.

MON FEB 4, 1805

Act for relief of John Steele; svcs as sec of the Miss Terr from May 7, 1802 to Mar 2, 1803; pay his salary & expenditures. Apprv'd: Th: Jefferson, Jan 31, 1805.

Hse of Reps: Petition of Jacob Greer of NC, comp for svcs rendered, for collection of taxes in Orange Co, NC; referred to committee.

Mrd: Jas Davidson Jr, esq, cashier of Ofc of Discount & Deposit, to Miss Mary Barber, of Wash, Feb 2, by Rev Mr McCormick.

Close of the impeachment of the Judges: Thos Shippen, Jasper Yeates & Thos Smith.
13 voted guilty & 11 not guilty.

Guilty:	Jos Hart	J Hartzellg	Heister W McArthur
	Montgomery	Th Morton	John Piper
	John Porter	Wm Reed	R Spangler
	John Steele	John Vance	R Whitehill
Not guilty	Jas Brady	Jas Gamble	Jas Harris
	J Heister	E Heston	John Kean
	P C Lane	C Mayer	Mewhorter
	Wm Pennell	John Richards	

Verdict: Acquitted-guilty votes were not two thirds.
-Lancaster, Jan 28

WED FEB 6, 1805
Jas A Bayard apptd to represent Delaware in Senate of U S.

FRI FEB 8, 1805
In Chancery-Benjamin R Morgan, exc of Benj Morgan, decd. v Wm Jones, exc of Wm Slubey, decd, Wm Ringgold, Jas Ringgold, & Richd Ringgold, exc of Jas Ringgold, decd, who was a creditor of the said Wm Slubey. Bill to establish a claim which clmnt sets in his own right & that of his fr, Benj Morgan, decd, against est of Wm Slubey late a co-partner in the hse of Morgan & Slubey; to compell production of bks of acc't of said hse; Morgan & Slubey gave their joint bond to Frederic Pigon for 5154L 3S 8D on Jan 20, 1785; Wm Jones resides in NY, NY. -Saml H Howard, Reg CC

Thos Barwise, declining his present business, has 2 coachees for sale. Apply to same at place formerly occupied by Geo Walker, nr Capitol.

MON FEB 11, 1805
Claims against Jos English, insolvent debtor, exhibit same. -Uriah Forrest, clk -R Parrott, trustee

Hse of Reps: Petition of Danl Clarke of Salem, Mass, in 1801 he loaded a schnr for St Jago De Cuba, where the Capt died, & Americ cnsl, Mr Blakely, took possession of the property & never accounted to him for same; prays for relief; referred to committee.

Claims against Jos English, insolvent debtor, exhibit same. -Uriah Forrest, clk -R Parrott, trustee

Impeachment trial of Saml Chase; witnesses for the prosecution,
Present:

*Alexander Jas Dallas	*Wm Lewis	Wm Rawle
Wm S Biddle	Edw Tilghman	Geo Read
John Taylor	John Montgomery	John Stephen
Wm Wirt	John Thompson Mason	Saml H Smith
Geo Hay	John Heath	

Absent:

Jas Lea	John Crow	Meriwether Jones
Jas Pleasants	Risdon Bishop	Aquila Hall
Philip Stewart	Thos Hall	Philip Norborne Nicholas
John Harvie		

Witnesses summoned by Judge Chase:

David M Randolph	Edmund Randolph	John A Chevale
Robt Gamble	John Marshall	Wm Marshall
Cyrus Griffin	David Robertson	Jas Winchester
Philip Moore	Cornelius Comegys	Thos Chase
John Stewart	Wm Rawle	John Purviance
Gunning Bedford	Nicholas Van Dyke	Wm C Frazier

Archibald Hamilton	Saml P Moore	Edw Tilghman
Wm Meredith	Jared Ingersol	Saml Wheeler
Saml Ewing	Walter Dorsey	Jas P Boyd
Nicholas Brice	Wm M Mechlin	Wm H Wynder
Wm Gwyin	Wm J Gavane	Edw J Coales
John Hall Jr	Thos Carpenter	Philip Gocch
John Bassett		

Not found:

Saml Wheeler	John Hopkins	Wm Minor
decd J C Barrett	[*of Philadelphia, Pa]	

WED FEB 13, 1805
Lost: Stock certificates of U S, No. 811, dated Oct 20, 1802 -$400; No. 1115 & 1116 -$100 ea, issued by Jos Nourse, Reg, in favor of Jas Paten, Alex, DC.

FRI FEB 15, 1805
Public sale. Decree of Crct Crt of Wash Co, DC, in suit of Saml Speake, cmplnt, v Joshua Gregg, dfndnt, in Chancery; lots in Thos Bealles Additon to Gtwn, #s 134 & 135. -Henry Whetcroft, trustee

Hse of Reps: 1-Petitions of John McFadon, & of John McFadon & Francis Johonnot, of Balt, Md; referred to sec of the Treas. 2-Peter Pedesclaux, of New Orleans, has leave to withdraw his petition. 3-Petition of Amy Dardin is reasonable & ought to be granted. 4-Petition of Benj Smith of Trenton, NJ & also that of (5-) Aaron Shepard of Orleans Co, Vt; both referred to committee of claims.

MON FEB 18, 1805
Map of Virginia by Wm Prentis, Petersburg, Va, Mr Wm Davis, draughts-man; explanatory ltr from J Madison, Wmsburg, Va, dated Feb 1, 1805.

For sale: negroes at Loudon March Crt, before the door of Mr Jones, innkpr, Leesburg. -Wm Byrd Page,
Trustee of Fairfax, Jeff. Co, Va

For sale: Young horse, Punch. -John Threlkeld, Gtwn.

Hse of Reps: Petition from Ishmael Giddens of Yorktown, Va; & also one from Nathan Putnam of Daveis, Essex Co, Mass; both referred.

WED FEB 20, 1805
Died: Woodbury Langdon, in Portsmouth, NH, Rpblcn & Rev Patriot.

Lost brother; of Sandford Edwards, or any of his chldrn, who resided abt 13 yrs ago within 30 miles of Edenton, NC, are living, will apply to me, they may hear of something to their advantage. -Ben Edwards, Bairdstown, Ky

Treaty bet U S & Delaware Indians, at Vincennes, Indiana Terr, Aug 18 last & ratified by the Pres of the U S on Jan 25, 1805.
Signed:

Sec to Comr	Wm Henry Harrison	John Gibson
Judge of the I.T.	Henry Vanderburgh	
Knox Co I.T. Militia	Col Vigo	
Atty Genrl of I.T.	B Parke	John Rice Jones
Prothonotary of Knox Co, I.T.	Robt Buntin	G Wallace Jr
	Antonie Marchal	
Interpreter	Jos Barron	
Atty at Law	Edw Hempstead	

Treaty bet the U S & the Piankashaw Tribe of Indians was signed at Vincennes, Indiana Terr, on Aug 27, 1804 & ratified by Pres of U S on Jan 21, 1805.
Signed:

Sec to Comr	Wm Henry Harrison	John Gibson
Judge of the I.T.	Henry Vanderburgh	
Knox Co I.T. Militia	Col Vigo	
Atty Genrl of I.T.	B Parke	John Rice Jones
Shrf of Knox Co, I.T.	Wm Prince	
Interpreter	Jos Barron	Abraham F Snapp
Atty at Law	Edw Hempstead	
Citizens of Knox co, I.T.	Geo Wallace Jr	Peters Jones

Runaway-Hannah, negro woman, lived with Mr Leonard abt 2 yrs past; her mthr's name is Fanny whom I set free, her fr's name is Harry belonging to Mr Edw Washington. -Simon Sommers, Alexandria, DC

FRI FEB 22, 1805
For sale: apple trees. -Thos McGrath, at Col Forrest's farm, 2 miles from Gtwn.

Resolutions passed by Leg of Ky; Signed-Wm Logan, S H R; Thos Posey, S S P. Approved-Christopher Greenup, Gov of Ky.

Orphans Crt of Wash Co, DC. Feb 19, 1805. Prsnl est of Jas Thompson, late of Wash co, decd. -Henry Herford & Thos Herty, adms. Prsnl prop of the same will be sold at Mr Danl Keely, tailor, at the Navy Yd.

Public sale of 10 acs of land, where I live, on upper road to Alexandria.
                                                      -Morris Newman

MON FEB 25, 1805
Ranaway from Mr Thos King, Fame, negro woman, age 38 yrs, PG Co, Md.
                                                  -Massey Simms, Chas Co, Md

Hse of Reps: Francis Mentges to have leave to withdraw his petition, together with the papers accompanying same.

WED FEB 27, 1805
Ltr from Cmdor Preble to sec of the Navy. Subj-Tyranny at Tripoli. -Edw Preble, U S Ship *Constitution*, Malta Harbor, Sep 18, 1804.

For sale: Lombardy poplars. -Theo Holt, Eastern Branch, Wash

FRI MAR 1, 1805
Ltr from Hon C C Pinckney to Gen Jas Wilkinson, dated Charleston, Oct 10, 1804. Subj: a sldr should wear his hair short.

Public sale: Decree of Chancellor of Md: plantation formerly owned by Allen Quynn, esq, decd, land cld: *Young's Chance, Dunkin's Luck, Hambleton, Hill's Good Luck, Timber Neck, Brompton,* & part of *Wardope,* abt 1000 acs, on South Rvr abt 4 miles from Annapolis. -John Johnson

Ltr from Gen W North to Gen Jas Wilkinson, dated, Duanesburg, Oct 25, 1804. Subj: cut & dress of the hair.

Ltr from Genrl Alexander Spotswood to Genrl Jas Wilkinson, dated Va, Fredericksburgh, Nov 17, 1804. Subj: order to cut men's hair short.

Ltr from Col Wm S Smith to Genrl Jas Wilkinson, dated NY, Oct 25, 1804. Subj: cut & dress of the hair.

Ranaway, Jos Stephens, his fr says he is above 20 yrs of age, apprentice.
-John Kedglei, plaisterer, Wash City

John Bausman, currier, 16 So Liberty St, Balt, Md.

MON MAR 4, 1805
Address of ofcrs of squadron under command of Cmdor Edw Preble on giving up his command of the Mediterranean Squadron to Cmdor Barron was signed at Syracuse Harbor on Nov 4, 1804 by:

Stephen Decatur jr	Capt	Frig - *Congress*
Chas Stewart	Master & Commandant	Brig - *Syren*
Isaac Hull	Master & Commandant	Brig - *Argus*
John Smith	Master & Commandant	Brig - *Vixen*
John H Dent	Lt Cmmdnt	Schnr - *Nautilus*
Thos Robinson	Lt Cmmdnt	*Enterprize*

Ofcrs of the *Constitution*
Lieutenants	Chas Gordon	Jas Tarbell
	Saml Elbert	Chas Morais
	Hechcote I Reie	Danl S Dexter
Mstr	Nath Haraden	
Capt of Marines	John Hall	
Lt of Marines	Robt Greenleaf	
Surg	Jas Wells	
Purser	N Norris	

Chaplain	P Leonard	
Ofcrs of the *John Adams*		
Lieutenants	Edw Bennet	J B Nicholson
	Marmaduke Dovebainbridge	J Thorn
	Thos McDonough	
Ofcrs of the *Siren*		
Lieutenants	Michael Carrol	Jos I Maxwell
	Robt Spence	J Thorn
Surgeon	Saml R Marshall	
Mstr	Wm Burrows	
Ofcrs of the *Argus*		
Lieutenants	Sybrant Vanschaiek	
Purser	Tim Winn	
Surgeon	L Griffin	N T Weems
	John W Dorsey	
Marines	John Johnson	
Ofcrs of the *Vixen*		
Lieutenants	John Tripp	Wm Crane
	Geo Wash. Reid	Chas Ridgely
	Ralph Izard	
Mstr	Richd Butler	Stephen Cassin
Purser	Jas Tootel	J Green
Surgeon	G Jacques	
Marines	J M Haswell	G Marcellin

Appointments: Robt Smith, Atty Genrl of U S, vice Levi Lincoln, rsgn'd; Jacob Crowninshield, sec of Navy, vice Robt Smith, [above]. Gen Hull, Gov of Terr of Michigan.

WED MAR 6, 1805
List of acts passed at 2d session of Eighth Cong, Mar 3, 1804
[Named petitioners extracted] Charlotte Hazen; John Steele; Alexander Murray; wid & chldrn of Robt Elliott; Richd Taylor; wid & chldrn of Thos Flinn; Geo Scoone & Alexander Cameron.

Copy of the Inaugural speech by Thos Jefferson, Pres of the U S, Mar 4, 1805. Thos Jefferson, Pres of the U S, took the oath of ofc, Mar 4. Geo Clinton, likewise, as VP.

Hse of Reps: Petitions from Thos Brickell of Gates Co, NC; from Cath Ansart of Mass, & from Benj Vicary of Edenton; all referred to the committee of claims.

Hse of Reps: Ltr from G F Saltonstall of Fayetville, NC, & papers on improvements he has made on boats & plan for sinking ships of war-praying the aid of Congress to complete the same.

FRI MAR 8, 1805

For sale, decree of High Crt of Chancery of Md, negroes, at late dwelling place of Mrs Mgt Bowie, nr Nottingham, PG Co, Md. -Philemon L Chew & Rd Marshall, trustees.

Public sale:-Order of Crt of Calvert Co, Md-prop of heirs of Capt Walter Smith, decd. Plantation where Smith formerly resided, 1225 1/8 acs, on St Leonard's Creek; plantation nr the former, 627 1/3 acs; on Parker's Creek, 536 1/2 acs. Apply to Mr John Turner who resides nr the first two, or Mr Richd Hance, who resides on last tract. -John Wilkinson, Jas Heighe, John Turner, comrs, Calvert Co, Md.

Mrs O'Reilly has remv'd her academy from Balt to Alexandria.

MON MAR 11, 1805

"Diomed", extraordinary horse, will stand at my stable, 3 miles below Richmond.
-Miles Selden, Tree Hill.

WED MAR 13, 1805

Died: Haydn, celebrated composer, at Vienna, age 79 yrs, early Dec.

For sale: dwlg hse of Peter Wood Jr, late of PG Co, Md.
-John T Wood, adm.

Elected to the Council of Alexandria: Aaron Hewes, Wm Harper, Jacob Hoffman, Alexander Smith, J Thompson, J Lumidon

FRI MAR 15, 1805

Died: Col W W Burrows, age 47 yrs, on Mar 6; Rev ofcr & late commandant of the Marine Corps.

An Act: Marshall of NY is directed to discharge John York, late a coll of the tax for the 83d coll dist of NY, from imprisonment.

Died: Mrs Anna Carroll, of Wash city, on Mar 12, after a lingering & painful illness; a wife, mthr & mistress.

Caution: do not receive 2 notes of hand, drawn in favor of Mr Wm Lovell, dated Mar 13, 1805, endorsed by Messrs Wm Woodward & Orlando Cook.
-Jos Huddleston

To be sold: at plantation of Jos Galloway, esq, decd: stock, utensels & furn; persons indebted to the est are to pay Mr John Galloway of West Rvr.
-David Lynn, adm., West Rvr

For sale: flour, corn meal, bran, etc, at warehse on NJ av, nr Barry's wharf.
-Peter Miller & Ebenezer Eliason

To let: hse now occupied by Mr John Wall on 11th st.
-Peter Lenox

MON MAR 18, 1805
Died: Mrs Sarah W Wood, w/o Col Jas G Wood, Nottingham, PG co, on Mar 6, age 26 yrs; ill since Feb; dght, wife & friend.

For rent: 3 story brick tavern, in Wash, lately occupied by Mr Wm Rhodes. Apply nr the Gtwn college to Mary Ann Fenwick.

Orphans crt of Wash co, DC: ltrs of adm de bonis non, on prsnl est of Wm Deakens, jr, late of said town, decd.   -John Hoye, adm, d b n

Orphans crt of Wash co, DC: ltrs of adm on prsnl est of Francis Deakens, late of said town, decd. John Hoye & Leo M Deakens, excs.

For sale: at present dwelling of Mrs Eliza Peacock, oppo Mr Lewis Morin on Pa av; sundry articles of hsehld & kitchen furn; collection of bks.
-Eliza Peacock, city of Wash

Stray cow taken up nr Mrs Cassiaeves; Jos Thomas, living on plantation, formerly occupied by Mr Down.

For sale: Paint Mills, 30 to 40 acs of land, mill hse-28 x 44, 2 stories high, in PG co on Big Paint Branch.   -Thos Edmonson, jr

For sale: all right & title of Wm McDono in hse & lot nr the war ofc, in sq #168, nrly oppo the hse occupied by Gabriel Duval. -Thos W Pairo, at the store at 7 bldgs.

WED MAR 20, 1805
Villard's Little Cottage & Spring Garden - open & providing ice creams, tea, coffee & other refreshments.

Wash Co. DC: Frederick Bette, insolvent debtor confined in prison of said co for debt.   -Uriah Forrest, clk.

Public sale: at late dwelling hse of the late Col Chas Beatty, decd, in Gtwn; the whole of his prsnl est.   -C A Beatty & A Ritchie,
adms with will annexed.

FRI MAR 22, 1805
Balt, Md, Mar 18: the Govnr & cncl have apptd Jeseph H Nicholson, esq, agent to negotiate stock in bank of Eng, belonging to this state.

For sale or rent: tavern for some yrs occupied by Dr Pontius D Stelle; on Capt. hill. Apply to Danl Carroll, of Dud'n.

Mon Mar 25, 1805

$100 reward for Rob't W Peacock, confined in Wash Co jail, on conviction of forgery, Dec term 1804; escaped from said jail. He is a stout man, 5' 10", abt 34 yrs of age, blue eyes & light hair. -Danl C Brent, Mrshl of DC.

Hse of Reps: Act passed for relief of Richd Taylor of Ky; in svc of the U S as an escort, spy & guide, daily pay $1.25, during hostilities with certain indians, in yr 1792; wounded in svc & placed on invalid pensioners list of the U S, rate of $20 per mo beginning Jan 1 in present yr. Apprv'd, Th. Jefferson.

Acts for relief: 1-Robt Patton & others; coll of Tappahannock is directed to pay Patton & Co, & Saml Pearson, owners of the schnr *Iris,* vessel of the U S, amt recd from them for foreign tonnage of said schnr; he is also directed to repay to Saml Gordon & others, owners of the cargo of said schnr, 10% additional duties, 1804. 2-The coll of Newport is to pay Edmund Briggs jr & others, mstr & crew of the schnr *Phebe,* amt of bounty arising on a fishing voyage, in 1804, schnr employed for 4 mos of the fishing season.

Wed Mar 27, 1805

Hse of Reps: 1-Act for relief of the widow & orphan chldrn of Robt Elliot, who was killed by hostile indians while conducting supplies to the army commanded by Maj Genrl Wayne, in 1794; sum of $2000. 2-Act for relief of Geo Scoone & Alex'r Cameron; Scoone late a cpl in 5th Md regt, in army of Rev, be placed on pension list & receive from Mar 5, 1790. 3-That Alex'r Cameron, late a sldr in 2d regt of NC line of the army of the Rev, be on pension list from Jan 1st last, pension of half pay of a pvt for & during his life. 4-Act for provisions for the widow & chldrn of Thos Flinn; sum of $518 with int from Jan 15, 1793; Flinn, interprete & guide was killed with Col John Harding while bearing messages of peace to hostile indians, in the yr 1792. Apprv'd-Th Jefferson

Sorrel gelding strayed from Nottingham. Reward will be pd any person delivering him to Jas G Wood, Nottingham.

Stolen: lg bay horse from my stable nr Balt. -Saml N Smith, Balt.

Public sale of 4 shares of stock of the Wash Bldg Co, part of the est of Jas Thompson, decd. -Henry Herford & Thos Herty, adms, Wash.

Wed Mar 27, 1805

Sale: land in Chas Co, Md; 275 acs. Apply to Jos Elgin.

Fri Mar 29, 1805

Traveller's Hall to be completed shortly for dining; R Bradley, Lexington, KY.

Mon Apr 1, 1805

Orphans Crt of PG co, Md: adm on prsnl est of Hyram Drane, late of said co, decd. Richd W Brashers, adm.

Ran away: Claiborne, negro boy abt 18 yrs old; from Nath'l Wilkinson living abt 7 miles from city of Richmond

WED APR 3, 1805
For sale: 800 acs of land named *Oakland Farm*, 22 miles from Fredricksburg. Mr Levan Oliver lives nr the place & will show the land; for terms apply to Mr John Love of said co.   -Thos Thorpe

John Langdon elected Gov of NH, in rm of Mr Gilman.

FRI APR 5, 1805
Alexandria, Apr 2. Votes for persons to rep the counties of Pr Wm, Loudon & Fairfax, in Hse of Reps of U S: Col W Elzy-180; Jos Lewis jr-75.

Ladies w. ltrs in Wash Post Ofc, Apr 1805:

Eliza Baker	Miss Ann H Baker
Mrs Loveday Buchanan	Mrs Zeporah Coming
Mrs Mgt Hugthrop	Miss Milly Ross
Miss Patience Smith	Betsey Shannon
Mrs Eliz Shorter	Miss Mary Taylor c/o Mr Cranch
Mrs Mary Tippet	Miss Eleanor Lee Wallace
Miss Prudence Williams.	

Ran away, Ben, negro, abt 20 yrs of age. Reward- $10.
-Wm Harrison, Charlotte Hall, St Mary's Co, Md.

MON APR 8, 1805
For sale: Sugar, gin, rum etc.   -Buller Cocke, Navy Yd.

Notice: Subscriber has rented the hse in F st, adj where the Hon Jas Madison resides, intends pursuing the practice of physic & surgery. Educated in Pa U; practiced for 5 yrs in Martinsburg, Va.   -Thos Patterson.

Runaway committed to Wash Co jail; Agnes, negro woman; says she is free & from Orange co, Va, where she lived with Mr Kyles.
   -N Rochester, shrf.

WED APR 10, 1805
Jared Shattuck, resid merchant in the Danish island of St Thomas, was born within the limits of the U S, but bec a Danish burgher abt the yr 1796.

Ranaway: Dick, negro man abt 40 yrs of age; was formerly the prop of widow Burch living in the Federal city. Dick has a wife at Kensey Beall's living in Montg. co, Md. -John Benson, nr the mouth of the Monocosy.

Edwin Gray & Thos Newton jr have been re-elected reps of Va to Congress without opposition.

Fri Apr 12, 1805

"Life of Washington" - gentlemen in Upper Marlbobo, Md, who signed a subscription for the above work held by David Por, jr, late postmstr of that place shd apply to John March's bkstore, Gtwn, or to Mr G Hill, bkseller, Balt, Md.

To let: for 2 1/2 yrs, the hse in which I reside, furnished as it is; $750 per annum; if agreeable to the tenant, I will reserve the lower rm now occupied by me as a store & deduct $100 from the annual rent.
-Chas Love, Gtwn, Jefferson St.

Mon Apr 15, 1805

Three stallions will be at Bowling Green this season.
-John Hoomes, Bowling Green.

Committed to Frederick co jail, runaway Gilbert Day, negro man; says he belongs to John Hodd of Balt co, md. -Geo Creager, shrf, Frederick Co, Md.

Wed Apr 17, 1805

Land sale-will & test of Anthony Holmead, decd; 40 acs adj Wash city.
-John Holmead, nr the premises

Va-Reps to Congress: Genrl John Smith re-elected w/o oppo.

Va County	Representative	Votes	Representative	Votes
Albemarle Co	Thos M Randolph	503	Walter Leak	140
Rockbridge Co	Alex'r Wilson	275	Robt Bailly	28
Mecklinburg Co	Mark Alexander	350	John Claiborne	150

Deserted on board the U S frig, *U S*, Balbrier Urree, speaks little or no English. Deliver to John Cassin, Wash Navy Yd.

Ranaway-Sandy, negro man, age abt 22 yrs. -H Rose, Alexandria.

Ranaway-Tom Daniel, negro man, abt 45 yrs of age.
-Ralph Lane, Fairfax Co, Va

Apr 19, 1805

Orphans Crt of Wash Co, DC. Apr 8, 1805. Prsnl est of Jas Carlan, late of said city, decd. -Mgt Carlan, admx

Committee apptd for bldg a dam from Mason's island to the Va shore: Thos Corcoran, Henry Foxhall & Nath. Lufborough.

Public auction of est cld *Chichester* on the Eastern Branch, oppo Wash city, 697 acs; apply to Col Hanson, Navy Yd; Capt John Davidson at Rhode's Hotel, or Chas Mayman, of Gtwn. Lots shown by Mr Wedden, living on the prem.
-Anthony Addison, Barnaby

Mon Apr 22, 1805
Run away-Henry Price, negro, purchased from Rev Bishop Nealle, of Gtwn. Reward-$20. -Peter Lenox, Wash

Pierpont Edwards, esq, atty, has remv'd from New Haven to NY. Attest: John H Lynde, clk, N Haven. -Jona. Ingersoll, chrmn, New Haven, Apr 2.

Wed Apr 24, 1805
Convention of Medical & Chirugical Faculty of Md, at Balt, Md, 1st Mon in Jun.
-Nat. Potter, sec Med & Chir; Fac Md

Fri Apr 26, 1805
Notice: Saddler & harness maker, John Lutz, has remv'd from Frederick Town & opened shop in High St, Gtwn, next to Abner Ritchie's.

Wash Co, DC. Jeremiah Conner, insolvent debtor, committed to Wash Co jail, for debt.   -Uriah Forrest, clk

Mrs Smith & Mrs Wily have remv'd their brdg school from Water St to Main St nr Mr Francis Lowndes, Gtwn.

Land surveying-Richd Freeman, Rhodes Hotel, Wash City.

Jos Rademaker is Charge Des Affaires of his Royal Highness, the Prince Regent of Portugal to U S.

The Life of Saml Johnson, DD, the first Pres of Kings College, in NY, now Columbia College; book by Thos Bradbury Chandler, DD, formerly rector of St John's chr, Elizabeth Town, NJ. Price-.87

Epitaph on monument in Christ chr, Startford: MS / Samuelis Johnson, D. D./ Collegii Regulis, Novi Eboraci; Praefidis Primi, / Et Hujus Ecclesiae /Najus Dire 14 Oct 1796, / Obiit 6 Jan 1772.

Mon Apr 29, 1805
Died: Rev Dr John Blair Linn, ntv of Pa, born in Shippensburg, Cumberland Co, in 1777; eldest s/o Rev Dr Wm Linn, who formerly settled in Pa but remv'd to NY; his mthr was d/o Rev John Blair; ordained by Presbyters of Phil on Jun 13, 1799; died Aug 30; affectionate & indulgent father.

High Crt of Appeals. Robt Reed, Collin Reed, Hugh Ballentine & Frances his wife, plntfs, v Mgt Reed, dfndnt. Robt Reed, ntv of Ire, settled in colony of Va prior to 1776; purchased 1/2 ac lot No. 7 in Staunton in 1763 & 740 acs of land in Augusta Co in 1767; wrote his bro, John Reed, of Ire, that he was childless & without heir in this country & wished him to send some of his chldrn to heir it; plntfs came over in 1784-Collin Reed arrv'g in 1786; [Frances Ballentine is d/o John Reed]; Robt Reed, the elder, died in 1787, without will & issue, leaving his wife, Mgt; 1799 the dist Crt decided in favour of the dfndnt-the plntfs did not become ctzns of this Commonwealth until after the descent of the lands in question.

WED MAY 1, 1805
For sale: hse belonging to me in west 10th St, Wash City, for $850; I am not proprietor of the ground. -A B Woodward

Elected Reps in Cong for Va:
Thos Newton Jr	John Randolph	Thos M Randolph	John Smith
Jos Lewis	John Clopton	John Dawson	Alex Wilson
Matthew Clay	Edwin Gray	John Claiborne	
Peterson Goodwyn			

Notice: Christopher Hilbourn, formerly resided in Loudon Co, Va, is informed by the death of his Aunt, Eliz Limebacker, of Northampton, Bucke Co, Pa, he is entitled to a considerable est in lands & cash. Apply to Gerardus Wynkoop or Leffert Leffert, excs.

For sale: 6000 acs of land in Holston, Wash Co, Va. -Francis Preston

FRI MAY 3, 1805
For sale: at the Navy Yard, 2 story brick hse, at present occupied by Mr Thos Mattingly, baker. -Samuel Russ

MON MAY 5, 1805
Ranaway-Armstead, negro man, age abt 25 yrs; has been hired to Mr John Woolfolk for last 3 yrs. -Lewis Collins, Caroline Co

WED MAY 8, 1805
For sale: hse & 2 acs, Bladensburg, PG Co, Md.
                    -Alexander McDonald, Bladensburg

FRI MAY 10, 1805
I would like to lease my propery nr the Navy Yd for 3 yrs. -A B Woodward

Warm Springs, Va, leased for 10 yrs, ready for at least 100 constant boarders.
                    -Robt & Geo Turner

Charlotte Cordee, assassinator of Marat; born at St Saturnin Des Lignerets in 1768; at age 23, she fell a self-devoted sacrifice; Belzunce, Maj-2nd of the Regt of Bourbon, quartered at Caen became devoted to her; he was massacred on Aug 11, 1789; Cordee arvd in Paris on Jul 9, 1793; she stabbed Marat in the heart; her hour of execution drew near & one man alone raised his voice in her praise; he was Addam Lux, he cried, "She is greater than Brutus!"; he was shortly after guillotined.

Mon May 13, 1805
This day is published by Samuel H Smith, price $2, the trial of Samuel Chase, Assoc Justice of Sup Crt of U S, impeached by the Hse of Reps for high crimes & misdemeanors. -Samuel H Smith & Thos Lloyd

Wed May 15, 1805
Died: Jacob Bryant, esq, age 89 yrs, Nov 13 last, in England.

Genrl Soc of Cincinnati meeting convened at Phil on May 7, 1805. Ofcrs elected:

Pres Genrl	Maj Gen'rl Chas Cotesworth Pinckney
Vp Genrl	Maj Genrl Henry Knox
Sec Genrl	Maj Wm Jackson
Assist Sec Genrl	Maj Wm D Bell
Treas Genrl.	Brig Genrl W MacPherson

Died: Mr Mark Stockwell, clk in Treas Dept, Apr 29, in Phil.

Reward-$5 for strayed cow. -Wm Wearey, Master of boat builders dept, U S Navy Yd, Wash.

Fri May 17, 1805
For sale: est of John Gardener, late of Wash City, deed dated Dec 28, 1804, land in Ohio, nr Zanesville. -Nicholas King

Mon May 20, 1805
Runaway-Jack, negro, abt 24 yrs of age; left his master, Claiborne, at Waterford, Va. -Geo Creager, shrf of Fred. Co

Died: Queen Dowager of Prussia, Feb 25, age 54 yrs, mthr of the Duchess of York.

For sale: hse in sq 905, Wash. -Barbaby Parsons, Wash

Reps of Va in Ninth Congress:

J W Eppes	John Smith	David Holmes	John Dawson
Walter Jones	*Jas M Garnett	Thos Newton Jr	Matthew Clay
T M Randolph	Edwin Gray	Paterson Goodwyn	Christopher Clark
John Randolph	*Burwell Bassett	Philip R Thompson	John G Jackson
*J Claiborne	Alex'r Wilson	Abram Trigg	*Col Morrow
John Clopton	Jos Lewis		

-all Rpblcn except Jos Lewis. *New mbrs.

Wed May 22, 1805
Sketch of Ephraim Kirby from the Mercury. Defender in Rev War; ntv of Conn; in 1804 he was nominated Chief Justice of Sup Crt of New Orleans when death arrested his course.

Longetivity in Va by Mr F of Crt of Appeals.
Thos Dance, late o/Chesterfield, died abt 1775, age 123 yrs, born in London;
John Halloway, died in 1791, Pr Edw Co, age 123 yrs, born in Eng;
John McBride, Irishman, died abt 1789 age 104 yrs, in Goochland, nr his nativity;
Anne Brown, born in Gloucester Co, Va, died in Hanover Co, abt 1717, age 110 yrs - [Possible typo for 1771];
Mary Merritt, died nr Ground Squirrell Bridge, Hanover Co, in 1777, age unkn, but lived with her 3d hsbnd for 83 yrs;
John Pool died in Powhatan Co in 1788, age 96;
Mary Pleasants, m/o late Thos Pleasants of Goochland Co, died abt 1792 or 93 age 96;
Jos Pollard, f/o late Jude Pendleton's widow & grfr of present clk of Hanover Crt, died in 1788, he had only 1 wife-mrd 68 yrs; Mathew Early, of Powhatan Co, born 1700, died 1791;
Saml Landrum died Dec 1803 age 87;
Mary Chastain, of Powhatan Co, died in 1800 age 95;
Judith Bingly of Powhatan Co now alive, age 101;
Chas Burton, living in Chesterfield, born in Sep 1700, now alive
Mr Edw Woodbridge has been mrd since 1742;
Mr M Clarke, who lives in Louisville, Ky, has 27 bros & 2 sisters, his fr thrice mrd was living in Lunenburgh Co, Va, as of 2 yrs ago.

FRI MAY 24, 1805

Havanna, Apr 30. Ltr from fellow ctzns at present in Havanna to Vincent Gray, Acting cnsl of the U S, Havanna; signed: Jno Morton-Chrmn; Nathl Fellowes Jr; John Murdock; Jas Gorham; Edw Landers; Amos Green, Jas Perry, J B Russell, a joint committee of the 60 americ merchants & mstrs of vessels. Subj: their support of Mr Gray. Dinner for Vincent Gray was given on Apr 30th at the Commercial Hotel in Havanna & was attended by John Morton of NY; N Fellows Jr of Boston; Capt Jas Perry of R I.

Alexandria, May 21. Sheep shearing prize ram belonged to Col Thos L Lee of Loudon, Va.

Died: Mr Jos Hodgson, May 20, mbr of City Cncl; hsbnd & parent. Funeral Jun 2 at Meth Meeting Hse, Gtwn, Rev John Chalmers.

MON MAY 27, 1805

Tkt for ensuing election for City Council-Wash:

Robt Alexander	Wm Emack	Wm Prout	John Dempsie
Geo Collard	Chas Minisie	Griffith Combs	John Chalmers
D Carrol	Peter Miller		
Adam Lindsey of Dun.			

For sale: 740 acs, Fairfax Co, Va; where I reside; desirous of moving to western country.   -Thomson Mason.

Candidates for the Easterly part of Wash City:

1st Chamber	Robt Alexander	John Dempsie	Saml Hamilton
	Chas Minisie	John Chambers	
2d Chamber	Alex'r McCormick	Wm Prout	Geo Collard
	Griffith Coombe		
Committee	W Cranch	H Ingle	Pontius D Stelle
	Alex. Cochran	W M Duncanson	

WED MAY 29, 1805

Chosen by the cncl: Associate judges of election for City Council-Wash:
Geo Blagden   Henry Ingle   Thos Herty
Benj Perkins   Clot. Stephenson   Jos Huddleston.

FRI MAY 31, 1805

Public auction of several lots, prop of late Benjamin Brookes, decd, in Upper Marlboro, PG Co, Md; on one stands the tavern lately occupied by Samuel Cooledge & the other the hse which Samuel Hepburn had occupied for some time past & has just moved from.   -Robt Bowie, trustee

Phil, May 28. Geo Hammaker, esq & bro, is apptd by the King of Denmark, cnsl for the eastern states, came passengers in the ship *Lydia*, Capt Treadwell; arvd on Sat last at NY from Tonningen, we are informed that J T Eckhart, esq, formerly vice cnsl at Phil, is apptd cnsl for the middle states by his Danish Majesty.

MON JUN 3, 1805

For sale: order from orphans Crt of Wash Co, DC; negro woman & 3 small boys, late the prop of John Young, decd.   -Chas Young, adm

Parents & guardians of pupils under Rev Mr McCormick, publicly express acknowledgment of their progress:

Jas H Kearney	Thos Carpenter	John Herford	David Shoemaker
Henry Ingle	John Coyle	Robt Underwood	Abraham Bradley Jr
Phineas Bradley			

WED JUN 5, 1805

Runaway negro, Ben, committed to jail in Allegany Co, Md: age abt 40 yrs, says he belongs to John Willcox, late of Montg Co but now of Ky. -L Hilleary, Shrff

Elected Jun 3, to City Council-Wash:

Chas Minisie	Geo Collard	Wm Prout
Jos Bromley	Alexander McCormick	John Dempsie
Wm Emack	John McGowan	John Chalmers
Jos Cassin	Saml Hamilton	Azariah Gatton
John Beckley	Peter Miller	Griffith Combs
Michael Nourse	Robt Cherry	Nicholas Voss
Robt Alexander		

Wash Co, DC-case of John Burns, insolvent debtor, confined in Wash Co jail for debt.
              -Uriah Forrest, clk

FRI JUN 7, 1805
Runaway negro committed to jail in Allegany Co, Md: Sam, 25 yrs of age, says he belongs to Samuel Minnis but was lent to Dr Timberlegs or Timberlain, of Va.
              -L Hilleary, Sheriff

Ltr dated - U S Gun Boat, No. 7, NY, May 30, 1805; to sec of the Navy from Midshipman P S Ogilvie, Commanding ofcr of same, built at NY; Subj: No. 7 is a fine vessel & capable of going to any part of the world.

MON JUN 10, 1805
Wash Co, DC. Confined to Wash Co jail, John Thomas Frost, insolvent debtor.
              -Uriah Forrest, clk

Mr Generes has opened his dancing school on Capitol Hill.

WED JUN 12, 1805
Died: Hon Thos Pownall, formerly Gov of NJ, in Bath, Eng; was Gov of Mass in 1757.

Died: Dr Miller, aet 72 yrs, in London; author of works on medicine.

FRI JUN 14, 1805
Wash Co, DC-In Chancery, Jun 12, 1805. John M Gantt, cmplnt, v Wm Pancoast, dfndnt. May 9, 1800, Gantt purch'd part of a tract of land in Wash Co cld *Pencotts Invention*, from Pancoast; deed has not been recorded.
              -Uriah Forrest, clk

Wash City-Meeting Jun 12;
Chrmn	Jos Stretch		
Sec	Tho Carpenter		
Cmtee	Nich. King	John Sessford	Jos Mechlin
	Jas Hoban	Peter Lenox	

MON JUN 17, 1805
Public auction in Piscataway-all the rl est, not heretofore sold, of Thos Clagett, esq, late of PG Co, Md: 225 acs, part of *Marlow's Resurvey*; 850 acs nr tobacco warehse.
              -Thos Duckett, PG Co, Md

WED JUN 19, 1805
Elections in NH:
Governor	John Langdon	*Treas*	Nath l Gilman
Pres of Senate	Clement Storer	*Sec of State*	Philip Carrigan Jr
Spkr o/Hse o/Reps	Saml Bell		

For sale at Gadsby's Hotel, Alex: land late of Presly Thornton, esq, in Northumberland Co, Va, 2,500 acs, large mansion hse. -Thos Robinson, W Lewis, Richd Peters Jr, Atty at Law, Phil.

Meeting of the stockholders of the Wash theatre at Rhodes City Tvrn-Jun 14, 1805;
Chrmn	Robt Brent	
Sec	Thos Herty	
Directors	Robt Brent	Wm Brent
	Thos Law	S H Smith
	John P Van Ness	

Samuel Forman, assignee of Richd Throckmorton, an insolvent debtor, will be at the hse of James Craig, inn kpr in Freehold Village, Monmouth Co, NJ, to make final settlement.

FRI JUN 21, 1805
Mrd: Mr Jesse Edwards, of Phil, to Miss Sarah Claxton, of Wash, Jun 13, in Phil, by Rt Rev Bishop White.

Treasurership of Rt Hon Lord Viscount Melville: [London Morning Chronicle] (amount follows the name)
London-Lord Melville has provided for himself & family since 1783 as follows: Lady Melville, 900; Mr Crawford, 250; Robt Dundas, s/o Lord M, 3000; R Dundas, son in law & nph to Lord M, 3000; W Dundas, nph to Lord M, 3000; Francis Dundas, nph to Lord M, 2000; Philip Dundas, nph to Lord M, 2000; Mrs Dundas, mthr to 4 last & sr-in-law to Lord M, 400; Archibald Cochran, bro-in-law to Lord M, 1280; Alexander MaClean, bro-in-law to Lord M, 2000; Geo Buchan, nph by marriage to Lord M, 1200; Robt Dundas, cousin & nph-in-law to Lord M, 1200; Robt Dundas, cousin & nph-in-law to Lord M, 400; Chas Hope, bro-in-law to Lady M, 2700; Sir Pat Murray, bro-in-law to Lady M, 1000; Alex. Hope, bro to Lady M, 600; _____ Oliphant, cousin to Lady M, 4500; Lord Lapier, cousin to Lady M, 2000.

MON JUN 24, 1805
For sale: 108 acs in PG Co, Md, nr Four Mile Run, adj Mr Baly Lannom, who will show it. -Chas Robertson

WED JUN 26, 1805
Runaway-negro, Jim, age 23 yrs, says he is the prop of John Chew Thomas.
-Geo Creager, Sheriff of Frederick Co

Died: Martha, age 120 yrs, wid of Zacharia, nobility of Mohegan Tribe of Indians, at Mohegan, nr New-London, Conn.

Robt Williams-inducted into ofc of Gov of Miss Terr, May 13.
-Gab. P. Van Horn, Justice of the Peace

Nelson's Fleet:
Bellesle	Capt Hargood	*Donnegal*	Capt Sir R Strachan, Bt
Kent	Capt Malcolm	*Le Tygre*	Capt B Hollwell
Excellent	Capt Sotheron	*Leviathen*	Capt Baynton
Superb	Capt Keats	*Spencer*	Capt Stopfard
Royal Sovereign	R A S R Bickerson, Capt J Stuart		
Canopus	R A G Campbell, Capt		
Victory	Royal V Nelson, R A G Murray, Capt T M Hardy		

PG Co, Md-Wm Prather, residing nr Vanville, brought before me a stray mare. -Gab. P. Van Horn, Justice of the Peace.

FRI JUN 28, 1805
Wm Esenbeck proposes to open a school in languages; Wash City.

Committed to Wash Co jail, Amos Smith, insolvent debtor, for debt.
-Uriah Forrest, clk

Hon Geo Nugent, esq, is Lt-Gov & Commander in Chief, in & over his Majesty's Island of Jamaica & Territories thereon.

Natches, May 17. Robt Williams, esq, was inducted into ofc as Gov of this territory on May 13th at the town of Washington; oath administered by Judge Rodney.

Died: Wm Petty, Marquis of Lansdown, May 6, in Eng.

MON JUL 1, 1805
For sale: cook & maid & her 2 yr old child. -John Coyle, Treas ofc, Wash City.

Protest of Capt John Willes, Sloop *Priscilla*, captured by a French privateer on his passage from Boston to Jamaica. which departed Feb 27, 1805 from Boston & on Mar 21, ordered out of my boat; found Capt J Carleton & 2 of his sailors from the *Savannah* in the Brig *Relief*, belonging to Newbury-Port; I was put on board the Brig *Newton*, from Phil -bound for New Orleans. Witnesses: John Willes, Mstr of *Priscilla*; John Carleton, Mstr of *Relief*; David Potter, Mate of *Relief*; John Jefferes, Mate of *Priscilla*.

WED JUL 3, 1805
For sale: at late dwelling hse of Jos Hodgson, decd, all his prsnl prop.
-Rebecca Hodgson, admx, Wash City

Sale by order of Crt of Calvert Co, Md; late mansion of Benj Ward, decd, 184 acs, on the Chesapeake Bay, Calvert Co, Md. -Wm M Carcaud, David L Weems, Chas Williamson, Cm'rs.

For sale: 530 acs, bet Richmond & Fredericksburg, Va, whereon I live.
-Anthony New

Stray cow found. -Jos Huddleston, Wash City

NY. Jun 29th the ship, *Mississippi*, Capt Skidmore, arvd at this port on Jun 28th, 30 days from Nantes, having on board his Excellency R R Livingston, late Mnstr from U S to French Gov't, his lady & suite.

Americ Philosophical Soc, Phil, Jun 29. Thanks to Capt Wm Mugford of Salem, Mass, for model of his temporary rudder; presented the Extra Magellanic Medal of $40 value or the same sum in money, his option. -T T Hewson, sec.

MON JUL 8, 1805
French Privateer schnr, *Matilda*, Capt Graffin, from Guadaloupe, captured on Jun 16, Americ Brig, *Comet*, John Chelton, master; owned in Norfolk by Mr Wm Pennock; Capt Chelton is now a prisoner on board.

Ladies with ltrs in Wash PO-Jul 1, 1805:
Mrs Lucy Addison	Miss Eliza Baker	Mgt Davies
Mrs Sarah M Biscoe	Miss Polly Evan	Miss Eliza R Fenwick
Mrs Eliza Dempsey	Sarah Gohagan	Miss Mary Hagan
Mrs Deborah Gardner	Miss Ann Lotts	Miss Rebecca Martin
Milley Lounox	Miss Eliz McKim	Mrs Peggy B Breston
Mrs Alexander McKim	Mrs Anna Thornton	Miss Esther Tooley
Mistress Simon		

Military school was opened in Canandaigua, NY, on Apr 30th, under the discipline of Gen Othniel Taylor.

Subscriptions towards a permanent institution for educ of youth in Wash City; sums recd were from $5 to $200:
Thos Jefferson	Robt Smith	Henry Dearborn
Jas Madison	Saml N Smallwood	Tho Tingey
Robt Brent	Buller Cocke	Benj More
Robt Alexander	Benj King	Josiah Fox
John Cassinnichs Voss	John Beckley	Chas Jonessam
Alex McCormick	Henry Herford	Peter Lenox
H Smith	Nich King	Jas Davidson Jr
John Hewitt	Geo Boyd	Jas Hoban
Alex Kerr	Jos Hodgson	John Davidson
Thos Munroe	Stanley Byus	W Cranch
Chas Love	Saml Burch	Pontius D Stelle
Wm Lambert	David Watterson	Jas Kenner
Wilson Bryan	Geo Burns	Jas Johnston
Geo St Clare	Jas Ford	Henry Tims
John Lenthall	Jas Middleton	Ch I Nourse
John Young	Thos G Hye	Franklin Wharton
P Farrall	Wm Kilty	Andrew Rheinhart

Geo Collard	Wm Coltman	Matthew Hart
Alls Th Kirk	David Peter	G Thompson
Clotworthy Stevenson	Isaac Pierce	John Sessford
John Threlkeld	Thos Herty	Thos Carpenter
Rob King	John Tayloe	Jas C King
Walter Hellen	Geo Thomson	Nich Travers
John Oakley	John Weems	C McLaughlin
Thos Corcoran	Nath. Lufborough	Richd Parrott
Saml Davidson	Corn. Coningham	Benj Perkins
Ben Stoddert	John Stephen	John Ardrey
Vincent King	Richd Gaines	A Bradley Jr
Thos Smith	Wm T Beall	Wm H Tuckfield
Z Farrell	Geo Blagden	Thos Thorpe
Henry Ingle	Danl Bailey	Jos Moor
Fred D May	Wm Howard	G Duvall
Peter Miller	J B Pickford	D Harper
Th T Tucker	Jos Thaw	Danl Rapine
Joshua I Moore	Jas Martin	Matthew Wright
Thos Claxton	Griffith Coombe	John Gardiner
Robt Cherry	Francis Clark	Geo Blount
Chas H Varden	Wm Woodward	Pierce Purcell
Lewis Morin	Edgar Patterson	John McGowan
Jos Huddleston	J B Anderson	B Betterton
Danl C Brent	Wm O Neale	Jos Harbough
Saml Brown	Jas Patterson	John Bullus
T J Caldwell	Jacob Cist	Robt F How
Phineas Bradley	David Shoemaker	Henry Whetcroft
Toppan Webster	S Pleasonton	Chris. S Thom
Jacob Wagner	C W Goldsborough	Wm Rhodes
Wm Simmons	Jas Hodnett	C Swan
P Hagner	T H Gillis	Jas Mechlin
Thos Turner	Henry Kramer	Jas McAllister
Saml Turner Jr	David Rawn	Jacob Laub
Wm Doughty	Andrew Ross	Lund Washington
John C Payne	Wm James	Jas MacClery
Jos Dawsen	Jos Stretch	John Litle
Jos Taylor	Chas Tomkins	Robt Underwood
Mich'l Nourse	Wm Brent	Clement Boswell
John Craven	Jas Webb	Jas Laurie
A & G Way	Robt Tilley	Solomon Myer
Ezra Varden	Orlando Cook	Hezekiah Rogers Sr
John Chalmers Jr	Saml Blodget-[One bridge share in Potomac]	

Ltr from Consulate of the U S, Island of Cuba, Havanna, Jun 11, 1805; Signed Henry Hill Jr. Subj: Reduction of the duties.

WED JUL 10. 1805
In Chancery, Jun 27, 1805. Thos P Wilson v Geo Beckwith, John Beckwith, Wm Lodge, *Elisha O Williams, *Simon Nicholls & *Barbara his wife, *Thos S Williams & *Anne his wife, *Edw O Williams, *Elemelick Beckwith & *John Lodge. Bill to obtain decree for sale of land in Montgomery Co, purch'd by Chas Beckwith, decd, from Elisha O Williams, for payment of debts of said Chas Beckwith. [*reside out of this state] -Saml H Howard, Reg CC

My wife, Eliz, absented herself from my bed & board, I am determined not to pay any of her debts.   -Thos Williams, Wash

Died: Genrl Forrest, Jul 6, clk of Crct Crt of Wash.

The marriage of Jerome Bonaparte has been annulled by the Pope; double motive of the hsbnd being a minor & the wife a heretic. The late Miss Patterson, being very pregnant, Mrs Bonaparte, attended by her bro, went to England rather than to Balt, Md.

FRI JUL 12, 1805
Died: David Rawn, esq, Jul 4, at Staunton, Va, age 35 yrs, clk in ofc of the comptroller of Treas; leaving a widow & 3 small children.

Party of Discovery, under Command of Capts Lewis & Clark, left the mouth of the Missouri on May 19, 1804. The Floyd Rvr was named after Chas Floyd, of their party, who died Aug 20.

For sale: my plantation on St Chas Branch, 800 acs, nr Upper Marlbro, PG Co, Md; *Strawberry Hill*, 180 acs nr same; 400 acs in Wash Co, Md, nr Hancock; lot 12 sq 652 in Wash.   -Wm B Beans, Upper Marlbro.

Lexington, Ky, Jun 18. Bks are opened in this place by Messrs John Jordan Jr, Alex'r Parker & John Bradford, comrs for subscriptions for opening a canal at the Falls of Ohio.

Consuls & Commercial agents of the U S.
In Great Britain & its Dominions:

Wm Lyman	London	Elias Vanderhorst	Bristol
Robt W Fox	Falmouth	Jas Maury	Liverpool
Jos Wilson	Dublin	Thos Auldio	Poole
Jas Holmes	Belfast	John Church	Cork
John Gavino	Gibraltar	Jos Pulis	Malta

In France & its Dominions-Commercial agents:

Fulwar Skipwith	Paris	Jacob Ridgway	Antwerp
Isaac Cox Barnet	Havre De Grace	John Mitchell	Do
Wm Lee	Bordeaux	Thos Aborn	Cayenne
Jas Anderson	Cette	Henry Wilson	Ostend
Etienne Cathalan	Marseilles	John Appleton	Calais

Wm Patterson	Nantz	Aaron Vale	L'orient
Thos Lovell	La Rochelle	Francis Coffyn	Dunkirk
Wm Buchanan	Isles of France & Bourbon		

In Spain & its Dominions-Consuls:

Moses Young	Madrid	Jos Yznardi	Cadiz
Robt Montgomery	Alicante	Wm Kirkpatrick	Malaga
Lewis O'Brien	St Andero	Henry Hill	Island of Cuba
John Leonard	Barcelona	John Jas Armstrong	Island of Teneriffe
John Martin Baker	Isles of Majorca, Monorca & Yvica		

In Portugal & its Dominions:

Wm Jarvis	Lisbon	John Street	Fayal
Marian Lemar	Madeira		

Within the Batavian Rpblc & its Dependencies:

Sylvanus Bourne	Amsterdam	Thos Hewes	Batavia

In Denmark & its Dominions:

Hans Saabye	Copenhagen	John F Brown	St Croix

In Germany:

John M Forbes	Hamburg	Philip Marck	Franconia
F J Wichlelhausen	Bremen	Wm Riggin	Triest

In Kingdom of Sweden:

Robt G Gardiner	Gottenburg	Isaac Prince	St Bartholomews

In the Italian States:

Thos Appleton	Leghorn	Frederick Degan	Naples
Peter Kuhn Jr	Genoa	John Broadbent	Messina
Abraham Gibbs	Palermo		

In Russia:

Levitt Harris	St Petersburg

In Turkey:

Wm Stuart	Smyrna

In Algiers:

Tobias Lear, cnsl Genrl.

MON JUL 15, 1805

Thos Williams, blacksmith, NJ Av, Wash City, whose wife is also Eliz, is not the one whose wife left him.

WED JUL 17, 1805

Wm Murray, insolvent debtor, confined to Wash Co jail, for debt.
                                                    -Wm Brent, clk.

Trustees elected-Permanent institution for the Educ of Youth in city of Wash:
Saml H Smith	Wm Cranch	Gabriel Duvall
Thos Munroe	Robt Brent	Thos Tingey.

Wm Brent is apptd clk of the Crct Crt, vice Genrl Forrest, decd. -Wash.

Ltr from Capt Meriwether Lewis to the Pres of the U S, Ft Mandan, Apr 7, 1805. Subj: Specimens & debt of Capt Clark's private journal; chart of the Missouri.

Dover, NH. Discovery made on Mr Danl Waldron's land, in this town, of quicksilver.

Phil, Jul 12. Don Jos Cabrera has lately been convicted of counterfeiting 3 cks on the Bank of Pa, in the name of the Marquis Yrujo, Spanish Mnstr.

FRI JUL 19, 1805
For sale: 100 acs, nr Hughs's Bridge on Rock Creek & nr Mr Leonard Jones & Chas Jones's Mills. Mr Wm Carroll on Rock Creek will show the land.
-Robt Brent, Wash.

To let-hse nr the Navy Yard. Contact Gustavus Higdon.

MON JUL 22, 1805
Lands & lots in PG Co-No prsnl prop-liable to pay the taxes for yrs 1802-4.
Allen Bowie heirs-Brooke Ridge, pt of Leith & Lee's Lodge-1026 acs;
Benj Brooke heirs-6 1/2 lots in Upper Marlboro town;
Eliz Brooke-her dower in above lots
Danl Carrolls heirs-part of Darnalls Chance-19 1/2 acs
Danl Dulany heirs-2 lots in Upper Marlboro
John Keadle-part of Beall's Chance-80 acs
Thos Sim Lee-part of a lot in Upper Marlboro
Grace Lyon-1 lot in do
Arnold Livers-1 lot in do
Frank Luke Sen heirs-4 3/4 lots in do; part of Darnalls Chance & Addition 92 7/8 acs
Samuel W Magruder heirs-part of a lot in Upper Marlboro
Dennis Scott heirs-part of 2 lots in do
John Campbell-part of Hogpen & Laffers Green-100 acs
Wm Grindell-Taylors Course-210 acs
Jane Eaton-part of Brookefield-100 acs
Dr Thos Gantt heirs-part of Turrell & Bowling Green/ part of Terraizcul Tabilus-178 1/2 acs
Priscilla Howington-Aaron's Reprieve-70 acs
Thos B Hodgkin-1 lot in Nottingham
Wm Mayhew heirs-part of Colibrook-196 1/2acs
Alex Magruder's heirs-pt of Coxhays 574 acs
Jas Mewbern-part of a lot in Nottingham
Laurence O'Neal-part of Liviver-112 acs
Josias Adams-part of Mkt Overton-102 1/2 acs
Jas Adams-part of Mkt overton-50 acs
Chas Boarman-part of the Upper part of Wynns Chance; part of Indian Fields; part of Gardiners Meadows; part o/Indian Fields & Wynns Chance-229 1/2 acs
Nicholas Blacklock heirs-Blacklocks Venture; part of the Widows Trouble; part of Gantts Enlargement, Enlarged; part of Strife & Boston-629 acs

John Bowling heirs-part of Piscataway Manor & Downs's Neglect-267 1/2 acs
Saml Berry-part of Aix-116 acs
Geo Dyer-part of Edelins Hogpen Enlarged-200 acs
Thos Dyer heirs-part of same land-100 acs
Henry Davidson-1 lot in Piscataway; part of Lieth & Pittsburgh-3 3/4acs
Mary Fenwick-part of Hills Recovery-400 acs
Elvina Hardy-part of Leith-1 ac
Rev Geo Ralph-part of Lempter; West quarter enlarged-400 1/2 acs
Richd B A Webster-part of the Ridge-73 acs
Judson Clagett heirs-part of Dublin; part of Stony Harbour-297acs
Danl Hurly-Weavers Delight-93 acs
John Hepburn-part of Outlet-70 acs
Thos Jenkins of Danl-Oxmantown & part of Maiden Bradley; pt of Magruders Choice; pt of Refuse; pt of What You Please-447 acs
Chas King-a small part of svr'l tracts-2 acs
Wm Mansfield-part of Lusbys Discovery-75 acs
Eliz McDonough-part of Majors Choice-57 1/2 acs
Jas Morris heirs-part of Silver Hills-449 acs
David Stone-part of Chance-166 acs
Sarah Spinks-The Ridge; Hurlys Fancy; Weavers; So. part of the White Marshes-347 acs
Eliz Beall-part of Fife Enlarged-367 acs
John Free-part of lot No 3 in Bladensburgh
Geo Fries heirs-part of the same lot
John Murray-land above-22 acs
Jesse Taylor-adjoining the town of Bladensburgh-1/2 ac
Wm Bayly-part of Barbadoes-80 acs
Jesse Carpenter-part of Jas & Mary; Worse Than Nothing; Plummers Jack-200 acs
Francis Deakins heirs-part of Resurvey on Millers Begining-105 acs
Cath Free-1 lot nr Bladensburgh-2 acs
Eliz Jones-part of Elizabeth's Portion-41 1/4 acs
Andrew Leitch heirs-part of Deakins's Hall; Little Meadows Forceput; Point Branch-235 1/2 acs
Jas Scagg-part of Chews Folly-81 1/2 acs
Geo Wilson-part of Flag Bottom-52 3/4 acs
Geo Brian-Burch's Venture-100 acs
Zepheniah Masters-part of Discovery-16 acs
John Masters-part of Discovery-26 acs
Basil Lucas-part of Hughs Discovery & Little Meadows-20 acs
Jas Ryon-part of Flag Bottom-25 acs
Thos Rhodes-part of Batchelors Forrest Enlarged, Rhodes's Purchase, Batchelors Forrest, pt of Millers Beginning & Resurvey on do; Hall's Chance Resurved, pt of the Resurvey on Isaacs Park-123 1/4 acs
Jas Prather-part of Batchelors Forrest & Millers beginning. part of Millers Begining-77 1/4 acs
John Witheral-Witherals Beginning-10 acs.
-Richd Duvall, Collector, Sam Hepburn, clk.

WED JUL 24, 1805

David Astin, insolvent debtor, confined to Wash Co jail for debt. -Wm Brent, clk.

Died: Fr Gabriel Gruber, Genrl of the Society of Jesuits, Mar 20, in Russia; born at Vienna.

Phil, Pa-Jul 19. Pa. v Jos Cabrera, Jul 6, 1805; charge of forgery; verdict-guilty; fine-$2000 & 2 yrs in imprisonment at hard labor.

FRI JUL 26, 1805

Died: Richd Hipkins Smoot, age 8 yrs, s/o Mr Alexander S Smoot of Wash, Jul 2, of dropsey.

Ltr to Gov Harrison from Capt Clark; dated-Ft Mandin, Apr 2, 1805. Subj: summary view of the Missouri, etc.   -Wm Clark

Ltr to Mr Jeremiah Powell, dated Point Petre, Guadaloupe, Jun 20, from David G Gillers. Subj: his capture on May 9th by the *Grand Decide*, cruiser; also captured were the schnr *Mary*, Capt Bunker; *Unity*, Capt Harding; *Sally*, Capt Gilpin; report is that we all will be hung; Capt Wells, of the Ship, *Dolphin*, of Phil, got admission into the prison; prison is too bad for any Christian to be in.
-David G Gillers [has friends in NY]

Ranaway-Moses, alias Lanham, negro, age 30 yrs, from Fredericktwn, Md; sold by Mr Burress to the late Jas Marshall, decd, of Frederick Co, Md.
-John L Harding

Wm King, insolvent debtor, confined in Wash Co jail for debt. -Wm Brent, clk.

August Von Kotzebue has published "Travels Through Switzerland to Paris in the Year 1804."

Ltr from the Commander of Gun Boat, No 8, at sea, May 27, 1805. Signed: Nath'l Haraden to Cmdor Edw Preble, Boston. Subj: Gale encounterd in crossing the Gulph Stream; the boat behaved well.

MON JUL 29, 1805

Elias B Caldwell, Atty at law, remv'd his ofc to hse lately occupied by Mr Law on Capitol Hill.Wash.

For sale: lots 18 & 26, prop of Jas Wigfield, of Wash Co, DC.
-Benson L McCormick.

Mississippi Herald-meeting at Claiborne Co, Apr 25; Capt Wm McCaleb,chrmn; Robt Williams, Gov of Miss Terr gave the address.

Protest was made by the late Capt Isaac Bridges, of Andover, his mate & crew, before the Americ cnsl at Fayal; this unfortunate man died of his wounds at said Island on Apr 18th after lanquishing 19 days in extreme distress. Bridges was Mstr of the Brig *Hannah*, of Newbury-port; John Street, vice cnsl for the U S at Islands of Fayal & Azores. Mate of the *Hannah*-Jos Gazneau; Mariners: Philip Pepple, Anthony Robert, Wm Brown & John Colere.

WED JUL 31, 1805
Robbery at the bank-ofc of Discount & Deposit, Balt, Md. Reward-$1000.
-David Harris, cashier.

Orphans Crt of Wash Co, DC-Jul 29, 1805. Prsnl est of Patrick Lynch, late of Marine Corps, decd.   -T H Gilliss

Ltr from Saml G Bailey, Mstr of the Brig Hudson, dated Cadiz Rds, Jun 2d, to his owner. Subj: boarded by a Spanish privateer on May 10th; I have remained under quarantine for 23 days; greasing the fingers of the guard, permitted me to send this ltr on board an Americ Vessel.

FRI AUG 2, 1805
New York Comm Advertiser-account of the Russian & Mass. Enterprize along the west Coast of N Americ, drawn up by Jacob Crowinshield, esq, of Salem. Extract-almost 20 yrs since the ship *Columbia*, Capt Kendrick, & the sloop, *Mary Washington*, Capt Gray, left from Boston to the N W coast of Americ; Capt K lost his life on the coast; Capt Metcalf, of NY, commanded the Brig *Elenora*, he too lost his life on his 2d trip on the coast; Capt Roberts & others from Boston, followed Capt K's voyages. Capt Ingraham sailed under Hendrick in the *Columbia* & his journal was presented to Gen'l Washington; Capt Magee's journal may be preserved by his relations who reside in Boston.

Mr John Peter, ofcr of Bank of Columbia, was robbed bet Wash & Alex, shot through the body with a pistol. Reward-$1500. [See Aug 14]

Lottery for St John's Church in Frederick town will commence, tkts are $5-purchase from Rev Wm Mathews, Petery Heally & Co, & Capt John Coyle, Wash City, & Bishop Neill, Gtwn.

Mr Andrew Reinhard will be keeping the public pumps in Washington repaired.
-Robt Brent, Mayor of Wash.

MON AUG 5, 1805
Died: Gen John Andre Hanna, age 44, in Harrisburgh, Jul 30; for many yrs a respectable inhabitant of that borough; buried Jul 31st; hsbnd & fr.

Paramaribo, Jun 9, 1805. Proceedings of the Gov of the British Colony of Paramaribo, So Americ. Rgrd: clearance only if I took 2 criminal negroes on board. Signed, J Havens Horton, Mstr of the schnr *Julian*, of Newbury-Port. Sworn Jul 15, 1805, before me, Matthew Lawler, Mayor, Phil.

Chas Erdmann, interpreter of foreign languages, in & for Pa, sworn in Phil, Jul 19th, 1805.

Ltr from Jona. Cowdery, esq, surg of the late frig, *Philadelphia*, to Dr Mitchill, dated Nov 24, 1804. Subj: Tripolitan captivity.

WED AUG 7, 1805
John Deterly, insolvent debtor, confined to Wash Co jail, for debt.
-Wm Brent, clk.

Detroit, Jun 14, 1805. Ltr from Robt Munro; entire conflagration of the town of Detroit on Tue; the furn of the est of Col Hamtramock was nrly consumed by fire; Mr Dodemead lives in a corner of the public store hse at the Ship Yd; Mr Donavan with his family have gone to Sandwich, Mr Oudrain occupies the hse below Mr Mays. Mr McIntosh & May's hse cld not be saved; no lives were lost.

Died: Mr Wm Carlton, age 33, printer & prop of Salem Register, in Salem.

Died: Sir Wm Pultney, Bart, May 31, at his hse in Picadilly.

Stephen Arnold, school mstr, convicted of the murder of a little girl by whipping, was sentenced to be executed at Cooperstown, Otsego Co, on Aug 19th; has been respited by the Govnr of NY.

Died: Schiller, German writer & many other theatrical pieces, on May 9th at Weimar.

Died: Dr Paley, age 62, at Sunderland on Sat last; Archdeacon of Carlisle, Sub-Dean of Lincoln & rector of Bishopwearmouth.

Bushrod Washington is elected a mbr of the Americ Philo Soc.

FRI AUG 9, 1805
John Minchin, boot maker, from Phil, wants 2 apprentices to the business-NJ Av, Wash City.

MON AUG 12, 1805
Ranaway: Nace, negro man, age 21 yrs. -Thos Mudd, PG Co, nr Piscataway, Md.

WED AUG 14, 1805
Duel bet Mr Enoch M Lyles, of Alexandria, & Mr John F Bowie, of Piscataway, Md, at Johnston's Spring, abt 6 miles from this town, on Va side of Potomac, on Aug 7; Mr Lyles died. -Alexandria, Aug 8.

Committed for trial-John A Burford, for wounding & robbing Mr Peter. [See Aug 2]

FRI AUG 16, 1805

Died: Mr Samuel Morse, Jul 25, age 28 yrs, in Savannah; ntv of Conn; editor of Georgia Republican.

Svcs of Thos Ewell, M D, practice of medicine & surgery-at the ofc lately occupied by Wm O Sprigg, esq, Gtwn.

Wm Davy, of Phil, apptd to superintend the trading hses of the U S with the Indian Nations within our limits.

MON AUG 19, 1805

Wash City. Our countryman, Joel Barlow, is arvd in NY.

Thos Corbett is Pres of So Carolina Ins Co. -Charleston, Jun 22, 1805.

Alexandria, Aug 16. Mr Peter, who was shot & robbed on Jul 30th, is now in a fair way to recover; he was remv'd from Mr Swift's hse to the county wharf, where he was recd by Mr Custis & placed on a bed under an awning in his elegant 10 oared barge & arvd at Gtwn.

Died: Arthur Murphy, Jun 18, nr London, barrister & writer.

Died: Mr Abraham Hodge, in Halifax, Aug 3, editor of NC Jrnl.

Wash City, Aug 19. Fire broke out on Sat in a hse occupied by Mr Wilson in E St; flames communicated to a hse belonging to Mr McDermot Roe.

WED AUG 21, 1805

Jane Burch, insolvent debtor, confined to Wash Co prison, for debt.
-Wm Brent, clk.

Robt Dill, insolvent debtor, confined in Wash Co prison, for debt.
-Wm Brent, clk.

For sale: 864 acs, 6 miles from Culpepper Crt hse, Va.
-Morton Pannell, Culpepper Co, Va.

Impeachment of Saml Chase-Feb 25. Hugh Holmes, sworn.

Ltr to Saml H Smith from John Chalmers Jr, dated Wash, Aug 17, 1805. Subj: the use of our own country hemp v Russian hemp. Also a ltr from John Gordon, dated Balt, Aug 14, 1805, on same subject.

Crt Martial has convened at New Orleans for the trial of Col Butler for disobedience of orders.

Hamilton Rowan has returned to Ireland, having recd his Majesty's pardon; he made promises of future loyalty in open court.

Wm Lattimore, Rpblcn, re-elected a Delg to rep the Miss Terr in Congress of the U S; he had 10 votes; Cato West-2 votes & John Ellis-1 vote.

FRI AUG 23, 1805
Ofcrs in Farmers' Bank, Balt, Md-Aug 17:

Pres	John Muir	*Cashier*	Jonathan Pinkney
Teller	Saml Maynard	*Bkpr*	Thos Shaw
Disc clk	Genrl John Davidson	*Runner*	Lewis Green
Porter.	Jas Cleary		

Directors of Farmers' Bank of Md, Western shore;

Calvert Co	Jos Wilkinson	**PG Co**	Robt Bowie
Charles Co	Henry H Chapman	**St Mary's Co**	Wm Somerville
Montgomery Co	Thos Davis	**Frederick Co**	John Tyler
Washington Co	Frisby Tilghman	**Baltimore Co**	Jas J Wilkinson
Harford Co	Benedict E Hall	**Alleghany Co**	Upton Bruce
Annapolis & Anne Arundel Co			
	Lewis Duvall	John Gibson	Wm Steuart
	Jas Mackubin	Horatio Ridout	Richd H Harwood
	John F Mercer	Arthur Shaff	

At the Sign of the Fan & Screen, 52 Front St, Old Town & Hanover St, nrly oppo Evans' Tavern, Balt; for sale-fans for cleaning wheat, wire safes, wire for milk houses. -Isaiah Baldonton & Son. Orders may be left with Wm Morgan, Gtwn.

For sale: at hse of David Rawn, decd, variety of furn.
-Eliza Rawn & John H Cheyney

MON AUG 26, 1805
Book Store-Jas Humphreys, 2d & Walnut Sts, Phil, Pa.

WED AUG 28, 1805
Tenn: Mr Sevier is elected Govnr; Messrs Campbell, Dickson & Rhea are re-elected Reps in Congress.

Runaway-Jim, negro, 23 yrs of age, says he belongs to Mr Evans, of Natchez, & that he was purch'd of Rezin Hammond, of A A Co, Md. -Geo Creager, sheriff of Frederick Co.

Caution-my wife Ellen has left my bed & board; I am determined to pay no debts of her. -John Bloor.

Ltr from John Shaw, esq, Commanding ofcr of the U S frig, John Adams, dated: Gibraltar, Jun 15, 1805. Subj: his arrival after 30 days from NY; on Jun 10th he fell in with No. 10, Lt Cartey out from Norfolk 27 days; found lying in anchor here-Gunboats No. 3-Lt Maxwell, No 6-Lt Lawrence & No. 5-Lt Harrison, all perfectly well. No. 2-Lt Izard, No 8-Lt Harraden & No 9-Lt Elbert, sailed for Tripoli yesterday; Capt Bainbridge, ofcrs & crew are well & not treated harshly; Capt Stewart sailed on the 2d; Cmdor Barron's health is perfectly restored. [Extracts]

For sale: 2 story brick hse & lot in Wash on 8th St. -John Bloor, on premises.

FRI AUG 30. 1805
Mrd: Mr Perrin Aldey, age 105 yrs, to Mrs Ann Tankesley, age 90 yrs, Jul 30, Charlotte Co, Va. She is his 3d wife & he her 3d hsbnd.

Died: Thos Percival, M D, at Manchester.

Died: Abbate Fontana, at Milan, Naturalists of Europe.

Died: Francis Dezoteux, age 79, at Versailles.

Died: Andrew Michaux, at Madagascar, author of History of Oaks of America.

Michael Zorger, York Co, Pa, has obtained the patent for the machine that cleans clover seed.

Maj Kenan is elected a Rep to Congress in rm of Mr Gillespie, decd.

J B Cordis, esq, of Bladensburgh, has added to the information on discoveries & settlements on the western coast of N A; he was an ofcr on board the same vessel with Capt Kendrick; Mr C's journals are in Mass. New York paper.

MON SEP 2, 1805
Brewery for sale: lot 10 sq 88, Wash City. Apply to Dr Conningham residing thereon.   -Marsham Waring.

WED SEP 4, 1805
For sale: 20,000 acs in Hardy Co, Va; good lots in west end of Wash City; his dwelling hse in Gtwn. Apply to Chas Wayman, Gtwn. I am determined to reside in Alleghany Co, Md & will be in Gtwn until Oct 5.
                                           -John Templeman, Gtwn.

Force at present in the Mediterranean employed against Tripoli:
Frig President	Com S Barron
Frig Constitution	Capt J Rogers
Frig Constellation	Capt H G Campbell
Frig Congress	Capt S Decatur
Frig Essex	Capt J Barron

Frig John Adams	Capt J Shaw
Brig Siren	Capt Stewart
Brig Argus	Capt Hullschner
Vixen	Capt Smith
Schnr Nautilus	Capt Dentschner
Enterprize	Capt Robinson

2 Americ bomb vessels, 9 Americ gun boats, 2 bomb vessels & 3 gun boats. Procured in the Mediterranean are 3,200 men.

For sale: *Brookefield*, 418 acs, large dwelling with 4 brick chimneys; 3 1/2 miles from port of Nottingham.   -Thos Brooke.

Reward-$10 for strayed or stolen bay horse nr the Navy Yard. -Mary Russell.

Robert Dillon-insolvent debtor. Claims to be made to trustee by order of Hon Wm Cranch, Crct Crt of DC. -Wm Brent. Chas Jones-Trust.

FRI SEP 6, 1805
Hon Nathan Macon is Spkr of Hse of Reps of Congress of U S.

MON SEP 9, 1805
Rpblcns of Delaware elected David Hall & Jas M Broom, Reps in Cong.

Address by Julien Poydras, Pres of the Leg Cncl of Orleans on its being prorogued on May 1st, 1805, address by same on Jul 3, 1805.

Address of the inhabitants of St Chas, La, to Gov Jas Wilkinson, Jul 12, 1805. Signed, E Hempstead. Subj: Gov's accession to ofc of Governor.

Hse of Reps, Feb 1. Debate on the Yazoo claims. At the end of the Indian war which broke out in 1763, a settlement was formed at Redstone Creek, Pa which settlers claimed to hold. Comrs, Gen Potter, Col Allison & Rev Mr Steel were sent to forbid settling same.

WED SEP 11, 1805
Appointed by the Pres for Terr of Orleans:
Governor	Wm C C Claiborne
Judges of Sup Crt	Hon J B Prevost
	Buckner Thruston
	Geo Duffield

Anacostia Library crnr of L St so. & 8th St east.
Trustees	Dr A McWilliams	Jas Burgess
	Azariah Gatton	Matthew Wright
	Adam Lindsay	
Lib	Gustavus Higdon	
Treas	Saml Fowler	
Sec	Robt Bunyie	

For sale or will exch for prop in Alex, Gtwn or Wash City; *Long Glades*, 1,350 acs, Fairfax Co, Va with hse cld the White House; also plantation, 400 acs, nr Winchester & Newtown; also tract of land, 356 acs, in dist of Col. - J Switt.

Runaway-Ralph-negro, age 23 yrs, committed to Wash Co jail; says he belongs to Jas Wyate nr the Red Hse, Pr Wm Co, Va. -L Hilleary-shrf, Allegany Co, Md.

In Chancery, Md, Aug 5, 1805. Hezekiah Berry, v *Samuel Smallwood, *Amastatia Smith & *Cornelius Smith her hsbnd & others. Bill is to obtain a decree to foreclose a mortage executed by Henry Smallwood on Jul 1, 1799 for conveying sundry tracts of land in Chas Co to cmplnt. [*Reside out of Md].
                                         -Saml H Howard, R C C.

Public sale at Mrs Kimbolls in Fredericktown, Frederick Co, Md, for benefit of creditors, 3 story brick dwelling-453 acs.   -John Ritchie, Tr.

Ltr from Robt Dennison, esq, sec to the Cmdor of the Mediterranean squad, dated Malta, Jun 15, 1805. Peace has been concluded betwixt the U S & the Bashaw of Tripoli & our countrymen restored to liberty.

FRI SEP 13, 1805
Public auction of furniture of Miss Sally Dashiel, next door to Mr Harrison Smith's on Pa Av   -John Travers, auct.

To be sold: order of orphans Crt of PG Co, Md-at plantation of Wm Hutchison nr Upper Marlbro, prsnl est of John T Willett, late of PG Co, Md, decd. -Ninian T Willett, adm.

Vindication of Mr Jefferson. Extractions: Col Wm Tatham being at Richmond in the time of Arnold's invasion 1780-1. Other names: A. Blair, late clk of the Cncl; Gen John Minor of Fredericksburg; Chas Symmes, present coll of the Port of Alexandria.

Address to Jas Wilkinson, Genrl & Commander in Chief of the U S Army & Gov of the Terr of La. Signed, Chas Gratiot, Augt. Choteau, Aut. Soulard, Robt Wescott & J Darneille. Jul 1, 1805.

Orphans crt of PG Co, Md.Sep 13, 1805-prsnl est of John Francis Hardy, decd. -Eliz Hardy & Richd S Gardiner, adms.

MON SEP 16, 1805
List of killed & wounded at taking of Derne: John Wilson, Marine-killed; Wm Eaton, Capt Lucca-a Greek, David Thomas & Bern'd O'Brien-Marines, & 9 Greek Christians-all wounded. [Argus, Derne-Apr 28]

Cmdor Barron, owing to the debilitated state of his constitution has rsgn'd the command of squadron to Capt Rodgers on May 22. [Norfolk Sep 11-Barron returned in ill health.]

Runaway: Campbell, negro, 32 yrs of age; says he is prop of Wm Smith of Faquier Co, Va, to whom he was sold by Geo Robinson. Also-Jim alias Richmond, mulatto, age 22 yrs, says his master Thos Strachan of Spotsyl-vania, Va sold him a month ago to John Crumson, from whom he escaped.
-Danl C Brent, Marshal of DC.

Name, date & data extracted from Richmond Enquirer on vindication of Mr Jefferson. [Sep 13 & Sep 16 papers]. Col Wm Tatham-at Richmond in 1780-1, time of invasion of Arnold; Maj Gen Baron Steuben was at Wilton, 6 miles below Richmond & stopped at Dl Truehart's plantation nr Meadow Bridges on Chickahominy also Mr Duval's hse at Mt Comfort; Richd Crouch referred me to Moses Tredway in Manchester. In 1796 Mr D Hylton made a deposition before Dr Wm Goushee that in 1781 he was living nr the foundery at Westham & his family was 8 miles up the rvr. Jas Currie, of Richmond recalls the yr 1781. Mr John Beckley was clk of Va Leg-Oct 12, 1796. Spring of 1781, Mr Richd O'Brien, late Americ cnsl at Algiers, certified that he was 1st Lt on board the state brig *Jefferson* & srvd 8 mos in svc of Va before the close of the Rev; was captive by the Algerines for 12 yrs, cnsl at Algiers for 8 yrs, arrv'd in Phil last spring. Capt Christopher Hudson, of Albermarle, an old vet, was attached to Capt Callis's troop of horse.

Died: Mr Hodgkinson, one of the most distinguished theatrical performers on the continent.

WED SEP 18, 1805

Died: Gen Christopher Gadsen, age 82 yrs, Aug 30, at Charleston; funeral svc at St Philip's Chr by Rev Dr Jenkins.

Died: John Churchman, age 53 yrs, Jul 24, on board the ship, *Wm Murdock*, Capt Thom, on passage from London to Phil; paralytic stroke suffered 5 mos before. -NY Adv

In Chancery-Md, Sep 7, 1805. Darius Gamble v Samuel Beck, Simon Beck, Wm Carroll & Mary his wife, Joshua Beck, Nathan Beck & Geo Beck, heirs of Joshua Beck. Bill is to obtain a decree for sale of debt of tract cld "*Gambles Farm* in Kent Co for payment of Joshua Beck from whom the said land descended to the dfndnts as his heirs. Some dfndnts reside out of Md.
-Saml H Howard, R C C.

Runaway-Celia, mulatto girl, abt 12 yrs of age; alias Nancy Adams. Reward
-Jas S Scott, Alexandria.

Dartmouth College: degree of Dr of law conferred on: Wm Paterson of NJ, John Langdon of NH; Stephen R Bradley of Vt. Same degree to Barnabas Bidwell of Mass, Providence College.

Wm Hull is Govnr of Michigan Terr.

Norfolk, Sep 11. Ofcrs who returned board the *"President"*:

Capt	Wm Bainbridge		
2d Lt	Jacob Jones		
Purser	Keith Spence		
Lts promoted	Benj P Read	Jas Gibbon	Danl T Patterson
Lt Marines	Wm Osborne		
Midshipmen	Jas Biddle	Robt Gamble	Wm Cutbush
	Wallace Wormly	Jas Renshaw	
Surg's Mates	Nicholas Harwood	Jonathan Cowdry	
Capt clk	Wm Anderson		
Boatswain	Geo Hodge		
Sailmkr	Jos Douglas		
Gunner	Richd Stevenson		

Remained in Mediterranean:

Lts	David Porter	Theodore Hunt	Benj Smith
Master	Bern'd Henry		
Midshipman	Simon Smith		
Carpenter	Wm Godby		

Dr John Ridgly remains as Chg De Affairs for U S for Tripoli.

Bills Drawn by the Americ Mnstr to satisfy claims adjusted under the La. Convention, up to Jul 3, 1805; to whose order livres-1805.

P W Livingston	Peter Torris	John Sinclair
Geo Lynham	Henry Jackson	Francois Robert
John Greenleaf	Vidal & Co	Bruneau Lorin
Saml Hatch	Lawrence Vial	Le Ray De Chaumont
Stephen Dutell	John Blagge	Bickley & Clarke
Murray & Mumford	John Leamey	Barthelemy Cabarrus
Fenwick Mason & Co	Peter Gilman	Jos White & Robt Stone
Jos White & Wm Kemball	David Tilden	Geo Dunham
Moses Myers	John Marrast	Benj Wilson
Wm Betts	David Spear	Geo Frost Blount
Jon Tilcomb	Henry Hodge	Smith & Ridgway
Ludwig Dupasquierpetit & Bayard		Henry L Waddell
John M Pintard	Nath'l Fellows	Anthony Butler
Gouverneur & Kemble	Jacob Shoemaker	Paul R Randal
Wm Duncan	John Judicott	Nichs Broughton
Wm R & Wm Lee	Wm Morgan	Saml Darby
John Johnson	Jas Gamble	Robt Mickle
Watson & Paul Eben Parsons	John Peters	Saml Watt
Pratt & Kintzing	Wm Patterson	Patrick Hogan

Abner Wood	J G Clark	Nath'l West
Stephen Girard	Stephen Marcy	John Plankinhorn
Wheaton & Tisdale	Edw Dunant	Saml & John Smith
Jos Young Jr	Saml Lewis	L Honore Guerlain
Gros Davilier & Co	Jos Fenwick	Jas Barry
Joshua Barney	Jos Russel	Anthony Laussat
Saml Hatch	Lawrence Vial	Jno Carriere & Wm Wyse
Saml Aborn & Jas Rhodes	Stephen Higginston & Wm Parsons	
Jno Holmes & Ch Ghesquier	Wm Prestman & Abm M Causland	

Christian Mayer, representing Valeck & Co — Rd Salter & J Sheafe
Richd H Wilcocks, exr of John Wilcocks — John Low, adm of Jno Low
Luke Callaghan, transf of Wm Shaller — Perregaux & Co
Chaubry De La Roche, transf of Judas Hays — Jos White & And. Dunlap
Debora Stewart, exc of Gen W Stewart — Saml Toplif & Eben. Gay
Edw Staples for himself & adm of Thos Adams — John Dunlap & Thos Irwin
Harper, Snowden & Jas King — Wm & Jos Bell & Jos Watson
Josh Orne, repres'g Wm R Lee, Jos Wilson & J Sewall;
Jas Swan & same as transf of Jas Crawford & Jno Donaldson;
Josh Orne respres'g Saml Smith; also repres'g Jos Howard;
E Kendall & Jon Ingersoll, adms of P Hammond, Jr;
Rob Patton, transf of Josh Barney;
Mich'l Owealy, transf of J Swan;
M Owealy, transf of J Swan; & trans of John Holmes;
Elias Rowe & Hannah Davis, adms of Estiphalet Davis;
Dennis Laury & same as transf of Wm Macreery;
Anne Burrows & Jos Vansise, adms of John Burrows;
Mary Motley, admx of Alex'r Motley;
Thos Ogier, transf of Thos Wallace;
Stephen Higginson & Wm Parsons;
Tunno, Cox, Miller & Robertson;
Jacob Shoemaker, transf of Andrew Summers;
Henry Pratt for himself & as adm of Fredk W Sterman Dicker & Co;
Jas Ash for himself & as adm of Jas Craig, Robeson & Paul, Ann Carhart, **adms of Wm Carhart, & Jos Higbee, transf of Pearson Hunt;**
Wm Glover & John Tittermary & sons;
Jas Robertson, adm of Timothy Gay ;
Danl & Chas Jackson, Wm Sturtevant & Louis Marcy, adms of Stephen Marcy;
Titus Wells, transf of John Salter;
Jas Swan, transf of John C Jones;
Jas Boland, Thos W Francis & Jos Russel;
Verewock Gole & Eben Thayer.
John Townsend, transferee of Henry Sadler
Baquenault & Co, transf. of Jas Ducupley

Reply to Gov Hull's communication of Jul 8. Inhaitants of Detroit in Mich Terr; Subj: Recent fire that destroyed Detroit. Signed, Jas Henry, Elijah Brush, Geo McDougall, Chabere Joncaire, Geo Meldrum. Jul 15, 1805, Detroit.

Fri Sep 20, 1805

Orphans Crt of PG Co, Md, Sep 16, 1805. Est of John Baden, of Thos, late of said Co, decd. -Clement Baden, Jos N Baden, excs.

For sale: 500 acs in PG Co, 4 miles above Upper Marlborough, & framed dwlg hse. Desirous of removing from this part of the country. -Clement Brooke.

Dr Thos Ewell of Va, author of a "Dissertation on the Stomach & Secretion", is about to engage in a new work on chemistry.

Note: Ltr from R Calder, dated Prince of Wales, Jul 23, 1805. Subj: yesterday I was favored with a view of the combined squadrons of France & Spain; I immediately stood before the enemy.

Ships under vice admiral Sir Robt Calder, Bart., Jul 22, 1805:

Hero	Hon A H Gardner	*Ajax*	Wm Brown
Triumph	H Inman	*Barfleur*	Geo Martin
Agamemnon	John Harvey	*Windsor Castle*	Chas Boyle
Defiance	P C Durham	*Repulse*	Hon a K Legge
Risonable	Josias Rowley	*Dragon*	Edw Griffiths
Thunderer	W Lechmere	*Malta*	Edw Buller
Warrior	S Hood Linze	*Pr of Wales*	V Adm Sir R Calder & Capt W Coming
Frigs:			
Egyptienne	Hon C E Fleming	*Syrius*	W Prowse
Frisk Cutter	Lt J Nicholson	*Nile Lugger*	Lt Fennel

Signed, R Calder, Vice Adm.

For sale: plantation in PG Co on which Mr Michael Lowe now lives,"*Trial*" & "*Deer Pond Enlarged*", 408 acs. Apply to Mr Thos Mundel nr Piscataway.
-Robt Ferguson.

Mon Sep 23, 1805

Mr Jas Steptoe, Sen, of Bedford Co, Va, resided within 2 miles of Poplar Forest in 1781 & at that time the estate belonged to T Jefferson, esq. Ltr dated Aug 6, 1805 by Steptoe. Robt Bradfute, Aug 6, 1805, writes that in the yr 1781 he lived within 2 miles of Poplar Forest, an estate that belonged to Th Jefferson.

For sale: *Neabico Furnace*, 4 or 5000 acs, Pr Wm, Va. Apply to Mr Thos T Page living nr the premises. -John Tayloe.

Auction sale of furniture, at hse opposite Mr Lingan's, nr West Mkt, Wash City.
-John Wall.

Public sale of "*Enfield Choice*", 600 acs, PG Co, Md, & dwelling hse. Apply to Isaac Lansdale living on the premises.

Hugh Densley, insolvent debtor, confined in Wash Co, DC prison, for debt.
-Wm Brent, clk.

Stray grey mare found at Warren's Mill, PG Co, Md, where I reside.
-Jos Clark Addington.

WED SEP 25, 1805
Syracuse, Jun 29th, 1805. U S Ship *Constitution*. The Court are decidedly of opinion that Capt Wm Bainbridge acted with fortitude & conduct in the loss of his ship, U S frig-*Philadelphia*, on Oct 31, 1803, & no degree of censure shld attach itself to him from that event. Jas Barron, Pres. Wm Eaton, Acting Judge Advocate. Witnesses: Lt David Porter late of the frig *Philadelphia*; Lt Jacob Jones; Lt Theodore Hunt; Lt Benj Smith; Mr Wm Knight-sailing mstr; Lt Wm Osborn of Marine Corps; Mr Keith Spence-Purser; Danl J Patterson, Benj F Read & Jas Gibbons-Mstrs' Mates; Midshipmen-Jas Biddle, Jas Henshaw & _____ Anderson; Rich Stephenson-gunner; Geo Hodge-boatswain; Wm Godby-carpenter; all of said frig, sworn & approved as witnesses.

Isaac Tichenor, re-elected Govnr of Vt; Paul Brigham, Lt-Gov, both Federal.

Died: Genrl Christopher Gadsden, age 82, at his hse in Charleston, on Wed last; one of the earliest patriots of Carolina & the Revolution. Capt Kalteisen, Commandant of Ft Johnson, had the fort hung in mourning; Genrl G was founder of the First Regt of Artl in 1755. -Charleston, Aug 30.

FRI SEP 27, 1805
John Baptist-Baron of Rufini: Info wanted whether this gentleman be living, & where he resides. Request of Dept of State, for satisfaction of his relatives in Europe.

PG Co Crt, Md, Sep Term, 1805. Petition of Allen Brightwell & John Bean, pray that the rl est of Richd Brightwell, late of PG Co, decd, wld admit of division; was determined that division wld be prejudicial. Reps of said R Brightwell summoned to crt; Rhody Cave, resides out of Md in state of Va.
-John Read Magruder Jr, clk.

PG Co Crt, Md, Sep Term, 1805. Petition of Sarah Adams & Anne Adams, pray that the rl est of Geo Walter Gibbons, late of PG Co, decd, wld admit to division; was determined that division wld be prejudicial. Reps of said G Gibbons summoned to crt; Josias Kedwell, s/o Leonard, resides out of Md in State of Va.
-John Read Magruder Jr, clk.

Salem, Sep 10. Ltr from Mr Saml Williams to the late owner of the *Essex*, of this port, dated-London, Jun 22, 1805. Rgrd: Condemnation of the "*Essex*" pronounced by the vice admiralty crt.

Mon Sep 30, 1805

Persons warned against a note given by me to Wm Adams, dated Jul 22, 1805.
-Geo St Clare.

For sale: 7000 acs, Mason Co, Va; apply to Wm Craik, Alexandria who attended the surveying. -Jas Craik

Botanic Garden of So C is now ready for plants. Jas Simons, 56 King St; Robt Pringle, crnr of Friend & Broad Sts; Fred. Dalcho, 54 Meeting St; Benj B Simons, crnr of Longitude La & East Bay; Jos Johnson, 5 Broad St. The garden is located in Meeting St.

Wed Oct 2, 1805

Runaway, Will, negro, age abt 40 yrs; says he belongs to John Tyler, nr Leesburg, Va. -N Rochester, shrf, Wash Co, Md.

Ltr to Lt Saml Baldwin, Marines, New Orleans, Aug 20, 1805. Congrats for his acquittal at a Genrl Crt Martial. -Constant Freeman, Lt.Col Artil.

Fri Oct 4, 1805

List of ladies with ltrs in Wash Post ofc, Oct 1, 1805:

Betsy Bowen c/o Mr Moren		Mrs Hughes c/o Mr Bentley
Mrs Banpfield	Miss Eliz Brown	Eliz Nevit
Mrs Mgt Coone	Mrs Eliza Dempsey	Miss Polly Elvin
Miss Rosanna Fanagan	Joanna Gallaspy	Mrs Polly Gates
Miss Sophia Michael	Milly Lomax	Mrs Sares
Mrs Harriot Peden	Mrs Lucy Nash	Eliz Washington
Miss Eliz Tacker	Mrs Eliz Runnells	Miss Eliz Wilkinson
Miss Sally Thompson	Miss Tarlanson	Mrs Rebecca James

Balt, Sep 5. Sat, Aug 28, *Rockhall Packet*, Capt Humphreys, sailed from Balt, & met with a squall of wind. Swept away-the sufferers-R Hatcheson, past Delegate in Leg of Md for Kent Co; Richd Goodman, Mate, & C Ridgeley, of Balt.

For sale: at Robb's Tavern Montg Crt hse, 1000 acs, debt of *Bradford's Rest*, Montg Co, Md. -John Ronsby Plater

Mon Oct 7, 1805

Partnership bet Henry Polkinhorn & Wm Hall, sadlers, is dissolved by mutual agreement; business will be cont'd by Henry Polkinhorn.

For sale: by power given me by Robt Wigfield, I will sell at Henry Harshman's, bet 5 & 6 acs nr the Eastern Branch Bridge. -Alex'r Cochran Jr.

Edw J Coale is Register of the City of Balt, Md. [Flour, butter & lard inspected within the city & precincts of Balt]

Mr Edmund Randolph is engaged in writing a history of Virginia.

WED OCT 9, 1805
John A Blaire, insolvent debtor, confined to Wash Co, DC, prison, for debt; trustee to be apptd. —Wm Brent, clk.

Appointments by the Pres: Walter Jones, Maj in 2d Leg of Militia of dist of Col; Robt Young, Maj of same Leg; Wm Allen Dangerfield, Capt of Cavalry in same legion.

Prison, Tripoli, Jun 2. Ltr to Capt Wm Bainbridge, esq from Stephen Howell, Henry Johnson, Jas Freise & John Smith. Subj: Upwards of $300 has been subscribed for the purpose of their emancipation; up to Capt B. to advance money.

Wash Co, DC-Jul Term, 1805. John Hoye adm D B N of Wm Deakins, late, decd, & John Hove & Leonard M Deakins, excs of Francis Deakins, who was exc of said Wm Deakins, cmplnts, v Adam Murray Stewart, Deborah Stewart, exc of Walter Stewart, late decd, & Wm, Robt, Ann, Walter, Henry, Mary Ann Stewart, heirs & devisees of W Stewart decd, & Sabritt Scott, Walter Story Chandler & Thos Herty, dfndnts. Bill to establish a debt due to cmplnts & same pd out of rl & prsnl est of decd, Walter Stewart. Stewarts reside out of D C. Wm Brent, clk.

FRI OCT 11, 1805
For sale: the ofc & establishment of the Republican; annual income bet 4 & $5000; desiring to retire. Thos Field, Petersburg, Va. In short space of 1 yr & 9 mos, death has snatched from me 2 amiable consorts [both in bloom of youth] & 3 chldrn. —Thos Field

Orphans Crt of Wash Co, DC. Oct 10, 1805. Prsnl est of Wm Jenkins, late of said Co, decd. —Saml Brown, Mary Jenkins, adms.

For sale: prop adjoining the Bank of Col in Gtwn, now occupied by Mr Jos Semme, as the Indian King Tavern. —Wm O Sprigg, Capitol Hill, Wash.

Md election: Andrew Ellicott & John Stephen-re-elected reps of Balt in assembly. Others who recd votes: Robt Stewart, Theo Bland, E Aisquith & J J Wilkinson.

MON OCT 14, 1805
Died: Maj Gen Wm Moultrie, age 76 yrs, Sep 27, soldier & patriot of SC. —Charleston, Sep 28.

Brig *Betsey*, for Phil, Capt Jas Atkinson, owned by Mr J Leger D'Happart, a naturalised ctzn of Americ since Dec 1797, captured by the British on Jul 14 last.

Died: Royal Highness Prince Wm Henry, Duke of Glousester, Aug 25. —London, Aug 27.

Md Election - House of Delegates
Kent Co   Scot B Hunson   Cornelius Hurtt   Wm Gale
Queen Anne's Co Wm Gleaves   Plulemon C Blake   Jos Nicholson
                   Wm Sudler
Baltimore Co   T E Stansbury   Amos Ogden   Geo Harryman
                   Alexis Lemmon   Moses Brown.

WED OCT 16, 1805
Md election:
Frederick Co   Thos Hawkins   1000   Joab Waters   977
                   Joshua Cockey   965   Henry Kuhn   960

Ltr from Capt Jos Tyrrell, of Ship *Commerce*; dated: Yarmouth Rds, Eng-Aug 15. On Aug 8th I was boarded by the King's cutter *Badger*, Capt Panthorpe & brought into Rds; expect to be cleared tomorrow. Vessels detained for trial, Ship *Portsmouth*, Capt Lewis-Balt; Ship *Hope,* Capt Robertson, of Portland. Vessels liberated: ship *Hunter,* Capt Chase of Newburyport; ship *Hermoine,* Capt Hopkins of Biddeford; ship *Saml Jackson,* Capt Easterby of NY & Capt Waite of Portland.

Copy of genr'l orders transmitted to Lt Col John Ellis, commanding the Militia of Wilkinson Co. Hdqrtrs Washington, Miss Terr, Sep 9, 1805.

FRI OCT 18, 1805
Md election: delegates for Genrl Assembly.
Annapolis City   John Muir   Arthur Shaaff
Anne Arundel Co Richd Merriken   John F Mercer
                   Joshua C Higgins   Lloyd Dorsey
PG Co   Francis M Hall   Alex r Contee
                   Archibald Van Horn   Henry A Callis

Died: John O'Donnel, esq, age 56 yrs, Oct 5, at his country resid in Barrens of Balt; possessed of a large fortune; Col in the Militia; hsbnd & fr; after a long & excrutiating illness.

Mrd: Mr Stephen S Johns of Calvert, to Miss Eliza G Skinner, of PG Co, Md, Oct 10, by Rt Rev Thos I Claggett, nr Nottingham, Md.

I caution the public against trusting my wife Biddy Dent, or Biddy Jourdan; I fear she is in the habit of stealing from the neighbors & others; I will not be answerable.   -Chas Dent.

Notice-I prohibit all seine hauling at Kit's Point, or any landing of St Inigo's Manor, w/out my leave or that of my agent, Jos Daffin, lvng in St Inigo's Neck; extend same to St Geo's Island, debt of St Inigo's Manor. -Francis Neale.

Lund Washington, insolvent debtor, confined to Wash Co, DC, prison, for debt; trustee to be apptd.   -Wm Brent, clk.

Partnership of Wm S Nichols & Richd Beck was dissolved on Aug 21. Nichols will continue the bus.

Mon Oct 21, 1805
Ck payable to J Williamson for $132.29, dated Sep 26, 1805, given by Chas Wadsworth was lost.

New York, Oct 15. Death of his Imperial Majesty of Hayti, John Jas Dessalines, is at least premature.

Wed Oct 23, 1805
Died: Col Butler, Sep 7, suddenly, at estate of his nph, abt 20 miles from New Orleans, buried as a priv ctzn.

Fri Oct 25, 1805
Runaway-Thos Johnson, negro, says he was raised in Charleston, SC where he was set free by Alexander McGilbray, afterwards srvd a full appr to Jas Mitchel, hse carpenter of same place; says he belonged to the frig-*John Adams*; been here since 1801; age abt 29 yrs. -Danl C Brent, mrsh l of DC.

Americ Seaman detained by the British svc for want of documents to prove their citzenship-friends are requested to submit same to Dept of State:

John McConnell	Henry Williams	Robt Talman
Thos Thompson	Alex Kirkwood	Chas Williams
Thos Church	Saml Wilson	Nichs Powers
John Burmore	Emes Wright	Cato Martin
John Frederick	Wm Wheeler	John Bailey
John Farewell	John Truman	Joshua Porter
Timothy Small	Isaac Van Blaken	Mich'l Nugent
Richd Mathers	Benj Lusina	W S Board
Thos Patten	Mayhew Tilton	Richd Strainge
Bosworth Cole	Geo Sloan	Thos Crippen
John Dennis	Wm Clark	Jas Newall
Benj George	Jas Stud	John Stewart
Thos Jones	Nichs Coston	John Smith
Danl Dyson	Richd Smythe	Peter McFarlane
John Hunn	Wm Hayes	John Love
Jas Campbell	John Colbourn	Alex. Carlisle
Stephen Lewis	Francis Edmonds	Wm Cole
Geo Durant	Wm Podd	Jacob Rhan
Wm Lyons	Wm Wilson	Chas Chessen
Henry Bowling	Edw Robinson	Edw Westford
Geo Gray	Saml Hills	John M Walker
Saml Dunkin	Jabez Choat	Benj Noyes
J Huger alias Jack	Geo Birch	Saml Dalton
Anthony Rutcas	Henry Feathers	Henry Chapmon
John Lawson	Wm Armstrong	Saml Rowsen

Saml Lloyd	Chas Harrison	John Walker
Thos Jones	Henry Waters	Wm Sandiford
John Mashevay	John Reid	Frederick Rhoads
Jas Green	Geo Campbell	Nath'l Curtis
Wm Sherrard	Richd Johnson	Jos Wilson
Lawrence Hollander	Jas Riley	John Frish
Francis Bainacoat	Peter Lewis	John Mason
Asa Thompson	Wm Chojan	John Huet
John Boston	Peter Willsmott	John Griffin
Jas Goldsborough	Chas McBride	Richd Edwards
Jas McPherson	Henry Applewhite	John Holmes
Wm Jarvis	Jos McKedder	Nath'l Tolman
John Lowe	Jonathan Archer	Wm Smith
____ Hughes	Jos Muratt	Jos Woodson
John Jones	Jas Lassley	Chas Mitchell
Wm Blechford	John Ferguson	John Grant
Wm alias Jas Deale	Wm Wall Jr	Marens Stephens
Saml Jenkins	Wm Rowland	John Robinson
Godfrey Winslow	John Jackson	John Woolicot
Jas Leppen	John Seymour	Edw Rogers
Francis Davis	John Smith	Thos Manning
Jas Lynn	Lundonill or Lion Donell	
David Coleman	Zeneas Swift	Edw Miller
Wm Bully	Jas Wermsley	Fredk Rhodes
Archd. McKetchine	David Stafford	Jas Watts
Saml Sother	John Rice	Anthony Nelson
Wm Bond	Thos Simonton	John Mitchell
Thos Edwards	Jos Perrin	Wm Mines
Edw Moore	Henry Bowling	John Slocum
Geo Watson	Thos Morris	Saml Brown
Wm Wall	Jas Wilson	Josh Wildman
John Ready	John Walsh	John Thompson
Geo Walker	David Merridith	John Johnson
Wm Buck	John Howes	Jos Pierson
Saml Lloyd	Peter Johnson	Danl Johnson
John Thompson	Geo Mars	Geo Watson
Danl Merridith	Wm Finlay	Richd Dawson
Abraham Hainard	John Miller	Liff Young
Thos Pennock	Geo Walby	John Robinson
Josh Thompson	Jas Featherstone	Elias Hiett
Wm Sculla	Andrew Mansfield	Barns. McNutt
John Hankerson	Saml B Spencer	Jos Wilson
Wm Saunders	Jas Doyle	Jos Hexis
Isaac Gaines	Geo W Eddy	Geo Farrington
John Haniford	Jas Gray	Thos White
Ebenezar Buckingham	Thos Simonton	
Philip Ford alias Caroline	Thos White	

Mon Oct 28, 1805

Runaway-Jas Frazier, negro, committed to Wash Co jail, says he was raised in Carlisle Co, Pa & set free by Wm Frazier abt 1798 & went to sea; was on board the frig, *President*, age abt 35 yrs. -Danl C Brent, Mrshl-DC.

Mr Osborne, editor of the Witness, prosecuted by the Fed Grand Jury in Litchfield for publishing the trial of Genrl Wm Hart before the Superior Crt! -American Mercury

For sale: at dwelling hse of late Jas Weems, of Calvert Co, Md, decd: stock, furniture etc. -Nathl T Weems, adm.

Raleigh, Oct 14. Fri last, the suit brought by the editor of this paper against Wm Boyland, esq, editor of the Minerva, for assault committed on his person, was determined in Hillsborough Superior Crt; Judge Locke presided; verdict-100 pds damages.

Americ Seamen-See Oct 25: (cont'd)

Jas Campbell	Alex Carlisle	John Lindsay
Stephen Lewis	John Copeland	David Coleman
Francis Edmonds	Wm Cole	Geo Durant
Wm Podd	Jacob Rhan	Wm Lyons
Wm Wilson	Jas Chosson	Henry Bowling
Edw Robinson	Edw Westford	Geo Gray
Saml Hilis	John M Walker	Saml Dunkin
Benj Noyes	Jack Huger	Geo Birch
John Smith	Saml Dalton	Anthony Rutcas
Henry Feathers	Henry Champmon	John Lawson
Wm Armstrong	Saml Rowson	Peter Willsmott
Saml Lloyd	Chas Harrison	John Walker
Thos Jones	Henry Waters	John Mashevay
John Reid	Frederick Rhoads	Jas Green
Geo Campbell	Wm Sherrard	Richd Johnson
Jos Willson	Lawrence Hollander	Jas Riley
John Frish	Francis Bainacoat	Peter Lewis
John Mason	Asa Thompson	Wm Chejan
John Huet	John Boston	John Griffin
Jas Goldsborough	Chas McBride	Richd Edwards
Jas McPherson	Wm. Jarvis	Henry Applewhite
Wm Sandiford	John Downing	John Byrens
Francis Wood	John Davis	Martin Doll
Royal Tarbox	David Cuff	John Magratin
John Holmes	Saml Carr	Jno Baptiste Destando
John Greene	Wm Hawker	David Collins
Edw Moore	John Haley	Thos Rowe
Wm Herson or Harrison		

WED OCT 30, 1805

Died: Mr Samuel Riggs Jr, in Montg Co, Md; beginning of manhood. Funeral at fmly seat in Brookville; attended by his parents & numerous bros & srs; discourse by Rev Mr Wilmer.

Died: Arthur Fenner, Govnr of R I, Oct 15, in a fit.

Americ Seamen-See Oct 25: (cont'd)

Jos McKedder	Nathl Tolman	John Lowe
Jonathan Archer	Wm Smith	____ Hughes
Jos Muratt	Jos Woodson	John Jones
Jas Lassley	Chas Mitchell	Wm Blechford
Wm alias Jas Deale	John Ferguson	Wm Wall Jr
Marens Stephens	Saml Jenkins	Wm Rowland
John Robinson	John Jackson	John Woolicot
Jas Lepper	John Seymour	Edw Rogers
Francis David	John Smith	Thos Manning
Jas Lynn	Chas Lewis	John Slocum
Wm/Wilmouth Johnson	Chas Robinson	Benj Mosley
Levi Hall	Edw Owens	Edw Miller
Jos or Th Quenichet	David Coleman	Wm Bond
Lundonill or Lion Donell	Zeneas Swift	Jos Perrin
Wm Bulty	Jas Wormsley	Frederick Rhodes
Archd McKetchine	David Stafford	John Rice
Jas Watts	Saml Sother	Thos Edwards
Anthony Nelson	Thos Simonton	Henry Bowling
Wm Mines	Edw Moore	John Miller
John Slocum	Geo Watson	Wm Wail
Thos Morris	Saml Brown	Jas Wilson
Geo Walker	Eben. Buckingham	Wm Finlay
Josh Wildman	Wm Buck	John Walsh
Philip Ford alias Caroline	Geo Watson	Jos Pierson
Thos Simonton	John Ready	Thos White
John Thompson	Danl Merridith	Danl Johnson
John Johnson	John Howes	Geo Watson
Saml Lloyd	Peter Johnson	Wm Robertson
John Thompson	Geo Mars	Geo Walby
John Grant	Abraham Hainard	Jas Featherstone
Liff Young	Thos Pennock	Barns McNutt
John Robinson	Josh Thompson	Jos Wilson
Elias Huett	Wm Sculla	Geo W Eddy
John Hankerson	Saml B Spencer	Jas Gray
Jos Hexis	Isaac Gaines	Wm Thompson
Geo Farrington	John Haniford	John Brown
Thos White	Richd Dawson	Saml Brown
Richd Reed	John Brack or Brock	Francis Lamott
Benj S Hunt	Wm Wilson	Robt Crosbie

Isaac Gaines	Jos Hixs	Clement Coffin
Robt Coulson	Saml Bond	Ebenezar Turner
Peter Harvey	Wm Sherrard	Chas Low
Peter Lauries or Lewis	Jos Blake	Peter Wilson
Gilbert Lewis	John Rich Jr alias John Bensen	
Wm Jarvis alias Jos Tallman		-Dept of State, Oct 25

Oct 10th, arvd at Savannah from the Creek Nation, Col Benj Hawkins, with 4 Indian Chiefs & 3 interpreters; they left for Wash City Oct 11th.

FRI NOV 1, 1805
Robt Whitehall elected a Rep in Cong in U S, vice John A Hanna, decd; Saml Smith vice John B C Lucas, rsgn'd-both Rpblcns.

Reward-$20 for Nim, mulatto fellow, age abt 22 yrs.
-John Coles, Albemarle Co, Va.

Lost-nr Col Bank, a gold seal. Reward-$2.   -Geo Andrews

Strayed from the Commons of Wash City, a cow. -John Lanthall.

MON NOV 4, 1805
Lt Jas Biddle, of Phil, late prisoner in Tripoli, apptd to command of Gun Boat, No. 1.

Died: Arthur Murphy, some days ago at an advanced age; ntv of Ireland & educated at St Omers.   -London Literary Journal

Dickinson College, Carlisle. Degrees conferred Oct 25:

Salutatory	Jas Linn, Cumberland Co, Pa		
Oration	Mr G Buchanaan, York Co		
	Mr Stephen Duncan, Carlisle		
	Mr W Barr, Cumberland Co		
Bach of Arts	Stephen Duncan	Wm Barr	Jas Linn
	Alexander Mahon	Geo Buchanaan	
Mstr of Arts	Rev Robt Kennedy	Rev Jos Brady	Dr Wm Steel
	Rev Amos A McGinley		
	Mr Jas R Black, student of law in Dela State		

Tuition-$20, boarding-$100.

Mary Bull, insolvent debtor, confined to Wash Co prison for debt.
-Wm Brent, clk.

Died: Miss Mgt Dalton, age 116 yrs 3 mos 10 days, in Mifflin Co, Pa, Oct 10; ntv of Tyrone, Ire.

WED NOV 6, 1805

Elias B Caldwell, atty at law, has remv'd his ofc to hse lately occupied by Mr Law, on Capitol Hill, Wash.

Rockland farm, adj the Delaware paper mills, Oct 15, 1805. Subscribers waiting for completion of the thrashing mach, built by David Prentise on said farm in our neighborhood. Signed: Wm Armour, Caleb Kirk & Jas Brindley. Newcastle Co, Dela, Oct 12, 1805.

Runaways-Gerera & Peter, negro fellows. -Wm Alexander, Pr Wm Co, Va.

Ltr from Capt T Baker, of the *Phoenix*, at sea, Aug 13 to adm Cornwallie. Subj: Capture of French frig, *La Lidon*; ofcrs of Phoenix killed: Lt J Bounton; Mstr's Mate G Donelan; Qrtrmstr John Powers. Wounded dangerously: Lt H Steel, & Midshipmen Aaron Tozer & E B Curling.
-London, admiralty ofc.[His Majesty's ship-*Phoenix*]

WED NOV 8, 1805

Strayed or stolen-dk bay horse. Reward of $5. Deliver to Wm McNain at Little Falls of Potomac.   -John Glasco, Gtwn

Ltr from Robt Williams, dated: town of Washington, Miss Terr. Jul 30th, 1805, to a friend in Rockingham Co. Subj: Description of the country & reference to Cato West & his small party, who have attempted to embarass my administration.

Ltr from Lt Col Saml Ten Broeck, dated Clermont, Oct 9, 1805, to Hon R R Livingston, esq. Subj: ofcrs congratulate him on his return to his ntv state; his company is requested at the Regt Review at Johnstown on Oct 10; an escort of the Troop of Horse, Capt Livingston, will wait at Gale's Tavern in Clermont, to the place of the parade. Robt R Livingston, Clermont, Oct 11, 1805, replies in the affirmative.

MON NOV 11, 1805

Mrd: Mr Geo G MacDaniel to Miss Cath C Simmons, both of Wash City, Nov 7, by Rev Mr Sayrs.

Creed Taylor was apptd a Judge of the Genrl Crt, vice, Judge Jones, decd.
        -Richmond Argus.

Died: Col Francis Mentges, Oct 6, at Rocky Mount, on the Catawba Rvr; assistant to Col Sent.

Declaration Agreement of the Americ Cong, dated Oct 24, 1774, was signed by & in Phil: Peyton Randolph-Pres, John Sullivan, Nathaniel Folsom-NH; Thos Cushing, Saml Adams, John Adams, Robt T Paine, Mass Bay; Stephen Hopkins, Saml Ward-R I; Eliphalet Dyer, Roger Sherman, Silas Dean-Conn; Isaac Low, John Alsop, John Jay, Jas Duane, Wm Floyd, Henry Wisner, S Boerum, Philip Livingston-NY; Jas Kinsey, Wm Livingsten, Stephen Crane, Richd Smith, John

De Hart-NJ; Jos Galloway, John Dickinson, Chas Humphreys, Thos Mifflin, Edw Biddle, John Mortan, Geo Ross-Pa; Coesar Rodney, Thos McKean, Geo Read-New Castle; Matthew Tilghman, Wm Paca, Thos Johnson, Saml Chase-Md; Richd H Lee, Richd Bland, Geo Washington, Benj Harrison, P Henry Jr, Edmond Pendleton-Va; Wm Hooper, Jos Hewes, R Caswell-NC; Henry Middleton, Thos Lynch, Christ. Gadsden, John Rutledge, Edw Rutledge-SC.

Reward-$20 for Aaron, mulatto man abt 43 yrs of age, ran away from Edw Gantt living in Gtwn.

Actions were deposited in the shrf's ofc of this district. Suit of Thos McKean & others against: Matthew Lawler, Thos Leiper, Dr M Leib, Mr Jacob Mitchell late a mbr of the State Leg, & Wm Duane, printer. -Aurora

Trenton, Nov 4. Two hses went into joint meeting-Jas Cox, esq, chrmn; votes for sec of State: Jas Linn-31 & John Beatty-20; for clk of Burlington Co: Jos McIlvaine-28 & Reuben D Tucker-24; for clk of Gloucester Co: Chas Ogden-27 & Elisha Clark-25 votes.

Notice: Anxious to settle all accounts for medical svcs rendered. -Edw Gantt.

WED NOV 13, 1805
Archibald Vanhorn, chosen Spkr of the Hse of Dels of Maryland.

New dry goodstore. -Benj & Horatio Jones, Gtwn.

New Orleans, Sep 21-Elected to rep Orleans Co in Legislative Body:
Mr. Macarty	Hazeu Delerme Sr	Dominique Bouligny
John Watkins	Jas Carrick	Robt Havard
Mr. Bore		

Balt, Md. Nov 11. Gentlemen, we understand apptd to rep the Executive of the U S, the depredations committed on our commerce by foreign nations:
| Jas Calhoun | John Hollins | David Stewart |
| Saml Sterett | Alex. McKim | |

FRI NOV 15, 1805
For sale. 8000 weight of ship bread. Saml Lowdermilk & Co, crnr of north L & 8th Sts, nr the Navy Yard.

Hartford, Nov 7. Rpblcns paid tribute to Joel Barlow, esq, lately returned, after a long absence, to his native state, Conn. Abraham Bishop gave a handsome entertainment at his hse on Oct 29th for Barlow. Jos Wilcox was chrmn. Extract from the journal of Dr Cowdery, who was on board the *Philadelphia* when she was plundered by the Tripolitan Chiefs. Subj: His captivity in Tripoli.

New Mbrs of Hse of Reps for ensuing Congress:

Jos Barker	Burwill Basset	Barnabas Bidwell
John Blake Jr	Thos Blount	Jas M Broom
John Chandler	John Claiborne	Orchard Cock
Leonard Covington	Ezra Darby	T W Thompson
C Ellis	Wm Ely Fisk	Jas M Garnett
Isaiah L Green	Silas Halsey	Chas Goldsborough
John Hamilton	Jas Kelly	Thos Kenan
John Lambert	Christian Lower	Duncan MacFarlane
Patrick Magruder	Robt Whitehill	Uri Tracy
Eliphalet Wickes	Robt Marion	Josiah Masters
Cowles Mead	John Morrow	Jonathan O Mosely
Gurdon S Mumford	Jeremiah Nelson	Timothy Pitkin Jr
John Pugh	Josiah Quincy	John Russell
David R Williams	Nathan Williams	Peter Sailly
Martin G Schuneman	O'Brien Smith	Saml Smith
Lewis B Sturgis		

Mon Nov 18, 1805

Ltr of Wm Goodwin Jr, supercargo of brig, *Stork,* Walter Cornell, Mstr, belonging to Jas D'Wolff, esq of R I. Subj: Brought to by French Privateer of 14 guns & the *Stork* was plundered; Capt & his son were beaten; we lost all but our lives. [July 1805]

Just arrived-sloop *Mary Ann,* Capt Lee, from Guilford, Conn; for sale on board said vessel: potatoes, onions, cheese, fish. -Navy Yard, Wash City.

Public auction nr West Mkt, prsnl est of Wm Jenkins, decd.
          -Saml Brown, Mary Jenkins, adms.

Danl Purrell of PG Co, Md, brought before me a stray sorrel stud.
          -Wm Sprigg Bowie, PG Co, Md
          Justice of the Peace.

New ship, *Fair American,* Robt Davies, mstr, sailing for New Orleans.
          -Wm Taylor, Balt, Md

Died: Gov Pownall, age 85 yrs, at Bath, England, Feb 25.

Wed Nov 20, 1805

Orphans Crt of Wash Co, DC. Nov 17, 1805. Prsnl est of Mrs Cath Johnson, late of said Co, decd. -Wm Brent, Washington Boyd, adms. [Public sale of hsehld & kitchen furn; late dwelling hse is offered for rent.]

Boston, Nov 8. David Myrick, undersigned, late mstr of the ship *Indus,* of Boston, gives account of his capture off Bermudas on Aug 10th last, by John P Beresford, commanding his B M ship, *Cambrian.*

Hdqtrs, St Louis, Sep 20, 1803. Genrl orders, Genrl Crt Martial; Lt Col Freeman, President; held at New Orleans on the 1st 'til Jul 10, 1805; Col Thos Butler was tried for not cutting his hair-Apr 30, 1801. Feb 1, 1804, same sentence-suspended from all command, pay & emoluments for 12 calendar mos. Signed, Jas Wilkinson. Attested as a true copy by Thos H Cushing, Adj & inspec'r, St Louis, Sep 20, 1805.

Genrl Eaton arvd from Gibraltar on the brig *Franklin,* came on shore at Hampton on Sun; reached Richmond on Tue evening.

Robt Bowie is re-elected Gov of Md & Allen E Duckett, Reverdy Ghiselin, Richd T Earle, Francis Digges & Philip Reed, his cncl. Tobias E Stansbury is elected spkr of the Hse of Dels of Md, vice, Archibald Van Horn, rsgn'd.

Fri Nov 22, 1805
Reward-$25 for runaway, Len, negro, age abt 38 yrs; formerly belonged to Maj Chew, living at head of Herring Bay who disposed of him to Mr Wm Campbell nr Fredericktown, Md; Dr Manuel Kent who lives at Lower Marlboro, purchased him of Mr Campbell & sold him to Nichs Voss, Navy Yd, Wash City.

Wm Rutherford, insolvent debtor, confined in Wash Co prison, for debt.
-Wm Brent, clk.

John D Brashears, insolvent debtor, confined in Wash Co prison, for debt.
-Wm Brent, clk.

Spermaceti oil & candles. Bridge St,Gtwn. -John Goulding, groc store,

Hugh Drummond has just opened a hse of entertainment in hse lately occupied by D Dobbin nr the Navy Yard.

Mon Nov 25, 1805
Ltr from Edmund P Gaines, dated: Frankfort, Nov 4, collector's ofc, dist of Mobile, Port of Ft Stoddert, Aug 1, 1805-to Colo: Franco Maximo P Maxent, city of Mobile. Subj: Receipt of a ltr in Spanish, interpreted by Mr Wm Simpson, of Oct 29th - Regarding the schnr *Cato,* commanded by Cadet Freret which did not stop at this port.

Elias Earle, elected a mbr of Congress, to rep the dists of Pendleton & Grenville, SC, vice John B Earle, who declined taking his seat.

Strayed or stolen nr the West Mkt, brown horse. -John Kedglei, Wash

Wed Nov 27, 1805
Assignees apptd by the Judges of the Inferior Crt of Common Pleas for Cumberland Co, NJ, to settle est of Saml Dollas, insolvent debtor, meet at hse of Benj S Ogden in Fairfield, Cumberland Co, NJ. -David C Wood & Humphries Green, assigs.

For sale-the late resid of Nathan Smith, decd; 414 acs; nr Nottingham; by order of Calvert Co Crt. Jos Blake, Chas Williamson, Richd Ireland Jr, comrs.

Boarding & Lodging. Pa Ave, Washington -John Doyne

Meeting in Wash City into utility of opening the Tyber Creek; committee: Jos Huddleston, Robt Underwood-chrmn, Thos Thorpe, Alex'r McCormick, Lewis Morin, Geo Andrews & John P Van Ness. -Thos Herty, sec.

FRI NOV 29, 1805

Ranaway, Sophy, mulatto woman, age abt 25 yrs; from Edw Isaack, living nr Huntington, Calvert Co, Md. Reward-$30.

For sale-2 tracts of land in Montgomery Co cld *Magruders Purchase & Addition to Resurvey on Magruders Purchase,* but lately named *Fruit Hills*-295 1/2 acs.
-Nichs Brewer, trust.

Message from Christ. Greenup, Gov of Ky to the Leg; dated-Frankfort, Nov 5,1805. Rgrd: concerns of the Government.

Runaways-apprentice boys, John Wesiner & David Magahan; from John Layland, cooper at Federal Mills nr Gtwn.

MON DEC 2, 1805

Boarding hse-Miss Finagan, remv'd from Capitol Hill to hse Miss Dashields formerly occupied nr the Centre Mkt, Wash.

Wm Logan was chosen spkr of the Hse of Reps-Ky. Genrl John Adair was elected Sen of U S, vice, John Breckenridge, rsgn'd. Raleigh, NC,-Stephen Cabarrus was elected spkr of Hse of Commons & A. Martin, spkr of Senate.

Dinner given to Genrl Wm Eaton on Mon at Stelle's Htl in Wash; committee: Robt Brent, John Tayloe, Wm Simmons, Danl Carroll, Franklin Wharton, Thos Monroe, Wm Brent, Elias B Caldwell & Saml H Smith.

TUE DEC 3, 1805

Lost on Nov 30, ck in favor of Wm Clemens, seaman on board the *Constellation,* $247.89, payable at the City Bank.

Wash Co, DC. Public sale by decree of Crct Crt of Wash Co, DC: suit of Robt S Bickley against Thos Peter, Thos Munroe, Robt Brent, Benj Stoddert, Elias B Caldwell, Wm Thornton, John Stickney, Adam Lindsey, Edw Frithy, Jas Dougherty, Francis Lowndes, Saml Blodget, Thos McKewen, Wm Davidson & Wm Smith, dfndnts in Chancery - sale of numerous lots in Wash City.
-Danl C Brent, clk.

F Oliver takes the liberty to acquaint her friends with an assortment of millinery of newest fashions. Local ad.

Wm Waters has mv'd to Wash nr the West Mkt-grocery for sale.

FRI DEC 6, 1805
Runaway, Natt, negro man, age abt 35 yrs. Reward-$10. Nr the Eastern Branch Bridge, Wash.   -Lewin Talburtt

Mbrs of the present Congress
Senate of the U S:

NH	*Nicholas Gilman	Wm Plumer
Mass	John Q Adams	Timothy Pickering
Vt	Stephen R Bradley	Israel Smith
R I	*Jas Fenner	Benj Howland
Conn	Jas Hillhouse	Uriah Tracy
NY	Saml L Mitchill	John Smith
NJ	John Condit	*Aaron Kitchill
Pa	Geo Logan	Saml Maclay
Dela	Jas A Bayard	Saml White
Md	Saml Smith	Robt Wright
Va	Wm B Giles	Andrew Moore
Ky	*John Adair	David Buckner Thruston
NC	David Stone	*Jas Turner
SC	John Gaillard	Thos Sumter
Ga	Abraham Baldwin	Jas Jackson
Tenn	Jos Anderson	*Danl Smith
Ohio	John Smith	Thos Worthington

Representatives:

NH	Silas Betton	Saml Tenney	*C Ellis
	David Hough	T W Thompson	
Mass	Jacob Crowninshield	Richd Cutts	Eben. Seaver
	Wm Stedman	Jos B Varnum	Phanuel Bishop
	*Orchard Cook	Jos Barker	*Isaiah L Green
	*Barnabas Bidwell	*John Chandler	Peleg Wadsworth
	Saml Taggart	Seth Hastings	*Josiah Quincy
	*Wm Ely	*Jeremiah Nelson	
Vt	Gideon Olin	Jas Elliot	*Jas Fisk
	Martin Chittenden		
R I	Nehemiah Knight	Jos Stanton	
Conn	John Cotton Smith	Saml W Dana	Benj Talmadge
	John Davenport Jr	*Jonathan O Mosely	
	*Timothy Pitken Jr	*Lewis B Sturges	
NY	*John Blake Jr	*Silas Halsey	*Uri Tracy
	Henry W Livingston	*Josiah Masters	*John Russell
	*Peter Saily	Thos Sammons	David Thomas
	*Martin G Shuneman	*Eliphalet Wickes	
	Philip Van Cortlandt	Killian K Van Rensselaer	

	Danl C Verplanck	*Nathan Williams	
	*Gurdon S Mumford	Geo Clinton Jr	
NJ	Henry Southard	Ebenezer Elmer	*John Lambert
	Wm Helms	Jas Sloan	*Ezra Darby
Pa	Jos Clay	Mich'l Leib	Andrew Gregg
	John Rea	David Bard	Saml Smith
	*Christian Lower	John Whitehill	Isaac Anderson
	*John Hamilton	John Smilie	Jacob Richards
	*Jas Kelly	Wm Findley	*John Pugh
	Frederick Conrad	Robt Brown	*Robt Whitehill
Dela	*Jas M Broom		
Md	Jos H Nicholson	Nicholas R Moore	Wm McCreery
	*Patrick Magruder	Roger Nelson	John Campbell
	*Leonard Covington	*Chas Goldsborough	John Archer
Va	Jos Lewis Jr	John Smith	*John Claiborne
	Thos Newton Jr	John Randolph	John Dawson
	Thos M Randolph	John Clopton	Alex'r Wilson
	Matthew Clay	Edwin Gray	Walter Jones
	Peterson Goodwyn	Abram Trigg	*Burwell Basset
	Christopher Clark	*John Morrow	John W Eppes
	David Holmes	Philip R Thompson	*Jas M Garnett
	John G Jackson		
Ky	Geo M Bedinger	Matthew Lyon	Matthew Walton
	John Boyle	John Fowler	Thos Sandford
NC	Nath'l Macon	Wm Blackledge	Jas Holland
	Richd Stanford	Thos Wynns	*Thos Blount
	Marmaduke Williams	Jos Winston	Willis Alston Jr
	*Duncan MacFarland	Nath'l Alexander	*Thos Kenan
SC	*Robt Marion	Wm Butler	Levi Casey
	*David R Williams	*O'Brien Smith	Richd Winn
	Thos Moore	*Elias Earle	
Ga	Peter Early	Jos Bryan	*Cowles Mead
	David Meriwether		
Tenn	Geo W Campbell	Wm Dickson	John Rhea
Ohio	Jeremiah Morrow	*new mbrs	

Mon Dec 9, 1805

Dr Nathaniel Alexander, elected Gov of NC. Luther Martin, esq, has rsgn'd the ofc of Atty Genrl of Md.

Address of the Gov of N Carolina, to the Leg, Nov 19, 1805. Subj: Acts & journals of the last Congress.   -Jas Turner.

Partnership of John Crow & Thos C Wright, is dissolved by mutual consent; Wright will continue the business in Gtwn.

New York - St Andrews Soc to erect a monument, val $400; to the memory of Genrl Alex'r Hamilton, on the spot where he fell.

Orphans Crt of Anne Arundel Co, Md - sale of late dwelling plantation of Randolph Brandt Latimer, decd, in Chas Co, & debt of prsnl est of said decd -Richd H Harwood-adm, Annapolis, Md.

Luther Martin, esq, has rsgn'd the ofc of Atty Genrl of Md. John Scott, esq, is likely to succeed him. Baltimore, Md, Dec 6.

WED DEC 11, 1805
Sale by auction - prsnl prop of Wm Smilie, decd, at his late dwelling nr the Navy Yd. -Henry Ingle, adm.

Orphans Crt of Wash Co, DC. Dec 11, 1805. Prsnl est of Stanley Byus, late of Wash Co, decd. -T H Gilliss, exc.

Ltr from Henry Toulmin, Judge in Miss Terr, to sec of State, dated Jul 6, 1805. Subj: vessels paying 12% ad valorem on their cargo at Mobile by Spanish ofcrs; these vessels are bound to & clearing out of Ft Stoddert.

Ltr from Lt Wm Wilson to Gov Robt Williams, dated Point Coupee, Sep 5, 1805. Subj: Rescue of Reuben, Nathan & Saml Kemper from a party of Spanish subjects; taken by force from their residence at Pinckneyville.

FRI DEC 13, 1805
Ranaway - Jane, mulatto, age abt 22 yrs, from Frederick Spangler, living in Harrisonsburg, Rockingham Co, Va.

John Murdoch, Gtwn, is authorised to collect all debts due to est of John Dunlap, late of Gtwn, decd.

Orphans Crt of PG Co, Md-order to sell all prsnl est of Elijah Wood, late of PG Co, decd. -Isabella Wood & Osborn Belt Jr, adms.

Wm H Cabell is elected Gov of Va.

Ltr from Chas Pinckney, Mnstr at Madrid to sec of State, dated Aug 1805. List of Americ vessels captured by the Spaniards; vessels sent into Algeziras for adjudication:

Brig	*Anne Isabel*	Williams Mstr	Va
Brig	*Dido*	Shail Mstr	Marblehead
Brig	*Vereries Pesa*		
Ship	*Mary*	Robt Stevenson	
Ship	*Eagle*	Nehemech Shaler	Liverpool
Brig	*Jefferson*	Simon Bahmond	
Brig	*Polly & Nancy*	John Croan	Balt
Schr	*Molengue*	John Waterman	New York
Schr	*Leffen*	Wm Maret	Va
Brig	*Diana*	Silvester Simmons	New Haven.

Ltr from Lt Jos J Maxwell, commanding Gun Boat No. 3, to Cmdor Rodgers; dated Harbor of Syracuse, Jul 3, 1805. Subj: Jun 15th last, I was brought to by 4 Spanish gun boats; they brought me into Algeziras; I sailed from Gibraltar on Jun 18th.

MON DEC 16, 1805

Henry Hill Jr, Consul of U S for Island of Cuba, residnt of Havanna, certifies that John L Cranston, late Master of schnr, *Caroline* of Charleston; May 14 was captured by his Britannic Majesty's Ship of War *Fortune,* Henry Vancitart, Cmder, who took possession of said schnr, plundered same & returned it on May 25. He headed for Charleston & on Jul 15 was boarded by a Felucca pirate commanded by Paul Cazafranca who took his vessel & robbed him of all cargo; dropped at Mantua Pavola, where for promise of paying $100 Cranston secured a boat. Andrew Arbree, mate; Wm Wood & John Judson seamen of said schnr. [Havanna, Aug 19, 1805, Henry Hill Jr.]

Documents signed before Henry Hill Jr, Cnslate of the U S island of Cuba, L S; protests signed in Havanna by: John L Cranston, late mstr of schnr *Caroline* of Charleston; Andrew Arbree, mate; Wm Wood & John Judson, seamen. On Aug 19, 1805; John Date, late mate of the Brig *Success* of NY; Nicholas Brum, mstr; John Fuller & Josiah Pelt, seamen; Jas Ferguson & John Smith, passengers on Jul 31, 1805; Henry Palmer, mstr of the brig *Jason* of Phil; Nath'l Houston, Chief Mate on Aug 20, 1805 at Havanna. Jacob Paiddrick, ctzn of the U S, born in Camden Co, NC, late mate of the schnr *Mary* of Camden; Stephen Charles, mstr; John Davis & Jeremiah Greave, both ctzns of U S & late mariners of schnr *Mary* onun 14, 1805. John Evans, mstr of ship *Eliza,* of Norfolk; Chas Simmons Jr & Edw Lowrie, seamen, on Aug 2, 1805.

Ranaway, Ben & Dick, negroes; Ben purch'd from Jos Ennalls, Dick, from Mr Driver. Deliver to our residence in Sumner Co on Station Camp, Tenn.
                                        -Jas Norris & Jas Laudadale.

WED DEC 18. 1805

Merchants of town of Boston, Dec 3: Jas Lloyd Jr, Hon J C Jones, Hon Geo Cabot, Arnold Weiles, David Green, Hon T H Perkins & David Sears.
                                        -Isaac Winslow Jr, sec.

Affidavit of Wm Flanagan Jr, of Wilkinson Co, Miss Terr. Aug 21st last, Spanish light horses, Lt Glascock, came over the line of demarkation to his hse on Tichtau Creek; took him & his wife abt 5 miles; his wife was dismissed the next morning & taken home by her bro who was sent after them by her fr; I returned home on foot. The party consisted of: John Glascock, Benj Le Near, Abraham Jones s/o Capt Kennada, Wm Lee, John Bates, ____Hale, Obiel Brewer, ____Conner & others. Signed [his mark] Wm Flanagan, Sep 7, 1805, town of Washington, Miss Terr. Note-the within deponent, Thos Holden, says that it was reported that Wm Flanagan Sr, had killed a certain John Sharp; Wm Flanagan Jr is nph to Wm Flanagan Sr & son-in-law to said Thos Holden. Signed, Thos Rodney. Affidavit of Thos Holden Sr of the county of Wilkinson, Miss Terr; part of Capt Jones' company came over to his hse & enquired for Wm Flanagan Sr & as they said, had killed a certain Jos Sharp. Signed, Thos Holden Sr, Sep 7, 1805, at the town of Washington, Miss Terr. Affidavit of Arthur Cobb Jr signed before Joshua Baker, (J P); Wilkinson Co, Miss Terr: Sep 3. He was at the hse of Saml Kemper; pistol was left belonging he believes to Ira Cook Kneeland.

Affidavit of Wm Westberry before Joshua Baker, (J P), Sep 3. He saw 5 men actually beating Saml Kemper with a stick. Affidavit of Jas Latta, before Joshua Baker, (J P), Sep 3. He heard some men requesting to see Saml Kemper. Affidavit of John Atkinson, Henry Gamheart, Richd Richardson & John Whittaker, before Joshua Baker, (J P), Sep 3. They were at the hse of Nathan Kemper. Affidavit of Nathan Kemper, before Ebenezer Cooley, (J P); Terr of Orleans, county of Point Coupe, Sep 5, 1805. Sep 3, he & his bro, Reuben, were seized by 18 or 20 men & taken as far as the plantation of Mr. Abraham Haton; found their bro, Saml Kemper, in custody; they were delivered to Capt Soloman Alston; he recognized the following persons who surrounded his hse: Minor Butler & his bro-in-law Ritchie, Abraham Horton, svr'l negroes, all inhabitants of the Miss Terr. Affidavit of Saml Kemper; same as above. Affidavit of Wm Barker; same as above. Affidavit of Adam Bingaman, same as above. Affidavit of Reuben Kemper; same as above; he recognized Louis Ritchie, Miner Butler, Abraham Horton, Jas Horton, Marcus Carr, Jas Say & Philip Say. The 3 bros were put on board a Piroque, commanded by Wm Breher, & manned by Chas Stuart, Adam Bengaman, John Ratcliff, Geo Rowe & John Morris.

FRI DEC 20, 1805

Ltr-Campte, dist of Natchitoches, Sep 14, 1805. Appeared before me, John Sibley, Magistrate for Co of Natchitoches. Mary Pulegie Grape Fontineau, age 46 yrs, believes she was born at ancient Caddo Village, [French inhabitants] & had lived there with her family. Other inhabitants of Campte who appeared before Sibley: Julian Beson, age 57; Louis Lamalaty, age 66 yrs, saw Mr Grappe & his family; Mary Louisa Brevell, wid of Antoine Grillette, decd, after she mrd Mr G. They went to ancient Village of Caddo; John Baptiste Grappe, of Campte, went with his fr to Caddo Village. Francis Grappe, born nr Caddo Village on the Red Rvr remembers a Mr Francois Hervey, a French gentleman, who lived there. Gaspard Bodin & Andrew Chamar, of Natchitoches, Madam Bodin who was with them spoke Spanish, & Lewis Bodin; Francis Roban, age 21 yrs. Story includes assault on Nathan Kemper & his bros, Reuben & on Saml Kemper in his own hse, & other incidents in the area. Sworn before John Sibley, (J P). Signed - John Horn. Julian Beson, age 57 yrs, inhabitant of Campte, Nachitoches Co, appeared before John Sibley, (J P); Sep 16, 1805. He too went with his fr to Caddo Village. Louis Lamalaty, age 66 yrs, of same Co, appeared before John Sibley, (J P), Sep 16, 1805. He was born at the place now cld Natchitoches; he saw Mr Grappe & his family when they returned from Caddo Village; he has knowledge of a Mr Verge & a Mr Bourne, who lived in the area. Mary Louisa Brevell, widow of Antoine Brevell, decd, appeared before John Sibley, (J P). She said that after she mrd Mr Brevell, they went to Caddo Village for abt 18 mos. Mr Grappe was a French Commandant. Her mark - Sep 16, 1805, Natchitoches. John Baptiste Grappe, inhabitant of Campte, age 42 yrs; went with his fr to Caddo Village; remembers the French families of Mr Verge & Mr De Coto, living at Yatasse Point. Appeared before John Sibley, (J P), Sep 16, 1805. Also appeared, same place & time: Francis Grappe, age 57; he remembers a French man, Mr Francois Hervey, who was the first white man that settled in the ancient Caddo Village. His fr was Commandant of the place for many yrs & succeeded by Mr Gloso. Gaspard Bodin & Andrew Chamar appeared before John Sibley, (J P); all of Natchitoches, on Oct 2, 1805. They were travelling from Natchitoches to Oppolousa & met with 5 Spanish sldrs. Also appeared before the same on Oct 3, 1805, Francis Roban of Natchitoches, age 21 yrs. He was in the employ of Messrs Oliver & Case & was with Jos Lucas when they stopped for the night at the plantation of a Mr Pisot.

John A Burford was found not guilty for robbery & attempted murder of Mr Peter, of Bank of Col.   -Alexandria, Dec 18.

Mrd: Mr Jos Cassin to Miss Eliza Wilcox, both of Wash, by Rev Mr Matthews, Dec 18.

Orphans Crt of St Mary's Co, Md.   Dec 14, 1805.   Prsnl est of Augustine Spalding, late of St Mary's Co, decd.   -Barbara Spalding, adm.

Order from Orphans Crt of PG Co, Md, will be sold: 2 women & 2 chldrn, hsehld furn & some cattle at Mrs Ann Greenwell's Tavern in PG Co, prop of Justiman Greenwell, decd.   -Ann Greenwell, adm.

MON DEC 23, 1805

J J Rey, by repeated misfortunes in a mercantile career & stript of his prop, seeks a new support of life, teaching.   -Gtwn & Wash.

Public sale: 900 acs in Jefferson Co, Va, cld "*The Rocks*", formerly the prop of Jas Wormeley, esq; also "*The Meadow Farm*" -300 acs; & 115 acs nr the former.
                                  -Ferdinando Fairfax, Chas Town, Va

Furnished lodgings. F St nr St Patrick's chr.   -Hady Hogan,

Hse of Reps. Petition of Nath'l Ellicott, praying that the Post ofc at Colchester, Va, be discontinued & an ofc established at Occoquan.

WED DEC 25, 1805

Merchants meet at NY; John Broome, esq, chrmn; committee:

John Murray	Matthey Clarkson	John B Coles
Archibald Gracie	Wm Edgar	Benj G Minturn
Wm Bayard	Gulian Ludlow	Wm W Woolsey
John P Mumford	Henry Post	Renselaer Havens
Eben. Stevens	Chas Wright	Wm Lovett
Geo Griswold	Wynant Van Zant Jr	Wm Henderson
Benj Baily	John R Livingston	Isaac Clason
John Broome	John Ferrers, sec.	

Thos Terry, of Buckingham Co, Va, found gold while ploughing.
-Lynchburg Vir. paper

Norfolk, Dec 14. In the *"Geo Barclay"* from Liverpool, came passenger Col John Mercer, late one of the comrs for the U S at Paris.

Fisher Ames elected Pres of Harvard Univ

FRI DEC 27, 1805
Indians have arrived from Missouri-do not give them wine or strong drink as they may become troublesome. By order of sec of War, H Rogers-Wash.

Public sale: Right, title, int of Ignatius Boone in sq 907 with 3 hses at suit of Thos H Hanson, Overton Carr & Aquilla Johns for use of Azariah Gaton & Nichs. L Queen. Int of Thos Jones in lot 55 sq 651 at suit of Saml Baker. Right, title, int of Wm Dyer in lot 6 sq 906 at suit of Saml Baker. Right, title, int of Wm Coglan in lot 10 sq 224 at suit of John M Gantt & Robt Brent. Right, title, int of John Harrison in part of sq 432 at suit of Sarah Crookshanks & Chas Glover, adms of Jno Crookshanks. Rght, title, int of John A Burford in part of lot 1 sq 881 at suit of Wm S Gantt. Rght, title, int of John Addison, 200 acs cld *"Gesberry Manor"* at suit of John W Pratt for use of Thos Pratt. Rght, title, int of John S Higden in lot 5 sq 118, suit of Walter S Chandler. Danl C Brent-mrshl.

Ranaway-Dick, negro, from Henry Woodward, living in Ann Arundel Co, Md. Reward-$30.

MON DEC 30, 1805
The Brig, *Mary*, Capt Crocker, arrv'd from Nantz this morning; passenger, Pinckney Horry, esq. Charleston, Dec 14.

Apptd by Govnr & Cncl of Md-Wm Pinckney, esq, Atty Genrl of Md, vice, Luther Martin, esq, rsgn'd.

—A—

Abbe, 109, 134
Abbot, 115
Aborn, 41, 48, 101, 236, 250
Abraham, 88, 106
Abrahams, 84
Abram, 49, 102, 110
Abrams, 115
Aburn, 84
Adair, 265, 266
Adams, 1, 10, 18, 22, 23, 28, 30, 42, 79, 97, 103, 114, 118, 120, 122, 127, 128, 145, 148, 150, 170, 175, 177, 200, 238, 245, 248, 250, 252, 253, 261, 266
Adamson, 81, 86, 130
Addington, 97, 252
Addison, 22, 24, 27, 55, 68, 77, 80, 88, 89, 90, 120, 127, 187, 192, 225, 234, 272
Addletong, 19
Adkins, 29
Adlin, 139
Adlum, 139
Agilvie, 77
Agnew, 112
Aiken, 191
Aikin, 54, 88
Air, 107
Aisquith, 254
Aitkin, 192
Albemarle, 31, 51, 200, 225, 260
Albers, 81
Albert, 45
Albright, 14, 142
Alburtis, 123
Alcock, 23, 205
Alden, 117
Alder, 14
Alderson, 73
Aldey, 245
Aldrich, 181, 205
Alexander, 8, 22, 24, 30, 31, 42, 46, 80, 90, 91, 92, 114, 118, 120, 136, 147, 165, 194, 195, 196, 200, 205, 206, 225, 229, 230, 234, 261, 267
Alexiowna, 40
Alexis, 49, 96
Alford, 10
Alger, 82, 100, 176
Allan, 25
Allein, 34, 190
Allen, 9, 23, 46, 65, 67, 73, 78, 81, 92, 96, 105, 109, 134, 149, 169, 176, 181, 185, 202, 205, 254
Alley, 43, 94, 198
Allison, 14, 45, 96, 187, 246
Alliston, 118
Allston, 5, 6, 147, 204
Ally, 200
Alricks, 161
Alsop, 261
Alsquith, 145
Alston, 8, 64, 105, 107, 190, 204, 267, 270
Altinson, 42
Amblet, 176
Ambroise, 193, 196
Ames, 97, 164, 200, 272
Amory, 172
Andaulle, 172
Anderson, 5, 7, 11, 90, 100, 101, 117, 124, 126, 127, 128, 146, 147, 156, 168, 169, 172, 178, 235, 236, 249, 252, 266, 267
Andrew, 30
Andrews, 18, 32, 38, 86, 122, 128, 213, 260, 265
Andrey, 31
Angue, 96
Angus, 169
Ansart, 220
Ansley, 92
Antes, 53, 55, 139
Appleton, 48, 85, 101, 122, 187, 236, 237
Applewhite, 257, 258
Arazer, 138
Artree, 269
Arcambal, 49, 102
Archer, 27, 36, 39, 64, 146, 169, 207, 257, 259, 267
Arden, 97
Ardrey, 235
Aris, 41
Armistead, 30
Armour, 261
Armstead, 114, 227
Armstrong, 4, 10, 24, 71, 72, 89, 105, 137, 140, 194, 237, 256, 258
Arnold, 17, 20, 45, 53, 156, 176, 204, 242, 247, 248
Arthur, 27
Asbury, 45, 81
Ash, 250
Ashe, 7, 10, 111, 113, 204
Ashley, 120, 176
Ashman, 30
Ashton, 91, 92, 106, 135
Asley, 200
Astir, 240
Astley, 134
Atkins, 92
Atkinson, 151, 211, 254, 270
Atlee, 65
Attwood, 81
Atwater, 7, 41
Atwood, 25, 45, 61
Auldio, 236
Auldji, 48, 100
Aupaumut, 159
Aurent, 149
Austin, 81, 89, 95, 109, 134, 138, 150, 171, 183, 198, 200, 203
Austis, 138
Aveilhe, 141, 163
Avilhe, 193
Ayres, 92, 194

—B—

Bache, 2, 170, 186
Backham, 156

Backman, 48
Backus, 50, 103, 196
Bacoa, 204
Bacon, 7, 16, 18, 63, 144, 198
Baden, 40, 251
Badger, 168, 213
Badollet, 196
Baggot, 61
Bahmond, 268
Bailenger, 27
Bailey, 3, 46, 106, 121, 145, 170, 178, 212, 235, 241, 256
Bailly, 225
Baily, 5, 63, 71, 80, 81, 271
Bainacoat, 257
Bainbridge, 12, 31, 96, 167, 168, 245, 249, 252, 254
Bainbringe, 178
Baker, 31, 36, 39, 47, 68, 71, 76, 82, 100, 118, 120, 124, 127, 145, 154, 162, 169, 176, 181, 187, 200, 209, 224, 234, 237, 261, 269, 270, 272
Balch, 27, 39, 85, 148, 174
Baldonton, 244
Baldwin, 2, 5, 38, 78, 90, 92, 103, 109, 115, 125, 134, 137, 138, 146, 176, 206, 253, 266
Balfour, 169
Ball, 17, 68, 93, 176, 203
Ballard, 106
Ballenger, 38
Ballentine, 226
Baltimore, 200
Banker, 201
Banks, 39, 124, 186
Baptist, 168
Baptiste, 48, 101, 102, 129, 141
Baquenault, 250
Barack, 176
Barber, 56, 131, 215
Barbour, 23

Barclay, 37, 49, 83, 172
Barcley, 101
Bard, 1, 146, 266
Barde, 30
Bare, 110
Baritz, 49, 102
Barker, 16, 17, 122, 123, 183, 262, 266, 270
Barkley, 137
Barlett, 80
Barlow, 243, 262
Barnabeau, 49
Barnabeu, 102
Barnard, 109, 119, 176
Barnes, 4, 21, 30, 35, 47, 82, 85, 100, 101, 119, 134, 174, 187
Barnet, 19, 124, 163, 236
Barnett, 62, 85, 100, 101, 187
Barney, 3, 17, 76, 99, 160, 161, 250
Barns, 109, 166, 176
Barnum, 154
Barnwell, 91, 112
Baron, 74, 252
Barr, 260
Barrein, 176
Barrell, 129
Barret, 84
Barrett, 217
Barron, 3, 30, 45, 158, 162, 169, 205, 206, 218, 219, 245, 248, 252
Barry, 17, 18, 22, 56, 86, 119, 123, 126, 141, 144, 150, 159, 193, 198, 206, 221, 250
Bartgiss, 122, 124
Bartlet, 205
Bartlett, 3
Barton, 28, 29, 35, 47, 67, 80, 117, 120, 135, 160, 172, 211, 213
Bartram, 105
Barwise, 216
Bass, 156
Basset, 47, 262, 267

Bassett, 19, 28, 129, 217, 228
Bastian, 161
Bates, 196, 269
Bath, 27
Batton, 185
Bausman, 219
Bavington, 42
Bay, 73
Bayard, 19, 64, 70, 72, 183, 184, 216, 249, 266, 271
Bayley, 147
Baylies, 9
Baylor, 128
Bayly, 21, 61, 76, 188, 239
Baynton, 16, 233
Beachum, 51
Beal, 30, 55, 95, 193
Beale, 39, 61
Beall, 4, 9, 22, 51, 72, 81, 92, 95, 113, 119, 121, 128, 131, 158, 179, 181, 187, 224, 235, 239
Bealle, 90, 214
Bean, 252
Beanes, 197
Beans, 187, 236
Bear, 5, 115
Beardslee, 204
Beatty, 7, 87, 90, 112, 148, 166, 177, 199, 222, 262
Beaufort, 52
Beauharnois, 94
Beavers, 140
Beck, 132, 248, 255
Beckitt, 76
Beckley, 70, 107, 187, 191, 203, 230, 234, 248
Beckwith, 236
Becraft, 136
Bedel, 98, 104
Bedford, 42, 43, 47, 77, 100, 216, 251
Bedinger, 142, 147, 267
Bee, 20, 28, 29, 47, 100
Beeler, 142
Beers, 20, 41
Beeston, 141

Begg, 147
Begley, 147
Belcher, 41, 176
Belfour, 105
Bell, 30, 83, 99, 113, 127, 206, 228, 231, 250
Bellechaffe, 201
Bellybreaker, 55
Belt, 22, 24, 37, 55, 80, 90, 106, 108, 170, 179, 199, 268
Belzunce, 227
Ben, 12
Benack, 167
Benedix, 112
Bengaman, 270
Benger, 165
Benkson, 68
Bennet, 30, 141, 163, 220
Bennett, 33, 34, 96, 107, 109, 169
Bensen, 260
Benson, 19, 28, 47, 209, 224
Bent, 176
Benthuisen, 150
Bentley, 203
Benton, 7
Beresford, 263
Bergen, 7, 26, 201
Berkeley, 30, 34, 200
Berry, 46, 206, 239, 247
Berthoud, 175
Beson, 270
Beston, 22
Bettan, 104, 146
Bette, 222
Betterton, 235
Betton, 68, 98, 179, 214, 266
Betts, 78, 157, 249
Betz, 157
Bevan, 42
Beverist, 198
Bezeler, 212
Biays, 32
Bickerson, 233
Bickley, 175, 249, 265
Bickwall, 53

Biddle, 168, 216, 249, 252, 260, 261
Bidwell, 262, 266
Bienvenu, 32
Bigelow, 6
Biggs, 50, 103
Bill, 87
Billaps, 73
Billington, 2
Billton, 172
Bindon, 25, 65, 67
Bingaman, 9, 270
Bingamin, 28
Bingham, 35, 57
Bingly, 229
Binkeley, 85
Binnet, 170
Birch, 90, 122, 256, 258
Birchett, 162
Birkhead, 54
Bisco, 168
Biscoe, 125, 234
Bishop, 5, 6, 7, 35, 41, 51, 63, 82, 120, 123, 140, 146, 154, 163, 216, 226, 262, 266
Bissell, 30, 124
Blachard, 172
Black, 260
Blackbourn, 20
Blackburn, 34, 83, 119, 129, 209
Blackiston, 37
Blackledge, 147, 190, 267
Blacklock, 32, 238
Blackston, 214
Blagden, 16, 86, 129, 132, 143, 171, 193, 207, 230, 235
Blagge, 141, 249
Blaine, 169
Blair, 23, 72, 134, 226, 247
Blaire, 254
Blake, 30, 41, 47, 48, 59, 77, 82, 84, 88, 89, 96, 100, 107, 137, 140, 183, 184, 254, 259, 262, 264, 266
Blakeley, 169

Blakely, 48, 96, 101, 216
Blakeman, 34
Blanch, 112
Blanchard, 89
Bland, 254, 261
Blauveit, 122
Bleakly, 67
Blechford, 257, 259
Bleecker, 20, 127
Bliss, 182
Blodget, 106, 116, 171, 175, 187, 204, 235, 265
Bloodworth, 84
Bloom, 85, 131
Bloomer, 144
Bloomfield, 95, 112
Blount, 145, 165, 177, 190, 204, 235, 249, 252, 267
Blue, 17, 21, 30
Blyth, 54
Blythe, 11
Board, 256
Boardman, 78
Boarman, 171, 187, 191, 238
Boden, 81
Bodin, 270
Bodley, 39
Boehm, 16
Boerum, 261
Bogart, 25, 66, 67
Bogert, 167, 212
Bohrer, 148
Boileau, 10
Bokee, 144
Boland, 250
Bollman, 102
Bolls, 14
Bolton, 176
Bonaparte, 94, 127, 139, 236
Bond, 14, 29, 49, 101, 103, 120, 145, 185, 187, 194, 208, 257, 259
Bone, 173
Bonifant, 99
Bonnau, 145
Boone, 81, 173, 174, 187, 272

Boote, 179
Bootes, 9, 79, 119
Booth, 21, 96, 104, 150, 199
Boots, 23, 136
Bordman, 117
Bore, 201, 262
Borham, 14
Boss, 98
Boston, 16, 23, 122, 257, 258
Boude, 1, 64
Boudinot, 7, 20, 21
Bouligny, 262
Bouman, 132
Bounton, 261
Bouquet, 207
Bour, 53
Bourne, 19, 28, 29, 47, 48, 82, 101, 237, 270
Boush, 156
Boutz, 102
Bowdoin, 89, 128, 131, 171, 183, 204
Bowen, 47, 53, 98, 100, 176, 180, 253
Bower, 32, 210
Bowers, 211, 212
Bowie, 54, 56, 75, 81, 90, 110, 113, 134, 146, 152, 165, 173, 187, 199, 207, 208, 221, 230, 238, 242, 244, 263, 264
Bowles, 136
Bowling, 239, 256, 257, 259
Bowman, 73, 166, 170
Bowne, 20, 127
Bowyer, 158
Boyd, 22, 24, 36, 60, 80, 90, 116, 139, 158, 170, 187, 192, 203, 213, 217, 234, 263
Boyer, 187
Boyes, 214
Boyland, 258
Boyle, 8, 142, 147, 160, 205, 251, 267
Boyne, 187
Brace, 2, 3, 9, 81, 109, 134

Brack, 259
Brackenridge, 11
Brackett, 170
Brackinridge, 146
Brackman, 42
Bradbury, 9
Brade, 150
Bradford, 15, 25, 28, 47, 53, 65, 67, 86, 100, 126, 128, 142, 187, 236, 253
Bradfute, 251
Bradley, 3, 41, 47, 90, 99, 109, 113, 123, 138, 145, 185, 187, 204, 223, 230, 235, 249, 266
Brady, 215, 260
Brag, 124
Bragg, 69
Brahan, 30
Brainard, 210
Brandon, 14
Brashears, 120, 264
Brashers, 223
Brashiers, 58
Brazer, 183
Breckenridge, 90, 265
Breese, 49, 101
Breher, 270
Brenan, 157
Brengle, 50, 136, 138
Brent, 8, 22, 24, 25, 29, 30, 35, 40, 45, 47, 51, 53, 54, 57, 59, 61, 62, 64, 68, 70, 73, 76, 77, 79, 80, 83, 86, 88, 89, 90, 98, 100, 104, 111, 112, 116, 121, 128, 129, 130, 133, 135, 139, 141, 152, 164, 171, 174, 175, 177, 181, 185, 191, 193, 195, 198, 201, 205, 209, 210, 213, 214, 223, 232, 234, 235, 237, 238, 240, 241, 242, 243, 246, 248, 252, 254, 255, 256, 257, 260, 263, 264, 265, 272
Brerely, 20

Breston, 234
Brevard, 181
Brevell, 270
Brevitt, 140
Brevoort, 31
Brewer, 125, 191, 265, 269
Breyfogel, 14
Brice, 152, 187, 217
Brickell, 220
Bridges, 241
Briggs, 121, 163, 180, 198, 223
Brigham, 1, 58, 107, 252
Bright, 16
Brightwell, 252
Brindley, 10, 30, 261
Brinton, 44
Briscoe, 175, 178
Bristow, 135
Britts, 140
Broadbent, 237
Brobson, 88
Brobst, 127
Broch, 19
Brock, 259
Brockenbrough, 166, 185
Brodhag, 150
Brodie, 132
Broeck, 4, 261
Brohawn, 37, 112, 129
Bromley, 213, 230
Bronson, 127
Brook, 199, 201
Brooke, 24, 70, 112, 113, 128, 162, 170, 172, 238, 246, 251
Brookes, 44, 187, 195, 230
Brooks, 25, 30, 65, 67, 125, 173, 203
Broom, 246, 262, 267
Broome, 87, 164, 173, 271
Broomfield, 33
Broughton, 249
Broughtou, 128
Brown, 1, 5, 7, 8, 12, 19, 24, 42, 44, 53, 54, 58, 61, 64, 68, 73, 75, 80, 86, 88,

89, 90, 105, 110, 113, 114, 122, 125, 128, 131, 132, 133, 135, 146, 156, 161, 162, 163, 170, 171, 176, 177, 187, 191, 194, 197, 201, 202, 213, 229, 235, 237, 241, 251, 254, 255, 257, 259, 263, 267
Browne, 105, 110, 115, 151
Brownell, 46
Brownson, 31
Bruce, 146, 156, 164, 244
Bruff, 179
Bruin, 50, 103
Brull, 79
Brum, 269
Brunson, 150
Brush, 213, 250
Brussels, 26
Brussit, 55
Bryan, 8, 50, 57, 148, 156, 200, 234, 267
Bryant, 228
Bryden, 23
Buchan, 50, 78, 187, 232
Buchanaan, 260
Buchanan, 48, 85, 101, 109, 145, 224, 237
Buck, 31, 158, 257, 259
Buckens, 19
Buckingham, 257, 259
Buckley, 15, 48, 187
Buckly, 157
Budicomb, 187
Bulkely, 32
Bull, 14, 88, 260
Buller, 251
Bulloch, 19, 62, 176
Bullock, 6
Bulls, 62
Bullus, 110, 111, 235
Bully, 257
Bulty, 259
Bundy, 162
Bunker, 240
Bunkers, 130
Buntin, 218
Bunting, 37

Bunyie, 246
Buonaparte, 34
Burbridge, 143
Burch, 59, 108, 224, 234, 239, 243
Burchan, 179, 184
Burchett, 87
Burd, 135
Burdett, 41
Bureau, 97
Burford, 75, 86, 109, 242, 271, 272
Burgess, 14, 57, 246
Burke, 4, 77, 85, 147
Burkhart, 50
Burlingame, 207
Burnore, 256
Burne, 149
Burnet, 105, 162
Burnett, 41, 177, 186
Burns, 80, 90, 231, 234
Burr, 18, 21, 46, 76, 99, 169, 183, 186
Burress, 240
Burrill, 31, 98
Burrils, 184
Burroughs, 116
Burrowes, 112
Burrows, 111, 135, 164, 220, 221, 250
Burt, 4, 58, 125
Burton, 181, 200, 229
Burwell, 127
Bury, 55
Bushel, 187
Busher, 73
Bussard, 104, 185
Bussay, 104
Butler, 5, 17, 30, 54, 56, 62, 64, 73, 77, 96, 116, 132, 136, 146, 147, 169, 179, 188, 201, 220, 243, 249, 256, 263, 267, 270
Butters, 3
Byrd, 49, 102, 109, 115, 125, 151
Byrens, 258
Byrn, 39
Byrne, 63, 111, 122, 147, 175
Byron, 37

Byus, 112, 129, 234, 258

—C—

Cabarrus, 202, 249, 265
Cabell, 8, 31, 64, 181, 205, 268
Cabot, 80, 145, 200, 269
Cabrera, 238, 240
Caffery, 143
Caffin, 135
Cain, 142
Cairnes, 42
Calbert, 42
Calder, 251
Caldwell, 15, 38, 42, 47, 48, 53, 55, 56, 75, 84, 100, 110, 115, 175, 186, 194, 199, 203, 210, 235, 240, 260, 265
Calhoun, 149, 262
Callaghan, 250
Callender, 107, 116
Callier, 141
Callis, 248, 255
Calvert, 11, 30, 52, 73, 115, 158, 187, 192
Calvet, 9
Calvit, 14
Cameron, 220, 223
Camp, 33, 187
Campbell, 20, 27, 36, 39, 53, 56, 59, 64, 111, 118, 146, 147, 151, 169, 172, 175, 187, 205, 207, 208, 233, 238, 244, 245, 248, 256, 258, 264, 267
Campfield, 7
Cannon, 205
Cantine, 146
Cantrell, 201
Carcaud, 56, 233
Carey, 70, 76, 105, 136
Cargill, 172
Carhart, 250
Carlan, 225
Carleton, 56, 60, 93, 233

Carlile, 98, 179
Carlisle, 27, 256, 258, 260
Carlton, 121, 242
Carnalt, 125
Carmichael, 125, 204
Carmichaels, 79
Carne, 144
Carnes, 62
Carney, 132, 147
Carol, 24
Caroline, 259
Carpenter, 12, 16, 23, 61, 110, 115, 130, 190, 192, 217, 230, 231, 235, 239
Carr, 10, 23, 51, 56, 71, 106, 111, 144, 169, 181, 189, 258, 270, 272
Carre, 105, 157
Carrere, 172
Carrick, 262
Carriere, 250
Carrigan, 231
Carrington, 15, 72
Carrol, 12, 13, 22, 33, 54, 80, 86, 152, 188, 220, 229
Carroll, 25, 33, 54, 79, 93, 94, 106, 116, 126, 129, 133, 135, 139, 141, 171, 187, 193, 215, 221, 222, 238, 248, 265
Carson, 30, 154, 202
Carter, 3, 8, 89, 93, 94, 116, 135, 143, 160, 182, 187, 201
Carteret, 182, 200
Carty, 45, 81
Caruthers, 166
Cary, 51, 72
Case, 271
Casenave, 75, 93
Casenev, 187
Casenove, 81
Casey, 96, 136, 168, 187, 267
Casine, 128
Caspeder, 55
Cass, 97
Cassenave, 130

Cassiaeves, 222
Cassin, 152, 153, 154, 159, 160, 181, 183, 211, 212, 214, 220, 225, 230, 271
Casson, 213
Casting, 45
Caswell, 42, 262
Cate, 97
Cathalan, 41, 48, 85, 101, 236
Cathcart, 49, 85, 101, 114, 162, 163
Caton, 172
Cattenhead, 116
Causland, 250
Cavacheche, 106
Cave, 252
Cavendish, 97
Caw, 23
Cazafranca, 269
Cazean, 25
Cazeau, 66, 67
Cellers, 56
Chaberlain, 107
Chace, 187
Chadwick, 172
Chafe, 4
Challis, 156
Chalmers, 213, 229, 230, 235, 243
Chamar, 270
Chamberlain, 6, 14, 37, 42, 146
Chambers, 44, 52, 158, 196, 230
Chamblin, 10
Champion, 2, 134
Champlin, 3, 5, 53
Champmon, 258
Chamrion, 78
Chancellor, 33, 219
Chancey, 39
Chandler, 32, 145, 157, 184, 226, 254, 262, 266, 272
Chapin, 118, 127
Chapman, 54, 118, 145, 205, 244
Chapmon, 256
Chapone, 90
Charle, 136
Charles, 38, 269

Charleton, 89
Charlotte, 70
Charlton, 148
Chas I, 200
Chas II, 200
Chase, 8, 46, 61, 100, 160, 165, 166, 210, 216, 228, 243, 255, 261
Chastain, 229
Chauncey, 42, 81, 96, 169
Cheetham, 212
Chejan, 258
Chelton, 234
Chenn, 93
Cherry, 34, 141, 142, 230, 235
Cheseldine, 36
Chessen, 256
Chester, 25, 42, 43, 66, 67, 74, 78, 81, 83, 109, 134
Chevale, 216
Chevallie, 168
Cheves, 107
Chew, 19, 21, 69, 80, 113, 171, 221, 264
Cheyney, 244
Child, 53
Childs, 115
Chinn, 25, 65, 67
Chipman, 5, 60, 90
Chisley, 143
Chisman, 83
Chiswell, 187
Chittenden, 107, 134, 146, 266
Choat, 256
Choate, 42
Chojan, 257
Chosson, 258
Choteau, 247
Chribbs, 82
Chricles, 124
Christie, 5, 110
Church, 48, 55, 95, 101, 160, 183, 184, 211, 236, 256
Churchman, 248
Ciaccioche, 94
Cilley, 47, 84
Cist, 235

Cither, 130
Clagett, 95, 97, 98, 116, 187, 193, 231, 239
Clagget, 104, 146
Claggett, 69, 255
Clagott, 145
Claiborne, 5, 32, 39, 50, 64, 82, 87, 103, 119, 124, 129, 147, 180, 198, 224, 225, 227, 228, 246, 262, 267
Clairborne, 171
Clare, 147
Clarendon, 200
Claret, 3
Clark, 17, 20, 25, 28, 30, 31, 32, 39, 41, 48, 50, 52, 53, 65, 67, 82, 89, 101, 103, 106, 112, 113, 121, 122, 126, 134, 137, 162, 189, 197, 201, 228, 235, 236, 238, 240, 250, 256, 262, 267
Clarke, 39, 50, 61, 68, 86, 88, 104, 106, 123, 124, 136, 148, 156, 169, 172, 194, 216, 229, 249
Clarkson, 47, 71, 82, 184, 271
Clason, 271
Claxton, 9, 11, 232, 235
Clay, 3, 4, 14, 20, 28, 30, 64, 67, 82, 87, 91, 93, 146, 147, 160, 176, 196, 227, 228, 266, 267
Clayland, 122
Cleary, 186, 244
Clemens, 265
Clement, 37, 75, 90, 98, 112, 235, 251, 259
Clements, 22, 172, 177
Clemmons, 196
Clephan, 139, 192, 213
Clerklee, 177
Cline, 176

Clingan, 127
Clinton, 23, 38, 71, 72, 90, 93, 145, 164, 206, 208, 211, 220, 266
Clole, 20
Clopton, 64, 128, 129, 146, 227, 228, 267
Cloud, 90
Cloutman, 73
Clymer, 141
Coale, 169, 253
Coales, 217
Coates, 16, 75, 81, 105
Cobb, 2, 89, 157, 269
Cobentzel, 127
Coburn, 11, 207
Cocheran, 4
Cochlin, 78
Cochran, 11, 18, 47, 70, 85, 100, 124, 192, 204, 230, 232, 253
Cochrane, 197
Cock, 81, 262
Cocke, 5, 62, 90, 146, 169, 224, 234
Cockey, 194, 255
Cocks, 30
Codman, 9, 32, 49, 102, 132
Coffin, 140
Coffyn, 237
Coglan, 272
Cogswell, 98, 104, 144, 168
Cohen, 125, 168
Cohogen, 90
Cohran, 14
Coke, 67
Colbourn, 256
Colcock, 8
Colden, 50
Cole, 25, 45, 65, 91, 182, 256, 258
Colefax, 204
Coleman, 16, 125, 170, 257, 258, 259
Colere, 241
Coles, 161, 168, 180, 260, 271
Coleton, 200
Colhoun, 111

Collard, 196, 229, 230, 235
Collin, 49, 102, 117
Collingwood, 161
Collins, 10, 15, 62, 132, 170, 181, 182, 202, 227, 258
Colman, 235
Comb, 167
Combe, 133, 173
Combs, 15, 112, 113, 142, 229, 230
Comeford, 160
Comegys, 90, 216
Coming, 224, 251
Commandant, 214
Commer, 144
Compton, 175
Comstock, 201
Conaway, 21
Condie, 63
Condit, 142, 146, 151, 266
Cone, 25, 65, 67
Coningham, 116, 182, 194, 235
Conklin, 92
Connell, 172
Connelly, 105, 164
Conner, 27, 41, 98, 149, 152, 162, 226, 269
Conningham, 245
Connor, 27, 58, 126
Conrad, 5, 7, 9, 12, 13, 33, 53, 123, 146, 267
Contee, 134, 165, 184, 195, 255
Conter, 120
Conway, 22, 24, 187
Conwell, 42
Conynham, 86
Cook, 42, 90, 105, 109, 115, 130, 143, 147, 157, 161, 177, 178, 190, 192, 195, 204, 221, 235, 266
Cooke, 8, 68, 105, 125, 176
Cooley, 204, 270
Coombe, 230
Coombes, 108, 132

Coombs, 86, 90, 143, 171
Coone, 253
Cooper, 3, 6, 14, 30, 31, 48, 91, 93, 101, 139, 165, 183
Copeland, 258
Coppenheffer, 91
Copper, 187
Corbett, 107, 243
Corbit, 26
Corcoran, 24, 80, 90, 116, 148, 149, 161, 184, 225, 235
Cordee, 227
Cordis, 245
Corey, 191
Corlis, 17
Cornelius, 172
Cornell, 42, 263
Cornells, 119
Cornish, 191
Cornman, 65
Cornwallie, 261
Corp, 168
Corran, 94
Corry, 145
Cortland, 5
Cosk, 168
Coston, 256
Costor, 32
Cothoun, 90
Cotton, 199
Coulon, 162, 168
Coulson, 259
Courme, 38
Courne, 55
Coventry, 181
Covington, 51, 52, 110, 134, 207, 208, 262, 267
Covrington, 166
Cowan, 160
Coward, 140
Cowdery, 168, 242, 262
Cowdry, 249
Cowley, 149
Cowper, 33, 49, 102
Cox, 68, 101, 106, 144, 151, 154, 163, 169, 208, 250, 262

Coxe, 1, 7, 14, 33, 55, 67, 84, 92, 112, 113, 117, 160, 163, 183
Coyle, 27, 156, 230, 233, 241
Cozen, 209
Cozens, 14
Crafts, 32, 194
Craig, 3, 68, 73, 119, 177, 187, 189, 206, 232, 250
Craik, 5, 253
Cramer, 201
Cramfield, 13
Cramphin, 196
Cranch, 13, 22, 28, 29, 47, 100, 145, 165, 195, 224, 230, 234, 237, 246
Crane, 84, 220, 261
Cranston, 269
Crape, 13
Craufurd, 184
Craven, 145, 184, 200, 235
Crawford, 10, 25, 66, 67, 96, 119, 149, 201, 232, 250
Crawley, 63
Creager, 180, 189, 198, 214, 225, 228, 232, 244
Creggmiles, 12
Creigh, 127
Creighton, 96, 169
Cress, 84, 89
Creswell, 206
Criglar, 160
Crippen, 256
Croan, 268
Crocker, 42, 187, 211, 272
Crocket, 83, 117
Crockett, 100
Crockette, 47
Crone, 181
Crookshank, 118, 149, 153
Crookshanks, 272
Cross, 30
Crossley, 90
Croswell, 122
Croudson, 90

Crouise, 50
Croussillat, 97
Crow, 161, 216, 267
Crowinfield, 1
Crowinshield, 146, 241
Crowley, 56
Crowninshield, 60, 220, 266
Croxail, 209
Croxall, 140
Crumson, 248
Cruse, 173
Crymes, 182
Cudworth, 88
Cuff, 258
Cullen, 24, 80
Culman, 85
Culnan, 48
Cumming, 63
Cummings, 14
Cumpston, 87
Cumson, 209
Cundell, 53
Cunningham, 22, 24, 31, 79, 80
Curan, 89
Curling, 261
Curran, 147
Currie, 248
Curtis, 122, 256
Cushing, 46, 97, 100, 120, 122, 179, 261, 263
Custis, 165, 243
Cutbush, 168, 169, 249
Cuthill, 53
Cutler, 6, 63, 109, 115, 127, 146, 163, 181
Cutter, 32, 60, 170, 251
Cutting, 113
Cutts, 63, 146, 169, 266
Cuyler, 176
Cyrus, 68

—D—

D'arcy, 45
D'Happart, 254
D'ogenoir, 201
D'Vroom, 204
D'Wolf, 151
D'Wolfe, 32
D'Wolff, 263

Dabney, 169
Daboie, 169
Daffin, 255
Dagan, 145
Daggett, 81, 109, 134, 200
Daight, 141
Dailey, 181
Daily, 205
Daird, 127
Dalcho, 253
Dale, 14, 34, 69
Dall, 53
Dallas, 24, 32, 47, 53, 72, 83, 87, 100, 165, 216
Dalton, 22, 56, 79, 86, 90, 91, 121, 187, 256, 258, 260
Dana, 1, 9, 63, 78, 97, 107, 146, 266
Dancan, 83
Dance, 97, 135, 229
Dandridge, 15, 48, 84, 93
Danes, 142
Dangerot, 158
Danielson, 169
Danks, 25, 66, 67
Darby, 43, 45, 188, 204, 249, 262, 266
Darcey, 81
Dardin, 121, 217
Darke, 62
Darling, 122, 124
Darlington, 109, 110, 121
Darlinton, 115
Darnal, 187
Darnall, 35
Darne, 24, 90
Darneille, 247
Darnes, 131, 206
Darwin, 86, 108
Dashiel, 247
Dashields, 265
Date, 269
Daugherty, 15
Davall, 50
Davenport, 1, 5, 6, 7, 63, 107, 146, 204, 266
Davey, 3

Davice, 76
David, 9, 10, 42, 176, 194, 249, 259
Davids, 109
Davidson, 53, 56, 74, 90, 92, 94, 109, 116, 118, 139, 149, 155, 175, 176, 178, 187, 205, 213, 215, 225, 234, 235, 239, 244, 265
Davie, 37, 82
Davies, 28, 82, 95, 145, 176, 181, 234, 263
Daviess, 47, 100
Davilier, 250
Davis, 5, 14, 15, 19, 29, 34, 41, 42, 47, 51, 53, 56, 57, 63, 64, 73, 94, 95, 96, 100, 106, 123, 124, 136, 151, 153, 157, 160, 167, 173, 178, 179, 204, 217, 244, 250, 257, 258, 269
Davison, 152, 202
Davist, 3
Davit, 176
Davy, 97, 186, 243
Dawes, 9, 89, 98, 99
Dawney, 135
Daws, 127
Dawsen, 235
Dawson, 5, 25, 64, 81, 107, 122, 128, 146, 227, 228, 257, 259, 267
Day, 42, 154, 225
Dayton, 2, 15, 90, 125, 146
De Bealeau, 26
De Borghese, 162
De Carnap, 55, 60, 62, 108
De Chaumont, 249
De Chavla, 152
De Coto, 270
De Ferrer, 30
De France, 15
De Genlis, 33
De Hart, 261
De La Motte, 48, 85, 101

De La Roche, 250
de La Sale, 192
De Lambre, 129
De Pais, 30
De St Gemme, 105
De Vaisseau, 35
De Vroom, 7
De Wolfe, 41
De Yrujo, 49, 102
Deaderick, 203
Deadrick, 208
Deakens, 151, 222
Deakin, 187
Deaking, 76
Deakins, 3, 61, 105, 106, 160, 185, 199, 215, 239, 254
Deale, 257, 259
Dean, 86, 139, 161, 261
Deane, 204
Dearborn, 21, 26, 46, 71, 99, 129, 138, 153, 167, 234
Dearborne, 59
Deas, 107
Deaton, 68
Deblock, 106
Deblois, 22, 103, 187
Debut, 117
Decatur, 59, 71, 96, 178, 210, 219, 245
Declary, 187
Deering, 24
Degan, 237
DeHulf, 120
DeKrafft, 184
Delerme, 262
Delesdernier, 25, 65, 67
Delphey, 121
Deming, 97
Dempsey, 16, 20, 27, 35, 234, 253
Dempsie, 143, 229, 230
Demun, 130
Deneale, 51, 165, 205
Deneley, 86
Dennet, 91
Dennis, 36, 54, 64, 126, 146, 187, 256
Dennison, 187, 247
Denniston, 93
Denny, 57
Densley, 156, 252

Dent, 5, 13, 27, 33, 35, 58, 89, 96, 123, 148, 219, 255
Dentschner, 246
DePeyster, 172
Derby, 11
Dering, 14, 173, 201
Dermott, 11, 78, 105, 145
Deshon, 81
Despard, 128
Dessalines, 256
Destaing, 93
Destando, 258
Deterly, 242
Devicman, 119
Devoe, 203
Devotion, 109
Dewey, 6
DeWitt, 4, 88, 173
Dexter, 12, 13, 21, 27, 28, 67, 68, 75, 82, 96, 219
Deyen, 49, 102
Dezoteux, 245
Dick, 15, 24, 29, 149, 152, 153, 187, 206
Dickenson, 202
Dicker, 250
Dickerson, 70, 87, 183, 201
Dickert, 120
Dickins, 5
Dickinson, 97, 103, 260, 261
Dickson, 6, 64, 69, 122, 130, 147, 183, 244, 267
Didot, 193, 196
Digges, 106, 109, 136, 138, 187, 215, 264
Diggs, 125
Digno, 106
Dill, 10, 105, 243
Dillings, 157
Dillon, 246
Dingley, 77
Dinmore, 32, 35
Dinsmore, 23, 120
Dishon, 34
Divene, 112

Dixon, 13, 46, 55, 62, 94, 104, 119, 145, 190, 194
Doak, 69
Doane, 5
Dobbin, 55, 192, 264
Dobbon, 187
Dobell, 41, 48, 84, 101, 163
Docker, 45, 180, 201
Dodd, 88
Dodemead, 242
Dodge, 25, 45, 65, 67, 69, 81, 130, 132
Dohertie, 114
Dole, 20, 83, 149
Doll, 258
Dollas, 264
Donaldson, 57, 106, 110, 143, 171, 250
Donalson, 115
Donavan, 242
Done, 42, 115
Donelan, 261
Donell, 259
Donelly, 147
Donnahan, 198
Donnell, 39, 141, 142
Donnelly, 132
Donoughue, 98
Doran, 147
Dorey, 45
Dorhman, 22
Dormott, 143
Dorr, 72
Dorrance, 98
Dorsey, 8, 22, 24, 26, 47, 56, 75, 100, 112, 121, 148, 149, 177, 181, 184, 186, 210, 217, 220, 255
Dougal, 14
Dougherty, 97, 175, 265
Doughty, 70, 235
Douglas, 86, 128, 151, 249
Douglass, 24, 30, 38, 57, 113, 123, 138, 139, 142, 168
Doulery, 38
Dove, 169
Dovebainbridge, 220

Dover, 16
Dow, 201
Dowager, 228
Down, 222
Downes, 96, 169
Downing, 258
Dowson, 59, 155
Doyle, 35, 76, 147, 154, 157, 173, 257
Doyne, 52, 78, 108, 264
Drane, 223
Drayton, 73, 107
Driscoll, 74
Driver, 269
Drum, 14
Drummond, 264
Duane, 10, 37, 86, 137, 152, 199, 208, 261, 262
Dubourg, 162
Dubuys, 201
Ducker, 134
Ducket, 8, 109
Duckett, 3, 51, 52, 193, 231, 264
Duclairack, 175
Ducupley, 250
Dudley, 42, 75, 125, 163, 181, 205
Duer, 30, 187
Duffield, 57, 67, 211, 246
Dugan, 57, 194
Duggan, 25, 66, 67
Duhamel, 81
Duhamet, 45
Duhy, 187
Dulany, 93, 94, 238
Dulin, 29
Dumbar, 180
Dumoutet, 13, 58
Dunant, 250
Dunbar, 15, 124, 178, 201
Duncan, 15, 41, 82, 84, 149, 249, 260
Duncanson, 79, 86, 230
Duncle, 14
Dundad, 206
Dundas, 80, 97, 232
Dunham, 30, 42, 83, 249
Dunkin, 256, 258

Dunlap, 29, 56, 68, 121, 122, 197, 208, 212, 250, 268
Dunlavy, 70, 115
Dunn, 24, 112
Dupasquierpetit, 249
Duponceau, 14, 16, 160
Durant, 256, 258
Durfee, 163
Durham, 32, 251
Durkee, 168
Duskins, 36
Dutell, 249
Duval, 5, 52, 109, 112, 138, 168, 222, 248
Duvall, 2, 4, 27, 55, 78, 87, 143, 152, 164, 173, 185, 235, 237, 239, 244
Dwight, 146
Dyer, 26, 27, 75, 89, 134, 239, 261, 272
Dyler, 4
Dyson, 179, 256

—E—

Eacker, 4
Eaker, 63
Earl, 25, 201
Earle, 65, 67, 81, 132, 147, 153, 264, 267
Early, 105, 147, 160, 200, 229, 267
Easterby, 255
Eastin, 198
Easton, 9, 84, 101, 175, 191, 197, 211
Eastwood, 116
Eaton, 49, 101, 238, 247, 252, 264, 265
Eaw, 187
Eckhart, 230
Eddy, 20, 25, 31, 65, 67, 127, 257, 259
Edelin, 196
Eden, 80, 160, 187
Edgar, 25, 65, 67, 87, 152, 271
Edgmont, 77
Edie, 1
Edmond, 1, 6, 134, 136

Edmonds, 109, 256, 258
Edmondston, 177
Edmonson, 222
Edmundson, 120, 214
Edoet, 164
Edwards, 37, 42, 45, 47, 78, 88, 89, 90, 94, 100, 104, 120, 181, 191, 207, 217, 226, 232, 257, 258, 259
Edwin, 33
Ege, 10
Ehrenzeller, 187
Elam, 31, 53
Elbert, 219, 245
Eldridge, 43, 204
Eldrige, 203
Elgin, 223
Eliason, 187, 221
Elicott, 145
Eliot, 11, 108
Eliott, 187
Elldridge, 156
Ellers, 131
Ellery, 34, 90, 116, 145
Ellgey, 114
Ellicot, 117, 201
Ellicott, 14, 55, 194, 254, 271
Elliot, 130, 138, 146, 165, 200, 203, 223, 266
Elliott, 30, 52, 112, 194, 212, 220
Ellis, 4, 15, 21, 28, 105, 107, 150, 244, 255, 262, 266
Ellsworth, 12, 81, 109
Ellzey, 8, 181, 205
Elmendorf, 63, 85, 201
Elmendorg, 6
Elmer, 63, 158, 204, 210, 266
Elmes, 42
Elmslie, 48, 101
Eloridg, 92
Elsdune, 42
Elswort, 134
Elsworth, 3, 200
Eltonhead, 142
Elvin, 253

Elwis, 136
Elwyn, 145
Ely, 131
Elzy, 224
Emack, 229, 230
Emanuel, 155, 180, 206
Emery, 193
Emlin, 105
Emmerson, 156
Emmons, 203
Engle, 57
English, 27, 39, 54, 99, 116, 216
Ennalls, 269
Eno, 40, 165
Epler, 14
Eppes, 146, 174, 228, 267
Erb, 18
Erdmann, 242
Ernest, 15
Erskine, 50
Ervin, 132, 197
Erving, 41, 48, 100, 202
Erwin, 29, 85
Erwine, 31
Erwing, 14
Esenbeck, 233
Eskridge, 177, 187
Essex, 125
Essicks, 90
Estep, 56
Etting, 35, 47, 83, 100
Eustis, 6, 63, 146, 183
Evan, 234
Evans, 6, 41, 69, 81, 96, 156, 166, 169, 176, 185, 214, 244, 269
Evens, 15
Everitt, 31
Ewell, 243, 251
Ewing, 47, 97, 98, 100, 120, 217
Eyermann, 17
Eyre, 16

—F—

Facias, 112
Fagan, 159
Fairfax, 72, 143, 271

Fairlie, 87, 201
Fairman, 150
Falconer, 23
Fales, 25, 65, 66
Falkinburge, 112
Fanagan, 253
Farar, 180
Farewell, 256
Farley, 204
Farmer, 69
Farrall, 234
Farrel, 52, 147
Farrell, 235
Farrington, 257, 259
Farris, 106
Farrow, 205
Fatio, 49, 102
Faucet, 110
Faugeres, 144
Faulkner, 25, 65, 66, 67
Faw, 22, 24, 80, 136
Fay, 24, 47, 83, 100, 122, 187
Fearing, 64, 97
Feathers, 256, 258
Featherstone, 257, 259
February, 166
Fegarie, 157
Fellowes, 32, 229
Fellows, 89, 131, 138, 229, 249
Felton, 124
Fennel, 251
Fennell, 175
Fenner, 5, 31, 80, 176, 259, 266
Fenney, 198
Fenwick, 27, 34, 105, 164, 184, 197, 198, 211, 222, 234, 239, 250
Ferebee, 164, 195
Ferguson, 10, 16, 57, 251, 257, 259, 269
Fernandes, 8
Ferrers, 271
Ferson, 122
Fessenden, 60
Fevrier, 161
Few, 195
Fidelio, 11
Field, 129, 181, 205, 254

Fillebrown, 204
Finagan, 135, 265
Finch, 181
Findlay, 50
Findlaye, 49, 82, 102
Findley, 50, 103, 120, 146, 207, 267
Finlay, 112, 257, 259
Finney, 198
Fish, 83, 144, 184
Fishback, 198
Fisher, 10, 76, 99, 105, 129, 169, 187, 195
Fisk, 262, 266
Fitch, 83, 109
Fithian, 140
Fitz, 140
Fitzgerald, 106, 125, 149, 152, 177
Fitzhugh, 18, 22, 24, 29, 108, 185, 187, 192, 209
Fitzpatrick, 43, 196
Fitzsimons, 68
Flagg, 137
Flanagan, 214, 269
Flaut, 188
Fleetwood, 43
Fleming, 43, 72, 81, 251
Fletcher, 63, 71, 180
Fleurieu, 3
Flinn, 57, 206, 220, 223
Flmendorf, 173
Flora, 70
Floyd, 3, 4, 43, 201, 236, 261
Flurty, 132
Flyment, 204
Flyming, 176
Fohi, 211
Foley, 108
Follanche, 74
Follet, 43
Folsom, 261
Folsome, 84
Fome, 19
Fonerden, 92
Fontana, 245
Fontineau, 270
Foote, 73, 149
Forbes, 19, 84, 85, 101, 237

Ford, 3, 10, 23, 43, 153, 213, 234, 257, 259
Fording, 196
Forentan, 168
Forman, 48, 70, 101, 171, 232
Forney, 204
Fornsworth, 171
Forrest, 22, 63, 64, 75, 79, 89, 90, 99, 105, 106, 108, 118, 119, 120, 124, 131, 133, 141, 147, 148, 150, 155, 161, 164, 171, 172, 174, 175, 177, 178, 184, 185, 186, 187, 189, 190, 191, 192, 195, 196, 199, 202, 208, 210, 212, 216, 218, 222, 226, 231, 233, 236, 237
Forrester, 43
Forrreyre, 65, 67
Forster, 172
Forsyth, 105
Fort, 97
Fortier, 171
Forwood, 57, 194
Fosdeck, 125
Fosdick, 88
Fosset, 43
Foster, 1, 5, 7, 14, 19, 43, 46, 50, 52, 63, 90, 109, 116, 124, 155, 168
Foulk, 27
Foulke, 33
Foushee, 114, 125, 168
Fowler, 53, 64, 142, 147, 202, 246, 267
Fownes, 62, 103, 107, 150
Fox, 48, 100, 105, 135, 137, 234, 236
Foxall, 55
Foxhall, 225
Foxton, 167
Foyles, 173
Frailey, 170
Francis, 3, 4, 8, 10, 120, 128, 189, 247, 250, 257, 258

Frank, 40
Franklin, 2, 6, 7, 20, 90, 108, 127, 146, 186, 234
Fraser, 144
Frazer, 87, 117, 133, 136, 168, 177, 205
Frazier, 57, 77, 216, 257
Frederic, 45
Frederick, 256
Free, 239
Freeland, 169
Freeman, 3, 5, 27, 43, 73, 123, 159, 161, 179, 226, 253, 263
Freise, 254
Freleigh, 204
Frelinghuysen, 7, 83, 112
French, 79, 112, 149
Freneau, 99
Freret, 264
Frethy, 192
Freytag, 16
Fries, 166, 239
Frisbie, 88
Frish, 257, 258
Frithy, 265
Fritkey, 175
Frizell, 113
Fromm, 74
Frost, 34, 52, 58, 87, 119, 177, 231, 249
Frothingham, 103
Fry, 119, 150
Fuller, 27, 73, 269
Fulton, 27, 168, 201
Furguson, 130
Furlong, 73
Furman, 2, 140, 204

—G—

Gacon, 196
Gadsden, 169, 252, 262
Gadsen, 248
Gadson, 187
Gahn, 49, 102
Gaillard, 11, 266
Gaines, 31, 195, 235, 257, 259, 264
Gains, 158
Gaither, 79, 187
Galasspy, 35
Galbreath, 139
Galdy, 3
Gale, 254
Galer, 185
Gales, 123, 160
Galey, 43
Gallager, 205
Gallaspy, 253
Gallatin, 33, 46, 82, 99, 138
Galloway, 187, 221, 261
Galusha, 107
Gamble, 10, 16, 57, 120, 168, 215, 216, 248, 249
Games, 122
Gamheart, 270
Ganevoort, 4
Gangaivare, 187
Gannt, 37, 80
Gano, 110
Gansevoert, 84
Gant, 121
Gantt, 30, 48, 50, 80, 84, 86, 94, 101, 106, 126, 134, 169, 231, 238, 262, 272
Gardener, 228
Gardiner, 31, 43, 67, 85, 98, 115, 135, 174, 180, 235, 237, 247
Gardner, 25, 26, 47, 60, 65, 75, 83, 96, 100, 101, 135, 151, 169, 183, 234, 251
Garland, 23, 170, 171, 195
Garlaue, 83
Garnder, 81
Garnet, 52
Garnett, 70, 91, 228, 262, 267
Garrard, 53, 113
Garretson, 169
Garrett, 23, 159
Garteret, 182
Garuch, 91
Gaskaden, 150
Gaskins, 110
Gassaway, 110, 134, 152, 205
Gatch, 115
Gates, 3, 31, 150, 253
Gatlatin, 88
Gaton, 272
Gatton, 72, 108, 230, 246
Gavane, 217
Gavino, 48, 101, 210, 236
Gay, 65, 67, 250
Gayot, 34
Gayton, 14
Gaz, 31, 37, 42, 53
Gazneau, 241
Geddes, 96, 169
Geiger, 133
Gelston, 40, 83
Generes, 231
George, 149, 256
Gerard, 97
Gerry, 92, 128
Geyer, 212
Gheislin, 109
Gheny, 84
Ghequiere, 141
Ghesquier, 250
Gibbon, 168, 249
Gibbons, 46, 176, 180, 252
Gibbs, 237
Gibson, 14, 50, 103, 109, 159, 163, 205, 218, 244
Giddens, 217
Gilbert, 2, 161, 200, 205
Gilchrist, 187
Giles, 8, 15, 28, 64, 83, 96, 169, 206, 266
Gillers, 240
Gillespie, 147, 154, 190, 212, 245
Gilliam, 156
Gillick, 154
Gillis, 94, 187, 214, 235
Gilliss, 142, 186, 241, 268
Gilman, 23, 49, 87, 98, 102, 109, 115, 224, 231, 249, 266

Gilmor, 158
Gilpin, 5, 22, 24, 33, 47, 52, 80, 83, 100, 118, 206, 240
Girard, 32, 68, 73, 105, 171, 250
Giraud, 49, 102
Girault, 180
Gird, 25
Girdler, 130
Gist, 140
Given, 192
Glasco, 261
Glascock, 269
Glass, 19
Gleaves, 206, 254
Glen, 5, 169
Glenbervie, 97
Glenn, 117, 154
Gloso, 271
Glover, 95, 153, 193, 250, 272
Glynn, 194
Godby, 168, 249, 252
Goddard, 2, 63, 87, 107, 118, 146
Goddrich, 73
Godfrey, 63, 77, 149, 187
Godfroy, 167
Godwin, 169
Goetchius, 163
Goforth, 109, 115, 124
Gohagan, 234
Goil, 187
Golden, 125, 187
Golding, 43, 97
Goldsborough, 8, 54, 111, 194, 207, 235, 257, 258, 263, 267
Gole, 250
Gooch, 217
Goodal, 144
Goodale, 15, 54
Goodall, 143
Goodhue, 7, 9
Goodluck, 41
Goodman, 57, 137, 253
Goodrich, 1, 2, 3, 6, 27, 41, 54, 81, 82, 107, 109, 134, 181, 198, 204, 205

Goodwin, 16, 43, 99, 122, 263
Goodwyn, 147, 228, 267
Gordon, 3, 45, 47, 57, 76, 96, 106, 117, 181, 219, 223, 243
Gore, 156, 174
Gorham, 174, 229
Goss, 63
Goszler, 148
Gould, 92, 122
Goulding, 64, 264
Goushee, 248
Gover, 117, 141
Gowan, 187
Gracie, 18, 271
Graeff, 120
Graffin, 234
Graham, 31, 43, 48, 82, 100, 128, 175, 178, 187
Grainger, 58
Graisberry, 70
Grange, 30
Granger, 2, 82, 99, 138
Grant, 8, 48, 54, 92, 101, 111, 196, 257, 259
Grappe, 270
Gratiot, 247
Grattan, 20, 83
Graves, 49, 102, 204
Gray, 20, 30, 47, 64, 92, 99, 146, 176, 224, 227, 228, 229, 241, 256, 257, 258, 259, 267
Graybill, 10, 206
Grayham, 69
Grayson, 40, 89, 214
Greathead, 111
Greave, 269
Greaves, 23
Green, 5, 10, 14, 17, 23, 39, 43, 46, 87, 91, 96, 105, 109, 123, 139, 140, 187, 209, 220, 229, 244, 256, 258, 263, 264, 266, 269

Greene, 19, 29, 53, 80, 88, 109, 112, 121, 195, 258
Greenfield, 77, 180
Greenhow, 18, 123
Greenleaf, 3, 14, 19, 68, 120, 165, 187, 219, 249
Greenup, 218, 265
Greenwell, 142, 271
Greenworth, 129
Greer, 46, 215
Gregg, 1, 64, 146, 187, 202, 217, 266
Gregory, 143, 204
Grenell, 96, 169
Grenville, 181
Gresham, 170, 204
Gridley, 174, 187
Grierson, 52
Grieves, 124
Griffin, 20, 28, 43, 45, 47, 50, 88, 92, 100, 103, 109, 120, 129, 147, 169, 187, 216, 220, 257, 258
Griffiss, 133
Griffith, 2, 19, 28, 47, 57, 174, 235
Griffiths, 251
Griger, 90
Grillette, 270
Grindell, 238
Grinnan, 46
Griswold, 1, 2, 6, 17, 28, 63, 78, 85, 107, 109, 134, 146, 160, 176, 271
Groce, 143
Grochan, 81
Groff, 92
Gronevaldt, 187
Groom, 10
Grose, 76
Gross, 92, 155, 187
Grove, 14, 27, 64
Grubb, 115
Gruber, 240
Guerlain, 250
Guerrent, 114
Guillard, 88
Gulick, 37
Gumpp, 120

Gunn, 50, 121
Gunnell, 80, 90
Gurley, 164
Gurrle, 14
Guy, 23, 67
Guyler, 150
Gwyin, 217
Gwyn, 132

—H—

Habersham, 33, 58, 82, 105, 168
Hackett, 187
Hackley, 169
Hadfield, 86, 121, 133
Hadgessin, 76
Haeffer, 120
Haga, 63
Hagan, 234
Hagner, 213, 235
Hainard, 257, 259
Haincock, 43
Hale, 46, 269
Haley, 258
Hall, 4, 10, 15, 37, 43, 47, 52, 54, 56, 83, 87, 88, 92, 107, 109, 152, 156, 172, 185, 187, 195, 196, 201, 216, 217, 219, 224, 244, 246, 253, 255, 259
Haller, 14
Halliday, 43
Halloway, 229
Halpen, 149
Halsey, 17, 263, 266
Halstead, 25
Halsted, 65
Halsteda, 67
Halvert, 187
Ham, 11, 168
Hamilton, 8, 11, 24, 38, 43, 47, 52, 70, 76, 82, 83, 123, 133, 170, 183, 184, 186, 195, 197, 212, 217, 230, 263, 267
Hamlin, 29
Hamm, 99
Hammaker, 230
Hamman, 190

Hammand, 154
Hammell, 69, 187
Hammon, 161
Hammond, 22, 24, 39, 54, 99, 147, 184, 244, 250
Hampton, 8, 11, 132, 147, 195
Hamtramock, 130, 242
Hance, 185, 186, 221
Hand, 98, 142, 145, 156
Hands, 74
Handy, 12, 21, 96
Hanford, 178
Haniford, 257, 259
Hankerson, 257, 259
Hanna, 1, 64, 72, 94, 122, 146, 241, 260
Hannah, 169
Hanson, 22, 57, 58, 81, 86, 145, 171, 181, 192, 225, 272
Haraden, 219, 240
Harbaugh, 132, 148
Harbough, 235
Harden, 19, 148
Harding, 25, 65, 67, 124, 157, 223, 240
Hardy, 8, 106, 139, 233, 239, 247
Hare, 95, 160, 211
Hargood, 233
Hargrove, 24, 209
Haring, 201
Harkimer, 116
Harles, 57
Harper, 3, 22, 33, 62, 90, 126, 148, 170, 206, 221, 235
Harraden, 245
Harrie, 31
Harrington, 108
Harris, 3, 23, 60, 64, 75, 84, 87, 118, 120, 124, 150, 156, 163, 176, 215, 237, 241
Harrison, 3, 7, 8, 9, 18, 19, 20, 29, 32, 39, 46, 50, 76, 83, 94, 96, 99, 103, 106, 112, 122, 124, 138, 158, 159, 177, 184, 211, 218, 224, 240, 245, 256, 258, 261, 272
Harry, 59, 187
Harryman, 194, 255
Harshman, 253
Harshorne, 36
Hart, 2, 88, 109, 128, 133, 159, 172, 178, 204, 215, 235, 258
Hartley, 3, 10, 12, 13, 17, 209
Hartshorn, 24, 41
Hartshorne, 96, 185
Hartzell, 10, 120
Hartzellg, 215
Harvey, 22, 52, 63, 251, 259
Harvie, 125, 152, 169, 216
Harvy, 154
Harwood, 8, 13, 31, 54, 134, 138, 168, 192, 244, 249, 267
Hasam, 157
Hasbrouck, 4
Hasket, 70
Hass, 187
Hastings, 63, 121, 146, 266
Haswell, 10, 220
Hatch, 125, 249, 250
Hatcher, 87
Hatcheson, 194, 253
Hatfield, 9
Hathorn, 85, 154
Haton, 270
Hatz, 120
Hauer, 120, 177
Haughman, 22
Haurton, 73
Havard, 262
Havens, 271
Haviland, 144
Havis, 207
Hawkens, 177
Hawker, 258
Hawkins, 37, 56, 77, 79, 82, 91, 105, 118, 119, 136, 140, 194, 255, 260
Hawley, 181
Hawthorne, 192, 204

Hay, 2, 72, 79, 87, 116, 134, 216
Haydn, 221
Hayes, 256
Haymaker, 127
Haymond, 137
Hays, 28, 47, 100, 250
Hayward, 54, 184
Haywood, 47, 100, 209
Hazard, 96, 98, 191
Hazen, 125, 199, 209, 213, 214, 220
Hazlehurst, 197
Hazlet, 144
Heally, 241
Healy, 198, 206
Heard, 34, 54, 83, 84, 85, 125
Heath, 16, 92, 171, 204, 216
Heatly, 43
Heaton, 165
Hebb, 56
Hedges, 90, 177, 197
Hege, 146
Heighe, 185, 221
Heineken, 13, 49, 102
Heiskell, 30
Heisley, 143
Heister, 5, 10, 27, 36, 64, 120, 122, 143, 146, 166, 194, 215
Hellen, 163, 235
Hellingsworth, 172
Helm, 5, 172, 181
Helme, 205
Helms, 2, 63, 158, 204, 266
Hembold, 33
Hemmersly, 187
Hemphil, 1
Hemphill, 64
Hempstead, 40, 218, 246
Henderson, 5, 16, 64, 77, 95, 105, 121, 149, 180, 187, 205, 210, 271
Hendley, 37
Hendrickson, 150
Henkle, 123
Henley, 76
Henly, 123

Henning, 34
Henry, 46, 68, 72, 76, 120, 157, 167, 168, 249, 250, 254, 261
Hensey, 85
Henshaw, 252
Hepburn, 162, 187, 207, 230, 239
Hepburne, 13
Herald, 127
Herbert, 8, 22, 24, 80, 83
Herford, 53, 133, 192, 218, 223, 230, 234
Herman, 178
Herndon, 24
Herner, 3
Herod, 133
Heron, 111
Herron, 104
Herschell, 29
Hersmon, 33
Herson, 211, 258
Hersy, 90
Herty, 10, 85, 86, 87, 164, 180, 192, 218, 223, 230, 232, 235, 254, 265
Hervey, 270
Heston, 7, 215
Heuster, 187
Hewell, 172
Hewes, 84, 101, 121, 206, 221, 237, 262
Hewett, 32, 100
Hewit, 192
Hewitt, 28, 47, 54, 60, 74, 81, 83, 86, 90, 93, 106, 109, 123, 130, 133, 140, 162, 164, 178, 234
Hewsom, 117
Hewson, 30, 160, 234
Hexis, 257, 259
Heye, 187
Heyleger, 120
Hickey, 38
Hickman, 137, 187
Hienesey, 86
Hieter, 122
Hiett, 257
Higbee, 250
Higden, 272

Higdon, 59, 188, 238, 246
Higgins, 10, 142, 255
Higginson, 250
Higginston, 250
Higinbotham, 96, 169
Hilbourn, 227
Hildrith, 201
Hilhouse, 134
Hilis, 258
Hill, 3, 12, 20, 29, 32, 43, 44, 64, 72, 119, 148, 157, 187, 225, 231, 235, 237, 269
Hillary, 113, 161, 167, 187
Hilleary, 230, 231, 247
Hillen, 45
Hillhouse, 5, 81, 90, 109, 145, 266
Hills, 256
Hinch, 211
Hinckley, 145
Hinderwell, 111
Hindman, 11, 187
Hinkley, 172
Hinson, 30
Hitchburn, 168
Hitchcock, 19, 28, 47, 78, 109, 171
Hite, 169
Hixs, 259
Hoban, 26, 40, 79, 86, 133, 171, 178, 192, 213, 231, 234
Hobart, 47, 97
Hobby, 95, 206
Hodd, 225
Hodgdon, 129
Hodge, 168, 243, 249, 252
Hodgins, 139
Hodgkin, 238
Hodgkinson, 248
Hodgson, 68, 86, 108, 130, 132, 133, 185, 192, 213, 229, 233, 234
Hodnett, 235
Hoffman, 14, 50, 71, 106, 184, 185, 192, 196, 221
Hogan, 36, 88, 249, 271

Hoge, 50, 64, 103
Hoggins, 106
Hoit, 150
Holbrook, 43
Holden, 269
Holford, 171
Holgate, 57
Holiday, 132
Holland, 56, 64, 190, 267
Hollander, 257
Holliday, 90, 113, 193
Hollingsworth, 13, 37, 47, 100, 172, 175
Hollins, 172, 262
Hollinsworth, 54
Hollowell, 183
Hollurry, 149
Hollyday, 96
Holmead, 90, 126, 188, 225
Holmes, 5, 8, 16, 22, 44, 48, 64, 98, 99, 101, 111, 129, 135, 136, 146, 181, 205, 228, 236, 243, 250, 257, 258, 267
Holmesin, 8
Holsey, 198
Holstien, 187
Holt, 61, 62, 73, 74, 155, 172, 219
Holyday, 54
Homboldt, 180
Hoockey, 132, 166
Hood, 159
Hooe, 22, 84, 126, 185, 187, 192
Hoof, 90, 206
Hoofnagle, 55
Hook, 83
Hooker, 9
Hooma, 158
Hoomes, 225
Hooper, 172, 262
Hope, 232
Hopkins, 6, 23, 28, 31, 47, 58, 81, 83, 91, 100, 106, 182, 217, 255, 261
Horlbeck, 107
Horn, 270
Horne, 10

Horry, 272
Horton, 241, 270
Hoskins, 164
Hosmer, 109, 134
Hoss, 187
Hostetter, 170
Hotckhiss, 120
Houfman, 86
Hough, 98, 104, 112, 146, 266
Houghinen, 24
Houghman, 80
Houreman, 39
Houston, 20, 57, 81, 203, 208, 269
Houstoun, 148, 176
Hove, 19, 254
Hoven, 187
How, 25, 65, 67, 111, 235
Howard, 5, 13, 17, 21, 22, 23, 26, 28, 30, 34, 35, 36, 37, 39, 47, 51, 59, 67, 75, 77, 80, 81, 89, 90, 91, 94, 95, 100, 108, 113, 114, 119, 126, 128, 130, 139, 148, 160, 162, 163, 164, 176, 179, 184, 193, 205, 216, 235, 236, 247, 248, 250
Howel, 2
Howell, 2, 43, 47, 79, 82, 100, 139, 254
Howes, 257, 259
Howington, 238
Howison, 153
Howland, 73, 80, 266
Howman, 41
Hoxie, 18
Hoxsie, 31, 80
Hoye, 222, 254
Hozey, 16
Hubband, 114
Hubbard, 2, 159
Hubley, 10
Huddleston, 178, 192, 221, 230, 234, 235, 265
Hudgins, 155
Hudson, 122, 139, 248
Huet, 257, 258

Huett, 259
Hufty, 204
Huger, 5, 7, 64, 73, 82, 132, 147, 160, 181, 256, 258
Hugh, 149
Hughe, 179
Hughes, 30, 142, 187, 257, 259
Hughesm, 161
Hughs, 14, 124, 187, 238
Hugthrop, 224
Huling, 48, 101
Hull, 48, 78, 219, 220, 249, 250
Hulling, 139
Hullschner, 246
Hulson, 3
Humboldt, 192
Humer, 145
Humphrey, 30, 45, 53, 115
Humphreys, 37, 84, 118, 132, 196, 244, 253, 261
Humrukhausen, 122
Hunn, 256
Hunnewell, 131
Hunson, 254
Hunt, 4, 6, 9, 30, 98, 104, 112, 117, 146, 156, 168, 169, 174, 249, 250, 252, 259
Hunter, 11, 14, 35, 43, 53, 74, 87, 98, 112, 152, 201
Huntingdon, 33, 78
Huntington, 88, 115, 200, 204
Hurdle, 196
Hurly, 239
Hurrin, 122
Hurtt, 254
Husk, 138
Huston, 69
Hutchins, 206
Hutchinson, 18, 135
Hutchison, 247
Hyde, 78, 88, 109, 127, 140. 148, 173
Hye, 234
Hylton, 31, 88, 248

17

Hynson, 140

—I—

I-ish, 170
Illsley, 125
Ilsley, 163
Imlay, 3, 6, 7, 47, 100, 204
Ingersol, 2, 19, 29, 217
Ingersoll, 28, 226, 250
Ingle, 7, 16, 62, 86, 90, 108, 110, 196, 230, 235, 268
Ingles, 57
Ingold, 23
Ingraham, 63, 241
Inman, 16, 251
Innes, 9, 47, 62, 100
Inston, 86
Ireland, 156, 264
Irvine, 46, 163, 168, 185, 207
Irving, 113
Irwin, 10, 14, 38, 137, 250
Irwine, 24
Isaack, 265
Isaacs, 92
Island, 161
Isnardi, 85
Israel, 123, 210
Ives, 109, 115, 120
Izard, 178, 220, 245

—J—

Jack, 18, 27, 90, 118, 138, 144, 153, 256, 258
Jacks, 60
Jackson, 4, 5, 9, 19, 23, 25, 31, 35, 43, 47, 53, 55, 58, 64, 85, 88, 90, 94, 108, 111, 131, 135, 136, 137, 146, 147, 155, 160, 177, 185, 186, 201, 228, 249, 250, 255, 257, 259, 266, 267
Jacob, 108, 130
Jacobs, 69, 91, 117, 127
Jacques, 68, 220

Jafey, 10
Jameison, 206
James, 39, 43, 67, 75, 117, 160, 168, 192, 235
Jameson, 16, 198
Jamieson, 118
Janney, 106, 138, 185, 192, 206
Jansen, 122
Jarret, 187
Jarrit, 17
Jarvis, 41, 85, 89, 91, 92, 101, 138, 183, 237, 257, 258, 260
Jasorn, 191
Jauncey, 150
Jay, 9, 12, 18, 28, 261
Jee, 172
Jefferes, 233
Jefferson, 4, 8, 9, 14, 18, 19, 21, 23, 24, 33, 46, 63, 67, 68, 76, 77, 79, 87, 99, 107, 117, 119, 120, 124, 127, 149, 159, 160, 162, 163, 167, 168, 174, 200, 206, 208, 211, 214, 215, 220, 223, 234, 247, 248, 251
Jenckes, 53, 169
Jenings, 68
Jenkins, 2, 16, 46, 91, 163, 201, 239, 248, 254, 257, 259, 263
Jenkinson, 97
Jenks, 25, 66, 67, 122
Jenners, 188
Jennet, 43
Jennings, 110, 134, 138, 187
Jerkins, 157
Jesse, 76
Jeton, 79
Jewitt, 91
Jinney, 156
Johns, 4, 90, 113, 187, 255, 272
Johnson, 5, 21, 22, 23, 26, 29, 32, 39, 43, 54, 61, 64, 65, 67, 78, 80, 83, 99, 104, 106, 109, 110, 120, 123, 127, 135, 139, 153, 157, 158, 159, 168, 173, 182, 184, 187, 206, 210, 219, 220, 226, 249, 253, 254, 256, 257, 258, 259, 261, 263
Johnston, 25, 45, 54, 73, 82, 89, 90, 105, 113, 120, 127, 161, 169, 173, 182, 188, 212, 234, 242
Johonnot, 217
Joint, 90
Joliet, 192
Joncaire, 250
Jones, 3, 4, 8, 13, 14, 16, 27, 28, 31, 34, 36, 37, 38, 41, 43, 47, 48, 51, 62, 64, 72, 74, 77, 79, 82, 84, 87, 90, 93, 100, 101, 116, 120, 122, 123, 125, 126, 127, 131, 133, 136, 147, 148, 150, 156, 158, 159, 168, 169, 170, 171, 181, 183, 193, 196, 197, 201, 204, 207, 212, 216, 217, 218, 228, 238, 239, 246, 249, 250, 252, 254, 256, 257, 258, 259, 261, 262, 267, 269, 272
Jonessam, 234
Jonti, 192
Jordan, 189, 199, 236
Jorden, 43
Jos, 68
Jouett, 167
Jourdan, 255
Joy, 172, 199
Joyce, 37
Joyeuse, 143
Judd, 191, 202, 204
Judicott, 249
Judson, 78, 198, 204, 269
Julian, 105
Junior, 43
Junkin, 207

—K—

Kahokia, 152
Kaldenbach, 173
Kalender, 196
Kalteisen, 252
Kaminsky, 50
Kane, 68
Karney, 169
Karrick, 188
Kaskaskias, 152, 153
Keadle, 238
Kean, 10, 72, 120, 180, 215
Kearnes, 61
Kearney, 3, 5, 20, 26, 86, 108, 147, 149, 191, 192, 230
Kearny, 96
Keats, 233
Kedglei, 264
Kedwell, 252
Keehmle, 105
Keely, 218
Keen, 140
Keene, 114, 156, 175
Keets, 142
Keighler, 208
Keith, 105, 106, 125, 128, 148, 185, 192
Keland, 188
Keller, 50
Kelly, 14, 91, 116, 147, 263, 267
Kemball, 249
Kemble, 14, 249
Kemp, 56, 105, 188
Kemper, 268, 270
Kempt, 188
Kempton, 169
Kenan, 245, 263, 267
Kendall, 250
Kendrick, 241, 245
Kennada, 269
Kennaday, 27
Kennard, 190
Kennedy, 16, 147, 150, 173, 183, 188, 260
Kenner, 15, 201, 234
Kennon, 10
Kent, 80, 164, 182, 264
Kenyon, 82
Ker, 16, 124, 128
Kerblay, 87
Kerby, 61, 90
Kercheval, 211
Kerr, 24, 42, 70, 90, 180, 234
Kerschner, 6
Kersein, 139
Kesler, 188
Kessler, 156
Ketland, 152, 207
Ketman, 43
Key, 8, 19, 28, 29, 47, 64, 80, 133, 195
Kicker, 110
Kid, 11
Kiehl, 14
Kikendall, 118
Kilgore, 170
Kilty, 25, 47, 69, 82, 100, 135, 152, 175, 184, 205, 234
Kilwarden, 149
Kimbolls, 247
Kinder, 149
Kindle, 198
King, 23, 35, 39, 40, 48, 61, 70, 73, 75, 77, 79, 86, 100, 103, 104, 110, 130, 133, 138, 160, 161, 163, 170, 171, 172, 176, 180, 188, 189, 195, 199, 200, 206, 213, 218, 228, 231, 234, 235, 239, 240, 250
Kingsbury, 81
Kingstand, 130
Kingston, 42, 45, 48, 68
Kinsbury, 140
Kinsey, 261
Kinson, 188
Kintzing, 172, 249
Kipp, 112
Kipps, 157
Kirby, 42, 78, 81, 83, 109, 196, 201, 207, 228
Kirk, 122, 183, 235, 261
Kirker, 115
Kirkland, 4, 30, 56, 105
Kirkpatrick, 48, 101, 151, 237
Kirkwood, 256
Kirtz, 64
Kirvan, 149
Kirwin, 147
Kitchel, 110
Kitchell, 142, 156
Kitchen, 115
Kitchill, 266
Kiterra, 36
Kitter, 83
Kittera, 3, 19, 29
Kittridge, 204
Kleirschmidt, 50
Klinger, 188
Knap, 130
Knapp, 18
Kneeland, 269
Knight, 58, 80, 98, 126, 146, 156, 168, 181, 191, 199, 252, 266
Knox, 45, 48, 81, 101, 122, 125, 130, 173, 228
Koath, 97
Koch, 117
Kohn, 32
Kollock, 122
Kontz, 188
Kramer, 27, 235
Kreeger, 188
Kremer, 14
Kuder, 17
Kuhn, 10, 50, 94, 135, 160, 237, 255
Kurrack, 59
Kurtz, 127
Kyles, 224

—L—

L'enfant, 16, 152, 188
L'Hommdieu, 93
L'Hommedieu, 173
La Bellona, 162
Lacey, 96
LaChiapella, 171
Lacoste, 45
Lacy, 112, 194
Ladd, 58, 121, 159, 177, 192
Laight, 141
Laird, 22, 106, 149, 153

Laithe, 188
Lamalaty, 270
Lamar, 71
Lamb, 25, 66, 67, 117, 173
Lambert, 112, 173, 204, 234, 263, 266
Lamkin, 30
Lamott, 259
Lamson, 48, 85
Lanberger, 91
Lancaster, 145
Lanchester, 73
Landais, 30, 209
Landers, 229
Landford, 87
Landon, 74
Landrum, 229
Lane, 4, 10, 24, 47, 106, 114, 115, 172, 188, 203, 213, 215, 225
Langdon, 5, 6, 35, 86, 87, 98, 217, 224, 231, 249
Langford, 81
Langley, 38, 188
Langston, 180
Langtey, 192
Lanham, 181, 240
Lannam, 145
Lanneau, 107
Lannom, 232
Lansdale, 152, 251
Lansdalk, 122
Lansing, 87, 164
Lanthall, 260
Lanthois, 162, 171
Lanusse, 171
Lany, 200
Lapier, 232
Larkin, 10, 169, 181, 199
Larkins, 180
Larue, 212
Lassley, 257, 259
Latimer, 17, 22, 25, 34, 84, 92, 98, 267
Latimore, 124
Latouche, 52
Latrobe, 67, 138
Latta, 270
Lattimore, 147, 244

Laub, 235
Laudadale, 269
Lauffat, 162
Laurie, 235
Lauries, 259
Laury, 250
Laussat, 158, 250
Lavater, 26
Law, 1, 9, 16, 17, 47, 51, 59, 100, 106, 119, 149, 152, 161, 171, 174, 191, 200, 211, 232, 240, 260
Lawler, 70, 170, 183, 241, 262
Lawrance, 30, 184
Lawrence, 3, 4, 43, 74, 106, 178, 245, 250, 258
Lawrie, 213
Laws, 96, 178
Lawson, 27, 107, 176, 188, 256, 258
Lawton, 191
Layborne, 32
Layland, 265
Laytons, 70
Le Briton, 130
Le Clerc, 162
Le Near, 269
Lea, 2, 216
Leak, 225
Leake, 176
Leamey, 249
Leaming, 7
Lear, 48, 61, 81, 84, 123, 137, 163, 237
Leary, 76
Leavenworth, 150
Leaycraft, 96, 169
Lechmere, 251
Leck, 188
Leclerc, 94
Lecompte, 53
Ledyard, 4, 208
Lee, 5, 6, 19, 22, 24, 28, 29, 31, 36, 41, 47, 48, 68, 71, 73, 82, 83, 84, 85, 88, 89, 92, 96, 100, 101, 106, 122, 126, 136, 161, 163, 165, 177, 181, 185, 205, 206,

215, 229, 236, 238, 249, 250, 261, 263, 269
Leffert, 227
Leffingwell, 150
Legaux, 94
Legge, 251
Lehman, 71
Leib, 10, 31, 64, 70, 146, 196, 262, 266
Leigh, 168
Leileh, 68
Leiper, 16, 135, 137, 262
Leister, 167
Leitch, 188, 239
Leith, 48, 101, 168
Leland, 68
Lelman, 124
Lemar, 124, 237
Lemmon, 56, 104, 194, 255
Lenox, 48, 86, 90, 133, 143, 186, 192, 196, 213, 222, 226, 231, 234
Lenthall, 234
Leonard, 43, 65, 96, 218, 220, 237
Leppen, 257
Lepper, 259
Leslie, 14, 67, 117
Lettimore, 180
Levering, 73
Levitre, 25
Levittre, 65, 67
Levrault, 213
Levy, 31
Lewden, 45, 81, 176
Lewes, 144
Lewis, 18, 22, 23, 27, 30, 33, 37, 39, 41, 47, 48, 50, 82, 84, 96, 100, 101, 103, 105, 138, 146, 147, 153, 161, 163, 165, 168, 173, 174, 181, 182, 190, 207, 214, 216, 224, 227, 228, 232, 236, 238, 250, 255, 256, 257, 258, 259, 260, 266, 267
Leyburn, 166

Lieb, 5
Light, 65
Lilleen, 147
Lillie, 30
Limebacker, 227
Lincoln, 1, 6, 16, 21, 47, 71, 100, 137, 138, 220
Lindo, 12, 163, 188
Lindray, 23
Lindsay, 50, 125, 175, 246, 258
Lindsey, 105, 265
Lingan, 22, 55, 82, 83, 93, 106, 251
Lingenfelter, 188
Linn, 37, 135, 226, 260, 262
Linnard, 84
Linze, 251
Liot, 49, 102
Lipinard, 4
Lippitt, 98
Liston, 6
Litle, 235
Little, 10, 59, 142, 199, 214
Littlefield, 43
Littlepage, 92
Lively, 33, 43
Livermire, 171
Livermore, 5, 19, 29, 82, 84
Livers, 141, 238
Livingston, 4, 21, 25, 26, 46, 47, 48, 66, 67, 83, 85, 100, 113, 138, 146, 171, 234, 249, 261, 266, 271
Lloyd, 7, 11, 57, 110, 137, 194, 228, 256, 257, 258, 259, 269
Locke, 57, 258
Lockwood, 43
Lodge, 128, 236
Logan, 38, 90, 146, 183, 218, 265, 266
Lomax, 253
Long, 3, 120, 135, 165, 170, 203
Longcope, 122
Loomis, 107, 204
Lorin, 249

Loring, 75, 133, 145, 183
Lotts, 234
Loud, 92
Lougdon, 90
Loughty, 147
Louis, 26
Lounox, 234
Love, 11, 56, 58, 63, 104, 148, 179, 202, 224, 225, 234, 256
Loveil, 124
Loveless, 62
Lovell, 75, 111, 183, 198, 221, 237
Lovering, 26
Lovett, 53, 77, 271
Low, 43, 45, 73, 92, 250, 259, 261
Lowdermilk, 262
Lowe, 138, 251, 257, 259
Lowell, 19, 28, 29, 47, 80, 131
Lower, 263, 267
Lownde, 76, 103
Lowndes, 2, 64, 80, 93, 94, 95, 106, 107, 132, 147, 158, 175, 179, 226, 265
Lowrie, 269
Lowring, 69
Lowry, 47, 57, 83, 214
Lt Medar, 169
Lucas, 63, 146, 173, 239, 260, 271
Lucca, 247
Lucia, 40
Ludlow, 50, 71, 103, 169, 271
Ludwick, 37
Lufborough, 95, 225, 235
Lukens, 32
Lull, 30
Lumidon, 221
Lumpkin, 10
Lunt, 74
Lush, 183
Lusina, 256
Lusk, 207
Lutz, 226
Lutze, 48, 101

Lux, 188, 227
Lyles, 90, 133, 148, 158, 188, 242
Lyman, 3, 53, 78, 84, 92, 158, 202, 236
Lynch, 106, 241, 262
Lynchcomb, 7
Lynchecomb, 6
Lynde, 226
Lynn, 61, 83, 90, 133, 221
Lyon, 35, 64, 103, 147, 186, 204, 238, 267
Lyone, 191
Lyons, 72, 256, 258
Lytle, 57, 194
Lytton, 58, 153

—M—

M'Cormick, 60
Macarty, 262
Macauly, 150
Macay, 8
MacBean, 128
MacClery, 235
MacCreery, 145, 146, 194
MacDaniel, 261
MacDougall, 167
Mace, 157
MacFarland, 267
MacFarlane, 263
MacGill, 77, 138, 139
Mack, 64
Mackal, 54
Mackall, 21, 56, 61, 71, 76, 113, 162
Mackay, 176
Mackenzie, 40
Mackey, 14, 164
Mackie, 188
Mackubin, 244
Macky, 24
Maclay, 120, 146, 266
MaClean, 232
Macley, 173
MacNamara, 128
Macomb, 79, 119, 167
Macon, 5, 64, 76, 78, 147, 162, 190, 246, 257
MacPherson, 228

MaCrae, 205
MacRea, 179
Macreery, 250
Macubin, 161
Madan, 48, 101
Maddox, 27, 55, 59, 62, 134
Madison, 8, 21, 22, 46, 77, 79, 99, 119, 120, 126, 127, 138, 159, 217, 224, 234
Maffie, 115, 135
Magahan, 265
Magaw, 31, 105, 117, 135
Magee, 144, 149, 241
Magill, 24, 29, 47
Magrath, 139, 196
Magratin, 258
Magruder, 34, 56, 112, 119, 120, 148, 161, 166, 167, 177, 179, 186, 207, 208, 238, 252, 263, 267
Maguire, 147
Magurder, 148
Mahan, 119
Mahn, 122
Mahon, 52, 260
Mail, 214
Main, 200
Maitland, 94
Makepeace, 172
Malcolm, 233
Malcom, 79, 184
Maley, 57, 77
Mall, 214
Mandeville, 133
Manley, 160
Manly, 25
Manning, 89, 105, 172, 198, 204, 257, 259
Mansfield, 50, 163, 239, 257
Manton, 5, 10
Mantz, 174, 177, 188
Marat, 227
Marbury, 22, 33, 62, 126, 192
Marcellin, 220
March, 63, 122, 160, 225
Marchal, 218

Marchant, 53
Marck, 48, 101, 237
Marcy, 250
Maret, 34, 268
Marion, 263
Maris, 29
Mark, 17, 215
Markley, 14
Markwan, 89
Marquette, 192
Marrast, 249
Mars, 257, 259
Marsh, 37, 58, 79, 83, 84
Marshal, 100, 124, 128, 188
Marshalk, 172
Marshall, 9, 11, 15, 16, 22, 28, 29, 46, 47, 52, 54, 72, 116, 154, 169, 172, 183, 196, 197, 216, 220, 221, 240
Marsteller, 90
Marten, 160
Martin, 8, 24, 44, 53, 57, 65, 81, 83, 112, 118, 123, 143, 151, 169, 188, 191, 198, 208, 234, 235, 251, 256, 265, 266, 267, 268, 272
Martinez, 91
Marton, 85
Mashevay, 256, 258
Mason, 7, 9, 22, 24, 25, 47, 56, 57, 62, 68, 74, 80, 83, 90, 100, 112, 115, 118, 121, 131, 133, 134, 149, 150, 160, 161, 174, 184, 187, 207, 216, 225, 229, 249, 257, 258
Massey, 172, 208
Masters, 239, 263, 266
Mather, 6
Mathers, 57, 88, 256
Mathews, 97, 110, 241
Matlack, 139
Matter, 65
Matthews, 54, 157, 210, 213, 271

Matthiew, 48, 101
Mattingly, 227
Mattocks, 151
Matton, 98
Mattoon, 63
Maund, 93
Maurice, 79
Mauro, 198
Maury, 48, 100, 236
Maxcey, 178
Maxent, 264
Maxson, 80
Maxwell, 12, 23, 25, 38, 47, 65, 67, 83, 100, 206, 220, 245, 268
May, 6, 43, 77, 90, 235, 242
Maybrook, 69
Mayer, 215, 250
Mayhew, 238
Maylan, 47
Mayman, 225
Maynard, 57, 244
Mayo, 8
Mayor, 45
Mc Call, 105
Mc Cormick, 11
Mc Illvain, 105
Mc Kissock, 105
McAdow, 194
McAllister, 62, 135, 148, 176, 235
McArthur, 215
McAverhill, 42
McBride, 229, 257, 258
McCabe, 149
McCable, 96
McCaleb, 240
McCalla, 128
McCalley, 37
McCance, 168
McCandless, 81
McCarty, 24, 68, 123
McCashlen, 76
McClallen, 179
McClan, 76, 86, 95, 97, 110, 115, 121, 128
McClann, 189
McClary, 84, 100
McClay, 139
McClean, 116
McClelland, 200, 209

McClenachan, 93, 172
McClentock, 87
McClung, 20, 28, 62
McClure, 185, 190, 195
McComas, 194
McComb, 30
McConnell, 111, 132, 166, 256
McCord, 85, 146
McCorkls, 122
McCormick, 18, 23, 34, 54, 70, 122, 132, 145, 171, 173, 180, 188, 190, 192, 215, 230, 234, 240, 265
McCoskey, 110
McCoun, 128
McCow, 94
McCoy, 5, 6, 68
McCraw, 168
McCree, 57
McCreery, 144, 188, 267
McCulloch, 54
McCullock, 51
McCutcheon, 175
McDermot, 16
McDonald, 3, 43, 53, 58, 106, 125, 150, 181, 227
McDonnough, 171
McDono, 222
McDonough, 49, 101, 178, 220, 239
McDougal, 154
McDougall, 90, 250
McDowell, 50, 83, 127, 169
McElroy, 101, 150
McElvoy, 85
McElwee, 193
McEntire, 97
McEowen, 112
McEwen, 175
McFaden, 140
McFadon, 217
McFarland, 190, 203
McFarlane, 181, 205, 256
McGilbray, 256
McGillis, 151
McGinley, 260
McGirk, 107

McGowan, 180, 192, 213, 230, 235
McGown, 25, 65, 67
McGrath, 188, 218
McGrew, 28, 141
McGuire, 90
McGuirk, 96
McHenry, 54, 79, 106
McHughes, 18
McIheney, 138
McIlvain, 142
McIlvaine, 169, 262
McIntire, 26, 109, 115, 150, 199
McIntosh, 169, 176, 242
McKaraher, 15
McKean, 7, 29, 139, 208, 261, 262
McKeaver, 175
McKedder, 257, 259
McKee, 10, 79, 99
McKennan, 171
McKenney, 44
McKenny, 147, 206
McKensie, 26
McKetchine, 257, 259
McKewen, 265
McKim, 234, 262
McKinley, 181, 205
McKinney, 14
McKinny, 88
McKissick, 140
McKiver, 32
McKnight, 90
McKun, 140
McLaring, 3
McLarty, 44
McLaughlin, 23, 61, 68, 90, 98, 99, 144, 164, 195, 214, 215, 235
McLean, 122, 178
McLellan, 114
McLeod, 144, 176
McLinnan, 3
McMahian, 111
McMahon, 168, 208
McMechen, 57
McMellon, 7, 9
McMillan, 49, 82, 102, 137
McMullen, 16, 88, 170
McMunn, 7, 9, 123

McNain, 261
McNairy, 47
McNai-y, 100
McNally, 121, 147
McNantz, 174, 192
McNeally, 24
McNeill, 154
McNish, 117
McNutt, 257, 259
McFherson, 92, 199, 204, 257, 258
McRae, 87, 114
McRee, 84
McWilliams, 169, 194, 246
Mcylan, 100
Mead, 174, 200, 263, 267
Meads, 150
Mease, 91, 94, 129
Meason, 105
Mechlin, 143, 217, 231, 235
Mecklin, 148
Meem, 161
Mees, 187
Megee, 79
Meigs, 37, 38, 50, 60, 97, 102, 109, 196, 204
Meizard, 91
Melanderhjelm, 129
Melbeck, 33
Melco, 154
Meldrum, 167, 250
Melone, 148
Melville, 232
Memim, 165
Mertges, 218, 261
Mercer, 52, 60, 67, 70, 72, 109, 116, 131, 138, 179, 207, 244, 255, 272
Merchant, 87, 183
Mercier, 25, 65, 66
Meredith, 15, 46, 52, 61, 82, 217
Merick, 123
Merieult, 171
Meriwether, 23, 62, 257
Merky, 188
Merriam, 122

Merridith, 257, 259
Merriken, 255
Merritt, 229
Merriwether, 112, 147, 200
Merry, 153
Merryman, 198
Mesler, 105
Messencope, 65
Metcalf, 241
Metzgar, 14
Mewbern, 238
Mewburn, 188
Mewhorter, 215
Meyer, 197, 210
Meyers, 172
Michael, 253
Michaux, 245
Michel, 141
Michin, 10
Mickle, 140, 249
Middleton, 37, 67, 105, 107, 234, 262
Miercken, 29, 208
Mifflin, 261
Miles, 23, 69, 116
Mill, 84
Millar, 58, 172
Mille, 86
Milledge, 31, 64, 110, 136, 155, 180
Millen, 114, 151
Miller, 21, 25, 30, 46, 66, 67, 78, 90, 99, 105, 106, 107, 117, 120, 121, 123, 128, 138, 141, 149, 169, 175, 176, 184, 188, 194, 200, 201, 221, 229, 230, 231, 235, 250, 257, 259
Milligan, 32, 115
Mills, 52, 67, 105, 126, 188, 222
Milns, 23
Milten, 158
Milton, 16
Minchin, 25, 54, 242
Mines, 257, 259
Minisie, 119, 133, 229, 230
Minnis, 231

Minor, 55, 118, 181, 205, 217, 247
Minot, 25, 66, 67
Minturn, 271
Mirror, 121
Mishaun, 183
Mitchel, 79, 84, 215, 256
Mitchell, 2, 4, 54, 63, 85, 93, 98, 100, 111, 125, 135, 136, 141, 146, 168, 169, 176, 193, 199, 203, 208, 236, 257, 259, 262
Mitchill, 211, 242, 266
Mocree, 149
Moffat, 75
Moffett, 36
Moffit, 122
Molier, 85, 101
Monday, 27
Monroe, 33, 47, 100, 114, 265
Montgomery, 4, 14, 28, 37, 48, 52, 57, 101, 137, 170, 194, 215, 216, 237
Montmollin, 94
Montz, 120
Moodie, 49, 101
Moody, 98, 168
Mooney, 164
Moor, 235
Moore, 2, 4, 5, 8, 14, 15, 22, 28, 33, 41, 44, 45, 47, 56, 64, 73, 78, 79, 81, 83, 85, 86, 90, 96, 99, 100, 104, 106, 132, 142, 144, 145, 146, 147, 149, 153, 168, 172, 192, 194, 206, 207, 208, 210, 216, 217, 235, 257, 258, 259, 266, 267
Morais, 219
More, 11, 24, 40, 80, 90, 116, 133, 139, 191, 198, 234
Moreau, 197
Moreton, 140

Morgan, 8, 16, 88, 89, 103, 166, 170, 171, 201, 216, 244, 249
Morin, 97, 173, 186, 192, 222, 235, 265
Morphy, 49, 102
Morrell, 33
Morris, 2, 4, 15, 18, 39, 41, 47, 63, 68, 75, 90, 100, 105, 114, 116, 120, 121, 129, 165, 168, 176, 178, 188, 239, 257, 259, 270
Morrison, 10, 86, 211
Morrow, 109, 115, 137, 147, 228, 263, 267
Morse, 210, 243
Morsel, 126
Morsell, 88
Mortan, 261
Morton, 48, 53, 120, 184, 188, 215, 229
Morveau, 136
Mosby, 183
Moscrop, 188
Moseley, 125
Mosely, 2, 43, 107, 263, 266
Moses, 131, 136
Mosley, 259
Mot, 2
Motley, 250
Mott, 63, 158
Moulton, 172
Moultrie, 88, 254
Mounger, 62
Mountflorence, 20, 85
Mountz, 189
Moylan, 188
Mudd, 215, 242
Mugford, 234
Muhburg, 1
Muhlenberg, 5, 25, 36, 38, 84, 92
Muhlenburg, 58
Muir, 106, 138, 205, 244, 255
Mulbrean, 43
Mulford, 30
Mullen, 37
Mullowny, 59
Mulso, 90

Mumbower, 63
Mumford, 80, 86, 98, 176, 191, 192, 249, 263, 266, 271
Muncaster, 206
Mundel, 251
Munhall, 185
Munmkhuysen, 140
Munn, 53
Munro, 242
Munroe, 41, 56, 83, 111, 114, 121, 135, 152, 163, 175, 213, 234, 237, 265
Munsell, 78
Munson, 88, 109, 120, 144
Murat, 94
Muratt, 257, 259
Murdoch, 5, 268
Murdock, 4, 106, 119, 173, 229, 248
Murehead, 69
Murphy, 104, 198, 243, 260
Murray, 3, 8, 20, 30, 41, 48, 53, 59, 84, 101, 109, 127, 156, 157, 168, 169, 172, 196, 199, 202, 220, 232, 233, 237, 239, 249, 271
Mutzenbecher, 166
Myer, 188, 235
Myers, 89, 123, 125, 183, 188, 249
Myrick, 263

—N—

Nace, 1, 242
Nagle, 65
Naisalis, 120
Nance, 171
Nash, 105, 116, 253
Nathans, 39
Nauche, 190
Naylor, 40, 74, 86, 89, 95
Neal, 52, 172
Neale, 29, 56, 182, 235, 255
Neall, 52

Neill, 241
Neilson, 7
Nell, 59
Nelson, 34, 47, 50, 52, 56, 100, 105, 143, 168, 194, 207, 208, 233, 257, 259, 263, 266, 267
Nesmith, 36, 75, 126, 196
Netherclift, 176
Neufville, 47
Neusville, 100, 189, 195
Nevan, 44
Neville, 140, 215
Nevitt, 189
New, 2, 5, 64, 129, 137, 147, 153, 169, 204, 233
Newall, 256
Newberry, 109
Newbery, 81
Newbold, 204
Newbury, 43, 134, 233
Newcomb, 214
Newell, 204
Newington, 88
Newlum, 8
Newman, 180, 196, 218
Newsum, 165
Newton, 8, 56, 64, 97, 112, 121, 147, 197, 224, 227, 228, 267
Nicholas, 5, 11, 31, 51, 90, 146, 166, 168, 183, 185, 191, 195, 216
Nicholls, 96, 116, 155, 236
Nichols, 37, 84, 88, 129, 255
Nicholson, 5, 11, 27, 36, 59, 64, 82, 88, 96, 100, 120, 146, 157, 159, 160, 165, 166, 169, 171, 177, 187, 188, 190, 207, 220, 222, 251, 254, 267
Nicklin, 174
Nicoll, 194
Nielson, 106

Niles, 201
Noble, 65, 169
Noel, 142, 176
Noland, 30
Norbury, 16
Norman, 122
Norment, 157
Norris, 150, 219, 269
North, 44, 71, 135
Norton, 27
Notly, 92
Nott, 81
Nourse, 4, 9, 15, 46, 99, 135, 180, 217, 230, 234, 235
Nouse, 138
Novle, 25
Nowland, 31
Noyes, 16, 17, 256, 258
Noys, 201
Nugent, 233, 256
Nutting, 172
Nyles, 148

—O—

O'Brien, 48, 49, 52, 85, 101, 139, 169, 173, 210, 237, 247, 248
O'Conner, 76
O'Connor, 27
O'Donnel, 255
O'Farrel, 52
O'Hara, 13
O'Neal, 11, 238
O'Neale, 147
O'Niel, 106
O'Reilly, 92, 128, 221
O'Reily, 90
O'Riely, 76
O'Riley, 42
Oakley, 55, 80, 82, 235
Oates, 176
Oden, 152, 187
Odenheimer, 57
Offery, 78
Ogden, 7, 90, 142, 204, 255, 262, 264
Ogier, 250
Ogilvie, 70, 78, 168, 174, 231
Ogle, 5, 93, 94
Olcott, 90, 145, 172

Oldfield, 197
Olfen, 91
Olgood, 83
Olin, 146, 266
Oliphant, 208, 232
Oliver, 97, 224, 265, 271
Olivier, 81
Olmstead, 78
Olney, 17, 53, 92
Olsen, 102
Opie, 51
Orang, 153
Orme, 128
Orne, 32, 250
Orono, 26
Orr, 81
Orrell, 57
Osborn, 168, 252
Osborne, 70, 129, 174, 179, 249, 258
Osborse, 11
Osburn, 210
Osgood, 4, 41, 163, 202
Oswald, 135
Otis, 3, 19, 29, 82, 89, 131, 156
Ott, 30, 56, 90, 123, 149
Oudrain, 242
Outhour, 4
Outwater, 7, 112
Owealy, 250
Owen, 22, 33, 37, 52, 62
Owens, 30, 73, 259
Owings, 32
Oxley, 56

—P—

Paca, 261
Packet, 56
Paddock, 151
Page, 5, 8, 24, 92, 96, 114, 127, 147, 168, 181, 205, 207, 217, 251
Pagram, 205
Paiddrick, 269
Paine, 3, 44, 45, 47, 56, 100, 108, 131, 169, 261
Paiolean, 107
Paire, 142
Pairo, 155, 192, 222
Paleske, 77
Paley, 242
Pallatson, 106
Palmatary, 55
Palmer, 74, 78, 85, 109, 135, 146, 269
Pancoast, 16, 151, 231
Pannell, 243
Pannill, 118
Panthorpe, 255
Paoly, 77
Parke, 158, 218
Parker, 15, 34, 40, 44, 47, 52, 98, 100, 104, 105, 110, 145, 161, 162, 169, 221, 236
Parkers, 108, 179
Parkins, 53
Parkinson, 73, 114, 182, 188
Parkman, 131
Parks, 30, 140, 167
Parnham, 206
Parrish, 127
Parrot, 173
Parrott, 203, 216, 235
Parrow, 121
Parry, 170
Parsons, 7, 19, 32, 69, 228, 249, 250
Pascalis, 143
Paskel, 66
Paskell, 25, 67
Pasteur, 103, 159
Paten, 217
Paterson, 44, 100, 249
Patten, 19, 256
Patterson, 14, 32, 33, 46, 65, 67, 84, 85, 90, 97, 117, 118, 124, 128, 138, 146, 151, 160, 168, 209, 211, 224, 235, 236, 237, 249, 252
Patton, 185, 192, 223, 250
Paul, 109, 115
Paulding, 26
Pauling, 188
Paulovits, 40

Pawling, 201
Paxton, 199
Payne, 137, 192, 235
Paysen, 140
Peacock, 1, 29, 39, 75, 79, 194, 203, 222, 223
Peal, 44
Peale, 14, 67, 117, 160, 208, 211
Pearce, 119, 140, 212
Pearcy, 167
Pearl, 39
Pearse, 191
Pearsee, 87
Pearson, 27, 45, 112, 120, 223
Peck, 4, 9, 15, 17, 47, 93, 100, 173, 177
Peckham, 86, 191
Peden, 39, 253
Pedesclaux, 217
Peelis, 41, 48
Peggy, 73
Pegram, 181
Peirce, 44, 116, 161
Pelham, 97, 128
Pelly, 42
Pelt, 269
Pelton, 110
Peltz, 16
Pendegraft, 135
Pendelton, 8
Pendleton, 61, 72, 150, 156, 157, 159, 184, 186, 212, 229, 262
Penman, 172
Penn, 8, 38, 181, 200, 205
Pennell, 215
Pennington, 105, 112, 122
Pennock, 46, 234, 257, 259
Penrose, 57, 188
Pepin, 167
Pepple, 241
Percival, 59, 245
Perkins, 1, 47, 63, 78, 100, 107, 143, 189, 193, 200, 213, 230, 235, 269
Perregaux, 250

Perrin, 257, 259
Perrott, 41
Perry, 169, 229
Persons, 18, 34, 67, 77, 78, 109
Pesinger, 16
Peter, 4, 7, 13, 15, 16, 22, 24, 29, 30, 56, 80, 83, 86, 90, 109, 111, 113, 133, 160, 161, 175, 188, 213, 235, 241, 242, 243, 258, 259, 265, 271
Peters, 22, 30, 47, 59, 78, 84, 100, 104, 112, 117, 145, 160, 165, 166, 232, 249
Peterson, 140
Petis, 44
Petit, 48, 185
Pettigare, 214
Pettit, 68
Petty, 233
Peyton, 22, 24, 69, 76, 80, 88, 105, 133, 176, 177
Phelan, 16, 17
Phelps, 85, 93, 127, 146, 182, 203, 204
Philemon, 26, 53, 69
Philips, 39, 71, 88, 101, 131, 183
Phillips, 9, 48, 53, 122, 171, 182
Phinney, 122
Physick, 91
Pic, 111, 156, 195
Pichon, 28, 49, 102, 107
Pick, 64
Pickens, 79, 82
Pickerell, 145
Pickering, 9, 15, 25, 28, 32, 47, 71, 78, 100, 122, 145, 159, 170, 171, 172, 266
Pickeron, 86
Pickett, 45
Pickford, 235
Pickins, 119
Pickman, 125, 174
Pieper, 120

Pierce, 63, 80, 83, 97, 98, 99, 122, 161, 188, 235
Piercey, 191
Piercy, 17, 51, 119, 188, 191
Pierson, 257, 259
Piestman, 140
Pigon, 216
Pinckney, 1, 2, 3, 8, 18, 30, 40, 48, 84, 92, 100, 107, 133, 138, 206, 209, 219, 228, 268, 272
Pindell, 141
Pinkney, 1, 74, 124, 205, 244
Pintard, 249
Piper, 215
Pisot, 271
Pitcairn, 48, 85
Pitchleynn, 120
Pitchlynn, 16
Pitken, 266
Pitkin, 2, 107, 263
Pitman, 98
Pitot, 185
Pitt, 20, 44, 139, 184
Plaisterers, 175
Plankinhorn, 250
Plater, 27, 36, 64, 146, 253
Platt, 5
Pleasants, 123, 125, 166, 207, 216, 229
Pleasonton, 147, 235
Pleni, 21, 40, 48, 84, 91, 92, 119, 153, 158, 163, 202
Plowden, 5
Plowman, 126
Plumb, 43, 111
Plumer, 170, 172, 266
Plumstead, 119
Plunket, 105
Podd, 256, 258
Pole, 10, 108
Polk, 54, 110, 111, 202
Polkinghorne, 148
Polkinhorn, 152, 253
Pollard, 121, 166, 229
Pollock, 55, 112, 162

Polock, 55, 106, 160, 188
Polt, 44
Poltlethwait, 128
Pool, 229
Poole, 48, 100, 121
Pooler, 176
Pooley, 144
Poor, 95
Pope, 11, 53
Por, 225
Porter, 16, 20, 31, 57, 120, 168, 188, 215, 249, 252, 256
Posey, 98, 203, 218
Posser, 168
Post, 20, 55, 67, 76, 88, 136, 253, 271
Postlethwait, 142
Porter, 31, 33, 47, 53, 80, 82, 84, 98, 100, 109, 145, 197, 226, 233, 246
Potts, 22, 52, 69, 71, 142
Pouselding, 44
Powel, 5, 188
Powell, 22, 24, 29, 30, 73, 80, 83, 118, 120, 162, 185, 192, 240
Power, 54, 73, 96
Powers, 49, 73, 101, 137, 256, 261
Pownall, 35, 231, 263
Poydras, 201, 246
Prahl, 148
Prather, 233, 239
Pratt, 42, 68, 120, 151, 176, 188, 194, 249, 250, 272
Praw, 44
Prebble, 19, 59
Preble, 85, 137, 167, 219, 240
Premir, 132, 166
Prentice, 86, 188
Prentis, 217
Prentise, 261
Prentiss, 195
Prescot, 40
Prestman, 250
Preston, 8, 127, 181, 205, 210, 214, 227

27

Prevost, 113, 201, 246
Price, 25, 66, 67, 125, 166, 226
Prichard, 166
Priestley, 14, 164
Priestly, 37, 143, 213
Prince, 183, 218, 237
Pringle, 77, 140, 253
Priscilla, 82
Proffet, 162
Pront, 143
Prosperin, 129
Prout, 11, 81, 86, 110, 133, 150, 176, 188, 229, 230
Provaux, 31
Prowse, 251
Prunty, 24
Pugh, 263, 267
Pulis, 84, 101, 236
Pultney, 242
Purcell, 147, 235
Purcival, 188
Purdie, 122
Purdon, 105
Purrell, 263
Purviance, 15, 61, 104, 145, 147, 157, 216
Putman, 97
Putnam, 109, 115, 163, 174, 176, 217
Pye, 27, 76

—Q—

Quackenbush, 87, 183, 201
Queen, 35, 90, 208, 272
Quenichet, 259
Quincy, 171, 200, 263, 266
Quinlan, 93
Quinn, 56, 81, 133, 138, 177
Quynn, 219

—R—

Raborg, 140
Rachery, 185
Rademaker, 226
Ragan, 188
Ralph, 60, 190, 203, 205, 215, 239
Ramsay, 22, 62, 126, 180
Ramsey, 3, 169, 196
Ranault, 200
Randal, 50, 249
Randall, 44, 185, 188
Randel, 150
Randolph, 64, 83, 146, 151, 157, 160, 216, 225, 227, 228, 253, 261, 267
Raniolini, 94
Rankin, 106
Rapine, 5, 13, 33, 123, 133, 174, 235
Ratcliff, 270
Rathmahler, 54
Raves, 199
Rawle, 216
Rawlings, 154
Rawn, 75, 193, 235, 236, 244
Ray, 18, 51, 119, 130, 191, 193
Raynton, 203
Rea, 266
Read, 1, 3, 6, 9, 20, 29, 47, 63, 100, 119, 122, 166, 179, 181, 205, 216, 249, 252, 261
Ready, 257, 259
Rebecca, 171
Redd, 205
Redgate, 187
Redman, 14, 67, 211
Redmond, 18, 78, 159
Reed, 5, 8, 44, 111, 120, 157, 162, 168, 215, 226, 259, 264
Reeder, 116
Reeve, 2, 151
Regnier, 93
Reid, 188, 220, 256, 258
Reie, 219
Reily, 90, 115
Reinhard, 241
Reinhart, 104
Reintzel, 22, 30, 80, 161
Reintzell, 24, 90
Relf, 53, 99
Remington, 181, 205
Rengel, 49, 102
Renner, 90, 104, 185
Renshaw, 96, 168, 249
Renssalaer, 4, 30
Renssalear, 4
Rentzel, 103
Retallick, 75
Revere, 58
Rewbell, 202
Rey, 271
Reynell, 52
Reynold, 44
Reynolds, 25, 30
Rhan, 256, 258
Rhea, 146, 147, 244, 267
Rheinhart, 234
Rhoades, 138
Rhoads, 256, 258
Rhode, 40, 165, 225
Rhodes, 21, 28, 53, 58, 75, 92, 93, 95, 99, 184, 188, 192, 213, 222, 226, 232, 235, 239, 250, 257, 259
Rice, 10, 31, 159, 176, 257, 259
Rich, 260
Richard, 153
Richards, 15, 62, 73, 120, 146, 196, 215, 267
Richardson, 21, 44, 54, 68, 155, 270
Richmond, 191
Richter, 60
Ricker, 50
Ricketts, 96, 118
Riddick, 99
Riddie, 185
Riddle, 53, 192, 206
Rideout, 109
Ridgeley, 253
Ridgely, 54, 56, 96, 168, 220
Ridgley, 39, 104
Ridgly, 249
Ridgway, 236, 249
Ridley, 188, 208
Ridout, 5, 244

Ried, 106
Riederer, 3
Riggin, 85, 101, 237
Riggs, 93, 105, 121, 149, 195, 205, 258
Right, 143
Riker, 212
Riley, 257, 258
Rinalde, 92
Rind, 79, 129, 177
Ringgold, 6, 52, 54, 216
Ripley, 74, 105
Rippely, 130
Ritchie, 48, 105, 161, 164, 222, 226, 247, 270
Ritenover, 188
Rittenhouse, 139
Rivers, 132, 169
Rivet, 158
Rivington, 89
Roane, 57
Roban, 270, 271
Robbins, 9, 128, 171
Roberson, 97
Robert, 19, 30, 241, 249
Roberts, 14, 22, 41, 65, 92, 105, 148, 156, 183, 188, 207, 209, 241
Robertson, 7, 62, 87, 90, 106, 117, 133, 155, 180, 212, 213, 215, 216, 232, 250, 255, 259
Robeson, 250
Robinet, 40
Robins, 53
Robinson, 36, 53, 54, 59, 96, 126, 183, 188, 219, 232, 246, 248, 256, 257, 258, 259
Robison, 108
Robson, 172
Roche, 33
Rochester, 189, 224, 253
Rodger, 73
Rodgers, 52, 154, 169, 248, 268

Rodman, 120, 156
Rodney, 93, 146, 163, 233, 261, 269
Rodwell, 95
Roe, 27, 243
Roebuck, 91
Roger, 51
Rogers, 8, 28, 32, 45, 52, 62, 69, 140, 205, 235, 245, 257, 259, 272
Romain, 201
Ronels, 181
Roney, 150
Roosevelt, 16
Root, 2, 69, 85, 146
Roots, 175
Ropes, 32
Rormdell, 30
Rose, 29, 57, 68, 78, 130, 149, 225
Ross, 52, 73, 90, 91, 95, 97, 119, 123, 137, 142, 164, 172, 188, 224, 235, 261
Rossell, 204
Rosseter, 9
Roulhac, 202
Roulston, 209
Roume, 91
Rourke, 147
Rouse, 117
Rousselet, 48
Rowan, 57, 86, 244
Rowe, 178, 250, 258, 270
Rowland, 257, 259
Rowles, 106
Rowley, 251
Rowsen, 256
Rowson, 258
Roxburgh, 91
Royston, 215
Rozier, 188
Rufus, 109
Rumbold, 210
Rumsey, 153
Rundle, 19
Runlet, 10
Runnells, 253
Runsberg, 50
Rush, 16
Rusk, 119

Russ, 227
Russel, 73, 77, 82, 188, 250
Russell, 24, 77, 92, 169, 171, 196, 229, 246, 263, 266
Rust, 78
Rustan, 181
Ruteas, 256, 258
Rutgers, 173
Rutherford, 23, 129, 206, 264
Rutland, 108, 110
Rutledge, 8, 64, 116, 262
Rutter, 196
Ryerson, 127
Ryland, 175
Ryon, 239

—S—

Saabye, 48, 101, 237
Sabb, 169
Sackett, 39
Sadler, 250
Safford, 107
Sailly, 263
Saily, 266
Sales, 25, 67
Salter, 250
Saltonstall, 134, 220
Sammons, 85, 146, 266
Sampson, 44, 156, 176
Sanborn, 16
Sanders, 8, 46
Sandford, 19, 142, 147, 201, 267
Sandiford, 256, 258
Sands, 83, 85, 146
Sanford, 30, 163
Sansbury, 151
Santoreous, 136
Sappington, 52
Sares, 253
Sargeant, 57
Sargent, 34, 54, 115, 163, 201
Sartori, 48, 101
Sasseer, 82
Saul, 60, 94, 108, 198
Saunders, 179, 257
Saunier, 35

Sauve, 171
Savage, 45
Savery, 181
Saw, 80, 163
Sawyer, 84, 204
Saxen, 90
Say, 129, 270
Sayrs, 261
Scagg, 239
Scarbrough, 102
Schebly, 52
Schell, 188
Schells, 188
Schiller, 242
Schimmelpendick, 187
Schmiddt, 43
Schmidt, 17
Schneider, 122
Schoell, 213
Schriver, 52
Schultz, 49, 77, 102
Schuneman, 263
Schureman, 5
Schuyler, 31, 202, 203
Scolfield, 188
Scoone, 220, 223
Scott, 11, 12, 13, 15, 25, 32, 47, 55, 68, 75, 83, 90, 100, 106, 115, 123, 125, 128, 133, 135, 154, 155, 166, 167, 194, 196, 206, 207, 210, 238, 248, 254, 268
Scrivern, 44
Sculla, 259
Scully, 59
Seamen, 32
Searin, 7
Sears, 269
Seaton, 30
Seaver, 146, 200, 266
Sedgwick, 3, 5, 15, 23
Seely, 127
Seger, 124
Segul, 113
Seitz, 86, 128
Selby, 163, 175
Selden, 125, 221
Seldon, 127
Sellers, 129
Semme, 254

Semmes, 4, 35, 64, 71, 76, 148, 165, 198
Sen, 238
Senes, 10
Seney, 80
Seraphin, 94
Sergeant, 87
Serjeant, 82
Serraire, 141
Sessford, 231, 235
Seton, 113, 157
Sever, 9
Sevier, 147, 244
Sewall, 9, 44, 47, 85, 100, 250
Sewell, 90, 195
Sextion, 128
Seybert, 14, 67, 91, 117, 160
Seyle, 120, 177, 186
Seymour, 81, 109, 171, 182, 257, 259
Shaaff, 188, 255
Shackelford, 54
Shad, 111, 176
Shade, 53
Shaff, 109, 185, 244
Shaffer, 19, 108
Shail, 268
Shaler, 268
Shallcross, 172
Shaller, 250
Shamson, 91
Shank, 188
Shannon, 91, 108, 148, 185, 224
Shannonhouse, 84
Shanwiler, 17
Sharadine, 158
Sharler, 44
Sharp, 7, 73, 269
Sharpless, 61, 104
Shattuck, 96, 169, 224
Shaumburgh, 79
Shaw, 8, 17, 29, 55, 123, 188, 201, 205, 244, 245, 246
Shawanese, 62
Sheafe, 118, 250
Shearman, 78
Shease, 90
Shee, 24, 26, 131, 137
Shelby, 11, 207

Sheldon, 173
Shelton, 204
Shent, 142
Shepard, 63, 168, 217
Shephard, 5, 169
Shepherd, 16, 39, 202, 203
Sheppard, 7
Sherbourne, 47, 82, 100
Sherburne, 31, 92, 159, 169, 172
Sheridine, 52, 194
Sherman, 122, 261
Sherrard, 257, 258, 259
Sherwood, 47, 169
Shicard, 188
Shields, 4, 44, 166, 169
Shipley, 156, 197
Shipman, 41
Shippen, 59, 192, 211, 215
Shiras, 32
Shoeder, 140
Shoemaker, 33, 94, 135, 165, 171, 186, 192, 208, 230, 235, 249, 250
Shorter, 224
Shriver, 50, 56, 105, 143
Shroyer, 9, 20
Shubrick, 114, 117
Sibley, 28, 160, 270
Sillman, 170
Silvester, 21
Sim, 6, 26, 77, 96, 169, 215
Simkins, 11, 99
Simmes, 103, 116, 188
Simmonds, 3
Simmons, 29, 46, 98, 99, 111, 138, 164, 208, 213, 235, 261, 265, 268, 269
Simms, 24, 89, 90, 133, 214, 218
Simon, 194, 234
Simonds, 156
Simons, 107, 137, 176, 253
Simonton, 257, 259

Simpson, 14, 49, 101, 110, 119, 132, 134, 156, 264
Sims, 117
Sinclair, 167, 249
Singer, 33
Sinnickson, 2
Site, 140
Sitgreaves, 20, 28, 29, 47, 74, 82
Skidmore, 234
Skinn, 89
Skinner, 30, 109, 121, 146, 188, 195, 255
Skipwith, 41, 48, 85, 101, 236
Skriven, 116
Skynner, 172
Slacum, 80
Slater, 188
Slaughter, 39, 46, 118
Slesman, 63
Sley, 188
Sloan, 21, 158, 168, 204, 256, 266
Slocum, 84, 191, 257, 259
Sloss, 47, 96, 100
Slubey, 216
Sluby, 188
Small, 188
Smallwood, 35, 72, 90, 99, 132, 160, 171, 177, 195, 196, 205, 213, 214, 234, 247
Smart, 81
Smilie, 5, 64, 146, 267, 268
Smith, 1, 2, 3, 4, 5, 6, 7, 9, 10, 14, 15, 16, 17, 19, 20, 24, 25, 26, 27, 28, 29, 31, 36, 37, 40, 44, 45, 46, 47, 53, 54, 56, 57, 59, 60, 61, 63, 64, 67, 69, 70, 76, 80, 81, 82, 83, 85, 86, 87, 89, 90, 91, 92, 93, 95, 96, 98, 99, 100, 104, 106, 107, 109, 110, 113, 114, 115, 124, 125, 128, 129, 131, 132, 133, 134, 135, 138, 145, 146, 147, 154, 160, 162, 168, 169, 170, 171, 172, 173, 175, 176, 179, 180, 181, 183, 184, 188, 192, 196, 200, 204, 205, 208, 212, 213, 215, 216, 217, 219, 220, 221, 223, 224, 225, 226, 227, 228, 232, 233, 234, 235, 237, 243, 246, 247, 248, 249, 250, 252, 254, 256, 257, 258, 259, 260, 261, 263, 264, 265, 266, 267, 269
Smithson, 52
Smock, 68
Smoot, 190, 240
Smyth, 31, 136
Smythe, 256
Snapp, 218
Sneider, 16
Snow, 209
Snowden, 12, 104, 118, 122, 166, 188, 250
Snyder, 137, 155, 188
Soderstrom, 49, 102
Sohonnot, 138
Solomon, 128
Somerfall, 107
Somers, 4, 210
Somerville, 46, 58, 244
Sommers, 218
Soper, 159
Sorenson, 73
Sother, 257, 259
Sothern, 117
Sotheron, 233
Sothoron, 1
Sotin, 87
Soulard, 247
Southard, 2, 63, 158, 204, 266
Southen, 105
Southwick, 183
Sowden, 205
Spaight, 6, 103
Spalding, 78, 92, 105, 119, 131, 271
Spangle, 122
Spangler, 215, 268
Speake, 27, 68, 173, 199, 217
Spence, 73, 168, 220, 249, 252
Spencer, 5, 32, 67, 71, 108, 109, 125, 135, 194, 201, 206, 257, 259
Spendler, 102
Spering, 170
Spiers, 76
Spiker, 188
Spinks, 239
Spooner, 9, 107
Spotswood, 24, 96, 219
Sprague, 23
Sprigg, 24, 27, 36, 64, 70, 75, 90, 112, 121, 129, 161, 214, 243, 254, 263
Spyker, 14
St Clair, 20, 28, 49, 74, 102, 203, 212
St Clare, 234, 253
St George, 52
St John, 8, 70
Staats, 121
Stack, 149
Stackhouse, 111, 176
Stacy, 19, 85
Stafford, 3, 44, 257, 259
Stagg, 46
Stahler, 17
Staler, 44
Stall, 188
Stamp, 96
Stampley, 28
Stanard, 128
Stanford, 4, 5, 44, 64, 147, 149, 190, 267
Stanhope, 2
Stanley, 45, 64
Stanly, 103
Stansbury, 51, 56, 104, 194, 206, 255, 264
Stanton, 38, 63, 98, 146, 161, 172, 181, 191, 266
Stanwood, 130
Staples, 250
Stare, 188

Stark, 30, 212
Starke, 162
Starr, 25, 65, 67, 88
Stasaph, 197
Steally, 24
Stedham, 146
Stedman, 105, 176, 177, 266
Steel, 162, 246, 260, 261
Steele, 39, 46, 50, 99, 103, 109, 120, 125, 169, 172, 205, 215, 220
Steil, 179
Steiner, 120, 177
Steinmeitz, 102
Stelle, 37, 62, 123, 135, 181, 222, 230, 234
Stephen, 194, 216, 235, 254
Stephens, 82, 100, 127, 147, 176, 204, 219, 257, 259
Stephenson, 24, 26, 40, 81, 110, 129, 134, 135, 147, 168, 192, 207, 230, 252
Steptoe, 251
Sterett, 15, 63, 262
Sterling, 34
Sterret, 188
Steuart, 27, 97, 131, 244
Steuben, 248
Stevens, 23, 51, 84, 106, 122, 125, 156, 158, 271
Stevenson, 45, 178, 235, 249, 268
Steward, 139, 168, 173
Stewart, 1, 17, 39, 44, 52, 64, 76, 77, 85, 90, 93, 97, 103, 106, 114, 137, 140, 146, 161, 164, 169, 171, 213, 216, 219, 245, 246, 250, 254, 256, 262
Steymets, 46
Stickney, 21, 37, 75, 164, 175, 265
Stier, 40
Stille, 6, 113
Stillman, 29, 84
Stiner, 188
Stites, 176
Stitwell, 44
Stock, 151
Stocker, 98, 99, 106
Stockton, 2, 16, 47, 100, 112
Stockwell, 147, 215, 228
Stocton, 169
Stoddard, 172, 188
Stodderd, 44
Stoddert, 22, 24, 26, 51, 71, 82, 94, 106, 161, 175, 187, 235, 265
Stokes, 37, 204
Stone, 8, 44, 46, 90, 112, 136, 143, 146, 154, 160, 197, 212, 239, 249, 266
Stoops, 176
Stopfard, 233
Storer, 91, 98, 104, 231
Storm, 71
Storrs, 125
Story, 125, 140, 141
Stoughton, 49, 102
Stout, 118, 128
Stover, 120, 177
Stow, 78, 109, 129
Strachan, 233, 248
Strainge, 256
Strange, 188
Stratton, 64
Strawbridge, 14, 105
Street, 48, 69, 101, 237, 241
Streeves, 188
Stretch, 184, 186, 231, 235
Stricker, 188
Strigg, 190
Striker, 56
Strong, 30, 107, 128, 171, 178, 211
Stuart, 8, 27, 29, 57, 114, 138, 169, 181, 188, 194, 205, 233, 237, 270
Stubblefield, 127
Stud, 256
Sturges, 2, 200, 266
Sturgis, 138, 263
Sturgus, 131
Sturtevant, 250
Suckley, 45
Sudler, 254
Sullivan, 59, 138, 171, 178, 204, 261
Summerl, 114
Summers, 22, 90, 250
Summervill, 154
Sumpter, 5, 90
Sumter, 5, 33, 48, 64, 82, 100, 146, 266
Sunday, 161
Suttle, 211
Sutton, 90, 124, 190, 194, 197
Swain, 157
Swaine, 60, 94, 170
Swan, 30, 58, 74, 83, 107, 235, 250
Swanks, 55
Swann, 63, 72, 165, 185
Swanton, 53
Swartwout, 26, 47, 93, 100, 212
Swartwowt, 83
Swearingen, 56, 143, 169
Sweeny, 134, 156, 186
Sweet, 176
Sweetman, 127
Swett, 30
Swift, 22, 49, 102, 243, 257, 259
Swingle, 188
Switt, 247
Sybert, 188
Syires, 124
Sylvester, 2, 4
Symmes, 15, 49, 68, 69, 102, 247

—T—

Tabb, 114
Taber, 5, 98, 114, 151, 181, 191, 205
Tabor, 86
Tacker, 253

Taggart, 151, 266
Tait, 126
Talbert, 74, 90
Talbied, 112
Talbot, 45, 59
Talburtt, 54, 59, 126, 140, 266
Taliaferro, 24, 64, 112, 181, 205
Talleyrand, 111
Talliafaro, 6
Talliaferro, 3, 4, 31
Tallmage, 63, 95
Tallman, 260
Talmadge, 56, 266
Talmage, 2, 107, 146
Talman, 256
Taney, 48, 84, 101, 131, 189
Tankesley, 245
Tanner, 106
Tappan, 143
Tapscott, 163
Tarascon, 32, 175
Tarbell, 219
Tarbox, 258
Tarlanson, 253
Tarlton, 205
Tarrascon, 32
Tarris, 73
Tarvin, 188
Tasker, 93
Tate, 8, 125
Tatham, 247, 248
Tatnall, 19, 62
Tatom, 5, 6, 8
Tatton, 35
Tayler, 127, 173
Tayloe, 208, 235, 251, 265
Taylor, 5, 6, 8, 10, 19, 22, 24, 25, 28, 31, 45, 47, 53, 76, 78, 80, 84, 89, 93, 95, 110, 111, 120, 127, 129, 132, 134, 144, 146, 147, 154, 155, 162, 165, 166, 181, 199, 201, 204, 205, 207, 213, 216, 220, 223, 224, 234, 235, 239, 261, 263

Tazewell, 9, 22, 72, 89, 131
Telfair, 148, 176, 206
Templeman, 39, 106, 148, 188, 245
Tenant, 140, 208
Tenbroeck, 125, 203
Tenney, 63, 98, 146, 170, 266
Terr, 7
Terry, 73, 271
Tew, 80
Thacher, 97
Thackett, 142
Thatcher, 112, 146
Thaw, 235
Thayer, 250
Theveatt, 87
Thom, 235, 248
Thomas, 5, 8, 19, 21, 26, 27, 30, 51, 53, 54, 57, 63, 65, 96, 98, 117, 122, 123, 128, 145, 146, 155, 169, 178, 188, 194, 222, 232, 247, 266
Thomee, 159
Thompson, 5, 6, 22, 23, 25, 31, 36, 44, 55, 57, 64, 65, 67, 68, 73, 76, 90, 106, 107, 122, 136, 147, 151, 152, 156, 159, 160, 163, 170, 181, 201, 203, 218, 221, 223, 228, 235, 253, 256, 257, 258, 259, 262, 266, 267
Thoms, 188
Thomson, 24, 32, 53, 127, 168, 173, 181, 189, 235
Thorn, 130, 178, 220
Thornton, 18, 22, 24, 40, 49, 59, 64, 69, 80, 86, 90, 101, 112, 116, 127, 161, 175, 192, 232, 234, 265
Thorpe, 192, 193, 224, 235, 265
Threlkald, 22
Threlkeld, 27, 39, 103, 161, 217, 235

Thrift, 205
Throop, 62, 120, 130
Thruston, 246, 266
Thunn, 97
Thuriot, 202
Thweatt, 97
Tibbets, 85, 146
Tibbits, 80
Tichenor, 1, 58, 107, 252
Tilden, 78
Tidyman, 68
Tiernan, 141
Tiffany, 150
Tiffin, 109, 115, 153
Tilcomb, 249
Tilden, 109, 131, 170, 171, 204, 249
Tilghman, 29, 47, 56, 93, 96, 188, 206, 216, 217, 244, 261
Tilley, 172, 192, 235
Tillinghast, 63, 98, 156
Tillotson, 46, 57
Tilton, 30, 50, 103, 256
Timberlain, 231
Timberlegs, 231
Tims, 188, 234
Tingey, 15, 27, 56, 63, 86, 121, 135, 145, 152, 164, 165, 234, 237
Tippet, 224
Tisdale, 250
Tisdall, 169
Titcomb, 30, 156
Tittermary, 37, 250
Tocker, 25
Todd, 92
Tolch, 136
Tolman, 257, 259
Tom, 51
Tomkins, 182, 188, 235
Tomlinson, 198, 204
Tompkins, 27, 87
Tongue, 64
Tonkin, 12
Tonkins, 16
Toole, 32
Tooley, 234
Toomer, 107
Tootel, 220
Topham, 139

Topless, 207
Toplif, 250
Toppoen, 74
Torbert, 99
Torreyre, 25
Torris, 249
Touifard, 86
Toulman, 196
Toulmin, 155, 268
Tousard, 78
Town, 11, 114
Townsend, 22, 126, 176, 250
Townshend, 99
Tozer, 261
Tracey, 81
Tracy, 5, 45, 81, 90, 145, 157, 263, 266
Trapier, 54
Trask, 180
Traver, 63
Travers, 148, 153, 177, 235, 247
Traverse, 148
Traversie, 26
Treadwell, 2, 81, 200, 230
Treat, 119, 191
Tredway, 248
Trenchard, 169
Tricou, 171
Trigg, 6, 16, 64, 147, 183, 228, 267
Trilamer, 158
Triplett, 136, 137, 169
Tripp, 220
Trippe, 96
Trist, 23, 125, 163, 170, 171, 195
Triste, 198
Trotter, 202
Troup, 18, 148
True, 97
Truehart, 248
Trueman, 26, 77, 124, 206
Truman, 256
Trumbull, 2, 78, 81, 122, 151, 200
Truston, 106
Truxton, 31, 75, 106
Tryon, 11, 95, 140, 149
Tschudy, 8

Tubman, 57
Tucker, 66, 67, 82, 88, 99, 130, 138, 159, 174, 235, 262
Tuckfield, 123, 235
Tufts, 84
Tunicliff, 60, 99, 185
Tunnicliff, 8, 20, 21, 76
Tupper, 170
Turberille, 127
Turner, 39, 46, 90, 99, 110, 112, 136, 138, 155, 163, 169, 176, 179, 204, 221, 227, 235, 259, 266, 267
Tutt, 68
Tutuall, 138
Twedy, 27
Twiggs, 168
Twitty, 114
Tyler, 44, 54, 72, 108, 114, 134, 179, 206, 208, 244, 253
Tyng, 92
Tyrrell, 255

—U—

Underwood, 230, 235, 265
Unwin, 33
Updegraff, 115
Updike, 53
Upham, 1, 6, 63, 91, 204
Upshear, 136
Upshire, 105
Usher, 3

—V—

Valch, 102, 172
Valck, 49
Vale, 55, 124, 237
Valeck, 250
Valentine, 17, 91
Valenzin, 152, 168, 180
Valkman, 134
Valle, 197
Vallsau, 184
Van Allen, 62, 96
Van Berkel, 13
Van Beuren, 62

Van Bibber, 104
Van Bomel, 122
Van Braam, 61
Van Cortland, 146
Van Cortlandt, 4, 63, 167, 266
Van Courtlandt, 85
Van Doren, 37
Van Duyn, 112
Van Dyke, 96, 216
Van Horn, 64, 232, 233, 255, 264
Van Horne, 10, 56, 146
Van Logan, 112
Van Manninck, 188
Van Meter, 129
Van Ness, 4, 63, 88, 132, 133, 135, 137, 148, 186, 192, 199, 211, 212, 214, 232, 265
Van Polanen, 49
Van Ransaeler, 113
Van Ransselaer, 63
Van Renselaer, 17
Van Rensellear, 16
Van Rensselaer, 17, 23, 146, 164, 266
Van Swearingen, 170
Van Vechten, 4
Van Vollen, 187
Van Wart, 26
Van Zant, 271
Vanbibber, 93
Vance, 95, 215
Vancitart, 269
Vancleve, 87, 112
Vander Heyden, 25, 65, 67
Vander Waller, 187
Vanderburg, 158
Vanderburgh, 20, 28, 50, 103, 218
Vandergrist, 140
Vanderhorst, 48, 100, 236
Vanderslice, 14
Vandwser, 156
Vaneman, 41
Vanhorn, 134, 158, 262
Vanhorne, 40, 58
Vanloghen, 55
Vanness, 80

Vansandt, 12, 87
Vanschaiek, 220
Vansise, 250
Varden, 12, 23, 61, 73, 126, 192, 235
Varick, 184
Varnum, 5, 6, 63, 146, 266
Vattier, 151
Vaughan, 14, 67, 106, 117, 142, 160, 203, 208, 211
Vcyo, 158
Veatch, 56
Veawck, 73
Veazy, 194
Veich, 171
Veitch, 160
Venable, 155, 183
Vercnock, 49, 102
Verey, 208
Verge, 270
Vernon, 17, 81, 86, 111, 144
Verplanck, 266
Verplank, 146
Vew, 127
Vezey, 158
Vial, 249
Vicary, 220
Vickers, 81
Vidal, 249
Vidler, 175
Vigo, 218
Villalobus, 49, 102
Villard, 79, 152, 222
Vincent, 14, 54, 235
Vining, 71
Vinnard, 157
Von Heer, 25, 66, 67, 117
Von Kotzebue, 59, 240
Voss, 27, 29, 40, 90, 193, 230, 234, 264
Vowell, 53, 56, 185, 192
Vroom, 7, 112

—W—

Wable, 131
Waddel, 156
Waddell, 249
Wade, 8, 34, 44, 156, 161
Wadsworth, 5, 63, 146, 148, 160, 169, 175, 210, 256, 266
Wagler, 123, 168
Wagner, 46, 99, 235
Wail, 259
Wait, 109
Waite, 31, 255
Wakefield, 44, 88
Walbach, 30, 79
Walback, 79
Walbergh, 27
Walby, 257, 259
Walden, 91
Waldo, 19, 84
Waldron, 238
Walker, 3, 8, 15, 21, 23, 25, 44, 51, 62, 63, 65, 67, 71, 72, 119, 122, 134, 135, 141, 142, 147, 157, 169, 189, 204, 205, 216, 256, 257, 258, 259
Wall, 100, 128, 140, 173, 222, 251, 257, 259
Wallace, 7, 12, 30, 49, 97, 101, 106, 218, 224, 250
Walloston, 48, 101
Walls, 110
Walmsley, 135
Waln, 6
Walsh, 141, 257, 259
Walter, 41, 188
Walton, 62, 142, 147, 215, 267
Wand, 188
Ward, 23, 89, 112, 163, 211, 233, 261
Waring, 22, 167, 189, 245
Warman, 188
Warner, 20, 88, 94, 116, 122, 127, 153, 155, 204
Warren, 3, 4, 34, 38, 43, 46, 51, 91, 92, 163, 204, 252
Warrington, 96

Wartman, 44
Washington, 1, 3, 4, 5, 6, 11, 31, 46, 59, 77, 81, 86, 90, 97, 100, 103, 104, 105, 124, 152, 156, 161, 199, 201, 209, 218, 235, 241, 242, 253, 255, 261
Waterhouse, 37
Waterman, 27, 31, 68, 74, 80, 137, 268
Waters, 19, 30, 45, 71, 135, 194, 198, 255, 256, 258, 265
Waterstone, 129
Wathen, 35
Watkins, 88, 201, 262
Watson, 18, 31, 62, 84, 88, 157, 249, 250, 257, 259
Watt, 81, 157, 249
Watterson, 234
Watts, 2, 152, 257, 259
Waugh, 104, 127, 188
Way, 92, 94, 192, 235
Wayal, 76
Wayman, 36, 170, 245
Wayne, 97, 223
Wearey, 228
Weaver, 43
Webb, 14, 172, 235
Webster, 24, 32, 235, 239
Wederstrandt, 96, 169
Wedgewood, 108
Weeks, 9, 99, 157
Weems, 80, 106, 190, 220, 233, 235, 258
Weiles, 269
Weisger, 86
Welch, 30, 78, 109
Welebar, 215
Welles, 92, 138, 200, 204
Wells, 5, 17, 68, 90, 109, 115, 146, 159, 204, 219, 240, 250
Welscher, 176
Welsh, 35
Welsher, 148
Wendell, 40, 83, 171
Wendover, 173

Wentworth, 98, 159
Wermsley, 257
Wescott, 90, 247
Wesiner, 265
West, 47, 92, 93, 100, 124, 125, 134, 142, 149, 184, 244, 250
Westberry, 270
Westford, 256, 258
Weston, 208
Wetheral, 44
Wetherill, 10, 57, 105
Wetmore, 103
Weymouth, 182
Whann, 57, 121, 165, 177
Wharton, 15, 189, 234, 265
Wheat, 27, 126
Wheaton, 80, 250
Wheelen, 139
Wheeler, 14, 31, 217, 256
Wheelock, 42
Whelan, 89, 163
Whelen, 46
Whetcroft, 25, 51, 59, 90, 205, 217, 235
Whetmore, 91
Whiling, 8
Whipp, 156
Whipple, 20, 26, 30, 83, 159, 172
Whistler, 90
Whitaker, 152, 194
White, 4, 22, 24, 32, 57, 88, 90, 91, 107, 118, 122, 125, 131, 146, 160, 170, 176, 183, 189, 196, 199, 205, 213, 232, 249, 250, 257, 259, 266
Whiteby, 53
Whitehair, 188
Whitehall, 260
Whitehill, 120, 146, 155, 170, 215, 263, 267
Whitely, 54
Whitfield, 8, 204
Whithill, 10
Whiting, 89, 150, 156, 169, 172, 204, 206

Whitlock, 30
Whitman, 191
Whitney, 121
Whittaker, 270
Whittelsey, 42
Whittemore, 125
Whitten, 97
Whittlesey, 78, 83, 109
Wichelhausen, 48, 101
Wichlelhausen, 237
Wickes, 263, 266
Wicket, 176
Wickham, 24, 44, 156
Widgery, 93
Wigell, 188
Wigfield, 240, 253
Wignell, 123
Wikoff, 201
Wilcocks, 40, 135, 250
Wilcox, 100, 262, 271
Wilde, 9, 38
Wildman, 259
Wiley, 39, 69, 142, 148
Wilkins, 15, 83
Wilkinshaw, 10
Wilkinson, 31, 32, 37, 46, 69, 79, 82, 119, 120, 122, 158, 160, 168, 179, 206, 219, 221, 224, 244, 246, 247, 253, 254, 263
Willard, 24, 47, 83, 100, 195
Willcox, 230
Willes, 233
Willets, 61
Willett, 165, 182, 247
Williams, 5, 6, 10, 15, 26, 30, 31, 38, 40, 44, 45, 52, 54, 63, 64, 68, 81, 85, 92, 98, 99, 107, 115, 117, 137, 142, 143, 146, 147, 150, 152, 153, 163, 164, 166, 168, 189, 191, 193, 195, 204, 209, 224, 232, 233, 236, 237, 240, 252, 256, 261, 263, 266, 267, 268
Williamson, 2, 35, 73, 75, 88, 121, 135, 141, 156, 189, 233, 256, 264
Willing, 29, 176, 208
Willis, 4, 48, 69, 91, 101, 130, 132, 137, 145, 152, 170, 182
Willoughby, 154
Willsmott, 257, 258
Willson, 258
Wilmarth, 31, 80
Wilmer, 57, 169, 258
Wilmore, 5, 88
Wilson, 12, 18, 21, 30, 44, 48, 53, 56, 61, 71, 76, 79, 91, 95, 98, 100, 105, 106, 108, 109, 111, 113, 115, 119, 121, 122, 124, 125, 130, 134, 135, 136, 137, 140, 143, 146, 148, 149, 150, 151, 156, 157, 163, 167, 169, 171, 176, 177, 178, 181, 187, 188, 189, 195, 204, 206, 225, 227, 228, 236, 239, 243, 247, 249, 250, 256, 257, 258, 259, 267, 268
Wilsons, 29
Wily, 132, 226
Winchester, 47, 100, 216
Winder, 53, 189
Wing, 108
Wingate, 91, 111, 133, 152, 214
Winn, 112, 132, 147, 189, 220, 267
Winner, 169
Winnsett, 189
Winnston, 147
Winslow, 169, 200, 257, 269
Winston, 8, 157, 190, 267
Winters, 188, 207
Winthorp, 204
Winthrop, 34, 49, 102, 181
Winton, 35
Winut, 170

Wirgman, 213
Wise, 24, 80, 90, 96
Wiseman, 49, 102
Wisner, 261
Wistar, 14, 160, 211
Wister, 67, 117
Witheral, 239
Witherell, 107
Witherill, 108
Withington, 161
Witmer, 127
Wittich, 123
Wock, 16
Wolbert, 16
Wolcot, 19, 83
Wolcott, 4, 12, 13, 28, 47, 95, 108, 184
Wollcott, 42
Wood, 11, 14, 27, 49, 53, 56, 96, 101, 103, 110, 124, 127, 128, 134, 153, 158, 190, 201, 221, 222, 223, 250, 258, 264, 268, 269
Woodbridge, 229
Woodfall, 144
Woodhouse, 67, 164, 211
Woodhull, 2, 116
Woodman, 73, 204
Woods, 5, 47, 64, 100, 115
Woodside, 26, 186, 196
Woodson, 257, 259
Woodward, 51, 79, 86, 144, 164, 173, 178, 213, 221, 227, 235, 272
Woodworth, 4, 173, 212

Woolfolk, 227
Woolicot, 257, 259
Woolley, 15
Woolridge, 30
Woolsey, 18, 271
Woosley, 169
Wooster, 116
Wooten, 189
Work, 127
Worm, 134
Wormeley, 127, 168, 271
Wormly, 249
Wormsley, 259
Worrel, 165
Worrell, 16, 165
Worsley, 199
Worthingotn, 125
Worthington, 50, 51, 54, 84, 87, 103, 109, 115, 146, 148, 184, 266
Wotton, 54
Wragg, 54, 68
Wraxall, 91
Wright, 54, 90, 146, 201, 235, 246, 256, 266, 267, 271
Wyate, 247
Wyckoff, 112
Wyer, 145, 169
Wyeth, 122
Wylley, 47, 82
Wylls, 81
Wyman, 151
Wynder, 217
Wynkoop, 227
Wynne, 52
Wynns, 8, 110, 147, 190, 267
Wyse, 250

Wythe, 8, 72, 166, 168, 181, 205

—X—

Xaupi, 130, 208

—Y—

Y'Nooky, 69
Yancey, 23
Yarnall, 129
Yates, 53, 54, 189
Yearts, 55
Yeates, 215
Yellot, 34
Yoe, 175
York, 200, 221
Youghman, 189
Young, 10, 11, 27, 37, 39, 48, 51, 59, 74, 76, 77, 81, 85, 90, 93, 101, 104, 105, 135, 140, 159, 168, 173, 175, 176, 185, 187, 189, 198, 199, 213, 217, 219, 230, 234, 237, 250, 254, 257, 259
Yrujo, 238
Yznardi, 48, 101, 237

—Z—

Zane, 76
Zeigler, 125
Zimmerman, 174
Zorger, 245

Other Heritage Books by the author:

National Intelligencer *Newspaper Abstracts, Special Edition: The Civil War Years, 1861-1863*

National Intelligencer *Newspaper Abstracts 1846*

National Intelligencer *Newspaper Abstracts 1845*

National Intelligencer *Newspaper Abstracts 1844*

National Intelligencer *Newspaper Abstracts 1843*

National Intelligencer *Newspaper Abstracts 1842*

National Intelligencer *Newspaper Abstracts 1841*

National Intelligencer *Newspaper Abstracts 1840*

National Intelligencer *Newspaper Abstracts, 1838-1839*

National Intelligencer *Newspaper Abstracts, 1836-1837*

National Intelligencer *Newspaper Abstracts, 1834-1835*

National Intelligencer *Newspaper Abstracts, 1832-1833*

National Intelligencer *Newspaper Abstracts, 1830-1831*

National Intelligencer *Newspaper Abstracts, 1827-1829*

National Intelligencer *Newspaper Abstracts, 1824-1826*

National Intelligencer *Newspaper Abstracts, 1821-1823*

National Intelligencer *Newspaper Abstracts, 1818-1820*

National Intelligencer *Newspaper Abstracts, 1814-1817*

National Intelligencer *Newspaper Abstracts, 1811-1813*

National Intelligencer *Newspaper Abstracts, 1806-1810*

National Intelligencer *Newspaper Abstracts, 1800-1805*

www.ingramcontent.com/pod-product-compliance
Lightning Source LLC
Chambersburg PA
CBHW070722160426
43192CB00009B/1280